ANALYSIS FOR FINANCIAL MANAGEMENT

Fifth Edition

ROBERT C. HIGGINS
The University of Washington

Irwin McGraw-Hill

Boston, Massachusetts   Burr Ridge, Illinois
Dubuque, Iowa   Madison, Wisconsin
New York, New York   San Francisco, California
St. Louis, Missouri

Irwin/McGraw-Hill

A Division of The **McGraw·Hill** Companies

ANALYSIS FOR FINANCIAL MANAGEMENT

This book is printed on acid-free paper.

5 7 8 9 0 DOC/DOC 9 0 9

ISBN 0-256-16703-6

Vice president and editorial director: *Michael W. Junior*
Publisher: *Gary Burke*
Senior sponsoring editor: *Gina M. Huck*
Editorial assistant: *Holly K. Zemsta*
Senior marketing manager: *Katie Rose Matthews*
Project manager: *Jim Labeots*
Production supervisor: *Karen Thigpen*
Designer: *Matthew Baldwin*
Compositor: *GAC/Shepard Poorman*
Typeface: *11/13 Times Roman*
Printer: *R. R. Donnelley & Sons Company*

Library of Congress Cataloging in-Publication Data

Higgins, Robert C.
    Analysis for financial management / Robert C. Higgins.—5th ed.
        p.   cm.
    Includes index.
    ISBN 0-256-16703-6 (alk. paper)
    1. Corporations—Finance.
    HG4026.H496 1998
    658.15′1—dc21   97-17268

http://www.mhhe.com

THE IRWIN/McGraw-Hill Series in Finance, Insurance, and Real Estate

Stephen A. Ross
Sterling Professor of Economics and Finance
Yale University
Consulting Editor

FINANCIAL MANAGEMENT

Benninga and Sarig
Corporate Finance: *A Valuation Approach*

Block and Hirt
Foundations of Financial Management
Eighth Edition

Brealey and Myers
Principles of Corporate Finance
Fifth Edition

Brealey, Myers, and Marcus
Fundamentals of Corporate Finance

Brooks
PC FinGame: *The Financial Management Decision Game*
Version 2.0—DOS and Windows

Bruner
Case Studies in Finance: *Managing for Corporate Value Creation*
Second Edition

Chew
The New Corporate Finance: *Where Theory Meets Practice*

Grinblatt and Titman
Financial Markets and Corporate Strategy

Helfert
Techniques of Financial Analysis: *A Modern Approach*
Ninth Edition

Higgins
Analysis for Financial Management
Fifth Edition

Hite
A Programmed Learning Guide to Finance

Kester, Fruhan, Piper, and Ruback
Case Problems in Finance
Eleventh Edition

Nunnally and Plath
Cases in Finance
Second Edition

Parker and Beaver
Risk Management: *Challenges and Solutions*

Ross, Westerfield, and Jaffe
Corporate Finance
Fourth Edition

Ross, Westerfield, and Jordan
Essentials of Corporate Finance

Ross, Westerfield, and Jordan
Fundamentals of Corporate Finance
Fourth Edition

Smith
The Modern Theory of Corporate Finance
Second Edition

White
Financial Analysis with an Electronic Calculator
Third Edition

INVESTMENTS

Ball and Kothari
Financial Statement Analysis

Bodie, Kane, and Marcus
Essentials of Investments
Third Edition

Bodie, Kane, and Marcus
Investments
Third Edition

Cohen, Zinbarg, and Zeikel
Investment Analysis and Portfolio Management
Fifth Edition

Farrell
Portfolio Management: *Theory and Applications*
Second Edition

Gibson
Option Valuation

Hirt and Block
Fundamentals of Investment Management
Fifth Edition

Jarrow
Modelling Fixed Income Securities and Interest Rate Options

Lorie, Dodd, and Kimpton
The Stock Market: *Theories and Evidence*
Second Edition

Morningstar, Inc. and Remaley
U.S. Equities OnFloppy Educational Version
Annual Edition

Shimko
The Innovative Investor
Version 2.0—Lotus and Excel

FINANCIAL INSTITUTIONS AND MARKETS

Flannery and Flood
Flannery and Flood's ProBanker: *A Financial Services Simulation*

James and Smith
Studies in Financial Institutions: *Non-Bank Intermediaries*

Rose
Commercial Bank Management: *Producing and Selling Financial Services*
Third Edition

Rose
Money and Capital Markets: *Financial Institutions and Instruments in a Global Marketplace*
Sixth Edition

Rose and Kolari
Financial Institutions: *Understanding and Managing Financial Services*
Fifth Edition

Santomero and Babbel
Financial Markets, Instruments, and Institutions

In memory of Alex Robichek
teacher, colleague, and friend.

PREFACE

Like its predecessors, the fifth edition of *Analysis for Financial Management* is for nonfinancial executives and business students interested in the practice of financial management. It introduces standard techniques and recent advances in a practical, intuitive way. The book assumes no prior background beyond a rudimentary and perhaps rusty familiarity with financial statements, although a healthy curiosity about what makes business tick is also useful. Emphasis throughout is on the managerial implications of financial analysis.

Analysis for Financial Management should prove valuable to individuals interested in sharpening their managerial skills and to participants in executive programs. The book has also found a home in university classrooms as the sole text in applied finance courses, as a companion text in case-oriented courses, and as a supplementary piece in more theoretical finance courses.

Analysis for Financial Management is my attempt to translate into another medium the enjoyment and stimulation I have experienced over the past three decades working with executives and college students. This experience has convinced me that financial techniques and concepts need not be abstract or obtuse; that recent advances in the field such as market signaling, market efficiency, and capital asset pricing are important to practitioners; and that finance has much to say about the broader aspects of company management. I also believe any activity in which so much money changes hands so quickly cannot fail to be interesting.

Part I looks at the management of existing resources, including the use of financial statements and ratio analysis to assess a company's financial health, its strengths, weaknesses, recent performance, and future prospects. Emphasis throughout is on the ties between a company's operating activities and its financial performance. A recurring theme is that a business must be viewed as an integrated whole and effective financial management is possible only within the context of a company's broader operating characteristics and strategies.

The rest of the book deals with the acquisition and management of new resources. Part II examines financial forecasting and planning with particular emphasis on managing growth and decline. Part III considers the financing of company operations, including a review of the principal security types, the markets in which they trade, and the proper choice of security type by the issuing company. The latter requires a close look at financial leverage and its effect on the firm and the firm's shareholders.

Part IV deals with the use of discounted cash flow techniques, such as the net present value and the internal rate of return, to evaluate investment opportunities. It also addresses the difficult task of incorporating risk into investment appraisal. The book concludes with an examination of business valuation and company restructuring within the context of the ongoing debate over the proper roles of shareholders, boards of directors, and incumbent managers in governing America's public corporations.

CHANGES IN THE FIFTH EDITION

Readers familiar with earlier editions of *Analysis for Financial Management* will note several changes and refinements in this edition, including

- An introduction to currency and interest rate swaps with emphasis on the ability of swaps to increase corporate financing flexibility
- A thorough rewrite of "Using Financial Markets to Manage Corporate Risks" to simplify and clarify the exposition
- Increased emphasis on the important tie between present value and creating shareholder wealth
- Increased emphasis on the significance of real options in investment appraisal
- An extensive revision of Chapter 9, "Business Valuation and Corporate Restructuring," to expand the treatment of discounted cash flow approaches to valuation, summarize empirical studies of mergers and leveraged buyouts, and de-emphasize the significance of hostile takeovers.

A word of caution: *Analysis for Financial Management* emphasizes the application and interpretation of analytic techniques in decision making. These techniques have proved useful for putting financial problems into perspective and for helping managers anticipate the consequences of their actions. But techniques can never substitute for thought. Even with the best technique, it is still necessary to define and prioritize issues, to modify analysis to fit specific circumstances, to strike the proper balance between quantitative analysis and more qualitative considerations, and to evaluate alternatives insightfully and creatively. Mastery of technique is only the necessary first step toward effective management.

I want to thank Bill Alberts, David Beim, Dave Dubofsky, Bob Keeley, George Parker, Megan Partch, Alan Shapiro, and Nik Varaiya for insightful help and comments on this and prior editions. I also want to thank my daughter, Sara Higgins, for her advice and editorial assistance, my wife for her patience, and my students and colleagues at the University of Washington, the Darden Graduate School of Business, the University of Hawaii Advanced Management Program, Bank of America, Advanced Technology Laboratories, and Microsoft, among others, for stimulating my continuing interest in financial management.

Robert C. Higgins
rhiggins@u.
washington.edu

BRIEF CONTENTS

CONTENTS

PART II

PLANNING FUTURE FINANCIAL PERFORMANCE

Chapter 3

Financial Forecasting   91

Chapter 4

Managing Growth   119

PART III

FINANCING OPERATIONS

Chapter 5

Financial Instruments and Markets   149

Chapter 6

The Financing Decision   191

PART IV

EVALUATING INVESTMENT OPPORTUNITIES

Chapter 7

Discounted Cash Flow Techniques   231

Chapter 8

Risk Analysis in Investment Decisions   269

ASSESSING THE FINANCIAL HEALTH OF THE FIRM

CHAPTER 1

INTERPRETING FINANCIAL STATEMENTS

Financial statements are like fine perfume; to be sniffed but not swallowed.

Abraham Brilloff

$\mathbf{A}$ccounting is the scorecard of business. It translates a company's diverse activities into a set of objective numbers that provide information about the firm's performance, problems, and prospects. Finance involves the interpretation of these accounting numbers for assessing performance and planning future actions.

The skills of financial analysis are important to a wide range of people, including investors, creditors, and regulators. But nowhere are they more important than within the company. Regardless of functional specialty or company size, managers who possess these skills are able to diagnose their firm's ills, prescribe useful remedies, and anticipate the financial consequences of their actions. Like a ballplayer who cannot keep score, an operating manager who does not fully understand accounting and finance works under an unnecessary handicap.

In this and the following chapter, we look at the use of accounting information to assess financial health. We begin with an overview of the accounting principles governing financial statements and a discussion of one of the most abused and confusing notions in finance: cash flow. In Chapter 2, we look at measures of financial performance and ratio analysis.

THE CASH FLOW CYCLE

Finance can seem arcane and complex to the uninitiated. However, a comparatively few basic principles should guide your thinking. One is that *a company's finances and operations are integrally connected*. A company's

3

F I G U R E   1-1

The Cash Flow–Production Cycle

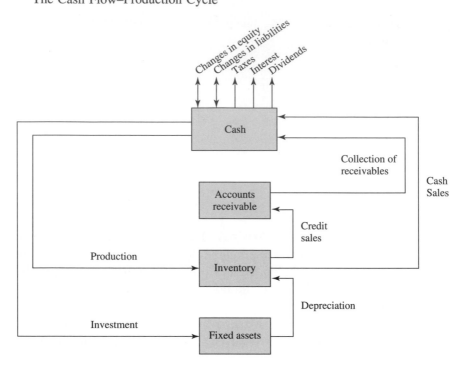

activities, method of operation, and competitive strategy all fundamentally shape the firm's financial structure. The reverse is also true: Decisions that appear to be primarily financial in nature can significantly affect company operations. For example, the way a company finances its assets can affect the nature of the investments it is able to undertake in future years.

The cash flow production cycle in Figure 1–1 illustrates the close interplay between company operations and finances. For simplicity, suppose the company shown is a new one that has raised money from owners and creditors, has purchased productive assets, and is now ready to begin operations. To do so, the company uses cash to purchase raw materials and hire workers; with these inputs, it makes the product and stores it temporarily in inventory. Thus, what began as cash is now physical inventory. When the company sells an item, the physical inventory changes back into cash. If the sale is for cash, this occurs immediately; otherwise, cash is not realized until some later time when the account receivable is collected.

This simple movement of cash to inventory, to accounts receivable, and back to cash is the firm's *operating*, or *working capital, cycle.*

Another ongoing activity represented in Figure 1–1 is investment. Over a period of time, the company's fixed assets are consumed, or worn out, in the creation of products. It is as though every item passing through the business takes with it a small portion of the value of fixed assets. The accountant recognizes this process by continually reducing the accounting value of fixed assets and increasing the value of merchandise flowing into inventory by an amount known as *depreciation.* To maintain productive capacity, the company must invest part of its newly received cash in new fixed assets. The object of this whole exercise, of course, is to ensure that the cash returning from the working capital cycle and the investment cycle exceeds the amount that started the journey.

We could complicate Figure 1–1 further by including accounts payable and expanding on the use of debt and equity to generate cash, but the figure already demonstrates two basic principles. First, *financial statements are an important window on reality.* A company's operating policies, production techniques, and inventory and credit-control systems fundamentally determine the firm's financial profile. If, for example, a company requires prompter payment on credit sales, its financial statements will reveal a reduced investment in accounts receivable and possibly a change in its revenues and profits. This linkage between a company's operations and its finances is our rationale for studying financial statements. We seek to understand company operations and predict the financial consequences of changing them.

The second principle illustrated in Figure 1–1 is that *profits do not equal cash flow.* Cash—and the timely conversion of cash into inventories, accounts receivable, and back into cash—is the lifeblood of any company. If this cash flow is severed or significantly interrupted, insolvency can occur. Yet the fact that a company is profitable is no assurance that its cash flow will be sufficient to maintain solvency. To illustrate, suppose a company loses control of its accounts receivable by allowing customers more and more time to pay, or suppose the company consistently makes more merchandise than it sells. Then, even though the company is selling merchandise at a profit in the eyes of an accountant, its sales may not be generating sufficient cash soon enough to replenish the cash outflows required for production and investment. When a company has insufficient cash to pay its maturing obligations, it is insolvent. As another example, suppose the company is managing its inventory and receivables carefully, but rapid sales growth is necessitating an ever-larger investment in these assets. Then, even though the company is profitable, it may have too little cash to meet its obligations. The company will literally be "growing broke." These brief examples illustrate why a manager must be concerned at least as much with cash flows as with profits.

We will return to these themes repeatedly in later chapters and will consider cash flow analysis shortly. But first, we need to review the basics of financial statements. If this is your first look at financial accounting, buckle up because we will be moving quickly. If the pace is too quick, take a look at one of the accounting texts recommended at the end of the chapter.

THE BALANCE SHEET

The most important source of information for evaluating the financial health of a company is its financial statements, which consist principally of a balance sheet, an income statement, and a cash flow statement. Let us look at each statement briefly.

A *balance sheet* is a financial snapshot, taken at a point in time, of all the assets the company owns and all the claims against those assets. The basic relationship is

$$\text{Assets} = \text{Liabilities} + \text{Shareholders' equity}$$

It is as if a herd (flock? covey?) of auditors run through the business on the appointed day, making a list of everything the company owns, and assigning each item a value. After tabulating the firm's assets, the auditors list all outstanding company liabilities, where a liability is simply any obligation to make a payment or, alternatively, any form of an "IOU." Having thus totaled up what the company *owns* and what it *owes*, the auditors call the difference between the two *shareholders' equity*. Shareholders' equity is the accountant's estimate of the value of the shareholders' investment in the firm just as the value of a homeowner's equity is the value of the home, less the mortgage outstanding against it. Shareholders' equity is also known as *owners' equity*, *stockholders' equity*, *net worth*, or simply *equity*.

To illustrate the techniques and concepts presented throughout this book, I will refer whenever possible to Analog Devices, Inc. (ADI), a high-tech manufacturer of specialized semiconductors and integrated circuitry headquartered in Norwood, Massachusetts. ADI's street address,

One Technology Way, says much about the company's image and aspirations. Tables 1–1 and 1–2 present ADI's balance sheets and income statements, respectively, for 1994 and 1995. If the precise meaning of every asset and liability category in Table 1–1 is not immediately apparent, be patient. We will discuss many of them in the following pages.

ADI's basic balance sheet equation for 1995 is

$$\text{Assets} = \text{Liabilities} + \text{Shareholders' equity}$$
$$\$1,001.6 \text{ million} = \$345.7 \text{ million} + \$656.0 \text{ million}$$

Current Assets and Liabilities

Accountants arbitrarily define any asset or liability that will turn into cash within one year as *current* and all other assets or liabilities as *long-term*. Inventory is a current asset because there is reason to believe it will be sold and will generate cash within the year. Accounts payable are short-term liabilities because they must be paid within the year. Note that even though ADI is a manufacturer, over half of its assets are current. We will say more about this in the next chapter.

Shareholders' Equity

A common source of confusion is the large number of accounts appearing in the shareholders' equity portion of the balance sheet. ADI has four, beginning with common stock and ending with cumulative translation adjustment (see Table 1–1). Unless forced to do otherwise, my advice is to forget these distinctions. They keep accountants and attorneys employed, but seldom make much practical difference. Just add up everything that is not an IOU and call it shareholders' equity.

A WORD TO THE UNWARY

Nothing puts a damper on a good financial discussion (if such exists) faster than the suggestion that if a company is short of cash, it can always spend some of its shareholders' equity. Equity is on the liabilities side of the balance sheet, not the asset side. It represents owners' claims against existing assets. In other words, that money has already been spent.

T A B L E 1–1

Analog Devices, Inc., Balance Sheets ($ millions)

	October 30 1994	October 30 1995	Change in Account
Assets			
Cash	$109.1	$ 69.3	$ (39.8)
Short-term investments	72.7	81.8	9.2
Accounts receivable	162.3	181.3	19.0
Inventories	130.7	144.0	13.2
Prepaid expenses and other current assets	30.6	49.6	19.0
Total current assets	505.5	526.0	
Property, plant, and equipment, at cost	658.9	856.3	197.4
Less accumulated depreciation	(377.1)	(424.3)	(47.2)
Net property, plant, and equipment	281.8	432.0	150.1
Intangible assets	19.3	17.2	(2.0)
Other long-term assets	9.3	26.4	17.1
Total assets	$815.9	$1,001.6	
Liabilities and Shareholders' Equity			
Short-term borrowings and current maturities of long-term obligations	$ 23.2	$ 2.4	$ (20.8)
Accounts payable	74.5	100.2	25.7
Deferred income on shipments to domestic distributors	18.9	27.6	8.7
Income taxes payable	29.4	50.1	20.7
Accrued liabilities	60.2	74.1	13.9
Total current liabilities	206.2	254.4	
Long-term obligations less current maturities	80.1	80.0	(0.1)
Deferred income taxes	3.2	5.0	1.8
Other long-term liabilities	4.5	6.3	1.8
Total liabilities	294.0	345.7	
Common stock	12.5	19.1	
Additional paid-in capital	141.2	149.5	
Retained earnings	362.2	481.5	
Cumulative translation adjustment	6.0	5.9	
Total shareholders' equity	521.9	656.0	134.1
Total liabilities and shareholders' equity	$815.9	$1,001.6	

T A B L E 1–2

Analog Devices, Inc., Income Statements ($ millions)

	October 30	
	1994	**1995**
Net sales	$773.5	$941.5
Cost of sales	394.4	464.6
Gross profit	379.0	477.0
Research and development	106.9	134.3
Selling, marketing, general and administrative expenses	170.3	184.9
Total operating expenses	277.2	319.2
Operating income	101.8	157.8
Interest expense	(7.1)	(4.2)
Interest income	5.2	8.1
Other income (expense)	(2.9)	(2.2)
Total nonoperating income (expense)	(4.9)	1.7
Income before income taxes	96.9	159.4
Provision for income taxes	22.4	40.2
Net income	$ 74.5	$119.3

THE INCOME STATEMENT

A balance sheet is a snapshot at a point in time. An income statement, on the other hand, records the flow of resources over time. The basic relationship is

$$\text{Net sales} - \text{Cost of goods sold} - \text{Operating expenses} + \text{Nonoperating income (expense)} - \text{Taxes} = \text{Earnings}$$

$$\$941.5 - \$464.6 - \$319.2 + \$1.7 - \$40.2 = \$119.3$$

Earnings measure the extent to which revenues generated during the accounting period exceeded expenses incurred in producing the revenues. For variety, earnings are also commonly referred to as *profits* or *income*, frequently with the word *net* stuck in front of them, and net sales are often called *revenues*, or *net revenues*. I have never found a meaningful distinction between these terms. Why so many words to describe the same thing? My personal belief is that accountants are so rule-bound in their calculations of the various amounts that their creativity runs a bit amok when it comes to naming them.

Income statements arc commonly divided into operating and nonoperating segments. As the names imply, the operating segment reports the results of the company's major, ongoing activities, while the nonoperating segment summarizes all secondary activities. In 1995, ADI reported operating income of $157.8 million and nonoperating income, principally interest income, of $1.7 million (see Table 1–2).

Measuring Earnings

This is not the place for a detailed discussion of accounting. But because earnings, or lack of same, are a critical indicator of financial health, several technical details of earnings measurement deserve mention.

Accrual Accounting
The measurement of accounting earnings involves two steps: (1) identifying revenues for the period and (2) matching the corresponding costs to revenues. Looking at the first step, it is important to recognize that revenue is not the same as cash received. According to the *accrual principle* (a cruel principle?) of accounting, revenue is recognized as soon as "the effort required to generate the sale is substantially complete and there is a reasonable certainty that payment will be received." The accountant sees the timing of the actual cash receipts as a mere technicality. For credit sales, the accrual principle means that revenue is recognized at the time of sale, not when the customer pays. This can result in a significant time lag between the generation of revenue and the receipt of cash. Looking at ADI, we see that revenue in 1995 was $941.5 million but accounts receivable increased $19.0 million over the year. We conclude that the cash received from sales during 1995 was only $922.5 million ($941.5 million − $19.0 million). The other $19.0 million still awaits collection.

Depreciation
Fixed assets and their associated depreciation present the accountant with a particularly challenging problem in matching. Suppose that in 1997, a company constructs for $50 million a new facility that has an expected productive life of 10 years. If the accountant assigns the entire cost of the

---

WHEN IS A SALE A SALE?

ADI also illustrates an even thornier issue in revenue recognition, one that exemplifies the power of accountants to alter apparent financial performance. Consistent with standard accounting practice, ADI recognizes revenue for product sales on shipment. However, a portion of these sales goes to domestic distributors under an agreement that, under certain conditions, allows the distributors to return unsold merchandise. The ability to return merchandise makes it difficult to decide when "there is a reasonable certainty that payment will be received" and, hence, when a sale truly occurs. Conservative accounting says ADI should not record a sale until the distributor does. In the meantime, the merchandise should remain part of ADI's inventory. Aggressive accounting, on the other hand, ignores the return option and books a sale on shipment to the distributor. Interestingly, ADI splits the difference, recognizing the revenue and relevant costs when it ships merchandise to distributors but deferring recognition of any profit until the distributor sells the goods. This is the origin of the entry on the liabilities side of ADI's balance sheet entitled "deferred income on shipments to domestic distributors." Had ADI used aggressive accounting, income before taxes in 1995 would have been about 17 percent higher and deferred income would have vanished.

---

facility to expenses in 1997, some weird results follow. Income in 1997 will appear depressed due to the $50 million expense, while income in the following nine years will look that much better as the new facility contributes to revenue but not to expenses. Thus, charging the full cost of a long-term asset to one year clearly distorts reported income.

The preferred approach is to spread the cost of the facility over its expected useful life in the form of depreciation. Because the only cash outlay associated with the facility occurs in 1997, the annual depreciation listed as a cost on the company's income statement is not a cash outflow. It is a *noncash charge* used to match the 1997 expenditure with resulting revenue. Said differently, depreciation is the allocation of past expenditures to future time periods to match revenues and expenses. Although the precise numbers cannot be confirmed from the data presented so far, you will see momentarily that ADI acquired $212.7 million of property, plant, and equipment in 1995 and included a $64.1 million noncash charge for depreciation among the expenses on its income statement.

To determine the amount of depreciation to take on a particular asset, three estimates are required: the asset's useful life, its salvage value, and the method of allocation to be employed. These estimates should be based on economic and engineering information, experience, and any other objective data about the asset's likely performance.

Broadly speaking, there are two methods of allocating an asset's cost over its useful life. Under the *straight-line* method, the accountant depreciates the asset by a uniform amount each year. If an asset costs $50 million, has an expected useful life of 10 years, and has an estimated salvage value of $10 million, straight-line depreciation will be $4 million per year ([$50 million − $10 million]/10).

The second method of cost allocation is really a family of methods known as *accelerated depreciation*. Each technique charges more depreciation in the early years of the asset's life and correspondingly less in later years. Accelerated depreciation does not enable a company to take more depreciation in total; rather, it alters the timing of the recognition. While the specifics of the various accelerated techniques need not detain us here, you should recognize that the life expectancy, the salvage value, and the allocation method a company uses can fundamentally affect reported earnings. In general, if a company is conservative and depreciates its assets rapidly, it will tend to understate current earnings, and vice versa.

Taxes

A second noteworthy feature of depreciation accounting involves taxes. Most U.S. companies, except very small ones, keep at least two sets of financial records: one for managing the company and reporting to shareholders and another for determining the firm's tax bill. The objective of the first set is, or should be, to accurately portray the company's financial performance. The objective of the second set is much simpler: to minimize taxes. Forget objectivity and minimize taxes. These differing objectives mean the accounting principles used to construct the two sets of books differ substantially. Depreciation accounting is a case in point. Regardless of the method used to report to shareholders, company tax books will minimize current taxes by employing the most rapid method of depreciation over the shortest useful life the tax authorities allow.

This dual reporting creates complications on U.S. companies' published financial statements. To illustrate, the "provision for income taxes" of $40.2 million appearing on ADI's 1995 income statement does not equal taxes paid; rather, it is the tax payable according to the accounting techniques used to construct ADI's published statements. But because the company used different accounting techniques when reporting to the tax authorities—techniques intended to defer the payment of tax until future years—taxes paid are less than $40.2 million. To confirm this, note that the company has two tax accounts on the liabilities side of its balance sheet called "income taxes payable" and "deferred income taxes." The changes in these accounts indicate that ADI's tax liability increased $22.5 million over the course of the year; hence, taxes paid must have been only $17.7 million. Here is a more detailed accounting:

Provision for income taxes	$40.2
– Increase in income taxes payable	(20.7)
– Increase in deferred income taxes	(1.8)
Taxes paid	$17.7 million

Because the $22.5 million in taxes is only postponed, not eliminated, it appears as an increase in liabilities on Analog Devices' 1995 balance sheet. In the meantime, ADI has use of the money; thus, tax deferral techniques create the equivalent of an interest-free loan from the government. In Japan and other countries that do not allow the use of separate accounting techniques for tax and reporting purposes, these complications never arise.

Research and Marketing
Now that you understand how accountants use depreciation to spread the cost of long-lived assets over their useful lives to better match revenues and costs, you may think you also understand how they treat research and marketing expenses. Because R&D and marketing outlays promise benefits over a number of future periods, it is only logical that an accountant would show these expenditures as assets when they are incurred and then spread the costs over the assets' expected useful lives in the form of a noncash charge such as depreciation. Impeccable logic, but this isn't what accountants do, at least not in the United States. Because the magnitude and duration of the prospective payoffs from R&D and marketing expenditures are difficult to estimate, accountants typically duck the problem by forcing companies to record the entire expenditure as an operating cost in the year incurred. Thus, although ADI's $134 million in research and development expenses in 1995 might have produced technical breakthroughs that will benefit ADI for decades to come, all of the costs must be shown on the income statement in 1995. The requirement that companies expense all research and marketing expenditures when incurred commonly understates the profitability of

high-tech and high-marketing companies and complicates comparison of American companies with those in other nations that treat such expenditures more liberally.

SOURCES AND USES STATEMENTS

Two very basic but valuable things to know about a company are where it gets its cash and how it spends the cash. At first blush, it might appear that the income statement will answer these questions because it records flows of resources over time. But further reflection will convince you that the income statement is deficient in two respects: It includes accruals that are not cash flows, and it lists only cash flows associated with the sale of goods or services during the accounting period. A host of other cash receipts and disbursements do not appear on the income statement. Thus, Analog Devices added $197.4 million to property, plant, and equipment during 1995 (Table 1–1); yet the only trace of this expenditure on the company's income statement is a modest increase in depreciation. ADI also reduced its short-term borrowings $20.8 million, and the only income statement effect is a modest decline in interest expense.

To gain a more accurate picture of where a company got its money and how it spent it, we need to look more closely at the balance sheet or, more precisely, two balance sheets. Use the following two-step procedure. First, place two balance sheets for different dates side by side, and note all of the changes in accounts that occurred over the period. The changes for ADI in 1995 appear in the rightmost column of Table 1–1. Second, segregate the changes into those that generated cash and those that consumed cash. The result is a *sources and uses statement*.

Here are the guidelines for distinguishing between a source and a use of cash:

• *A company generates cash in two ways: by reducing an asset or by increasing a liability.* The sale of used equipment, the liquidation of inventories, and the reduction of accounts receivable are all reductions in asset accounts and are all sources of cash to the company. On the liabilities side of the balance sheet, an increase in a bank loan and the sale of common stock are increases in liabilities, which again generate cash.

• *A company also uses cash in two ways: to increase an asset account or to reduce a liability account.* Adding to inventories or

T A B L E 1–3

Analog Devices, Inc., Sources and Uses Statement, 1995 ($ millions)

Sources	
Reduction in cash	$ 39.8
Reduction in intangible assets	2.0
Increase in accounts payable	25.7
Increase in deferred income on shipments to domestic distributors	8.7
Increase in income taxes payable	20.7
Increase in accrued liabilities	13.9
Increase in deferred taxes	1.8
Increase in other deferred liabilities	1.8
Increase in shareholders' equity	134.1
Total sources	**$248.5**
Uses	
Increase in short-term investments	$ 9.2
Increase in accounts receivable	19.0
Increase in inventories	13.2
Increase in prepaid expenses and other current assets	19.0
Increase in net property, plant, and equipment	150.1
Increase in other long-term assets	17.1
Reduction in short-term borrowings and current maturities of long-term obligations	20.8
Reduction in long-term obligations less current maturities	0.1
Total uses	**$248.5**

accounts receivable and building a new plant all increase assets and all use cash. Conversely, the repayment of a bank loan, the reduction of accounts payable, and an operating loss all reduce liabilities and all use cash.

Because it is difficult to spend money you don't have, total uses of cash over an accounting period must equal total sources.

Table 1–3 presents a 1995 sources and uses statement for ADI. It reveals that the company got most of its cash from a $134.1 million increase in shareholders' equity. ADI, in turn, spent most of this cash on a $150.1 million increase in net property, plant, and equipment. The table shows a conservative company investing heavily in capacity to support anticipated future growth. We will revisit this topic in more detail in later chapters.

HOW CAN A REDUCTION IN CASH BE A SOURCE OF CASH?

One potential source of confusion in Table 1–3 is that the reduction in cash during 1995 appears as a source of cash. How can a reduction in cash be a source of cash? Simple. It is the same as when you withdraw money from your checking account: You reduce your bank balance but have more cash on hand to spend. Conversely, a deposit to your bank account adds to your balance but reduces the spendable cash in your pocket.

The Two-Finger Approach

I personally do not spend a lot of time constructing sources and uses statements. It might be instructive to go through the exercise once or twice just to convince yourself that sources really do equal uses. But once beyond this point, I recommend using a "two-finger approach." Put the two balance sheets side by side, and quickly run any two fingers down the columns in search of big changes. This should enable you to quickly observe that the great majority of ADI's cash came from increased shareholders' equity while additions to property, plant, and equipment and, to a much lesser extent, a reduction in short-term borrowings were the principal uses to which the cash was put. In 30 seconds or less, you have the essence of a sources and uses analysis and are free to move on to more stimulating activities. The other changes are largely window dressing of more interest to accountants than to managers.

THE CASH FLOW STATEMENT

Identifying a company's principal sources and uses of cash is a useful skill in its own right. It is also an excellent starting point for considering the cash flow statement, the third major component of financial statements along with the income statement and the balance sheet.

Until about 10 years ago, the third element in the accounting triumvirate was a creature known as the *statement of changes in financial position*. Once described as "a random collection of pluses and minuses," the statement of changes in financial position was so confusing that even accountants were uncertain of its purpose. The cash flow statement is a quantum improvement, but I still wonder whether it really provides any more useful information than one can glean much more simply with a quick sources and uses analysis.

Basically a cash flow statement simply expands and rearranges the sources and uses statement, placing each source or use into one of three broad categories. The categories and their values for Analog Devices in 1995 are as follows:

Category	Source (or Use) of Cash ($ millions)
1. Cash flows from operating activities	$210.3
2. Cash flows from investing activities	($238.7)
3. Cash flows from financing activities	($10.9)

Double-entry bookkeeping guarantees that the sum of the cash flows in these three categories equals the change in cash balances over the accounting period. (For companies with international operations, a fourth category called "effect of exchange rate change on cash" also appears; more on this shortly.) Again, we see a conservative company devoting all of its operating cash flows and then some to increasing productive capacity.

Table 1–4 presents a complete cash flow statement for Analog Devices in 1995. The first category, "cash flows from operating activities," can be thought of as a rearrangement of ADI's financial statements to eliminate the effects of accrual accounting on net income. First, we add all noncash charges, such as depreciation and deferred taxes, back to net income, recognizing that these charges did not entail any cash outflow. Then we add the changes in current assets and liabilities to net income, acknowledging, for instance, that some sales did not increase cash because customers had not yet paid, while some expenses did not reduce cash because the company had not yet paid. Changes in other current assets and liabilities, such as inventories and prepaid expenses, appear here because the accountant, following the matching principle, ignored these cash flows when calculating net income. Interestingly, the cash generated by ADI's operations was almost double the firm's net income. The two principal cash generators mislabeled or ignored on the income statement were $64.1 million depreciation mislabeled as an expense and a $51.3 million increase in accounts payable and other short-term liabilities that was ignored on the income statement.

T A B L E 1–4

Analog Devices, Inc., Cash Flow Statement, 1995 ($ millions)

Cash Flows from Operating Activities	
Net income	$119.3
Adjustments to reconcile net income to net cash provided by operations:	
Depreciation and amortization	64.1
Deferred income taxes	1.8
Changes in current assets and liabilities:	
(Increase) decrease in accounts receivable	(18.3)
(Increase) decrease in inventories	(14.4)
(Increase) decrease in prepaid expenses and other current assets	(19.1)
Increase in accounts payable, deferred income, and accrued liabilities	51.3
Increase in income taxes payable	23.8
Increase (decrease) in other current liabilities	1.8
Net cash provided by operating activities	210.3
Cash Flows from Investing Activities	
Additions to property, plant, and equipment	(212.7)
Purchase of short-term investments	(173.4)
Maturities of short-term investments	164.3
Increase in other assets	(16.9)
Net cash used in investing activities	(238.7)
Cash Flows from Financing Activities	
Payments on long-term debt and capital lease obligations	(20.2)
Proceeds from employee stock plans	10.1
Other financing activities	(0.8)
Net cash used for financing activities	(10.9)
Effect of exchange rate changes on cash	(0.5)
Net increase (decrease) in cash	(39.8)
Cash at beginning of year	109.1
Cash at end of year	$ 69.3

WHAT IS CASH FLOW?

So many conflicting definitions of *cash flow* exist today that the term has almost lost meaning. At one level, cash flow is very simple: It is the movement of money into or out of a cash account over a period of time. The problem arises when we try to be more specific. Here are four common types of cash flow you are apt to encounter.

Net cash flow = Net income ± Noncash items

Often known in investment circles as *cash earnings*, net cash flow is intended to measure the cash a business generates, as distinct from the earnings—a laudable objective. Applying the formula to Analog Devices' 1995 figures (Table 1–4), net cash flow was $185.2 million, equal to net income plus depreciation and amortization and deferred income taxes.

A problem with net cash flow as a measure of cash generation is that it implicitly assumes a business's current assets and liabilities are either unrelated to operations or do not change over time. In ADI's case, the cash flow statement reveals that changes in a number of current assets and liabilities contributed about $25 million in cash to the company. A more inclusive measure of cash generation is therefore cash flow from operating activities as it appears on the cash flow statement:

Cash flow from operating activities = Net cash flow ± Changes in current assets and liabilities

A third type of cash flow popular in finance circles is

Free cash flow = Total cash available for distribution to owners and creditors after funding all worthwhile investment activities

As we will see in Chapter 9, free cash flow is a fundamental determinant of the value of a business. Indeed, one can argue that the principal means by which a company creates value for its owners is by increasing free cash flow.

Yet another type of cash flow, popular among finance specialists, is

Discounted cash flow = A sum of money today having the same value as a future stream of cash receipts or disbursements

Discounted cash flow refers to a family of techniques for analyzing investment opportunities that take into account the time value of money. This topic is the focus of two later chapters.

My advice when tossing cash flow terms about is to either use the phrase broadly to refer to a general movement of cash or define your terms.

One potentially confusing entry in Table 1–4 is "effect of exchange rate changes on cash" toward the bottom of the statement. It arises as follows. Companies engaged in international business commonly hold cash balances denominated in foreign currencies. When the value of the U.S. dollar changes relative to these currencies, the dollar value of these cash balances changes as well. For example, if a U.S. company has a

QUOTH THE BANKER, "WATCH CASH FLOW"

Once upon a midnight dreary as I pondered weak and weary
Over many a quaint and curious volume of accounting lore,
Seeking gimmicks (without scruple) to squeeze through some new tax
  loophole,
Suddenly I heard a knock upon my door,
   Only this, and nothing more.

Then I felt a queasy tingling and I heard the cash a-jingling
As a fearsome banker entered whom I'd often seen before.
His face was money-green and in his eyes there could be seen
Dollar-signs that seemed to glitter as he reckoned up the score.
   "Cash flow," the banker said, and nothing more.

I had always thought it fine to show a jet black bottom line,
But the banker sounded a resounding, "No,
Your receivables are high, mounting upward toward the sky;
Write-offs loom. What matters is cash flow."
   He repeated, "Watch cash flow."

Then I tried to tell the story of our lovely inventory
Which, though large, is full of most delightful stuff.
But the banker saw its growth, and with a mighty oath
He waved his arms and shouted, "Stop! Enough!
   Pay the interest, and don't give me any guff!"

Next I looked for non-cash items which could add ad infinitum
To replace the ever-outward flow of cash,
But to keep my statement black I'd held depreciation back,
And my banker said that I'd done something rash.
   He quivered, and his teeth began to gnash.

When I asked him for a loan, he responded, with a groan,
That the interest rate would be just prime plus eight,
And to guarantee my purity he'd insist on some security—
All my assets plus the scalp upon my pate.
   Only this, a standard rate.

Though my bottom line is black, I am flat upon my back,
My cash flows out and customers pay slow.
The Growth of my receivables is almost unbelievable;
The result is certain—unremitting woe!
And I hear the banker utter an ominous low mutter,
   "Watch cash flow."

Herbert S. Bailey, Jr.

1 million German mark deposit and the exchange rate changes over the year from DM1.00 = $0.50 to DM1.00 = $0.75, the dollar value of the mark deposit will rise from $500,000 to $750,000. This $250,000 increase will appear on the cash flow statement under the heading "effect of exchange rate changes on cash." The dollar value of ADI's foreign-denominated cash fell $500,000 in this manner during 1995.

Much of the information contained in a cash flow statement can be gleaned from a careful study of a company's income statement and balance sheet. Nonetheless, the statement has three principal virtues. First, accounting neophytes and those who do not trust accrual accounting have at least some hope of understanding it. Second, the statement provides more accurate information about certain cash flows than one can infer from income statements and balance sheets alone. Third, it casts a welcome light on the issue of firm solvency by highlighting the extent to which operations are generating or consuming cash.

FINANCIAL STATEMENTS AND THE VALUE PROBLEM

To this point, we have reviewed the basics of financial statements and grappled with the distinction between earnings and cash flow. To gain a further perspective and in anticipation of later discussions, let us conclude by examining a recurring problem in the use of accounting data for financial decision making.

Market Value versus Book Value

Part of what I will call the *value problem* involves the distinction between the market value and the book value of shareholders' equity. Analog Devices' 1995 balance sheet states that the value of shareholders' equity is $656 million. This is known as the *book value* of ADI's equity. However, ADI is not worth $656 million to its shareholders or to anyone else, for that matter. There are two reasons. One is that financial statements are *transactions based*. If a company purchased an asset for $1 million in 1950, this transaction provides an objective measure of the asset's value, which the accountant uses to value the asset on the company's balance sheet. Unfortunately, it is a 1950 value that may or may not have much relevance today. To further confound things, the accountant attempts to reflect the gradual deterioration of an asset over time by periodically subtracting depreciation from its balance sheet value. This practice makes sense as far as it goes, but depreciation is the only change in value an American accountant recognizes. The $1 million asset purchased in 1950 may be technologically obsolete and therefore virtually worthless today; or, due to inflation, it may be worth much more than its original purchase price. This is especially true of land, which can be worth several times its original cost.

It is tempting to argue that accountants should forget the original costs of long-term assets and provide more meaningful current values. The problem is that objectively determinable current values of many assets do not exist. Faced with a choice between relevant but subjective current values and irrelevant but objective historical costs, accountants opt for irrelevant historical costs. This means it is the user's responsibility to make any adjustments to historical-cost asset values she deems appropriate.

Prodded by the Securities and Exchange Commission, the Financial Accounting Standards Board, accounting's principal rulemaking fraternity, has recently begun to require that certain assets and liabilities appear on financial statements at their market values instead of at their historical costs. Such "marking to market" applies to all assets and liabilities that trade actively in markets, including many common stocks and bonds. The change has been greeted with howls of protest by commercial bankers, among others, concerned that the move will increase the apparent volatility of earnings and, more menacingly, may reveal that some enterprises are worth less than historical-cost financial statements suggest. The appearance of benign stability is apparently more appealing to these critics than the hint of an ugly reality.

To understand the second, more fundamental reason Analog Devices is not worth $656 million, recall that equity investors buy shares for the future income they hope to receive, not for the value of the firm's assets. Indeed, if all goes according to plan, most of the firm's existing assets will be consumed in generating future income. The problem with the accountant's measure of shareholders' equity is that it bears little relation to future income. There are two reasons for this. First, because the accountant's numbers are backward looking and cost based, they often provide few clues about the future income a company's assets might generate. Second, companies typically have a great many assets and liabilities that do not appear on their balance sheets but affect future income nonetheless. Examples include patents and trademarks, loyal customers, proven mailing lists, superior technology, and, of course, better management. It is said that in many companies, the most valuable assets go home to their spouses in the evening. Examples

T A B L E 1–5

The Book Value of Equity Is a Poor Surrogate for the Market Value of Equity Fiscal Year-End 1995, except Edison Brothers Stores and Wal-Mart Stores

Company	Value of Equity ($ millions) Book	Market	Ratio, Market Value to Book Value
American Pacific	$ 98	$ 45	0.5
Analog Devices	656	2,848	4.3
Boise Cascade	1,694	1,648	1.0
British Steel*	4,087	5,298	1.3
Coca Cola	5,392	92,983	17.2
Continuum	82	567	6.9
Cray Research	602	629	1.0
Edison Brothers Stores	140	33	0.2
Hudson's Bay Company†	1,772	1,427	0.8
Mid American Waste Systems	110	98	0.9
Silicon Graphics	1,346	6,399	4.8
Wal-Mart Stores	14,756	46,761	3.2

*Common equity in pounds sterling.

†Common equity in Canadian dollars.

of unrecorded liabilities include pending lawsuits, inferior management, and obsolete production processes. The accountant's inability to measure assets and liabilities such as these means that book value is customarily a highly inaccurate measure of the value perceived by shareholders.

It is a simple matter to calculate the market value of shareholders' equity when a company's shares are publicly traded: Simply multiply the number of common shares outstanding by the market price per share. At the end of fiscal year 1995, Analog Devices' common shares closed on the New York Stock Exchange at $24.88 per share. With 114.5 million shares outstanding, this yields a value of $2,848 million, or more than 4.3 times the book value ($2,848 million/$656 million). This $2,848 million is the *market value* of Analog Devices' equity.

Table 1–5 presents the market and book values of equity for a dozen representative companies. It demonstrates clearly that book value is a poor proxy for market value.

Goodwill

There is one instance in which intangible assets, like brand names and patents, find their way onto company balance sheets. It occurs when one company buys another at a price above book value. For example, suppose an acquiring firm pays $100 million for a target firm and the target's assets have a book value of only $40 million and an estimated replacement value of only $60 million. According to the most commonly used method of acquisition accounting, the accountant will allocate $60 million of the acquisition price to the value of the assets acquired and assign the remaining $40 million to a new asset commonly known as *goodwill*. Much as he would treat depreciation, the accountant will then write this goodwill off as a noncash expense against income over a period not exceeding 40 years. The acquiring company paid a handsome premium over the fair value of the target's recorded assets because it placed a high value on the target's unrecorded, or intangible, assets. But not until the acquisition created a piece of paper with $100 million written on it was the accountant willing to acknowledge this value.

Economic Income versus Accounting Income

A second dimension of the value problem is rooted in the accountant's distinction between *realized* and *unrealized* income. To anyone who has not studied too much accounting, income is what you could spend during the period and be as well off at the end as you were at the start. If Mary Siegler's assets, net of liabilities, are worth $100,000 at the start of the year and rise to $120,000 by the end, and if she receives and spends $70,000 in wages during the year, most of us would say her income was $90,000 ($70,000 in wages + $20,000 increase in net assets).

But not the accountant. He would say Mary's income was only $70,000. The $20,000 increase in the market value of assets would not qualify as income because the gain was not *realized* by the sale of the assets. Because the market value of the assets could fluctuate in either direction before the assets are sold, the gain is only *on paper*, and accountants generally do not recognize paper gains or losses. They consider *realization* the objective evidence necessary to record the gain, despite the fact that Mary is probably just as pleased with the unrealized gain in assets as with the $20,000 in wages,

It is easy to criticize accountants' conservatism when measuring income. Certainly the amount Mary could spend, ignoring inflation, and be as well off as at the start of the year is the commonsense $90,000, not the accountant's $70,000. Moreover, if Mary sold her assets for $120,000 and immediately repurchased them for the same price, the $20,000 gain would become realized and, in the accountant's eyes, become part of income. That income could depend on a sham transaction such as this is enough to raise suspicions about the accountant's definition.

However, we should note two points in the accountant's defense. First, if Mary holds her assets for several years before selling them, the gain or loss the accountant recognized on the sale date will just equal the sum of the annual gains and losses we nonaccountants would recognize. So it's really not total income that is at issue here but simply the timing of its recognition. Second, it is extremely difficult to measure the periodic change in the value of many assets unless they are actively traded. Thus, even if an accountant wanted to include "paper" gains and losses in income, she would often have great difficulty doing so. In the corporate setting, this means the accountant must be content to measure realized rather than economic income.

Imputed Costs

A similar but subtler problem exists on the cost side of the income statement. It involves the cost of equity capital. Analog Devices' auditors acknowledge that in 1995 the company had use of $656 million of shareholders' money, measured at book value. They would further acknowledge that ADI could not have operated without this money and that this money is not free. Just as creditors earn interest on loans, equity investors expect a return on their investments. Yet if you look again at ADI's income statement (Table 1–2), you will find no mention of the cost of this equity; interest expense appears, but a comparable cost for equity does not.

While acknowledging that equity capital has a cost, the accountant does not record it on the income statement because the cost must be imputed, that is, estimated. Because there is no piece of paper stating the amount of money ADI is obligated to pay owners, the accountant refuses to recognize any cost of equity capital. Once again, the accountant would rather be reliably wrong than make a potentially inaccurate estimate. The result has been serious confusion in the minds of less knowledgeable observers and continuing "image" problems for corporations.

Following is the bottom portion of Analog Devices' 1995 income statement as prepared by its accountant and as an economist might prepare it. Observe that while the accountant shows earnings of $119.3 million for the year, the economist records a profit of only $40.5 million. These numbers differ because the economist includes a $78.7 million cost of equity capital, while the accountant shows no cost. (We will consider ways to estimate a company's cost of equity capital in Chapter 8. Here I have assumed a 12 percent equity cost and applied it to the book value of ADI's equity [$78.7 million = 12% × $656 million].)

Analog Devices' 1995 Income as Seen by an Accountant and by an Economist ($ millions)

	Accountant	Economist
Operating income	$157.8	$157.8
Interest expense	(4.2)	(4.2)
Interest income	8.1	8.1
Other nonoperating expenses	(2.2)	(2.2)
Cost of equity		**(78.7)**
Income before tax	159.4	80.7
Provision for taxes	40.2	40.2
Accounting earnings	$119.3	
Economic earnings		**$ 40.5**

The distinction between accounting earnings and economic earnings might be only a curiosity if everyone understood that positive accounting earnings are not necessarily a sign of superior or even commendable performance. But when many labor unions and politicians view accounting profits as evidence that a company can afford higher wages, higher taxes, or more onerous regulation, and when most managements view such profits as justification for distributing handsome performance bonuses, the distinction can be an important one. Keep in mind, therefore, that the right of equity investors to expect a competitive return on their investments is every bit as legitimate as a creditor's right to interest and an employee's right to wages. All voluntarily contribute scarce resources, and all are justified in expecting compensation. Remember too that a company is not shooting par unless its *economic* profits are zero or above. By this criterion, Analog Devices had a fine but not fantastic year in 1995. On closer inspection, you will find that many companies reporting apparently large earnings are really performing like weekend duffers when the cost of equity is included.

In sum, those of us interested in financial analysis eventually develop a love-hate relationship with accountants. The value problem means that financial statements typically yield distorted information about company earnings and market value. This limits their applicability for many important managerial decisions. Yet financial statements frequently provide the best information available, and if we bear their limitations in mind, they can be a useful starting point for analysis. In the next chapter, we consider the use of accounting data for evaluating financial performance.

Inflation and the Assessment of Company Performance

'Tis the night before Christmas
and all through the nation
your bonus means nothing
because of Inflation

Mad Magazine

Assessing the financial performance of a company during inflation is like measuring the width of a table with a rubber band: The size of the yardstick keeps changing. Here we will briefly consider the ways inflation distorts historical-cost financial statements and the accounting techniques available to minimize these distortions.

Inflation and Company Profits

Inflation distorts a company's income statement in three distinct ways. The first involves historical-cost depreciation, the second the valuation of inventory, and the third accounting for interest expense. The first two sources of distortion are well known, while the third is more obscure and frequently misunderstood.

Historical-Cost Depreciation

Because depreciation expense under historical-cost accounting must be based on the original cost of the asset, the annual amount charged against income during inflation understates the true decline in the value of assets. Said differently, historical-cost depreciation is not sufficient to maintain the value of company assets during inflation. This understatement of annual depreciation causes an overstatement of reported earnings and an increase in corporate taxes due.

Inventory Valuation

An analogous problem arises with inventories. The two most widely used methods of inventory accounting in the United States are first-in, first-out (FIFO) and last-in, first-out (LIFO), although FISH (first-in, still-here) is still popular in some circles. In an inflationary environment, a company's reported earnings and its tax bill depend on which method it uses. To illustrate, suppose a company manufactures and sells boxes and keeps its inventory of finished boxes in a stack, as shown in Figure 1A–1. Each time a new box is completed, it is added to the top of the pile. The dollar

F I G U R E   1A–1

Inventory Valuation, Taxes, and Earnings under Inflation

Cost of Production	Finished Boxes		FIFO Accounting	LIFO Accounting
$1.50		Selling price	$2.00	$2.00
1.40		Cost of goods sold	1.00	1.50
1.30		Taxable income	1.00	0.50
1.20		Tax at 50%	0.50	0.25
1.10		Earnings after tax	$0.50	$0.25
1.00				

amounts to the left of the boxes are the cost the company incurs in making each box. Since prices are rising, the cost of each successive box is higher, starting with the oldest box in inventory at $1.00 and rising to the most recently produced box at $1.50.

When the company sells a box for, say, $2.00, the accountant must match the cost of the box sold against the revenue. If the company uses FIFO, the assigned cost of goods sold will be $1.00; if LIFO accounting is employed, the cost of goods sold will be $1.50. (Here we ignore all practical problems associated with removing a box from the bottom of the stack.) As the figure shows, the choice of the inventory valuation method significantly affects the company's tax liability and reported earnings. In our numerical example, FIFO accounting produces earnings and taxes of $0.50 as opposed to $0.25 for LIFO accounting.

Which earnings figure is correct? Since the current cost of manufacturing one box is much closer to $1.50 than to $1.00, the LIFO earnings figure is the more accurate measure of true earnings under inflation. Yet for reasons we need not go into here, a great many corporations use FIFO accounting. For these companies, inflation again causes an overstatement of reported earnings and an increase in taxes.

Gains to Net Debtors

The third distortion to a company's income statement under inflation involves the way accountants measure interest expense on a loan. Suppose you borrow $100 from a bank for one year. In the absence of inflation, the banker might be content for you to repay $104 at year end—$100 in principal and $4 in interest. But in an environment of, say, 50 percent inflation, $104 will no longer be sufficient. The banker will now want the $100 principal back *plus* enough to maintain the purchasing power of the principal, or $50. In addition, the banker will want a return on the loan of $4 *plus* enough to maintain the purchasing power of the return, or $2. So in total, you will be asked to repay $156 in one year. You and the banker both know that $150 of this amount is really the repayment of principal and only $6 represents interest on the loan. But the accountant, whether or not she knows the truth, does not report the transaction this way. Instead, she reasons that because you borrowed $100, this amount by definition is the principal and the rest must be interest expense. This overstatement of interest expense causes an understatement of reported earnings and a reduction of taxes due. Of course, these effects apply only to companies that are "net debtors," that is, companies that have more IOUs outstanding than "you-owe-me's."

The Net Effect

The overstatement of reported earnings caused by historical-cost depreciation and FIFO inventory accounting is well known. Indeed, for a number of years, U.S. national income accounts have included adjustments to aggregate corporate income required to remove these distortions. They are known as the *inventory valuation adjustment (IVA)* and the *capital consumption adjustment (CCA)*.

However, the understatement of reported earnings caused by the mislabeling of interest expense is not known precisely. One study suggests that *on average*, the understatement of company earnings due to the mislabeling of interest is about equal in magnitude, but opposite in sign, to the *total* overstatement due to FIFO accounting and historical-cost depreciation.[1] This means that for the economy as a whole, the three distortions to reported income approximately offset one another, leaving reported earnings about equal to true earnings. This, of course, does not suggest that such a conclusion applies to every company. Depending on the particular company's degree of capital intensity, accounting conventions, and capital structure, reported earnings can differ substantially from true earnings.

---

1 F. Modigliani and R. Cohn, "Inflation, Rational Valuation and the Market," *Financial Analysts Journal*, March/April 1979.

INFLATION BIASES COMPANY EARNINGS

During a period of rapid inflation, companies A and B both report earnings of $100 million. Company A uses LIFO accounting, has primarily current assets, and makes extensive use of debt financing. Company B uses FIFO accounting, has primarily fixed assets, and is very conservatively financed. Which company is probably the more profitable?

Answer: Company A. FIFO accounting and historical-cost accounting cause reported earnings to exceed true earnings during inflation. Company A suffers comparatively little from these biases. Debt financing and the resulting misstatement of interest expense cause reported earnings to understate true earnings. Company A does suffer from this bias. Hence, true earnings are probably above $100 million. By the same reasoning, company B's true earnings are probably below $100 million.

Inflation and Company Balance Sheets

The distortions to a company's balance sheet caused by inflation are the direct result of the three biases already discussed. Thus, historical-cost accounting tends to understate the balance sheet value of long-term assets. Similarly, a look back at Figure 1A–1 will convince you that LIFO accounting understates the balance sheet value of company inventories. Indeed, after the sale of one box in our example, finished goods inventory would be $6.50 under FIFO but only $6.00 under LIFO.

Finally, the accounting treatment of liabilities under inflation tends to overstate their balance sheet values. Consistent with the idea that borrowers repay debts with cheaper dollars during inflation, the true values of many liabilities decline during inflationary periods. However, the accountant ignores these declines, with the result that the apparent indebtedness of a company overstates reality.

Let me caution: I am not saying it is necessarily good to be a debtor during inflation. The true values of liabilities do decline, but if the inflation is anticipated, the interest rate rises to offset the declines. The accountant's error is including the higher interest rate but ignoring the fall in the values of the liabilities.

Inflation Accounting

In the late 1970s and early 1980s, as the U.S. inflation rate headed toward the moon, the accounting profession made a halfhearted attempt to remedy the problems cited here by requiring large corporations to report some of the effects of inflation on their historical-cost financial statements. How-ever, the information was relegated to a footnote, was presented in a confusing format, and did not include gains to net debtors. Not surprisingly, it was seldom used, and as soon as the inflation rate dipped to a tolerable level, the reporting requirement was eliminated entirely.

The intent here is not to ridicule historical-cost financial statements but simply to remind you that historical-cost statements are especially misleading under inflation. At the same time, inflation accounting admittedly is still controversial. One debate involves the extent to which it is proper to write up fixed assets under inflation; another surrounds the question of whether gains to net debtors should appear on the income statement. Until these and related controversies are resolved, and as long as inflation remains low, many executives are prepared to acknowledge that inflation distorts historical-cost statements while remaining skeptical about the objectivity and usefulness of available remedies.

CHAPTER SUMMARY

1. This chapter reviewed the accounting principles governing financial statements and described the relationship between earnings and cash flow.

2. A company's finances and its business operations are integrally related. We study a company's financial statements because they are a window on the firm's operations.

3. Earnings are not cash flow. The financial executive watches both.

4. A balance sheet is a snapshot of a company's assets and liabilities at a point in time. An income statement records sales, related expenses, and earnings over a period. Both documents are transactions based and use the accrual principle: Because accounting statements are transactions based, long-term assets and depreciation are listed at historical cost and paper gains and losses are ignored. Use of the accrual principle means that revenues and expenses do not always coincide with cash inflows and outflows.

5. A cash flow statement presents a company's cash receipts and disbursements over the accounting period.

6. A sources and uses statement can be thought of as a "poor man's" cash flow statement. Two steps are required to create one: (a) calculate changes in balance sheet accounts over the accounting period and (b) segregate the sources from the uses.

7. Two recurring problems in the use of accounting statements for financial analysis are that (*a*) accounting book values seldom equal market values and (*b*) the accountant's refusal to recognize unrealized gains and losses and imputed costs makes accounting income differ from economic income.

ADDITIONAL   READING

Anthony, Robert N. *Essentials of Accounting.* 5th ed. Reading, MA: Addison Wesley, 1993.
   By a distinguished emeritus Harvard professor. A very popular programmed text with
      over 500,000 copies in print. A great way to review or pick up the basics of financial
      accounting on your own. Available in paperback, about $29.95.
Bandler, James P. *How to Use Financial Statements: A Guide to Understanding the Num-
      bers.* Burr Ridge, IL: Irwin Professional Publishing, 1994. 147 pages.
   A practical guide to financial statements with basic yet thorough introductions to the
      accrual concept, financial statements, and special reporting issues. Available for
      about $18.95 (paperback).
Downes, John, and Jordan Elliot Goodman.*Dictionary of Finance and Investment Terms.*
      Fourth ed. New York: Barron's Educational Services, Inc., 1995. 682 pages.
   Over 3,500 terms clearly defined. Available in paperback, about $11.95.
Stickney, Clyde P. *Financial Accounting: An Introduction to Concepts, Methods, and Uses.*
      7th ed. Hinsdale, IL: HBJ College & School Division, 1994.
   A clearly written introduction to financial accounting. Part Two, "Accounting Concepts
      and Methods," provides a solid treatment of financial statements in about 200 pages.
      Hardback, about $73.00.

CHAPTER   PROBLEMS

1. What happens to a company's equity when assets rise $1 million and liabilities fall $2 million?

2. What does it mean when cash flow from operations on a company's cash flow statement is negative? Is this bad news? If so, is it dangerous?

3. *a.* Is a company better or worse off when the market value of its assets rises $10 million? Why?

   b. Is a company better or worse off when the market value of its liabilities falls $10 million? Why?

   c. If you owned a company, would you prefer the market value of its assets to rise $10 million or the market value of its liabilities to fall $10 million?

4. You manage a real estate investment company. One year ago the company purchased 10 parcels of land distributed throughout the community for $1 million each. A recent appraisal of the properties indicates that five of the parcels are now worth $600,000 each, while the other five are worth $1.5 million each.

    Ignoring any income received from the properties over the year, calculate the investment company's accounting earnings and its economic earnings in each of the following cases:
    a. The company sells all of the properties at their appraised values today.
    b. The company sells none of the properties.
    c. The company sells the properties that have fallen in value and keeps the others.
    d. The company sells the properties that have risen in value and keeps the others.
    e. Upon returning from a property management seminar, an employee recommends the bank adopt an end-of-year policy of always selling properties that have risen in value since purchase and always retaining properties that have fallen in value. The employee explains that with this policy the company will never show a loss on its real estate investment activities. Do you agree with the employee? Why or why not?

5. Selected information about Adams Wright Corporation follows.

| | ($ in millions) | |
	1996	1997
Net sales	$ 52	$ 78
Cost of goods sold	30	41
Depreciation	10	12
Net income	5	8
Finished goods inventory	6	5
Accounts receivable	10	15
Accounts payable	6	9
Net fixed assets	80	84

    a. During 1997, how much cash did Adams Wright collect from sales?

     b. During 1997, what was the cost of goods produced by the company?

     c. Assuming the company sold no assets during the year, what were its capital expenditures during 1997?

6. Why do you suppose financial statements are constructed on an accrual basis rather than a cash basis when cash accounting is so much easier to understand?

7. Table 3–1 in Chapter 3 presents financial statements over the period 1993–1996 for R&E Supplies, Inc.

     a. Construct a sources and uses statement for the company from 1993 through 1996 (one statement for all three years).

     b. What insights, if any, does the sources and uses statement give you about the financial position of R&E Supplies?

8. Use the following information to estimate ZTZ Corporation's net cash flow from operations as it would appear on the company's 1997 cash flow statement.

	1996	1997
Net sales	$600	$800
Cost of goods sold	320	400
Gross income	280	400
Depreciation	60	80
General, selling expenses	40	40
Income before tax	180	280
Provision for taxes @ 40%	72	112
Income after tax	108	168
Cash	$200	$100
Accounts receivable	100	200
Inventory	120	80
Accrued taxes	200	240
Accrued wages	120	60
Accounts payable	60	80

9. Following are summary cash flow statements for three roughly equal-size companies.

	($ millions)		
	A	**B**	**C**
Net cash flows from operations	$ (100)	$ (100)	$ 100
Net cash used in investing activities	(300)	(10)	(30)
Net cash from financing activities	400	70	(80)
Cash balance at beginning of year	50	50	50

    a. Calculate each company's cash balance at the end of the year.

    b. Explain what might cause company C's net cash from financing activities to be negative.

    c. Looking at companies A and B, which company would you prefer to own? Why?

    d. Is company C's cash flow statement cause for any concern on the part of C's management or shareholders? Why or why not?

10. You are responsible for labor relations in your company. During heated labor negotiations, the general secretary of your largest union exclaims, "Look, this company has $1 billion worth of assets, $500 million worth of equity, and made a profit last year of $40 million—due largely, I might add, to the effort of union employees. So don't tell me you can't afford our wage demands." How would you reply?

CHAPTER 2

EVALUATING FINANCIAL PERFORMANCE

You can't manage what you can't measure.

William Hewlett

T he cockpit of a 747 jet looks like a three-dimensional video game. It is a sizable room crammed with meters, switches, lights, and dials requiring the full attention of three highly trained pilots. When compared to the cockpit of a single-engine Cessna, it is tempting to conclude that the two planes are different species rather than distant cousins. But at a more fundamental level, the similarities outnumber the differences. Despite the 747's complex technology, the 747 pilot controls the plane in the same way the Cessna pilot does: with a stick, a throttle, and flaps. And to change the altitude of the plane, each pilot makes simultaneous adjustments to the same few levers available for controlling the plane.

Much the same is true of companies. Once you strip away the facade of apparent complexity, the levers with which managers affect their companies' financial performance are comparatively few and are similar from one company to another. The executive's job is to control these levers to ensure a safe and efficient flight. And like the pilot, the executive must remember that the levers are interrelated; one cannot change the business equivalent of the flaps without also adjusting the stick and the throttle.

THE LEVERS OF FINANCIAL PERFORMANCE

In this chapter, we analyze financial statements for the purpose of evaluating performance and understanding the levers of management control. We begin by studying the ties between a company's operating decisions, such as how many units to make this month and how to price them, and its financial performance. These operating decisions are the levers by which management controls financial performance. Then we broaden the discussion to consider the uses and limitations of ratio analysis as a tool for evaluating performance. To keep things practical, we will again use the financial statements for Analog Devices, Inc., presented in Tables 1–1, 1–2, and 1–4 of the last chapter, to illustrate the techniques. The chapter concludes with an evaluation of ADI's financial performance relative to its competition.

RETURN ON EQUITY

By far the most popular yardstick of financial performance among investors and senior managers is the *return on equity (ROE)*, defined as

$$\text{Return on equity} = \frac{\text{Net income}}{\text{Shareholders' equity}}$$

ADI's ROE for 1995 was

$$\text{ROE} = \frac{\$119.3}{\$656.0} = 18.2\%$$

It is not an exaggeration to say that the careers of many senior executives rise and fall with their firms' ROEs. ROE is accorded such importance because it is a measure of the *efficiency* with which a company employs owners' capital. It is a measure of earnings per dollar of invested equity capital or, equivalently, of the percentage return to owners on their investment. In short, it measures bang per buck.

Later in this chapter, we will consider some significant problems with ROE as a measure of financial performance. For now, let us accept it provisionally as at least widely used and see what we can learn.

The Three Determinants of ROE

To learn more about what management can do to increase ROE, let us rewrite ROE in terms of its three principal components:

$$\text{ROE} = \frac{\text{Net income}}{\text{Shareholders' equity}}$$
$$= \frac{\text{Net income}}{\text{Sales}} \times \frac{\text{Sales}}{\text{Assets}} \times \frac{\text{Assets}}{\text{Shareholders' equity}}$$

Denoting the last three ratios as the profit margin, asset turnover, and financial leverage, respectively, the expression can be written as

$$\frac{\text{Return on}}{\text{equity}} = \frac{\text{Profit}}{\text{margin}} \times \frac{\text{Asset}}{\text{turnover}} \times \frac{\text{Financial}}{\text{leverage}}$$

This says that management has only three levers for controlling ROE: (1) the earnings squeezed out of each dollar of sales, or the *profit margin*; (2) the sales generated from each dollar of assets employed, or the *asset turnover*; and (3) the amount of equity used to finance the assets, or the *financial leverage*. With few exceptions, whatever management does to increase these ratios increases ROE.

Note too the close correspondence between the levers of performance and company financial statements. The profit margin summarizes a company's income statement performance, while asset turnover and financial leverage do the same for the left side and the right side of the balance sheet, respectively. This is reassuring evidence that despite their simplicity, the three levers do capture the major elements of a company's financial performance.

We find that ADI's 1995 ROE was generated as follows:

$$\frac{\$119.3}{\$656.0} = \frac{119.3}{941.5} \times \frac{941.5}{1,001.6} \times \frac{1,001.6}{656.0}$$
$$18.2\% = 12.7\% \times \quad 0.94 \quad \times \quad 1.53$$

Table 2–1 presents ROE and its three principal components for 10 highly diverse businesses. It shows quite clearly that there are many paths to heaven: The companies' ROEs are very similar, but the combinations of profit margin, asset turnover, and financial leverage producing this end result vary widely. Thus, ROE ranges from a high of 20.6 percent for Hewlett-Packard to a low of 11.6 for Nordstrom Inc., while the range for the profit margin, to take one example, is from a low of 2.1 percent for Food Lion Inc. to a high of 15.3 percent for Duke Power. ROE differs by about 2 to 1 high to low, but the profit margin varies by a factor of over 7 to 1.

Why are ROEs similar across firms while profit margins, asset turnovers, and financial leverages differ dramatically? The answer, in a word, is competition. Attainment of an unusually high ROE by one company acts as a magnet to attract rivals anxious to emulate the superior performance. As rivals enter the market, the heightened competition drives the successful company's ROE back toward the average. Conversely,

T A B L E 2–1

ROEs and Levers of Performance for 10 Diverse Companies, 1995

	Return on Equity (ROE) (%)	=	Profit Margin (P) (%)	×	Asset Turnover (A) (times)	×	Financial Leverage (T) (times)
Analog Devices, Inc.	18.2	=	12.7	×	0.94	×	1.53
BankAmerica Corporation	13.2	=	13.1	×	0.09	×	11.49
Duke Power	14.9	=	15.3	×	0.35	×	2.79
Exxon Corporation	16.0	=	5.3	×	1.33	×	2.26
Food Lion Inc.	15.7	=	2.1	×	3.10	×	2.40
Hewlett-Packard	20.6	=	7.7	×	1.29	×	2.06
Nike	20.4	=	8.4	×	1.51	×	2.60
Nordstrom Inc.	11.6	=	4.0	×	1.51	×	1.92
Southwest Airlines	12.8	=	6.4	×	0.88	×	2.28
Tiffany & Company	14.8	=	4.9	×	1.23	×	2.48

unusually low ROEs repel potential new competitors and drive existing companies out of business so that over time survivors' ROEs rise toward the average.

To understand how managerial decisions and a company's competitive environment combine to affect ROE, we will examine each lever of performance in more detail. In anticipation of the discussion of ratio analysis to follow, we will also consider related commonly used financial ratios. See Additional Readings at the end of the chapter for published sources of business ratios.

The Profit Margin

The profit margin measures the fraction of each dollar of sales that trickles down through the income statement to profits. This ratio is particularly important to operating managers because it reflects the company's pricing strategy and its ability to control operating costs. As Table 2–1 indicates, profit margins differ greatly among industries depending on the nature of the product sold and the company's competitive strategy.

Note too that profit margin and asset turnover tend to vary inversely. Companies with high profit margins tend to have low asset turns, and vice versa. This is no accident. Companies that add significant value to a product, such as Duke Power, can demand high profit margins. However, because adding value to a product usually requires lots of assets, these same firms tend to have lower asset turns. At the other extreme, grocery stores that add little to product value, such as Food Lion, Inc., have very low profit margins but high asset turns. It should be apparent, therefore, that a high profit margin is not necessarily better or worse than a low one, for it all depends on the combined effect of the profit margin and the asset turnover.

Return on Assets

To look at the combined effect of margins and turns, we can calculate the *return on assets (ROA)*:

$$\text{ROA} = \frac{\text{Profit}}{\text{margin}} \times \frac{\text{Asset}}{\text{turnover}} = \frac{\text{Net income}}{\text{Assets}}$$

Analog Devices' ROA in 1995 was

$$\text{Return on Assets} = \frac{\$119.3}{\$1,001.6} = 11.9\%$$

This means ADI earned an average of 11.9 cents on each dollar tied up in the business.

ROA is a basic measure of the efficiency with which a company allocates and manages its resources. It differs from ROE in that it measures profit as a percentage of the money provided by owners *and* creditors as opposed to only the money provided by owners.

Some companies, such as Duke Power and Hewlett-Packard, produce their ROAs by combining a high profit margin with a low to moderate asset turn; others, such as Food Lion, adopt the reverse strategy. A high profit margin *and* a high asset turn is ideal, but can be expected to attract considerable competition. Conversely, a low profit margin combined with a low asset turn will attract only bankruptcy lawyers.

Gross Margin

When analyzing profitability, it is often interesting to distinguish between variable costs and fixed costs. Variable costs change as sales vary, while fixed costs remain constant. Companies with a high proportion of fixed costs are more vulnerable to sales declines than other firms, because they cannot reduce fixed costs as sales fall. This means falling sales will produce major profit declines in high-fixed-cost businesses.

Unfortunately, the accountant does not differentiate between fixed and variable costs when constructing an income statement. However, it is usually safe to assume that most expenses in cost of goods sold are variable, while most of the other operating costs are fixed. The gross margin enables us to distinguish, insofar as possible, between fixed and variable costs. It is defined as

$$\text{Gross margin} = \frac{\text{Gross profit}}{\text{Sales}} = \frac{\$477.0}{\$941.5} = 50.7\%$$

Roughly speaking, then, half of ADI's sales dollar is a *contribution to fixed cost and profits*; 50.7 cents of every sales dollar is available to pay for fixed costs and to add to profits.

Asset Turnover

Some newcomers to finance believe assets are a good thing: the more the better. The reality is just the opposite: Unless a company is about to go out of business, its value is in the income stream it generates, and its assets are simply a necessary means to this end. Indeed, the ideal company would be one that produced income without any assets; then no investment would be required, and returns would be infinite. Short of this fantasy, our ROE equation tells us that, other things constant, financial performance improves as asset turnover rises. This is the second lever of management performance.

The asset turnover ratio measures the sales generated per dollar of assets. Analog Devices' asset turnover of 0.94 means that ADI generated 94 cents of sales for each dollar invested in assets. This ratio is a measure of capital intensity, with a low asset turnover signifying a capital-intensive business and a high turnover the reverse.

The nature of a company's products and its competitive strategy undeniably contribute significantly to the company's asset turnover. But the process is not a mechanical one. Management diligence and creativity in controlling assets are also vital. When product technology is similar among competitors, control of assets is often the margin between success and failure.

Control of current assets is especially critical. You might think the distinction between current and fixed assets based solely on whether the asset will revert to cash within one year is artificial. But more is involved than this. Current assets, especially accounts receivable and inventory, have several unique properties. One is that if something goes wrong—if sales decline unexpectedly, customers delay payment, or a critical part fails to arrive—a company's investment in current assets can balloon very rapidly. When even manufacturing companies routinely invest one-half or more of their money in current assets, it is easy to appreciate that even modest alterations in the management of these assets can significantly affect company finances.

A second distinction is that unlike fixed assets, current assets can become a source of cash during business downturns. As sales decline, a company's investment in accounts receivable and inventory should fall as well, thereby freeing cash for other uses. (Remember, a reduction in an asset account is a source of cash.) The fact that in a well-run company current assets move in an accordionlike fashion with sales is appealing to creditors. They know that during the upswing of a business cycle rising current assets will require loans, while during a downswing falling current assets will provide the cash to repay the loans. In bankers' jargon, such a loan is said to be *self-liquidating* in the sense that the use to which the money is put creates the source of repayment.

It is often useful to analyze the turnover of each type of asset on a company's balance sheet individually. This gives rise to what are known as *control ratios*. Although the form in which each ratio is expressed may vary, every control ratio is simply an asset turnover for a particular type of asset. In each instance, the firm's investment in the asset is compared to net sales or a closely related figure.

Why compare assets to sales? The fact that a company's investment in, say, accounts receivable has risen over time could be due to two forces: (1) Perhaps sales have risen and simply dragged receivables along, or (2) management may have slackened its collection efforts. Relating receivables to sales in a control ratio corrects for changes in sales, enabling the analyst to concentrate on the more important effects of changing management control. Thus, the control ratio distinguishes between sales-induced changes in investment and other, perhaps more sinister causes. Following are some standard control ratios and their values for ADI in 1995.

Inventory Turnover
Inventory turnover is expressed as

$$\text{Inventory turnover} = \frac{\text{Cost of goods sold}}{\text{Ending inventory}} = \frac{\$464.6}{\$144.0} = 3.2 \text{ times}$$

An inventory turn of 3.2 times means that items in ADI's inventory turn over 3.2 times per year on average; said differently, the typical item sits in inventory almost four months before being sold (12 months/3.2 times = 3.75 months).

Several alternative definitions of the inventory turnover ratio exist, including sales divided by ending inventory and cost of goods sold divided by average inventory. Cost of goods sold is a more appropriate numerator than sales because sales include a profit markup that is absent from inventory. But beyond this, I see little to choose from among the various definitions.

The Collection Period

The *collection period* highlights a company's management of accounts receivable. For Analog Devices,

$$\text{Collection period} = \frac{\text{Accounts receivable}}{\text{Credit sales per day}} = \frac{\$181.3}{\$941.5/365} = 70.3 \text{ days}$$

Credit sales appear here rather than net sales because only credit sales generate accounts receivable. As a company outsider, however, I do not know what portion of ADI's net sales, if any, are for cash, so I assume they are all on credit. Credit sales per day is defined as credit sales for the accounting period divided by the number of days in the accounting period, which for annual statements is obviously 365 days.

Two interpretations of ADI's 70.3-day collection period are possible. We can say that ADI has an average of 70.3 days' worth of credit sales tied up in accounts receivable, or we can say that the average time lag between sale and receipt of cash from the sale is 70.3 days.

If we like, we can define a simpler asset turnover ratio for accounts receivable as just credit sales/accounts receivable. However, the collection period format is more informative, because it allows us to compare a company's collection period with its terms of sale. Thus, if ADI sells on 90-day terms, a collection period of 70.3 days is excellent, but if the terms of sale were 30 days, our interpretation would be quite different.

Days' Sales in Cash

Analog Devices' days' sales in cash is as follows:

$$\frac{\text{Days' sales}}{\text{in cash}} = \frac{\text{Cash \& securities}}{\text{Net sales per day}} = \frac{\$69.3 + \$81.8}{\$941.5/365} = 58.6 \text{ days}$$

> ## BEWARE OF SEASONAL COMPANIES
>
> Interpreting many ratios of companies with *seasonal sales* can be tricky. For example, suppose a company's sales peak sharply at Christmas, resulting in high year-end accounts receivable. A naive collection period calculated by relating year-end accounts receivable to average daily sales for the whole year will produce an apparently very high collection period because the denominator is insensitive to the seasonal sales peak. To avoid being misled, a better way to calculate the collection period for a seasonal company is to use credit sales per day based only on the prior 60 to 90 days' sales. This matches the accounts receivable to the credit sales actually generating the receivables.

ADI has 58.6 days' worth of sales in cash and securities. It is difficult to generalize about whether or not this amount is appropriate for ADI. Companies require modest amounts of cash to facilitate transactions and are sometimes required to carry substantially larger amounts as compensating balances for bank loans. In addition, marketable securities can be an important source of liquidity for a firm in an emergency. So the question of how much cash a company should carry is often closely related to the broader question of how best to provide needed liquidity. Nonetheless, almost two months' sales in cash and securities appears quite generous.

Payables Period

The *payables period* is a control ratio for a liability. It is simply the collection period applied to accounts payable. For Analog Devices,

$$\frac{\text{Payables}}{\text{period}} = \frac{\text{Accounts payable}}{\text{Credit purchases per day}} = \frac{\$100.2}{\$464.6/365} = 78.7 \text{ days}$$

The proper definition of the payables period uses credit purchases, because they are what generate accounts payable. However, credit purchases are seldom known by an outsider, so it is frequently necessary to settle for the closest approximation: cost of goods sold. This is what is done above for ADI; $464.6 million is ADI's cost of goods sold, not its credit purchases. Cost of goods sold can differ from credit purchases for two reasons. First, the company may be adding to or depleting inventory, that is, purchasing at a different rate than it is selling. Second, all manufacturers add labor and depreciation to material in the production process, thereby making cost of goods sold larger than purchases. Because of these differences, it is tricky to compare a manufacturing company's payables period, based on cost of goods sold, to its purchase terms. For ADI, it is almost a certainty that cost of goods sold overstates credit purchases per day and that ADI's suppliers are waiting a good bit longer than 78.7 days on average to receive payment.

Fixed-Asset Turnover
Fixed-asset turnover reflects the capital intensity of a business. The ratio in 1995 for Analog Devices was

$$\text{Fixed-asset turnover} = \frac{\text{Sales}}{\text{Net property, plant, and equipment}} = \frac{\$941.5}{\$432.0} = 2.2 \text{ times}$$

where $432.0 million is the book value of ADI's net property, plant, and equipment.

Financial Leverage

The third lever by which management affects ROE is financial leverage. A company increases its financial leverage when it raises the proportion of debt relative to equity used to finance the business. Unlike the profit margin and the asset turnover ratio, where more is generally preferred to less, financial leverage is not something management necessarily wants to maximize, even when doing so increases ROE. Instead, the challenge of financial leverage is to strike a prudent balance between the benefits and costs of debt financing. Later we will devote a full chapter to this important financial decision. For now it is sufficient to recognize that while companies have considerable latitude in their choice of how much financial leverage to employ, there are economic and institutional constraints on their discretion.

As Table 2–1 suggests, the nature of a company's business and its assets influence the financial leverage it can employ. In general, businesses with highly predictable and stable operating cash flows, such as Duke Power, can safely undertake more financial leverage than firms facing a high degree of market uncertainty, such as Hewlett-Packard. In addition, businesses such as commercial banks, which have diversified portfolios of readily salable, liquid assets, can also safely use more financial leverage than the typical business.

Another pattern evident in Table 2–1 is that ROA and financial leverage tend to be inversely related. Companies with low ROAs generally employ more debt financing, and vice versa. This is consistent with the previous paragraph. Safe, stable, liquid investments tend to generate low returns but substantial borrowing capacity. Commercial banks are extreme examples of this pattern. Bank of America combines what by manufacturing standards would be a horrible 1.2 percent ROA with an astronomical leverage ratio of 11.49 to generate a representative ROE of 13.2 percent. The key to this pairing is the safe, liquid nature of the bank's assets. Loans to Third World dictators and Arizona real estate speculators are, of course, another story—one the bank would just as soon forget.

The following ratios measure financial leverage, or debt capacity, and the related concept of liquidity.

Balance Sheet Ratios

The most common measures of financial leverage compare the book value of a company's liabilities to the book value of its assets or equity. This gives rise to the *debt-to-assets ratio* and the *debt-to-equity ratio*, defined as

$$\text{Debt-to-assets ratio} = \frac{\text{Total liabilities}}{\text{Total assets}} = \frac{\$345.7}{\$1,001.6} = 34.5\%$$

$$\text{Debt-to-equity ratio} = \frac{\text{Total liabilities}}{\text{Shareholders' equity}} = \frac{\$345.7}{\$656.0} = 52.7\%$$

The first ratio says that money to pay for 34.5 percent of Analog Devices' assets, in book value terms, comes from creditors of one type or another. The second ratio says the same thing in a slightly different way: Creditors supply ADI with 52.7 cents for every dollar supplied by shareholders. As the footnote demonstrates, the lever of performance introduced earlier, the assets-to-equity ratio, is simply the debt-to-equity ratio plus 1.[1]

Coverage Ratios

A number of variations on these balance sheet measures of financial leverage exist. Conceptually, however, there is no reason to prefer one over another, for they all focus on balance sheet values, and hence all suffer from the same weakness. The financial burden a company faces by using debt financing ultimately depends not on the size of its liabilities relative

---

[1] $$\frac{\text{Assets}}{\text{Equity}} = \frac{\text{Liabilities} + \text{Equity}}{\text{Equity}} = \frac{\text{Liabilities}}{\text{Equity}} + 1$$

For Analog Devices, 1.53 = 52.7% + 1.

to assets or to equity but on its ability to meet the annual cash payments the debt requires. A simple example will illustrate the distinction. Suppose two companies, A and B, have the same debt-to-assets ratio, but A is very profitable and B is losing money. Chances are that B will have difficulty meeting its annual interest and principal obligations, while A will not. The obvious conclusion is that balance sheet ratios are of primary interest only in liquidation, when the proceeds of asset sales are to be distributed among creditors and owners. In all other instances, we should be more interested in comparing the annual burden the debt imposes to the cash flow available for debt service.

This gives rise to what are known as *coverage ratios,* the most common of which are *times interest earned* and *times burden covered.* Letting EBIT represent *earnings before interest and taxes*, these ratios are defined as follows:[2]

$$\text{Times interest earned} = \frac{\text{EBIT}}{\text{Interest expense}} = \frac{\$163.6}{\$4.2} = 39.0 \text{ times}$$

$$\text{Times burden covered} = \frac{\text{EBIT}}{\text{Interest} + \left(\dfrac{\text{Principal repayment}}{1 - \text{Tax rate}} \right)}$$

$$= \frac{\$163.6}{\$4.2 + \$20.2/(1 - 40.2/159.4)} = 5.2 \text{ times}$$

Both ratios compare income available for debt service in the numerator to some measure of annual financial obligation. For both ratios, the income available is EBIT. This is the earnings the company generates that can be used to make interest payments. EBIT is before taxes because interest payments are before-tax expenditures, and we want to compare like quantities. Analog Devices' times-interest-earned ratio of 39.0 means the company earned its interest obligation 39 times over in 1995; EBIT was 39 times as large as interest. If this sounds high, it is.

The times-burden-covered ratio expands the definition of annual financial obligation to include debt principal repayments as well as interest.

---

2 To calculate Analog Devices' EBIT, I used Table 1–2, adding interest expense to income before tax ($4.2 million + $159.4 million). I found the company's 1995 principal payment on its cash flow statement under the heading "Payments on long-term debt and capital lease obligations." I approximated the company's tax rate as provision for income taxes divided by income before income taxes. Alternatively, I could have used the marginal corporate tax rate of 35 percent.

If a company fails to make a principal repayment when due, the outcome is the same as if it had failed to make an interest payment. In both cases, the company is in default and creditors can force it into bankruptcy. When including principal repayment as part of the company's financial burden, we must remember to express the figure on a before-tax basis comparable to interest and EBIT. Unlike interest payments, principal repayments are not a tax-deductible expense. This means that if a company is in, say, the 50 percent tax bracket, it must earn $2 before taxes to have $1 after taxes to pay creditors. The other dollar goes to the tax collector. For other tax brackets, the before-tax burden of a principal repayment is found by dividing the repayment by 1 minus the company's tax rate. Adjusting the principal repayment in this manner to its before-tax equivalent is known in the trade as *grossing up* the principal—about as gross as finance ever gets.

Analog Devices' times-burden-covered ratio of 5.2 times indicates that in 1995, the company earned its interest and principal obligations 5.2 times over.

An often-asked question is: Which of these coverage ratios is more meaningful? The answer is that both are important. If a company could always roll over its maturing obligations by taking out new loans as it repaid old ones, the *net* burden of the debt would be merely the interest expense, and times interest earned would be the more important ratio. The problem is that the replacement of maturing debt with new debt is not an automatic feature of capital markets. In some instances, when capital markets are unsettled or a company's fortunes decline, creditors may refuse to renew maturing obligations. Then the burden of the debt suddenly becomes interest plus principal payments, and the times-burden-covered ratio assumes paramount importance. This happened to Burmah Oil, a large British company, some years ago when it took out a large, short-term loan to finance an acquisition, thinking it could roll over the maturing short-term debt into more permanent financing. However, before Burmah could pull off the refinancing, a bank failure in Germany made creditors suddenly very skittish, and no one was willing to lend Burmah the money. A major crisis was averted only when the British government stepped into the breach. In sum, it is fair to conclude that the times-burden-covered ratio is too conservative assuming the company will pay its existing loans down to zero, but the times-interest-earned ratio is too liberal assuming the company will roll over all of its obligations as they mature.

Another common question is: How much coverage is enough? I cannot answer this question precisely, but several generalizations are possible. If a company has ready access to cash in the form of unused borrowing capacity, sizable cash balances, or readily salable assets, it can operate safely with lower coverage ratios than competitors without such reserves. The ready access to cash gives the company a means of payment it can use whenever operating earnings are insufficient to cover financial obligations. A second generalization is that coverage should increase with the *business risk* the firm faces. For example, Hewlett-Packard (HP) operates in a dynamic environment characterized by rapid technological change and high rates of product obsolescence. In view of this high business risk, HP would be ill advised to take on the added financial risk that accompanies low coverage ratios. Said another way, an electric utility that has very stable, predictable cash flows can operate safely with much lower coverage ratios than a company such as HP, which has trouble forecasting more than three or four years into the future.

Market Value Leverage Ratios

A third family of leverage ratios relates a company's liabilities to the *market value of its equity* or the *market value of its assets*. For Analog Devices in 1995,

$$\frac{\text{Debt}}{\text{Market value of equity}} = \frac{\text{Debt}}{\text{Number of shares of stock} \times \text{Price per share}}$$

$$= \frac{\$345.7}{\$2,848} = 12.1\%$$

$$\frac{\text{Debt}}{\text{Market value of assets}} = \frac{\text{Debt}}{\text{Market value of debt} + \text{Equity}}$$

$$= \frac{\$345.7}{\$345.7 + \$2,848} = 10.8\%$$

Careful readers will note that in the second ratio, I have assumed the market value of debt equals the book value of debt. Strictly speaking, this is seldom true, but in most instances the difference between the two quantities is small. Also, accurately estimating the market value of debt often turns out to be a tedious, time-consuming chore that is best avoided—unless, of course, you are being paid by the hour.

Market value ratios are clearly superior to book value ratios simply because book values are historical, often irrelevant numbers, while market values indicate the true worth of creditors' and owners' stakes in the business. Recalling that market values are based on investors' expectations about future cash flows, market value leverage ratios can be thought of as coverage ratios extended over many periods. Instead of comparing income to financial burden in a single year as coverage ratios do, market value ratios compare today's value of expected future income to today's value of future financial burdens.

Market value ratios are especially helpful when assessing the financial leverage of rapidly growing, start-up businesses. Even when such companies have terrible or nonexistent coverage ratios, lenders may still extend them liberal credit if they believe future cash flows will be sufficient to service the debt. McCaw Communications offers an extreme example of this. At year-end 1990, McCaw had over $5 billion in debt; a debt-to-equity ratio, in book terms, of 330 percent; and annualized interest expenses of *more than 60 percent of net revenues.* Moreover, despite explosive growth, McCaw had never made a meaningful operating profit in its principal cellular telephone business. Why did otherwise intelligent creditors loan McCaw $5 billion? Because creditors and equity investors believed it was only a matter of time before the company would begin to generate huge cash flows. This optimism was handsomely rewarded in late 1993 when AT&T paid $12.6 billion to acquire McCaw. Including the $5 billion in debt assumed by AT&T, the acquisition ranked as the second largest in corporate history.

Economists like market value leverage ratios because they are accurate indicators of company indebtedness at a point in time. But you should be aware that market value ratios are not without problems. One is that they ignore rollover risks. When creditors take the attitude that debt must be repaid with cash, not promises of future cash, modest market value leverage ratios can be of hollow comfort. Also, despite these ratios' conceptual appeal, few companies use them to set financing policy or to monitor debt levels. This may be due in part to the fact that volatile stock prices can make market value ratios appear somewhat arbitrary and beyond management's control.

Liquidity Ratios

As noted, one determinant of a company's debt capacity is the liquidity of its assets. An asset is liquid if it can be readily converted to cash, while a liability is liquid if it must be repaid in the near future. As the Burmah Oil debacle illustrates, it is risky to finance illiquid assets such as fixed plant and equipment with liquid, short-term liabilities, because the liabilities will come due before the assets generate enough cash to pay them. Such "maturity mismatching" forces borrowers to roll over, or refinance, maturing liabilities to avoid insolvency.

Two common ratios intended to measure the liquidity of a company's assets relative to its liabilities are the *current ratio* and the *acid test*. For Analog Devices,

$$\text{Current ratio} = \frac{\text{Current assets}}{\text{Current liabilities}}$$

$$= \frac{\$526.0}{\$254.4} = 2.1 \text{ times}$$

$$\text{Acid test} = \frac{\text{Current assets} - \text{Inventory}}{\text{Current liabilities}}$$

$$= \frac{\$526.0 - \$144.0}{\$254.4} = 1.5 \text{ times}$$

The current ratio compares the assets that will turn into cash within the year to the liabilities that must be paid within the year. A company with a low current ratio lacks liquidity in the sense that it cannot reduce its current assets for cash to meet maturing obligations. It must rely instead on operating income and outside financing.

The acid-test ratio, sometimes called the *quick ratio*, is a more conservative liquidity measure. It is identical to the current ratio except that the numerator is reduced by the value of inventory. Inventory is subtracted because it is frequently illiquid. Under distress conditions, a company or its creditors may realize little cash from the sale of inventory. In liquidation sales, sellers typically receive 40 percent or less of the book value of inventory.

You should recognize that these ratios are rather crude measures of liquidity, for at least two reasons. First, rolling over some obligations, such as accounts payable, involves virtually no insolvency risk provided the company is at least marginally profitable. Second, unless a company intends to go out of business, most of the cash generated by liquidating current assets cannot be used to reduce liabilities because it must be plowed back into the business to support continued operations.

IS ROE A RELIABLE FINANCIAL YARDSTICK?

To this point, we have assumed management wants to increase the company's ROE, and we have studied three important levers of performance by which they can accomplish this: the profit margin, asset turnover, and financial leverage. We concluded that whether a company is General Motors or the corner drugstore, careful management of these levers can positively affect ROE. We also saw that determining and maintaining appropriate values of the levers is a challenging managerial task that requires an understanding of the company's business, the way the company competes, and the interdependencies among the levers themselves. Now it is time to ask how reliable ROE is as a measure of financial performance. If company A has a higher ROE than company B, is it necessarily a better company? If company C increases its ROE, is this unequivocal evidence of improved performance?

ROE suffers from three critical deficiencies as a measure of financial performance, which I will refer to as the *timing* problem, the *risk* problem, and the *value* problem. Seen in proper perspective, these problems mean ROE is seldom an unambiguous measure of performance. ROE remains a useful and important indicator, but it must be interpreted in light of its limitations, and no one should automatically assume a higher ROE is always better than a lower one.

The Timing Problem

It is a cliché to say that successful managers must be forward looking and have a long-term perspective. Yet ROE is precisely the opposite: backward looking and focused on a single period. So it is little wonder that ROE can at times be a skewed measure of performance. When, for example, a company incurs heavy start-up costs to introduce a hot new product, ROE will initially fall. However, rather than indicating worsening financial performance, the fall simply reflects the myopic, one-period nature of the yardstick. Because ROE necessarily includes only one year's earnings, it fails to capture the full impact of multiperiod decisions.

The Risk Problem

Business decisions commonly involve the classic "eat well–sleep well" dilemma. If you want to eat well, you had best be prepared to take risks in search of higher returns. If you want to sleep well, you will likely have to forgo high returns in search of safety. Seldom will you realize both high returns and safety. (And when you do, please give me a call.)

The problem with ROE is that it says nothing about what risks a company has taken to generate it. Here is a simple example. Take-a-Risk,

Inc., earns an ROA of 6 percent from wildcat oil exploration in Cambodia, which it combines with an assets-to-equity ratio of 5.0 to produce an ROE of 30 percent (6% × 5.0). Never-Dare, Ltd., meanwhile, has an ROA of 10 percent on its investment in government securities, which it finances with equal portions of debt and equity, yielding an ROE of 20 percent (10% × 2.0). Which company is the better performer? My answer is Never-Dare. Take-a-Risk's ROE is high, but its high business risk and extreme financial leverage make it a very uncertain enterprise. I would prefer the more modest but eminently safer ROE of Never-Dare. Even if I preferred eating well to sleeping well, I would still choose Never-Dare and finance my purchase with a little personal borrowing to lever my return on the investment. In sum, because ROE looks only at return while ignoring risk, it can be an inaccurate yardstick of financial performance.

Return on Invested Capital

To circumvent the distorting effects of leverage on ROE and ROA, I recommend calculating *return on invested capital (ROIC)*, also known as *return on net assets (RONA):*

$$ROIC = \frac{EBIT(1 - Tax\ rate)}{Interest\text{-}bearing\ debt + Equity}$$

Analog Devices' 1995 ROIC was

$$\frac{\$163.6(1 - 40.2/159.4)}{\$2.4 + 80.0 + 656.0} = 16.6\%$$

The numerator of this ratio is the earnings after tax the company would report if it were all equity financed, and the denominator is the sum of all sources of cash to the company on which a return must be earned. Thus, while accounts payable are a source of cash to the company, they are excluded because they carry no explicit cost. In essence, ROIC is the rate of return earned on the total capital invested in the business without regard for whether it is called debt or equity.

To see the virtue of ROIC, consider the following example. Companies A and B are identical in all respects except that A is highly levered and B is all equity financed. Because the two companies are identical except for capital structure, we would like a return measure that reflects this fundamental similarity. The following table shows that ROE and ROA fail this test. Reflecting the company's extensive use of financial leverage, A's ROE is 18 percent, while B's zero-leverage position generates a lower but better-quality ROE of 7.2 percent. ROA is biased in the other direction, punishing company A for its extensive use of debt and leaving B unaffected. Only ROIC is independent of the different financing schemes the two companies employ, showing a 7.2 percent return for both firms. ROIC thus reflects the company's fundamental earning power before it is confounded by differences in financing strategies.

	Company	
	A	B
Debt @ 10% interest	$ 900	$ 0
Equity	100	1,000
Total assets	$1,000	$1,000
EBIT	$ 120	$ 120
– Interest expense	90	0
Earnings before tax	30	120
–Tax @ 40%	12	48
Earnings after tax	$ 18	$ 72
ROE	18.0%	7.2%
ROA	1.8%	7.2%
ROIC	7.2%	7.2%

The Value Problem

ROE measures the return on shareholders' investment; however, the investment figure used is the *book value* of shareholders' equity, not the *market value*. This distinction is important. Analog Devices' ROE in 1995 was 18.2 percent, and indeed this is the return you could have earned had you been able to buy the company's equity for its book value of $656.0 million. But that would have been impossible, for, as noted in the previous chapter, the market value of Analog Devices' equity was $2,848 million. At this price, your annual return would have been only 4.2 percent, not 18.2 percent ($119.3/$2,848 = 4.2%). The market value of equity is more significant to shareholders because it measures the current, realizable worth of the shares, while book value is only history. So even when ROE measures management's financial performance, it may not be synonymous with a high return on investment to shareholders. Thus, it is not enough for investors to find companies capable of generating high ROEs; these companies must be unknown to others, because once they are known, the possibility of high returns to investors will melt away in higher stock prices.

The Earnings Yield and the P/E Ratio

It might appear that we can circumvent the value problem by simply replacing the book value of equity with its market value in the ROE. But the resulting *earnings yield* has problems of its own. For Analog Devices,

$$\text{Earnings yield} = \frac{\text{Net income}}{\text{Market value of shareholders' equity}}$$

$$= \frac{\text{Earnings per share}}{\text{Price per share}} = \frac{\$1.04}{\$24.88} = 4.2\%$$

Is earnings yield a useful measure of financial performance? No! The problem is that a company's stock price is very sensitive to investor expectations about the future. A share of stock entitles its owner to a portion of *future* earnings as well as present earnings. Naturally, the higher an investor's expectations of future earnings, the more she will pay for the stock. This means that a bright future, a high stock price, and a *low* earnings yield go together. Clearly, a high earnings yield is not an indicator of superior performance; in fact, it is more the reverse. Said another way, the earnings yield suffers from a severe timing problem of its own that invalidates it as a performance measure.

Turning the earnings yield on its head produces the *price-to-earnings ratio*, or *P/E ratio*. Analog Devices' 1995 P/E ratio is

$$\text{P/E} = \frac{\text{Price per share}}{\text{Earnings per share}} = \frac{\$24.88}{\$1.04} = 23.9 \text{ times}$$

The P/E ratio adds little to our discussion of performance measures, but its wide use among investors deserves comment. The P/E ratio is the price of one dollar of current earnings and is a means of normalizing stock prices for different earnings levels across companies. At fiscal year end 1995, investors were paying $23.90 per dollar of Analog Devices' earnings. A company's P/E ratio depends principally on two things: its future earnings prospects and the risk associated with those earnings. Stock price, and hence the P/E ratio, rises with improved earnings prospects and falls with increasing risk. A sometimes confusing pattern occurs when a company's earnings are weak but investors believe the weakness is temporary. Then prices remain buoyant in the face of depressed earnings, and the P/E ratio *rises*. In general, the P/E ratio says little about a company's current financial performance, but it does indicate what investors believe about future prospects.

ROE or Market Price?

For years academicians and practitioners have been at odds over the proper measure of financial performance. Academicians criticize ROE for the reasons just cited and argue that the correct measure of financial performance is the firm's stock price. Moreover, they contend that management's goal should be to maximize stock price. Their logic is persuasive: Stock price represents the value of the owners' investment in the firm, and if managers want to further the interests of owners, they should take actions that increase value to owners. Indeed, the notion of "value creation" has become a central theme in the writings of many academicians and consultants.

Practitioners acknowledge the logic of this reasoning but question its applicability. One problem is the difficulty of specifying precisely how operating decisions affect stock price. If we are not certain what impact a change in, say, the business strategy of a division will have on the company's stock price, the goal of increasing price cannot guide decision making. A second problem is that managers typically know more about their company than do outside investors, or at least think they do. Why, then, should managers consider the assessments of less informed investors when making business decisions? A third practical problem with stock price as a performance measure is that it depends on a whole array of factors outside the company's control. One can never be certain whether an increase in stock price reflects improving company performance or an improving external economic environment. For these reasons, many practitioners remain skeptical of stock market–based indicators of performance even while academicians and consultants continue to work on translating value creation into a practical financial objective. One promising recent effort along these lines is *economic value added* (*EVA*), popularized by the consulting firm Stern Stewart Management Services. We will look more closely at EVA in Chapter 8.

CAN ROE SUBSTITUTE FOR SHARE PRICE?

Figures 2–1 and 2–2 suggest that the gulf between academicians and practitioners over the proper measure of financial performance may be narrower than supposed. The graphs plot the market value of equity divided by book value of equity against ROE for two representative groups of companies. The most recent year is 1995, and ROE is measured as a weighted average of the most recent three years' ROEs. The solid line in each figure is a regression line indicating the general relation between the two variables. The strong positive relationship visible in both graphs suggests that high-ROE companies tend to have high stock prices relative to book value, and vice versa. Hence, working to increase ROE appears to be largely consistent with working to increase stock price.

The proximity of the company dots to the fitted regression lines is also interesting. It shows the importance of factors other than ROE in determining a company's market-to-book ratio. As we should expect, these other factors play a significant role in determining the market value of a company's shares.

For interest, I have indicated the positions of several companies on the graphs. Note in Figure 2–1 that Analog Devices is somewhat above the regression line, indicating that based purely on historical ROEs, Analog's stock price is a little rich compared to those of other semiconductor manufacturers. Note too that Linear Technology Corporation and Altera Corporation have well-above-average ROEs and are accorded the highest market-to-book ratios.

In Figure 2–2, Coca-Cola takes the prize with an ROE of over 50 percent and an astronomical market-to-book ratio of almost 18. General Motors, on the other hand, appears to be the Rodney Dangerfield of the stock market. Despite an ROE of over 35 percent, it "can't get no respect" among investors who are unwilling to pay much more than book value for their shares. Evidently, investors are skeptical that the company can continue such performance.

To summarize, these graphs offer tantalizing evidence that despite its weaknesses, ROE may be a useful proxy for share price in measuring financial performance.

RATIO ANALYSIS

In our discussion of the levers of financial performance, we defined a number of financial ratios. It is now time to consider the systematic use of these ratios to analyze financial performance. This involves simply calculating a number of diverse ratios and comparing them to certain standards to gain insights into the company's operations and financial health.

Ratio analysis is widely used by managers, creditors, regulators, and investors. Used with care and imagination, the technique can reveal much about a company and its operations. But there are a few things to bear in mind about ratios. First, a ratio is simply one number divided by

F I G U R E   2-1

Market Value to Book Value of Equity Ratio versus Return on Equity for
22 Large Firms in the Semiconductor Manufacturing Industry

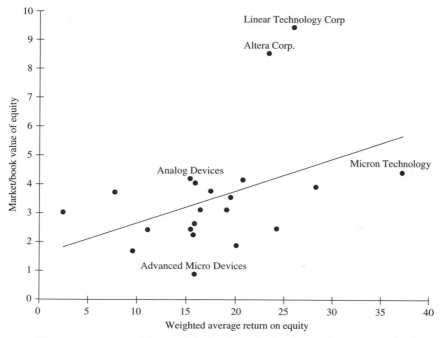

The regression equation is MV/BV = 1.51 + .11 ROE, where MV/BV is the market value of
equity relative to the book value of equity and ROE is a weighted average of return on equity in
1995 and the prior two years. Companies with negative ROE were omitted.
Adjusted $R^2 = .13$

another, so it is unreasonable to expect the mechanical calculation of one
or even several ratios to automatically yield important insights into anything as complex as a modern corporation. It is useful to think of ratios
as clues in a detective story. One or even several ratios might be misleading, but when combined with other knowledge of a company's management and economic circumstances, ratio analysis can tell a revealing
story.

A second point to bear in mind is that a ratio has no single correct
value. Like Goldilocks and the three bears, the observation that the value
of a particular ratio is too high, too low, or just right depends on the
perspective of the analyst and on the company's competitive strategy.
The current ratio, previously defined as the ratio of current assets to

F I G U R E 2–2

Market Value to Book Value of Equity Ratio versus Return on Equity for
81 Large Corporations

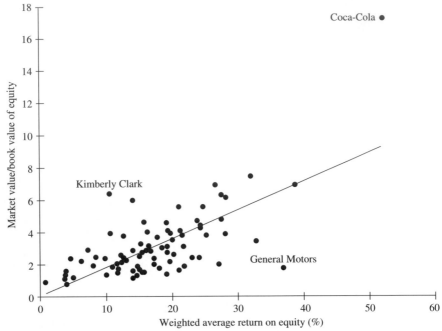

Companies are from the Fortune list of the 100 largest U.S. corporations. Those with negative ROEs
were eliminated. The regression equation is MV/BV = 0.0 + 17.9 ROE, where MV/BV is the market
value of equity relative to book value at the end of 1995 and ROE is a weighted-average of return on
equity for 1995 and the prior two years.
Adjusted R^2 = .47

current liabilities, is a case in point. From the perspective of a short-term
creditor, a high current ratio is a positive sign suggesting ample liquidity
and a high likelihood of repayment. Yet an owner of the company might
look on the same current ratio as a negative sign suggesting that the
company's assets are being deployed too conservatively. Moreover,
from an operating perspective, a high current ratio could be a sign of
conservative management or the natural result of a competitive strategy
that emphasizes liberal credit terms and sizable inventories. In this case,
the important question is not whether the current ratio is too high but
whether the chosen strategy is best for the company.

Using Ratios Effectively

Now that we have calculated a number of ratios, what shall we do with them? If ratios have no universally correct values, how do you interpret them? How do you decide whether a company is healthy or sick? There are three approaches: Compare the ratios to rules of thumb, compare them to industry averages, or look for changes in the ratios over time. Comparing a company's ratios to rules of thumb has the virtue of simplicity but has little else to recommend it conceptually. The appropriate ratio values for a company depend too much on the analyst's perspective and on the company's specific circumstances for rules of thumb to be very helpful. The most positive thing one can say about them is that over the years, companies conforming to these rules of thumb apparently go bankrupt somewhat less frequently than those that do not.

Comparing a company's ratios to industry ratios provides a useful feel for how the company measures up to its competitors. But it is still true that company-specific differences can result in entirely justifiable deviations from industry norms. Also, there is no guarantee that the industry as a whole knows what it is doing. The knowledge that one railroad was much like its competitors was cold comfort in the depression of the 1930s, when virtually all railroads got into financial difficulties.

The most useful way to evaluate ratios involves trend analysis: Calculate ratios for a company over several years, and note how they change over time. Trend analysis avoids the need for cross-company and cross-industry comparisons, enabling the analyst to draw firmer conclusions about the firm's financial health and its variation over time.

Moreover, the levers of performance suggest one logical approach to trend analysis: Instead of calculating ratios at random, hoping to stumble across one that might be meaningful, take advantage of the structure implicit in the levers. As Figure 2–3 illustrates, the levers of performance organize ratios into three tiers. At the top, ROE looks at the performance of the enterprise as a whole; in the middle, the levers of performance indicate how three important segments of the business contributed to ROE; and on the bottom, many of the other ratios discussed reveal how the management of individual income statement and balance sheet accounts contributed to the observed levers. To take advantage of this structure, begin at the top by noting the trend in ROE over time. Then narrow your focus and ask what changes in the three levers account for the observed ROE pattern. Finally, get out your microscope and study

F I G U R E 2–3

The Levers of Performance Suggest One Road Map for Ratio Analysis

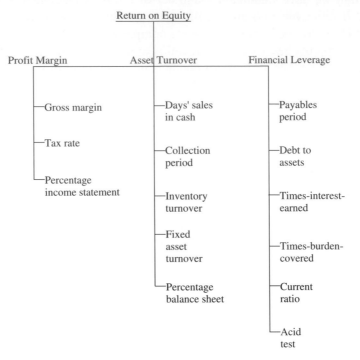

individual accounts for explanations of the observed changes in the levers. To illustrate, if ROE has plunged while the profit margin and financial leverage have remained constant, examine the control of individual asset accounts in search of the culprit or culprits.

Ratio Analysis of Analog Devices, Inc.

As a practical demonstration of ratio analysis, let us see what the technique can tell us about Analog Devices, Inc. Table 2–2 presents previously discussed ratios for Analog Devices over the years 1991 to 1995 and median industry figures for 1995. The comparison industry consists of the seven companies from the electronics (semiconductors) industry represented in the Standard & Poor's 500 stock averages.[3] As another example

---

3 The companies represented are Advanced Micro Devices, Applied Materials, Intel Corporation, Micron Technology, Motorola Inc., National Semiconductor, and Texas Instruments.

T A B L E   2–2

Ratio Analysis of Analog Devices, Inc., 1991–1995, and Industry Medians, 1995

	1991	1992	1993	1994	1995	Industry Median*
Profitability ratios:						
Return on equity (%)	**2.3**	**4.0**	**10.3**	**14.3**	**18.2**	**25.5**
Return on assets (%)	1.6	2.7	6.6	9.1	11.9	11.8
Return on invested capital (%)	3.1	4.4	9.4	12.8	16.6	21.8
Profit margin (%)	**1.5**	**2.6**	**6.7**	**9.6**	**12.7**	**12.4**
Gross margin (%)	49.3	46.8	47.3	49.0	50.7	46.0
Price to earnings (×)	53.2	51.8	27.3	23.7	23.9	10.1
Turnover-control ratios:						
Asset turnover (×)	**1.1**	**1.0**	**1.0**	**0.9**	**0.9**	**1.1**
Fixed-asset turnover (×)	2.4	2.4	2.7	2.7	2.2	2.5
Inventory turnover (×)	2.3	2.1	2.3	3.0	3.2	5.5
Collection period (days)	64.6	71.9	79.8	76.6	70.3	56.3
Days' sales in cash (days)	11.2	11.4	44.2	85.8	58.6	68.7
Payables period (days)	50.1	52.4	50.7	68.9	78.7	71.7
Leverage and liquidity ratios:						
Assets to equity (×)	**1.4**	**1.5**	**1.6**	**1.6**	**1.5**	**1.6**
Debt to assets (%)	29.6	33.3	36.3	36.0	34.5	37.1
Debt to equity (%)	42.0	49.8	57.1	56.3	52.7	58.9
Times interest earned (×)	3.0	4.2	8.7	14.6	39.0	34.7
Times burden covered (×)			1.9	14.6	5.2	12.3
Debt to assets (market value %)	24.9	19.3	16.9	14.3	10.8	25.9
Debt to equity (market value %)	33.2	24.0	19.6	16.7	12.1	34.9
Current ratio (×)	2.6	3.0	3.0	2.5	2.1	1.8
Acid test (×)	1.4	1.6	1.9	1.8	1.5	1.5

*Sample consists of seven firms in Standard & Poor's 500 stock index from the electronics (semiconductor) industry. The companies are Advanced Micro Devices, Applied Materials, Intel Corporation, Micron Technology, Motorola Inc., National Semiconductor, and Texas Instruments.

of readily available industry data, Table 2–4, at the end of the chapter presents similar ratios from Dun & Bradstreet Information Services for other representative industries, including median, upper-quartile, and lower-quartile values for the represented ratios.[4]

Beginning with Analog Devices' return on equity, we see that the number improved dramatically over the five years from 2.3 percent in 1991 to a robust 18.2 percent in 1995. The 1995 number is a healthy one relative to the average American corporation, which scored a 15.7 percent ROE in that year, but below the industry median of 25.5 percent.[5] ADI's return on invested capital also shows dramatic improvement to 16.6 percent but still lags the industry median of 21.8 percent. Looking next at the company's levers of performance, we see that the profit margin soared over the period from an anemic 1.5 percent to a hearty 12.7 percent, marginally outstripping the comparable industry figure of 12.4 percent. The asset turnover ratio tells a different story, falling from 1.1 in 1991 to 0.9 times in 1995 and lagging the industry median by about 20 percent (0.9 versus 1.1 times). To put ADI's turnover in perspective, had the company's asset turnover equaled the industry figure in 1995, ROE would have been 13 percent higher. Looking at the third lever of performance, we see a very conservatively financed company and industry. Although Analog Devices' assets-to-equity ratio rose modestly through 1994, the number fell in 1995 and is presently somewhat below the industry figure of 1.6 times. The industry's conservative financing is most apparent in a times-interest-earned ratio of 34.7, which is fully five to 10 *times* higher than the comparable figure for U.S. industry as a whole.

Our look at Analog Devices' ROE and levers of performance reveals that the source of the company's sharply improved financial performance is its income statement. ADI is selling more at much higher margins than it did in 1991. At the same time, its asset turnover has modestly undermined

---

4 For any ratio, if we array all of the values for the companies in the industry from the highest to the lowest, the figure falling in the middle of the series is the *median*, the ratio halfway between the highest value and the median is the *upper quartile*, and the ratio halfway between the lowest value and the median is the *lower quartile*. Data are from *Industry Norms and Key Business Ratios: Library Edition 1994–95*, Dun & Bradstreet Credit Services, 1995.

5 According to *Business Week* ("The Business Week 1000," March 25, 1996, p. 102), the 1995 all-industry composite return on equity for America's 1,000 most valuable companies, as measured by market value of equity, was 15.7 percent. The comparable figure for return on invested capital was 11.8 percent.

its operating improvements, while its persistently conservative financial posture has contributed little to improving ROE. Digging a little deeper into these broad trends, it appears from the relatively stable gross margin that the improving profit margin must be due to better control of operating expenses such as research, development, marketing, and administrative expenses. The declining asset turnover appears to be due principally to a major increase in property, plant, and equipment in 1995, which caused a sharp drop in fixed-asset turnover. However, it is worth noting that the company's inventory turnover and, to a lesser extent, its collection period are worse than comparable industry figures. An inventory turnover of 3.2 times when the industry figure is 5.5 connotes one of two things: Either ADI customizes many of its products and hence is stuck with large work-in-process inventories or its manufacturing processes and inventory management systems are inferior.

ADI's leverage and liquidity ratios show no cause for concern. Liquidity, as evidenced by the current and acid-test ratios, fell sharply in 1995 but are still at or above comparable industry figures. After rising somewhat in 1991 through 1993, the company's balance sheet leverage ratios have since trended downward and are modestly below industry figures.

Table 2–3 presents what are known as *common-size financial statements* for Analog Devices over the period 1991 to 1995, as well as industry averages for 1995. A common-size balance sheet simply presents each asset and liability as a percentage of total assets. A common-size income statement is analogous except that all items are scaled in proportion to net sales instead of to total assets. The purpose of scaling financial statements in this fashion is to concentrate on underlying trends by abstracting from changes in the dollar figures caused by growth or decline. In addition, common-size statements are useful for removing simple scale effects when comparing different-size companies.

Looking first at Analog Devices' balance sheet, note that although the company is a manufacturer, about half of its assets are short term, primarily accounts receivable and inventories. These numbers again highlight the importance of working-capital management to most businesses. When a high proportion of a company's investment is in assets as volatile as inventory and accounts receivable, that investment bears close watching. In this light, note that although ADI's inventories as a percentage of total assets has come down sharply, it still exceeds the industry average.

On the liabilities side of the balance sheet, we again see a conservatively financed company. Accounts payable have risen modestly to

T A B L E 2-3

Analog Devices, Inc., Common-Size Financial Statements, 1991–1995, and Industry Averages, 1995

	1991	1992	1993	1994	1995	Industry Average*
			Assets			
Cash	3.3%	3.2%	11.9%	13.4%	6.9%	9.0%
Short-term investments				8.9%	8.2%	7.9%
Accounts receivable	18.9%	19.9%	21.5%	19.9%	18.1%	18.3%
Inventories	23.3%	25.4%	22.2%	16.0%	14.4%	11.1%
Prepaid expenses and other current assets	4.0%	4.5%	3.9%	3.8%	5.0%	5.7%
Total current assets	49.4%	52.9%	59.4%	62.0%	52.5%	52.1%
Net property, plant, and equipment	44.5%	42.3%	36.6%	34.5%	43.1%	40.9%
Intangible assets	5.1%	4.2%	3.1%	2.4%	1.7%	1.5%
Other long-term assets	0.9%	0.7%	0.8%	1.1%	2.6%	6.7%
Total assets	100.0%	100.0%	100.0%	100.0%	100.0%	100.0%

TABLE 2-3 (continued)

Analog Devices, Inc., Common-Size Financial Statements, 1991–1995, and Industry Averages, 1995

	1991	1992	1993	1994	1995	Industry Average*
		Liabilities and Shareholders' Equity				
Sort-term borrowings and current maturities of long-term obligations	1.2%	0.5%	0.3%	2.8%	0.2%	2.3%
Accounts payable	7.4%	7.7%	7.2%	9.1%	10.0%	14.5%
Deferred income on shipments to domestic distributors	1.8%	2.3%	2.4%	2.3%	2.8%	
Income taxes payable	1.0%	0.3%	2.3%	3.6%	5.0%	3.9%
Accrued liabilities	8.0%	6.9%	7.4%	7.4%	7.4%	9.3%
Other current liabilities						2.6%
Total current liabilities	19.3%	17.7%	19.6%	25.3%	25.4%	27.4%
Long-term obligations less current maturities	7.3%	12.6%	14.8%	9.8%	8.0%	6.3%
Deferred income taxes	2.3%	2.3%	1.3%	0.4%	0.5%	2.7%
Other long-term liabilities	0.7%	0.7%	0.7%	0.5%	0.6%	3.7%
Total liabilities	29.6%	33.3%	36.3%	36.0%	34.5%	39.6%
Shareholders' equity	70.4%	66.7%	63.7%	64.0%	65.5%	60.4%
Total liabilities and shareholders' equity	100.0%	100.0%	100.0%	100.0%	100.0%	100.0%

T A B L E 2-3 (concluded)

Analog Devices, Inc., Common-Size Financial Statements, 1991–1995, and Industry Averages, 1995

	1991	1992	1993	1994	1995	Industry Average*
			Income Statement			
Net sales	100.0%	100.0%	100.0%	100.0%	100.0%	100.0%
Cost of sales	50.7%	53.2%	52.7%	51.0%	49.3%	57.4%
Gross profit	49.3%	46.8%	47.3%	49.0%	50.7%	42.6%
Research and development	16.6%	15.5%	14.1%	13.8%	14.3%	10.3%
Selling, marketing, general and administrative expenses	28.3%	26.7%	23.8%	22.0%	19.6%	13.9%
Total operating expenses	44.8%	42.2%	37.9%	35.8%	33.9%	21.3%
Operating income	4.5%	4.6%	9.4%	13.2%	16.8%	21.3%
Interest expense	– 0.9%	– 1.1%	– 1.1%	– 0.9%	– 0.4%	– 0.3%
Other income (expense)	– 1.9%	– 0.2%	0.0%	0.3%	0.6%	1.3%
Total nonoperating income (expense)	– 2.8%	– 1.3%	– 1.1%	– 0.6%	0.2%	1.1%
Income before income taxes	1.7%	3.3%	8.3%	12.5%	16.9%	22.4%
Provision for income taxes	0.2%	0.7%	1.7%	2.9%	4.3%	7.6%
Net income	1.5%	2.6%	6.7%	9.6%	12.7%	14.8%

*Sample consists of seven firms in Standard & Poor's 500 stock index from the electronics (semiconductor) industry. The companies are Advanced Micro Devices, Applied Materials, Intel Corporation, Micron Technology, Motorola Inc., National Semiconductor, and Texas Instruments.

10 percent of total assets, or a payables period of 78.7 days, but these figures do not appear out of line compared to industry figures.

Analog Devices' common-size income statement makes agreeable reading. Although not quite up to industry standards, operating margins have been steadily improving despite rapid sales growth. The company's biggest challenge over the period appears to have been control of operating expenses, especially selling, marketing, and general and administrative expenses, which fell dramatically from 28.3 percent of sales in 1991 to 19.6 percent in 1995 but are still high compared to an industry average of only 13.9 percent. One general observation: Although small percentage changes on an income statement may appear inconsequential, they seldom are. For example, ADI's research and development expenses declined 2.3 percentage points between 1991 and 1995—not a big deal until you compare the change to net income rather than sales. Because net income is only about 12 percent of sales, the decline in the R&D percentage equals a healthy 19 percent of what really matters.

Some beginners might fault Analog Devices for allowing operating expenses to rise with sales. Where are the economies of scale, they may ask? The answer is that scale economies are usually not so simple. If they were, very large companies, such as Sears, would quickly dominate smaller competitors and eventually monopolize markets. In fact, it appears that while some activities exhibit economies of scale, others are subject to diseconomies of scale, meaning the company becomes less efficient with size. Moreover, many activities exhibit scale economies over only a limited range of activity and then require a large investment to increase capacity. So Analog Devices' inability to hold operating expenses constant in the face of increased sales is not a major concern to me.

In sum, ratio analysis of Analog Devices reveals a company in the throes of a major renaissance. Faced with declining core military and industrial markets in 1990, ADI chief executive Ray Stata redirected the company toward consumer markets, developing specialized chips for burgeoning auto safety, wireless communications, and consumer electronics markets. The wisdom of this strategic shift is apparent in the company's rapid sales growth and sharply improving profit margins. The only apparent weakness is in asset turnover, especially inventory turns, where further improvement may be possible. With this modest caveat, Analog Devices' management should take pleasure in a job well done and hope fervently it can maintain its momentum. It certainly appears investors expect it to. Looking at Table 2–2, the company's price-to-earnings ratio in 1991 was a whopping 53.2 times, indicating that investors have believed all along that Analog's earnings problems were only temporary. And although the ratio has come back down to a more reasonable level in recent years as earnings have recovered, it is still more than double the industry median. The stock market clearly expects more good news.

TABLE 2–4

Selected Ratios for Representative Industries, 1995 (upper-quartile, median, and lower-quartile values)

Lines of Business and Number of Firms Reporting	Current Ratio (times)	Total Liabilities to Net Worth (%)	Collection Period (days)	Net Sales to Inventory (times)	Total Assets to Net Sales (%)	Profit Margin (%)	Return on Assets (%)	Return on Equity (%)
Agriculture, forestry, and fishing:								
Beef cattle feedlots (143)	2.2	39.2	15.3	17.8	36.3	6.8	7.1	18.5
	1.3	111.8	27.6	10.3	50.3	2.5	3.6	8.4
	1.1	213.0	45.1	4.2	75.2	0.5	0.3	0.1
Lawn and garden services (1,008)	3.2	38.2	17.3	107.4	23.1	9.4	23.1	52.4
	1.6	94.8	35.0	36.1	31.8	4.1	9.6	22.6
	1.0	200.3	54.9	14.1	46.8	1.2	2.7	7.3
Manufacturing:								
Men's and boys' shirts (90)	3.5	42.6	20.2	13.1	25.5	6.0	9.6	28.9
	2.2	84.2	36.3	7.8	34.7	2.2	4.9	12.6
	1.5	175.7	62.8	4.6	56.2	0.8	1.3	3.5
Motor homes (22)	2.2	92.0	11.1	11.9	17.2	3.2	9.7	32.1
	1.6	141.4	15.9	9.4	23.3	1.9	7.0	19.8
	1.1	325.8	27.1	8.0	31.9	0.7	1.6	3.4

T A B L E 2-4 (continued)

Selected Ratios for Representative Industries, 1995 (upper-quartile, median, and lower-quartile values)

Lines of Business and Number of Firms Reporting	Current Ratio (times)	Total Liabilities to Net Worth (%)	Collection Period (days)	Net Sales to Inventory (times)	Total Assets to Net Sales (%)	Profit Margin (%)	Return on Assets (%)	Return on Equity (%)
Semiconductors and related devices (288)	4.1	27.6	46.3	12.0	50.7	12.1	14.9	25.1
	2.6	56.1	57.9	7.9	73.6	6.4	8.5	15.7
	1.7	111.3	73.5	4.9	109.5	1.6	1.9	3.7
Electronic computers (222)	3.2	47.5	35.6	16.7	25.3	7.9	15.0	35.7
	1.9	106.2	56.6	9.3	53.4	3.7	7.5	17.3
	1.4	206.3	85.5	6.3	88.3	0.9	3.7	9.5
Wholesale trade:								
Sporting and recreational goods (574)	3.7	41.9	18.8	10.5	24.7	5.7	12.3	34.1
	2.0	102.1	32.1	6.3	35.4	2.1	5.5	12.3
	1.3	223.2	48.8	4.1	51.1	0.8	1.6	4.2
Women's and children's clothing (673)	3.8	34.3	17.2	14.6	20.5	6.0	16.3	38.1
	1.9	96.8	34.2	8.2	31.7	2.6	6.9	17.3
	1.4	206.0	54.0	4.8	46.9	0.9	2.0	4.8

T A B L E 2-4 (continued)

Selected Ratios for Representative Industries, 1995 (upper-quartile, median, and lower-quartile values)

Lines of Business and Number of Firms Reporting	Current Ratio (times)	Total Liabilities to Net Worth (%)	Collection Period (days)	Net Sales to Inventory (times)	Total Assets to Net Sales (%)	Profit Margin (%)	Return on Assets (%)	Return on Equity (%)
Retail trade:								
Department stores (499)	7.1	17.5	3.7	5.9	36.8	3.8	6.3	12.3
	3.9	50.8	16.8	4.5	49.2	1.5	3.1	5.3
	2.4	124.0	47.5	3.2	67.6	(0.1)	(0.2)	0.4
Grocery stores (2,013)	3.8	36.9	1.1	28.3	12.8	3.0	13.6	30.9
	1.9	93.3	2.6	19.0	19.5	1.3	6.1	13.4
	1.2	212.3	6.3	12.5	29.0	0.5	1.8	5.0
Jewelry stores (1,180)	5.9	24.5	8.4	3.9	45.8	8.9	11.9	22.9
	3.0	68.2	21.9	2.6	64.0	3.9	5.4	10.4
	1.8	148.5	50.7	1.7	92.4	1.0	1.3	2.8
Services:								
Beauty shops (240)	5.7	16.6	2.6	78.9	16.2	12.0	21.2	43.9
	2.2	63.7	25.2	35.9	27.7	4.2	9.1	18.5
	1.1	149.7	88.0	20.1	71.0	1.3	2.0	5.3

T A B L E 2–4 (concluded)

Selected Ratios for Representative Industries, 1995 (upper-quartile, median, and lower-quartile values)

Lines of Business and Number of Firms Reporting	Current Ratio (times)	Total Liabilities to Net Worth (%)	Collection Period (days)	Net Sales to Inventory (times)	Total Assets to Net Sales (%)	Profit Margin (%)	Return on Assets (%)	Return on Equity (%)
Legal services (772)	5.4	25.4	15.3	113.6	13.9	35.7	117.0	147.9
	1.9	66.5	51.8	63.1	25.4	11.5	19.8	28.6
	1.1	171.6	103.7	8.2	45.4	1.0	0.5	0.9
Colleges and universities (170)	4.9	15.7	10.2	124.8	102.6	10.0	8.0	11.9
	2.1	39.8	17.9	84.4	169.1	3.6	2.8	4.0
	1.1	79.0	43.1	50.7	218.4	0.7	0.4	0.4

Source: *Industry Norms & Key Business Ratios*, 1995–96, Desktop Edition. ©1996, Dun & Bradstreet, a company of The Dun & Bradstreet Corporation. Reprinted by permission.

International Differences in Financial Structure

Those French have a different word for everything.

Steve Martin

To this point, we have spoken almost entirely of American practices and norms. It is natural to ask how universal these customs are and to wonder how financial structure varies from one country to another. This appendix attempts to answer these questions and to review the more popular explanations for the differences observed. Definitive answers will not be possible in these few pages, but we will survey the most comprehensive data available and briefly summarize the best of emerging research.

Percentage Balance Sheets

The Organization for Economic Cooperation and Development (OECD) publishes the most comprehensive data available on company financial structure around the globe. Using these data, Figure 2A–1 shows aggregate, percentage balance sheets, in the form of bar charts, for nonfinancial companies in four countries in two different years. The countries are Germany, Japan, the United Kingdom, and the United States, and the most recent year for which data are available is 1994 for all countries except the United Kingdom, where the most recent year is 1990. I wanted to include an emerging economy such as South Korea or China, but neither is a member of the OECD, and I could not find reliable, comparable data elsewhere.

A four-country sample is hardly exhaustive, but the selected countries are economically important and offer some geographic and economic diversity. Germany and Japan in particular are often said to be "bank-oriented" economies in the sense that a high proportion of company financing in these countries comes from banks rather than financial markets. In contrast, Britain and the United States are referred to as "market oriented" because public financial markets play a more important role in company financing. As we will see, this differing orientation and its causes may be at the bottom of a number of the observed differences in financial structure

Looking first at the assets side of the balance sheet, several observations are noteworthy. First, German companies reveal much less information than others. This is not an aberration; rather, it evidences a long tradition of secrecy among companies in Germanic countries. Indeed, not many years ago *Fortune* magazine remarked of Hoffman LaRoche, the

F I G U R E   2A-1

Percentage Balance Sheets of Companies in Four Countries

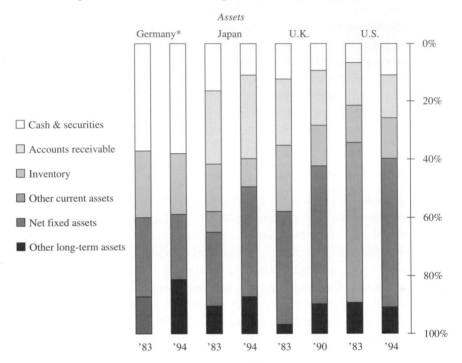

large Swiss pharmaceutical company, "The only number in Hoffman La-Roche's annual report you can believe is the year on the front." Note too the remarkable stability in the composition of German companies' assets over the decade. Either German industry was very stable over this period or German accounting numbers are slow to respond.

Second, Japanese companies have very large accounts receivable balances, although they have declined modestly over the decade. This is usually attributed to the importance of banks in financing Japanese business and a unique form of corporate organization known as *keiretsu*. A *keiretsu* is a form of mutual aid society composed of a number of companies, usually including a "main bank," that purchase sizable ownership interests in one another as a way to cement business relations. So many Japanese companies belong to *keiretsu* that the resulting cross-stock holdings among members has been estimated to account for as much as half of total shares outstanding

F I G U R E   2A–1 (concluded)

Percentage Balance Sheets of Companies in Four Countries

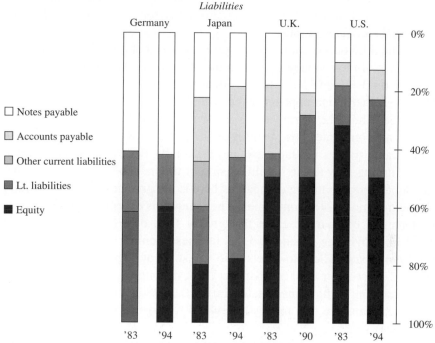

* Data do not distinguish among cash, securities, and accounts receivable.

Source: OECD, *Financial Statistics*, Part 3, *Non-Financial Enterprises Financial Statements*, various issues.

on the Japanese stock market.[1] A principal way to finance *keiretsu* has been for the main bank to lend generously to the major *keiretsu* members—companies such as Toyota, Sony, and so on—which then pass some of the money downstream to other *keiretsu* members in the form of liberal trade credit. Hence the large accounts receivable balances. The practice is so common that some observers suggest many large Japanese companies are really two companies in one, an operating business and a bank.

This financing system has several virtues. The banks need not take on the risks of lending to smaller, less-well-capitalized companies, and the large trade credit balances among *keiretsu* members bind them more

---

1 Brian Bremner, "High-Water Mark?" *Business Week*, September 2, 1996, p. 53.

firmly to one another. Reducing credit risk is especially important to Japanese banks when regulators limit the interest rates banks can charge on loans. By lending only to the most creditworthy companies, the system enables banks to continue lending profitably, on a risk-adjusted basis, despite the ceiling on rates.

The third observation from Figure 2A–1 is that American companies tie up less of their money in current assets—or, equivalently, invest more of their funds in long-term assets—than do companies in other countries. However, there also appears to be a tendency for all four countries to converge. Thus, the aggregate investment in current assets on the part of American companies rose to almost 40 percent over the period, while comparable figures for Japanese and especially British companies fell.

Turning now to the liabilities side of the balance sheet, we see that the big difference among companies here is the greater reliance on equity financing among U.S. companies. The contrast is especially stark relative to Japanese companies. Even though the U.S. debt-to-assets ratio rose noticeably over the decade and the Japanese number declined modestly, the 1994 Japanese debt-to-assets ratio still stood at *80 percent* compared to only 52 percent for U.S. companies. Thus, despite the great popularity of debt financing in the United States during the 1980s, these figures indicate that U.S. firms are still modestly levered relative to companies in other countries.

The willingness of Japanese companies to carry such high debt levels is usually attributed to lower costs of financial distress in Japan. When a Japanese company falls into financial difficulty, its *keiretsu* members and sometimes its main bank traditionally come to its aid with additional capital and possibly management talent, giving the troubled company time to work through its difficulties. In contrast, in more market-oriented economies such as the United States, lending relationships are more adversarial and nervous creditors can force distressed companies into bankruptcy and possibly liquidation. Where the costs of excessive financial leverage are high, as in the United States and Britain, it is thus logical to anticipate that use of debt financing will be correspondingly low, and vice versa.

Comparisons among Large, Publicly Traded Companies

Before accepting the OECD data as gospel, it is instructive to look at a second international data source consisting of large, publicly traded companies in various countries. Although consistent with the OECD evidence

T A B L E   2A–1

International Differences in Times-Interest-Earned Ratios, 1991

Country	Number of Companies	Median Times-Interest-Earned Ratio
U.K.	619	4.26
Germany	250	3.66
Japan	680	2.78
U.S.	2,580	2.40

Source: Raghuram G. Rajan and Luigi Zingales, "What Do We Know about Capital Structure? Some Evidence from International Data," *Journal of Finance*, December 1995, pp. 1421–60.

in many respects, this second data source supports markedly different conclusions regarding international differences in the use of debt financing. Table 2A–1 presents median times-interest-earned ratios in 1991 for large numbers of publicly traded businesses in each of four countries. Contrary to the OECD numbers, these data show U.S. companies to be the *most* indebted among the four countries, followed in order by Japanese, German, and British firms.

How do we reconcile these differing results? There are several possibilities. First, 1991 was a recessionary year in the United States, so earnings may have been depressed relative to firms in other countries. Second, because the U.S. sample of publicly traded companies is over four times as large as those of other countries, it likely includes many more small, aggressively levered firms. Third, the OECD data are balance sheet aggregates for the economy as a whole, while the data in Table 2A–1 are median coverage ratios for predominantly large, public companies, so strictly speaking we are not comparing like quantities.

In any event, the data on publicly traded companies suggest caution when generalizing about debt financing in one country relative to another. For our four countries, we can safely say that American companies significantly increased their financial leverage over the years in question. We can also probably add that despite the growing popularity of debt financing, American companies are still no more heavily levered than their counterparts elsewhere and may in fact remain somewhat less levered. This conclusion is broadly consistent with that of academic researchers who, after measuring leverage a number of different ways and subjecting the data to a

variety of statistical tortures, concluded that leverage appeared to be fairly
similar across the countries studied.

International Accounting Differences

A problem inherent in any cross-country comparison of accounting numbers is that accountants in different countries do not always keep score by
the same rules. Daimler-Benz, maker of Mercedes-Benz cars, provides a
vivid example of the distortions that can occur. Domiciled in Germany but
anxious to list on American stock exchanges, Daimler-Benz found it necessary to publish two sets of financial statements, one for German and one
for American authorities. The differences between accounting standards in
the two countries became startlingly apparent when the company estimated that 1993 profits on its German books would be DM 600 million as
opposed to an expected *loss* of DM 1.7 billion on its American statements.
When different accounting standards can have this big an effect (admittedly an extreme example), possible distortions in aggregate data from this
source should not be ignored.

To date, Kenneth French and Jim Poterba have done the best job of
grappling with such accounting distortions in a provocative study entitled
"Were Japanese Stock Prices Too High?"[2] A brief review of the accounting challenges they faced will provide a better idea of the nature and
magnitude of accounting distortions.

Between 1984 and 1989, the price-to-earnings (P/E) ratio of the
Nikkei index of Japanese stocks rose from 37.9 to 70.9 times; meanwhile,
the P/E of the Standard & Poor's 500 stock index of U.S. stocks mean-
dered upward from 10.4 to 14.8. French and Poterba asked why this large
discrepancy existed, why it had widened, and whether market fundamentals could explain the P/E differences.

One market fundamental the authors had to confront was different
accounting practices in the two countries. If Japanese company J and
American company A are identical except for location, their stock
should sell for the same P/E ratio. But suppose company J, reporting
under more conservative Japanese accounting rules, announces net
income of only half that of its American twin. Then, if rational investors

---

2 Kenneth R. French and James M. Poterba, "Were Japanese Stock Prices Too High?" *Journal of
Financial Economics*, October 1991, pp. 337–63.

see through the accounting veil to the true earning power of the two entities, company J should sell at twice the P/E multiple of company A. So before deciding whether Japanese shares were overpriced, French and Poterba had to adjust for accounting-induced differences in reported income. Without boring you with the details, here are the highlights of what they found.

Earnings Consolidation

When a parent company owns 20 percent or more of other companies, the parent's consolidated earnings include the earnings of those subsidiaries. The parent's *un*consolidated earnings, however, include only the dividends received from subsidiaries. The norm in the United States is to report consolidated earnings. Even though Japanese companies have been required to report consolidated earnings since 1977, it is still common to use the unconsolidated numbers for P/E calculations and elsewhere. Given the extensive cross-ownership of shares among Japanese companies, this can impart a significant downward bias to Japanese earnings relative to American earnings. The authors estimated that adjusting for this difference reduced the reported discrepancy between Japanese and American P/Es by almost one-half.

Special Reserves

The Japanese tax code allows companies to make annual tax-deductible contributions to a variety of special reserves for such future contingencies as product returns, payments on guarantees, and employee retirement benefits. This might be of only passing interest were it not for the fact that unlike in American and British practice, Japanese and German companies may not keep separate accounts for taxes and reporting. Thus, any strategies Japanese companies use to reduce taxes also reduce reported income. Reserve contributions of this type by large Japanese corporations appear to have averaged about 4 percent of net income over the 1975–1990 period, so the resulting adjustment to P/E ratios was correspondingly small.

Depreciation Accounting

In a similar vein, about three-quarters of American companies use accelerated depreciation for tax purposes and straight-line depreciation for public reporting. This generally reduces current taxes and increases current reported earnings. Unable to keep two sets of books, the great majority of Japanese companies use accelerated depreciation for taxes and public reporting, which leads to an understatement of reported earnings compared to those of American companies. French and Poterba estimate that this difference, when added to the others, collectively explains only about half of the disparity between Japanese and American P/E ratios in the decade of the 1980s, strongly suggesting that Japanese stock prices were indeed irrationally high throughout the period.

CHAPTER SUMMARY

1. Although a major corporation and the corner drugstore may seem vastly different, the levers by which managers in both firms affect performance are similar and few in number. This chapter studied the ties between these levers and the firm's financial performance.
2. Return on equity is the most popular single yardstick of financial performance, although it does suffer from timing, risk, and value problems.
3. The primary components of return on equity are the profit margin, the asset turnover ratio, and financial leverage. The profit margin summarizes income statement performance. The asset turnover ratio focuses on the left side of the balance sheet and indicates how efficiently management has used the firm's assets. Financial leverage looks at the right side of the balance sheet and how the company has financed its assets.
4. Turnover control ratios are very important for operating managers. They indicate the efficiency with which the company uses a specific type of asset, such as accounts receivable or inventories.
5. More financial leverage is not always better than less. Financial leverage can be measured by using balance sheet ratios or coverage ratios. The latter are usually superior for long-term debt.
6. Ratio analysis is the systematic examination of a number of company ratios in search of insights into the firm's operations and its financial vitality. Used creatively, ratios are useful tools, but they can be misleading if applied mechanically.

A D D I T I O N A L   R E A D I N G   A N D   R E C O M M E N D E D   W E B   S I T E S

Bernstein, Leopold A. *Financial Statement Analysis: Theory, Application, and Interpretation.* 5th ed. Burr Ridge, IL: Richard D. Irwin, 1992. 1,024 pages.

A detailed examination of financial statements and their uses from an accounting perspective. Not what I would call exciting reading, but particularly levelheaded and thorough. Can be yours for only $81.25.

Gallinger, George W. *Liquidity Analysis and Management.* 2nd. ed. Reading, MA: Addison-Wesley, 1991. 642 pages.

A textbook on the management of current assets and liabilities. Topics covered include cash flow analysis; off-balance sheet financing; international cash management; hedging with futures, options, and swaps; and asset-backed financing. Intended for advanced finance students and practicing professionals. A thorough look at an important but neglected topic. $61.25

Palepu, Krishna G.; Victor L. Bernard; and Paul M. Healy. *Business Analysis and Valuation: Using Financial Statements.* Cincinnati: South-Western College Publishing, 1996, 273 pages.

Part finance, part accounting. An innovative look at the use of accounting information to address selected financial questions. Available in paperback for $29.95.

Siegel, Joel G.; Jae K. Shim; and Stephen W. Hartman. *The McGraw-Hill Pocket Guide to Business Finance: 201 Decision-Making Tools for Managers.* New York: McGraw-Hill, 1992. 354 pages.

A reference book with 201 financial tools explained in a clear, straightforward manner. Available in paperback for $14.95.

Securities and Exchange Commission Filings: http://edgar.stern.nyu.edu/

Known in the trade as Edgar, this site contains virtually all company filings with the Securities and Exchange Commission. A treasure trove of financial information on most public companies, including annual and quarterly reports.

Federal Reserve Bank of St. Louis Economic Data: http://www.stls.frb.org/fred/

Lots of good economic data on interest rates, employment, and so on. Excellent historical data.

Sources for Business Ratios

Check your library for the following:

Compact Disclosure. *Annual Report Information for U.S. Companies.*

Extensive balance sheet and income statement information, including standard ratios, for virtually all publicly traded U.S. companies. Available on compact disk.

Dun & Bradstreet Business Credit Services. *Industry Norms and Key Business Ratios.* New York: published annually.

Percentage balance sheets and 14 ratios for over 1 million U.S. corporations, partnerships, and proprietorships, both public and private, representing 800 lines of business as defined by SIC codes. Median-, upper-, and lower-quartile values.

Robert Morris Associates. *Annual Statement Studies.* Philadelphia: published annually.

Common-size financial statements and widely used ratios in many business lines. Ratios broken out into six size ranges by sales and by assets. Also contains comparative historical data. One limitation is that only companies with assets of $250 million or less are included. Excellent bibliography entitled "Sources of Composite Financial Data."

Standard & Poor's. *Analysts Handbook.* New York: published annually, with monthly supplements.

Income statement, balance sheet, and share price data by industry for all companies in S&P 500 stock averages.

CHAPTER PROBLEMS

1. A company is considering the acquisition of a very promising biotechnology company. One executive argues against the move, pointing out that because the biotech company is presently losing money, the acquiring company's return on equity will fall.

   a. Is the executive correct in predicting that ROE will fall?

   b. How important should changes in ROE be in this decision?

2. Top management measures your division's performance by calculating the division's return on investment, defined as division operating income per period divided by division assets. Your division has done quite well lately; its ROI is 40 percent. You believe the division should invest in a new production process, but a colleague disagrees, pointing out that because the new investment's first-year ROI is only 35 percent, it will hurt performance. How would you respond?

3. Answer the questions that follow based on the following information.

	($ in millions)	
	Company A	**Company B**
Earnings before interest and taxes	$300	$560
Interest expense	20	160
Earnings before tax	280	400
Taxes at 40%	112	160
Earnings after tax	168	240
Debt	$200	$1,600
Equity	800	400

     a. Calculate each company's ROE, ROA, and ROIC.

     b. Why is company B's ROE so much higher than A's? Does this mean B is a better company? Why or why not?

     c. Why is company A's ROA higher than B's? What does this tell you about the two companies?

     d. How do the two companies' ROICs compare? What does this suggest about the two companies?

4. Table 3–1 in Chapter 3 presents financial statements over the period 1993 through 1996 for R&E Supplies, Inc.

     a. Use these statements to calculate as many of the ratios in Table 2–2 as you can.

     b. What insights, if any, do these ratios for R&E Supplies provide about R&E's financial performance? What problems, if any, does the company appear to have?

5. Selected information for DressMiss, Inc., a young women's clothing store, follows. (Assume all sales are credit sales, ratios are based on a 365-day year, and the payables period is based on cost of goods sold.)

	1996 ($ in millions)
Net sales	$1,200
Cost of goods sold	800
Net income after tax	100
Accounts receivable	200
Accounts payable	80
Ending inventory	400

     Calculate the collection period.

  a.

     b. Calculate the payables period.

     c. Calculate the inventory period, defined as

$$\text{Ending inventory/Cost of goods sold per day}$$

     d. How many days elapse, on average, between

       (1) The time the company is billed for a purchase and the time it receives cash from the sale of the items purchased?

(2) The time the company is billed for a purchase and the time it pays for the purchase?

(3) The time the company pays for a purchase and the time it receives cash from the sale of the items purchased?

e. The *cash cycle* is defined as

Inventory period + Collection period − Payables period.

What is DressMiss's cash cycle?

f. Suppose DressMiss's cash cycle increases. What does this imply about the company's need for financing?

g. Suppose DressMiss's cash cycle does not change but sales double. What does this imply about the company's need for financing?

h. DressMiss's assistant treasurer recommends reducing the company's cash cycle to zero days. Do you think this is necessarily a good idea? Why or why not?

6. Show that if a company's liabilities-to-equity ratio is 200 percent, its assets-to-equity ratio is 300 percent.

7. In 1996, Natural Selection, a nationwide computer dating service, had $80 million of assets and $50 million of liabilities. Earnings before interest and taxes were $10 million, interest expense was $5 million, the tax rate was 40 percent, sinking fund requirements were $2 million, and annual dividends were 40 cents per share on 5 million shares outstanding.

a. Calculate:

(1) Natural Selection's liabilities-to-equity ratio.

(2) Times interest earned.

(3) Times burden covered.

b. What percentage decline in earnings before interest and taxes could Natural Selection have sustained before failing to cover

(1) Sinking fund requirements?

(2) Common dividend payments?

8. Given the following facts, complete the balance sheet that follows. (Assume all sales are credit sales, ratios are based on a 365-day year, and the payables period is based on cost of goods sold.)

Collection period   30 days
Days' sales in cash   6.0 days
Current ratio   2.4 times
Inventory turnover   4.0 times
Liabilities to assets   50%
Payables period   30 days

Assets

Cash $50,000
Accounts receivable
Inventory   _600,000_
   Total current assets
Net fixed assets   _____
   Total assets $1,400,000

Liabilities and Owners' Equity

Accounts payable
Short-term debt   _____
   Total current liabilities
Long-term debt
Shareholders' equity   _____
Total liabilities & equity

PART II

PLANNING FUTURE
FINANCIAL PERFORMANCE

CHAPTER 3

FINANCIAL FORECASTING

Planning is the substitution of error for chaos.

Anonymous

T o this point we have looked at the *past*, evaluating existing financial statements and assessing past performance. It is now time to look to the *future*. We begin this chapter with an examination of the principal techniques of financial forecasting and a brief overview of planning and budgeting as practiced by large, modern corporations. In the following chapter, we look at planning problems unique to the management of company growth. Throughout this chapter our emphasis will be on the *technique*s of forecasting and planning; so as a counterweight, it will be important that you bear in mind that proper technique is only a part of effective planning. At least as critical is the development of creative market strategies and operating policies that underlie the financial plans.

PRO FORMA STATEMENTS

Finance is central to a company's planning activities for at least two reasons. First, much of the language of forecasting and planning is financial. Plans are stated in terms of financial statements, and many of the measures used to evaluate plans are financial. Second, and more important, the financial executive is responsible for a critical resource: money. Because virtually every corporate action has financial implications, a vital part of any plan is determining whether the plan is attainable given the company's limited resources.

Companies typically prepare a wide array of plans and budgets. Some, such as production plans and staff budgets, focus on a particular aspect of the firm, while others, such as pro forma statements, are much broader in scope. Here we will begin with the broader techniques and talk briefly about more specialized procedures later when we address planning in large corporations.

Pro forma financial statements are the most widely used vehicles for financial forecasting. A pro forma statement is simply a prediction of what the company's financial statements will look like at the end of the forecast period. These predictions may be the culmination of intensive, detailed operating plans and budgets or nothing more than rough, back-of-the-envelope projections. Either way, the pro forma format displays the information in a logical, internally consistent manner. A major use of pro forma forecasts, as will become apparent shortly, is to estimate the company's future need for external financing.

Percent-of-Sales Forecasting

As Victor Borge first noted, "Forecasting is always difficult, especially with regard to the future." One simple yet effective way to simplify the challenge is to tie many of the income statement and balance sheet figures to future sales. The rationale for this *percent-of-sales* approach is the tendency, noted in Chapter 2, for all variable costs and most current assets and current liabilities to vary directly with sales. Obviously, this will not be true for all of the entries in a company's financial statements, and certainly some independent forecasts of individual items will be required. Nonetheless, the percent-of-sales method does provide simple, logical estimates of many important variables.

The first step in a percent-of-sales forecast should be an examination of historical data to determine which financial statement items have varied in proportion to sales in the past. This will enable the forecaster to decide which items can safely be estimated as a percentage of sales and which must be forecast using other information. The second step is to forecast sales. Because so many other items will be linked mechanically to the sales forecast, it is critical to estimate sales as accurately as possible. Also, once the pro forma statements are completed, it is a good idea to test the sensitivity of the results to reasonable variations in the sales forecast. The final step in the percent-of-sales forecast is to estimate individual financial statement items by extrapolating the historical patterns to the newly estimated sales. For instance, if inventories have historically been about 20 percent of sales and next year's sales are forecast to be $10 million, we would expect inventories to be $2 million. It's that simple.

To illustrate the use of the percent-of-sales method, consider the problem faced by Suburban National Bank. R&E Supplies, Inc., a modest-size wholesaler of plumbing and electrical supplies, has been a customer of the bank for a number of years. The company has maintained average deposits of approximately $30,000 and has had a $50,000 short-term, renewable loan for five years. The company has prospered, and the loan has been renewed annually with only cursory analysis.

In late 1996, the president of R&E Supplies visited the bank and requested an increase in the short-term loan for 1997 to $500,000. The president explained that despite the company's growth, accounts payable had increased steadily and cash balances had declined. A number of suppliers had recently threatened to put the company on COD for future purchases unless they received payments more promptly. When asked why he was requesting $500,000, the president replied that this amount seemed "about right" and would enable him to pay off his most insistent creditors and rebuild his cash balances.

Knowing that the bank's credit committee would never approve a loan request of this magnitude without careful financial projections, the lending officer suggested that he and the president prepare pro forma financial statements for 1997. He explained that these statements would provide a more accurate indication of R&E's credit needs.

The first step in preparing the pro forma projections was to examine the company's financial statements for the years 1993 through 1996, shown in Table 3–1, in search of stable patterns. The results of this ratio analysis appear in Table 3–2. The president's concern about declining liquidity and increasing trade payables is well founded; cash and securities have fallen from 6 percent of sales to 2 percent, while accounts payable have risen from 9 to 16 percent. In terms of the payables period, defined as accounts payable divided by cost of goods sold per day, the increase has been from 39 to 66 days. Another worrisome trend is the increase in cost of goods sold and general, selling, and administrative expenses in proportion to sales. Earnings clearly are not keeping pace with sales.

The last column in Table 3–2 contains the projections agreed to by R&E's president and the lending officer. In line with recent experience, sales are predicted to increase 25 percent over 1996. General, selling, and administrative expenses will continue to rise as a result of an unfavorable

T A B L E 3–1

Financial Statements for R&E Supplies, Inc.,
December 31, 1993–1996 ($000)

Income Statements				
	1993	1994	1995	1996*
Net sales	$11,190	$13,764	$16,104	$20,613
Cost of goods sold	9,400	11,699	13,688	17,727
Gross profit	1,790	2,065	2,416	2,886
Expenses:				
General, selling, and administrative expenses	1,019	1,239	1,610	2,267
Net interest expense	100	103	110	90
Earnings before tax	671	723	696	529
Tax	302	325	313	238
Earnings after tax	$ 369	$ 398	$ 383	$ 291
Balance Sheets				
Assets				
Current assets:				
Cash and securities	$ 671	$ 551	$ 644	$ 412
Accounts receivable	1,343	1,789	2,094	2,886
Inventories	1,119	1,376	1,932	2,267
Prepaid expenses	14	12	15	18
Total current assets	3,147	3,728	4,685	5,583
Net fixed assets	128	124	295	287
Total assets	$ 3,275	$ 3,852	$ 4,980	$ 5,870
Liabilities and Owners' Equity				
Current liabilities:				
Bank loan	$ 50	$ 50	$ 50	$ 50
Accounts payable	1,007	1,443	2,426	3,212
Current portion long-term debt	60	50	50	100
Accrued wages	5	7	10	18
Total current liabilities	1,122	1,550	2,536	3,380
Long-term debt	960	910	860	760
Common stock	150	150	150	150
Retained earnings	1,043	1,242	1,434	1,580
Total liabilities and owners' equity	$ 3,275	$ 3,852	$ 4,980	$ 5,870

*Estimate.

T A B L E 3–2

Selected Financial Statement Items as a Percentage of Sales for R&E
Supplies, Inc., 1993–1997

	1993	1994	1995	1996*	1997†
Annual increase in sales	—	23%	17%	28%	25%
Percentage of sales:					
Cost of goods sold	84%	85	85	86	86
General, selling, and administrative expenses	9	9	10	11	12
Cash and securities	6	4	4	2	5
Accounts receivable	12	13	13	14	14
Inventories	10	10	12	11	10
Accounts payable	9	10	15	16	14
Tax/earnings before tax‡	0.45	0.45	0.45	0.45	0.45
Dividends/earnings after tax	0.50	0.50	0.50	0.50	0.50

*Estimate.

†Forecast.

‡Including state and local taxes.

labor settlement. The president believes cash and securities should rise to
at least 5 percent of sales, or 18 days' sales. Since much of this money will
sit in his bank, the lending officer concurs. The president also thinks
accounts payable should decline to no more than 14 percent of sales,
giving the company a payables period of 59 days.[1] The tax rate and the
dividends-to-earnings, or payout, ratio are expected to stay constant.

The resulting pro forma financial statements appear in Table 3–3.
Looking first at the income statement, the implication of the preceding
assumptions is that earnings after tax will decline to $234,000, down 20
percent from the prior year. The only entry on this statement requiring
further comment is net interest expense. Net interest expense will clearly
depend on the size of the loan the company requires. However, because we
do not know this yet, net interest expense has initially been assumed to
equal last year's value with the understanding that this assumption may
have to be modified later.

1

$$\frac{\text{Payables}}{\text{period}} = \frac{\text{Accounts payable}}{\text{Cost of goods sold per day}} = \frac{14\% \text{ sales}}{86\% \text{ sales}/365} = 59 \text{ days}$$

T A B L E 3–3

Pro Forma Financial Statements for R&E Supplies, Inc.,
December 31, 1997 ($000)

	Income Statement	
	1997	**Comments**
Net sales	$25,766	25% increase
Cost of goods sold	22,159	86% of sales
Gross profit	3,607	
Expenses:		
General, selling, and administrative expenses	3,092	12% of sales
Net interest expense	90	Initially constant
Earnings before tax	425	
Tax	191	At 45% tax rate
Earnings after tax	$ 234	

	Balance Sheet	
Assets		
Current assets:		
Cash and securities	$ 1,288	5% of sales
Accounts receivable	3,607	14% of sales
Inventories	2,577	10% of sales
Prepaid expenses	20	Rough estimate
Total current assets	7,492	
Net fixed assets	280	See text discussion
Total assets	$ 7,772	
Liabilities and Owners' Equity		
Current liabilities:		
Bank loan	$ 0	
Accounts payable	3,607	14% of sales
Current portion of long-term debt	100	See text discussion
Accrued wages	22	Rough estimate
Total current liabilities	3,729	
Long-term debt	660	
Common stock	150	
Retained earnings	1,697	See text discussion
Total liabilities and owners' equity	$ 6,236	
External funding required	$ 1,536	

Estimating the External Funding Required

To most operating executives, a company's income statement is more interesting than its balance sheet because the income statement measures profitability. The reverse is true for the financial executive. When the object of the exercise is to estimate future financing requirements, the income statement is interesting only insofar as it affects the balance sheet. To the financial executive, the balance sheet is key.

The first entry on R&E's pro forma balance sheet (Table 3–3) requiring comment is prepaid expenses. Like accrued wages, prepaid expenses is a small item that increases erratically with sales. Since the amounts are small and the forecast does not require a high degree of precision, rough estimates will suffice.

When asked about new fixed assets, the president indicated that a $43,000 capital budget had already been approved for 1997. Further, depreciation for the year would be $50,000, so net fixed assets would decline $7,000 to $280,000 ($280,000 = $287,000 + $43,000 − $50,000).

Note that the bank loan is initially set to zero. We will calculate the external funding required momentarily and will then be in a position to consider a possible bank loan. Continuing down the balance sheet, "current portion of long-term debt" is simply the principal repayment due in 1998. It is a contractual commitment specified in the loan agreement. As this required payment becomes a current liability, the accountant shifts it from long-term debt to current-portion long-term debt.

The last entry needing explanation is retained earnings. Since the company does not plan to sell new equity in 1997, common stock remains constant. Retained earnings are determined as follows:

$$\frac{\text{Retained}}{\text{earnings '97}} = \frac{\text{Retained}}{\text{earnings '96}} + \frac{\text{Earnings}}{\text{after tax '97}} - \text{Dividends '97}$$

$$\$1{,}697{,}000 = \$1{,}580{,}000 + \$234{,}000 - \$117{,}000$$

In words, when a business earns a profit larger than its dividend, the excess adds to retained earnings. The retained earnings account is the principal bridge between a company's income statement and its balance sheet; so as profits rise, retained earnings grow and loan needs decline. Sometimes companies will complicate this equation by charging nonrecurring gains or losses directly to retained earnings. But this is not a problem here.

The final step in constructing R&E's pro formas is to determine the size of the external funding required. We know from the principles of double-entry bookkeeping that

$$\frac{\text{Total}}{\text{assets}} = \text{Liabilities} + \frac{\text{Owners'}}{\text{equity}} + \frac{\text{External}}{\text{funding required}}$$

Using the forecasted amounts, this means that

$$\$7,772,000 = \$6,236,000 + \frac{\text{External}}{\text{funding required}}$$

$$\frac{\text{External}}{\text{funding required}} = \$1,536,000$$

According to our forecast, R&E Supplies needs not $500,000 but *over* *$1.5 million* to achieve the president's objectives.

The lending officer for Suburban National Bank is apt to be of two minds about this result. On the one hand, R&E has a projected 1997 accounts receivable balance in excess of $3.5 million, which would probably provide excellent security for a $1.5 million loan. On the other hand, R&E's cavalier attitude toward financial planning and the president's obvious lack of knowledge about where his company is headed are definite negatives.

PRO FORMA STATEMENTS AND FINANCIAL PLANNING

To this point, R&E's pro forma statements have displayed only the financial implications of the company's operating plans. This is the forecasting half of the exercise. Now R&E management is ready to do some financial planning. This involves reviewing the forecasts and considering whether to modify the operating plans. The first step is to decide whether the initial pro formas are satisfactory. This involves assessing the company's financial health as revealed in the pro formas, paying special attention to whether the estimated external funding required is too large. If the answer is yes, either because R&E does not want to borrow $1.5 million or because the bank is unwilling to grant such a large loan, management must modify its plans to conform to the financial realities. This is where operating plans and financial plans merge (or, too often, collide) to create a coherent strategy.

To illustrate, suppose R&E management wants to reduce its reliance on external financing. It might then decide to test the following revisions in its operating plans for their impact on the company's

WHY ARE LENDERS SO CONSERVATIVE?

Some would answer, "Too much Republican in-breeding," but there is another possibility: low returns. Simply put, if expected loan returns are low, lenders cannot accept high risks.

Let us look at the income statement of a representative bank lending operation with say, 100, $1 million loans, each paying 10 percent interest:

($000)

Interest income	$10,000
Interest expense	7,000
Gross income	3,000
Operating expenses	1,000
Income before tax	2,000
Tax at 40% rate	800
Income after tax	$ 1,200

The $7 million interest expense represents a 7 percent return the bank must promise depositors and investors to raise the $100 million lent. (In bank jargon, these loans offer a 3 percent lending margin, or spread.) Operating expenses include costs of the downtown office towers, the art collection, wages, and so on.

These numbers imply a minuscule return on assets of 1.2 percent. We know from the levers of performance that to generate any kind of reasonable return on equity, banks must pile on the financial leverage. Indeed, to generate a 12 percent ROE, our bank needs a 10-to-1 assets-to-equity ratio or, equivalently, $9 in liabilities for every $1 in equity.

Worse yet, our profit figures are too optimistic because they ignore the reality that not all loans are repaid. Banks typically are able to recover only about 40 percent of the principal value of defaulted loans, implying a loss of $600,000 on a $1 million default. Ignoring tax losses on defaulted loans, this means that if only two of the bank's 100 loans go bad annually, the bank's $1.2 million in expected profits will evaporate. Stated differently, a loan officer must be almost certain that each loan will be repaid just to break even. (Alternatively, the officer must be almost certain of being promoted out of lending before the loans start to go bad.) So why are lenders conservative? Because the aggressive ones have long since gone bankrupt.

external financing needs: (1) Moderate the buildup in liquidity so that cash and securities are only 4 percent of sales instead of 5, (2) tighten up collection of accounts receivable so that receivables are 12 percent of sales rather than 14 percent, and (3) settle for a more modest improvement in trade payables so that payables equal 15 percent of sales rather than 14 percent. In combination, these reductions in assets and increases in liabilities would reduce R&E's need for outside financing by just under $1 million ([3% reduction in assets + 1% increase in liabilities] × Net sales = $1 million).

Although each of these actions would reduce R&E's need for external financing, each clearly has offsetting disadvantages; thus, we cannot say for certain that the revised operating plan is necessarily better than the original one. It should be evident, however, that the pro forma format is useful for evaluating the financial dimensions of alternative operating strategies.

Sensitivity Analysis

Sensitivity analysis is the formal name for "what if" questions: What if R&E's sales grow by 15 percent instead of 25 percent? What if cost of goods sold is 84 percent of sales instead of 86 percent? It involves systematically changing one of the assumptions on which the pro forma statements are based and observing how the forecast responds. The exercise is useful in at least two ways. First, it provides information about the range of possible outcomes. For example, sensitivity analysis might reveal that depending on the future sales volume attained, the company's need for external financing could vary between $1.5 million and $2 million. This would tell management that it had better have enough flexibility in its financing plans to add an extra $500,000 in new debt as the future unfolds. Second, sensitivity analysis encourages management by exception. Sensitivity analysis enables managers to determine which assumptions most strongly affect the forecast and which are secondary. This allows managers to concentrate their data-gathering and forecasting efforts on the most critical assumptions. Subsequently, during implementation of the financial plan, the same information enables management to focus on those factors most critical to the plan's success.

Scenario Analysis

Sensitivity analysis has its uses, but it is important to realize that forecasts seldom err on one assumption at a time. That is, whatever events throw one assumption in a financial forecast off the mark will likely affect other assumptions as well. For example, suppose we want to esti- mate R&E Supplies' external financing needs assuming sales fall 15 percent below expectations. Sensitivity analysis would have us simply cut forecasted sales growth by 15 percent and recalculate the external financing required. However, this approach implicitly assumes the short- fall in sales will not affect any of the other estimates underlying the forecast. If the proper assumptions are that inventories will initially rise when sales drop below expectations and the profit margin will decline as the company slashes prices to maintain volume, failure to include these complementary effects will cause an underestimate of the need for out- side financing.

Instead of manipulating one assumption at a time, *scenario analy- sis* broadens the perspective to look at how a number of assumptions might change in response to a particular economic event. The first step in a scenario analysis is to identify a few carefully chosen events, or scenarios, that might plausibly befall the company. Common scenarios include loss of a major customer, successful introduction of a major new product, or entry of an important new competitor. Then, for each sce- nario identified, the second step is to carefully rethink the variables in the original forecast to either reaffirm the original assumption or substi- tute a new more accurate one. The last step in the analysis is to generate a separate forecast for each scenario. The result is a limited number of detailed projections describing the range of contingencies the business faces.

Simulation

Simulation is a computer-assisted extension of sensitivity analysis. To perform a simulation, begin by assigning a probability distribution to each uncertain element in the forecast. The distribution describes the possible values the variable could conceivably take on and states the probability of each value occurring. Next, ask a computer to pick at random a value for each uncertain variable consistent with the assigned probability distribu- tion and generate a set of pro forma statements based on the selected values. This creates one *trial.* Performing the last step many times pro- duces a large number of trials. The output from a simulation is a table or a graph summarizing the results of many trials. For example, the output from a simulation study of R&E's loan needs for 1997 involving 1,000 trials might be the following:

External Funding Required	Number of Trials Occurring	Percentage of Trials Occurring
$751,000–$1,000,000	150	15%
1,001,000–1,250,000	200	20
1,251,000–1,500,000	300	30
1,501,000–1,750,000	200	20
1,751,000–2,000,000	100	10
More than $2,000,000	50	5
Total	1,000	100%

These results suggest that there is a 30 percent chance that R&E's need for external financing will be in the $1.25 million to $1.50 million range but a 15 percent chance that it will top $2 million.

Simulation has enjoyed a burst of popularity in recent years, due largely to the advent of a new generation of computer software packages, such as @Risk and Crystal Ball, that easily convert a standard spreadsheet forecast into a full-blown simulation. The principal advantage of simulation relative to sensitivity analysis and scenario analysis is that it allows all of the uncertain input variables to vary at once. The principal disadvantage, in my experience, is that the results are often hard to interpret. One reason is that few executives are used to thinking about future events in terms of probabilities. In the above table, should the company be prepared to raise in excess of $2 million, or is the 5 percent chance that this need will arise too remote to warrant concern? What is a reasonable maximum external funding requirement the company should be prepared to meet?

A second difficulty with simulation in practice recalls President Eisenhower's dictum "It's not the plans but the planning that matters." With simulation much of the "planning" goes on inside a computer, and managers see only the results. Consequently, they may not gain the depth of insight into the company and its future prospects that they would if they used simpler techniques.

Interest Expense

One thing that bothers attentive novices about pro forma forecasting is the circularity involving interest expense and indebtedness. As noted earlier, interest expense cannot be estimated accurately until the amount of external funding required has been determined. Yet because the external funding depends in part on the amount of interest expense, it would appear one cannot be accurately estimated without the other.

There are two ways around this dilemma. One is to define a set of simultaneous equations to solve for interest expense and external funding together. If you use a computer spreadsheet, this is equivalent to asking the computer to work through the statements several times, with each pass coming closer to the simultaneous solution. The other, more pragmatic approach is to forget the whole problem with the expectation that the first-pass solution will be close enough. Given the likely errors in predicting sales and other variables, the additional error caused by a failure to determine interest expense accurately is usually not all that important.

To illustrate, R&E Supplies' first-pass pro formas assumed a net interest expense of $90,000, whereas the balance sheet indicates total interest-bearing debt as high as $2.2 million. At a 10 percent interest rate, this implies an interest expense of about $220,000, or more than $100,000 more than our first-pass estimate. But think what happens as we trace the impact of a $100,000 addition to interest expense through the income statement. First, the $100,000 expense is before taxes. At a 45 percent tax rate, the decline in earnings after tax will be only $55,000. Second, because R&E Supplies distributes half of its earnings as dividends, a $55,000 decline in earnings after tax will result in only a $27,500 decline in the addition to retained earnings. So after all the dust settles, our estimate of the addition to retained earnings and, by implication, the external funding required will be about $27,500 low. But when the need for new external financing is already over $1.5 million, what's another $27,500 among friends? Granted, increased interest expense has a noticeable percentage effect on earnings, but by the time the increase filters through taxes and dividend payments, the effect on the external funding needed is modest.

Seasonality

A more serious potential problem with pro forma statements—and, indeed, with all of the forecasting techniques mentioned in this chapter—is that the results are applicable only on the forecast date. The pro formas in Table 3–3 present an estimate of R&E Supplies' external financing requirements on December 31, 1997. They say nothing about the company's need for financing on any other date before or after December 31. If a company has seasonal financing requirements, knowledge of year-end loan needs may be of little use in financial planning, since the year end may bear no relation whatever to the date of the company's peak financing need. To avoid this problem, you should make monthly or quarterly forecasts rather than annual ones. Or, if you know the date of peak financing need, you can simply make this date the forecast horizon.

Forecasting with Computer Spreadsheets

Easy-to-use computer spreadsheets, such as Excel and Lotus 1-2-3, have revolutionized financial forecasting. Now anyone with a modicum of computer skill can spin out elegant (and occasionally useful) pro forma forecasts, scenario analyses, and even simulations.

    To demonstrate how easy spreadsheet-based forecasting is, Table 3–4 presents an abbreviated one-year forecast for R&E Supplies as it might appear on a computer screen. (If you are a computer novice, I suggest skipping this section or developing a basic understanding of spreadsheet programs before continuing.) The first area on the simulated screen is an *assumptions box*, containing all of the information and assumptions required to construct the forecast. (It is a good idea to leave some room here initially so that if you are unable to think of all the necessary information immediately, you can add it later.) Gathering all of the necessary input information in an assumptions box can be a real timesaver later if you want to change assumptions or do some scenario or sensitivity analysis. The 1997 data in the assumptions box correspond closely to the data used earlier in our handmade forecast for R&E Supplies.

    The forecast begins immediately below the assumptions box. The first column, labeled "Equations 1997," is included for explanatory purposes and would not appear on a conventional forecast. Entering the equations shown causes the computer to calculate the quantities appearing in the second column, labeled "Forecast 1997." The third column, labeled "Forecast 1998," is presently blank.

    Two steps are required to get from the assumptions to the completed forecast. First, it is necessary to enter a series of equations tying the inputs to the forecasted outputs. These are the equations appearing in the first column. Here is how to read them. The first equation for net sales is = B3 + B3 * C4. This instructs the computer to get the number in cell B3 and add to it that number times the number in cell C4, in other words, $20,613 + $20,613 × 25%. The second equation instructs the computer to multiply

T A B L E 3–4

Forecasting with a Computer Spreadsheet: Pro Forma Financial Forecast for R&E Supplies, Inc., December 31, 1997 ($000)

	A	B	C	D
1				
2	*Year*	*1996 Actual*	*1997*	*1998*
3	Net sales	$20,613		
4	Growth rate in net sales		25.0%	
5	Cost of goods sold/net sales		86.0%	
6	Gen., sell., and admin. expenses/net sales		12.0%	
7	Long-term debt	$ 760	$660	
8	Current portion long-term debt	$ 100	$100	
9	Interest rate		10.0%	
10	Tax rate		45.0%	
11	Dividend/earnings after tax		50.0%	
12	Current assets/net sales		29.0%	
13	Net fixed assets		$280	
14	Current liabilities/net sales		14.5%	
15	Owners' equity	$ 1,730		
16	**INCOME STATEMENT**			
17		*Equations*	*Forecast*	*Forecast*
18	*Year*	*1997*	*1997*	*1998*
19	Net sales	=B3+B3*C4	$25,766	
20	Cost of goods sold	=C5*C19	22,159	
21	Gross profit	=C19–C20	3,607	
22	Gen., sell., and admin. exp.	=C6*C19	3,092	
23	Interest expense	=C9*(B7+B8+C40)	241	
24	Earnings before tax	=C21–C22–C23	274	
25	Tax	=C10*C24	123	
26	Earnings after tax	=C24–C25	151	
27	Dividends paid	=C11*C26	75	
28	Additions to retained earnings	=C26–C27	75	
29				
30	**BALANCE SHEET**			
31	Current assets	=C12*C19	7,472	
32	Net fixed assets	=C13	280	
33	Total assets	=C31+C32	7,752	
34				
35	Current liabilities	=C14*C19	3,736	
36	Long-term debt	=C7	660	
37	Equity	=B15+C28	1,805	
38	Total liabilities and shareholders' equity	=C35+C36+C37	6,202	
39				
40	**EXTERNAL FUNDING REQUIRED**	=C33–C38	$ 1,551	

forecasted net sales by the forecasted cost of goods sold percentage. The third says to calculate gross profit by subtracting cost of goods sold from net sales.

There are only three tricky equations. Interest expense, row 23, is the interest rate times beginning-of-period long-term debt, including the current portion, plus the forecasted external funding required. As discussed earlier, the tricky part here is the interdependency between interest expense and external funding required. (I will talk more about this in step 2.) The other two equations are simple by comparison. The equity equation, row 37, is beginning-of-period equity plus additions to retained earnings; the external funding required equation, row 40, is total assets minus total liabilities and shareholders' equity.

The second required step is to incorporate the interdependence between interest expense and external funding required. Without some adjustment, the computer will likely signal "circular reference" and then stall when you enter the equation for interest expense. To avoid this, you need to shift to what spreadsheeters call *manual calculation*. With Excel software, you need to do the following. Select "Tools" from the menu, followed by "Options." Select the "Calculation" tab, then choose "Manual" calculation and click the "iteration" toggle. Finally, set the maximum number of iterations to something above, say, 5, and press OK. With the program no longer in automatic calculation mode, you will now need to tell the computer when to calculate. Do this by pressing the F9 key. (Lotus has a very similar protocol.) Your forecast should now be complete.

Now the fun begins. To perform a sensitivity analysis on the forecast, just change one of the entries in the assumptions box, press F9, and *voilà:* The computer instantly makes all the necessary changes and shows the revised forecast. To extend the forecast one more year, just complete the entries in the assumptions box, highlight the 1997 forecast, and copy or fill one column to the right. Then make some obvious changes in the equations for net sales and equity, press the F9 key, and the computer does the rest.

CASH FLOW FORECASTS

A cash flow forecast is simply a listing of all anticipated sources of cash to and uses of cash by the company over the forecast period. The difference between forecasted sources and forecasted uses is the external financing required. Table 3–5 shows a 1997 cash flow forecast for R&E Supplies.

T A B L E   3–5

Cash Flow Forecast for R&E Supplies, Inc., 1997 ($000)

Sources of Cash	
Net income	$ 234
Depreciation	50
Decreases in assets or increases in liabilities	
Increase in accounts payable	395
Increase in accrued wages	4
Total sources of cash	$ 683
Uses of Cash	
Dividends	$ 117
Increases in assets or decreases in liabilities:	
Increase in cash and securities	876
Increase in accounts receivable	721
Increase in inventories	310
Increase in prepaid expenses	2
Investment in fixed assets	43
Decrease in long-term debt	100
Decrease in short-term debt	50
Total uses of cash	$2,219

Determination of *external funding required*:

Total sources + External funding required = Total uses

$683,000 + External funding required = $2,219,000

External funding required = $1,536,000

The assumptions underlying the forecast are the same as those used to construct R&E's pro forma statements.

Cash flow forecasts are quite straightforward and easily understood. Their principal weakness compared to pro forma statements is that they are less informative. R&E's pro forma statements not only indicate the size of the external financing required but also provide information that is useful for evaluating the company's ability to raise this amount of money. Thus, a loan officer can assess the company's future financial position by analyzing the pro forma statements. Because the cash flow forecast presents only *changes* in the quantities represented, a similar analysis using cash flow forecasts would be much more difficult.

CASH BUDGETS

A *cash budget* is a list of all anticipated receipts of cash and disbursements of cash over the forecast period. It can be thought of as a detailed cash flow forecast in which all traces of accrual accounting have been eliminated.

Table 3–6 presents a monthly cash budget for TransInternational Manufacturing (TIM) for the third quarter of 1997. To purge the accounting data of all accrual effects, it is necessary to remember that a period of time elapses between a credit sale or a credit purchase and the receipt or disbursement of the associated cash. In TIM's case, a 60-day collection period on accounts receivable means there is an average lag of 60 days between a credit sale and the receipt of cash. Consequently, cash collections in any month equal credit sales two months prior. The analogous lag for credit purchases is one month. Note that depreciation does not appear on a cash budget because it is not a disbursement of cash.

The bottom portion of TIM's cash budget illustrates the determination of external financing needs. Observe that the ending cash balance for one month becomes the beginning balance for the next month. Comparing the ending cash balance to the desired minimum balance, as determined by management, yields an estimate of TIM's monthly cash surplus or deficit. The deficit corresponds to external funding required in a pro forma forecast; it is the amount of money that must be raised on the forecast date to cover disbursements and leave ending cash at the desired minimum. A forecasted cash surplus means the company will have excess cash on that date and ending cash will exceed the desired minimum by the forecasted amount.

Because a cash budget focuses so narrowly on the cash account, operating executives seldom use it as a general forecasting tool. Its principal application is use by treasury specialists for managing the company's cash balances. TIM's cash budget suggests that surplus cash will be available for investment in July and August, but the investments chosen had better be liquid, because all of the excess cash, plus $21 million from other sources, will be required in September.

THE TECHNIQUES COMPARED

Although the formats differ, it should be a relief to learn that all of the forecasting techniques considered in this chapter produce the same results. As long as the assumptions are the same and no arithmetic or accounting

T A B L E 3–6

Cash Budget for TransInternational Manufacturing, 3rd Quarter, 1997 ($000)

	Actual		**Forecast**		
	May	**June**	**July**	**August**	**September**
		Raw Data			
Credit sales	$10,000	$14,000	$16,000	$19,000	$15,000
Credit purchases	$ 5,000	$ 6,000	$ 5,000	$12,000	$ 6,000
		Cash Budget			
Cash receipts:					
Sales for cash			$ 1,000	$ 1,000	$ 1,000
Collections from credit sales			10,000	14,000	16,000
(assumes 60-day lag, sale to collection)					
Sale of used machinery				19,000	
Total cash receipts			11,000	34,000	17,000
Cash disbursements:					
Purchases for cash			1,000	1,000	2,000
Payments for credit purchases			6,000	5,000	12,000
(assumes 30-day lag, purchase to payment)					
Wages and salaries			4,000	4,000	4,000
Interest payments					12,000
Principal payments					26,000
Dividends					8,000
Tax payments			3,000		
Total cash disbursements			14,000	10,000	64,000
Net cash receipts (disbursements)			($ 3,000)	$24,000	($47,000)
Determination of cash needs:					
Beginning cash			$15,000	$12,000	$36,000
Net receipts (disbursements)			(3,000)	24,000	(47,000)
Ending cash			12,000	36,000	(11,000)
Minimum cash desired (assumed)			10,000	10,000	10,000
Cash surplus (deficit)			$ 2,000	$26,000	($21,000)

mistakes are made, all of the techniques will produce the same estimate of external funding required. Moreover, if your accounting skills are up to the task, it is possible to reconcile one format with another.

A second reassuring fact is that regardless of which forecasting technique is used, the resulting estimate of new financing needs is not biased by inflation. Consequently, there is no need to resort to elaborate inflation

A PROBLEM WITH DEPRECIATION

XYZ Corporation is forecasting its financing needs for next year. The original forecast shows an external financing need of $10 million. On reviewing the forecast, the production manager, having just returned from an accounting seminar, recommends increasing depreciation next year—for reporting purposes only, not for tax purposes—by $1 million. She explains, rather condescendingly, that this will reduce net fixed assets by $1 million and, because a reduction of an asset is a source of cash, this will reduce the plug by a like amount. Explain why the production manager is incorrect.

Answer: Increasing depreciation will reduce net fixed assets. However, it will also reduce provision for taxes and earnings after tax by the same amount. Since both are liability accounts and reduction of a liability is a use of cash, the whole exercise is a wash with respect to determination of external financing requirements. This is consistent with cash budgeting, which ignores depreciation entirely. Here is a numerical example:

	Original Depreciation	Increase in Depreciation	Change in Liability Account
Operating income	$10,000	$10,000	
Depreciation	4,000	5,000	
Earnings before tax	6,000	5,000	
Provision for tax @ 40%	2,400	2,000	– 400
Earnings after tax	3,600	3,000	
Dividends	1,000	1,000	
Additions to retained earnings	$ 2,600	$ 2,000	– $600
Total change in liabilities			– $1,000

adjustments when making financial forecasts in an inflationary environment. This is not to say that the need for new financing is independent of the inflation rate; indeed, as will become apparent in the next chapter, the financing needs of most companies rise with inflation. Rather, it means that direct application of the previously described forecasting techniques will correctly indicate the need for external financing even in the presence of inflation.

Mechanically, then, the three forecasting techniques are equivalent, and the choice of which one to use can depend on the purpose of the forecast. For most planning purposes and for credit analysis, I recommend pro forma statements because they present the information in a form suitable for additional financial analysis. For short-term forecasting and the management of cash, the cash budget is appropriate. A cash flow forecast lies somewhere between the other two. It presents a broader picture of company operations than a cash budget does and is easier to construct and more accessible to accounting novices than pro formas are, but it is also less informative than pro formas.

PLANNING IN LARGE COMPANIES

In a well-run company, financial forecasts are only the tip of the planning iceberg. Executives throughout the organization devote substantial time and effort to developing strategic and operating plans that eventually become the basis for the company's financial plans. This formalized planning process is especially important in large, multidivision corporations because it is frequently a key means of coordination, communication, and motivation within the organization.

In a large company, effective planning usually involves three formal stages that recur on an annual cycle. In broad perspective, these stages can be viewed as a progressive narrowing of the strategic choices under consideration. In the first stage, headquarters executives and division managers hammer out a corporate strategy. This involves a broad-ranging analysis of the market threats and opportunities the company faces, an assessment of the company's own strengths and weaknesses, and a determination of the performance goals to be sought by each of the company's business units. At this initial stage, the process is creative and largely qualitative. The role of financial forecasts is limited to outlining in general terms the resource constraints the company faces and testing the financial feasibility of alternative strategies.

In the second stage, division managers and department personnel translate the qualitative, market-oriented goals established in stage 1 into a set of internal division activities deemed necessary to achieve the agreed-upon goals. For example, if a stage 1 goal is to increase product X's market share by at least 2 percent in the next 18 months, the stage 2 plans define what division management must do to achieve this objective. At this point, top management will likely have indicated in general terms the resources to be allocated to each division, although no specific spending plans will have been authorized. So division management will find it necessary to prepare at least rough financial forecasts to ensure that its plans are generally consistent with senior management's resource commitments.

In the third stage of the planning process, department personnel develop a set of quantitative plans and budgets based on the activities defined in stage 2. This essentially involves putting a price tag on the agreed-upon division activities. The price tag appears in two forms: operating budgets and capital budgets. Although each company has its own definition of which expenditures are to appear on which budget, capital budgets customarily include expenditures on costly, long-lived assets, whereas operating budgets include recurring expenditures such as materials, salaries, and so on.

The integration of these detailed divisional budgets at headquarters produces the corporation's financial forecast. If management has been realistic about available resources throughout the planning process, the forecast will contain few surprises. If not, headquarters executives may discover that in the aggregate, the spending plans of the divisions exceed available resources and some revisions in division budgets will be necessary.

In Chapters 7 and 8, we will consider the financial analysis of investment opportunities in some detail. For now it is sufficient to acknowledge that corporate investment decisions are not made in a vacuum; rather, they are an integral part of the planning process described here. This means, among other things, that even though a capital expenditure opportunity may appear to be financially attractive, it is likely to be rejected by senior management unless it furthers the attainment of agreed-upon corporate objectives. The proper perspective with regard to investment analysis, therefore, is that a company's strategic plans should create an umbrella under which operating and capital budgeting take place.

CHAPTER SUMMARY

1. This chapter presented the principal techniques of financial forecasting and planning.
2. Pro forma statements are the best all-around means of financial forecasting. They are a projection of the company's income statement and balance sheet at the end of the forecast period.

3. Percent-of-sales forecasting is a simple and useful technique in which most income statement and many balance sheet entries are assumed to change in proportion to sales.

4. Most operating managers are concerned chiefly with the income statement. When the goal is forecasting the need for outside financing, the income statement is of interest only insofar as income affects the balance sheet.

5. Financial forecasting involves the extrapolation of past trends and agreed-upon changes into the future. Financial planning occurs when management evaluates the forecasts and considers possible modifications.

6. A cash budget is a less general way to forecast than pro forma statements. It consists of a list of anticipated cash receipts and disbursements and their net effects on the firm's cash balances. When done correctly and using the same assumptions, cash budgets and pro forma statements generate the same estimated need for outside financing.

7. Planning in most large companies involves three continuing cycles: (*a*) a strategic planning cycle in which senior management is most active, (*b*) an operational cycle in which divisional managers translate qualitative strategic goals into concrete plans, and (*c*) a budgeting cycle that essentially puts a price tag on the operational plans. Financial forecasting and planning are increasingly important in each succeeding stage of the process.

A D D I T I O N A L   R E A D I N G

Mayes, Timothy R., and Todd M. Shank. *Financial Analysis with Microsoft Excel*. Dryden Press, 1996. 294 pages.

McLaughlin, Hugh S., and J. Russell Boulding. *Financial Management with Lotus 1-2-3*. Englewood Cliffs, NJ: Prentice Hall, 1986. 224 pages.

Personal computers are playing an increasingly important role in financial analysis. These two books offer how-to instruction in constructing your own programs to take much of the drudgery out of the calculations recommended in this and following chapters.

CHAPTER PROBLEMS

1. Suppose you constructed a pro forma balance sheet for a company and a cash budget for the same time period and the external funding required from the pro forma forecast differed from the cash surplus (deficit) estimated on the cash budget. How would you interpret this result?

2. Suppose you constructed a pro forma balance sheet for a company and the estimate for external funding required was negative. How would you interpret this result?

3. Table 3–4 presents a computer spreadsheet for estimating R&E Supplies' external funding required for 1997. The text mentions that with modifications to the equations for equity and net sales, the forecast can easily be extended through 1998. Write the modified equations for equity and net sales.

4. Using a computer spreadsheet, the information that follows, and the modified equations determined in question 3, extend the forecast for R&E Supplies contained in Table 3–4 through 1998. Is R&E's external funding required in 1998 higher or lower than in 1997?

R&E Supplies Assumptions for 1998

Growth rate in net sales	30.0%	Tax rate	45.0%
Cost of good sold/net sales	86.0%	Dividend/earnings after tax	50.0%
General, selling, &		Current assets/net sales	29.0%
administrative expenses/net		Net fixed assets	$270
sales	11%	Current liabilities/net sales	14.4%
Long-term debt	$560		
Current portion long-term debt	$100		
Interest rate	10.0%		

5. The treasurer of Michigan Milling, a wholesale distributor of knitting supplies, wants to estimate his company's cash balances for the first three months of 1997. Using the following information, construct a monthly cash budget for Michigan Milling for January through March 1997. Does it appear from your results that the treasurer should be concerned about investing excess cash or looking for a bank loan?

Michigan Milling Selected Information

Sales (20 percent for cash, the rest on 30-day credit terms):

1996 actual

October	$240,000
November	280,000
December	800,000

1997 projected

January	$400,000
February	160,000
March	160,000

Purchases (all on 60-day terms):

1996 actual

October	$340,000
November	360,000
December	800,000

1997 projected

January	$200,000
February	80,000
March	80,000

Wages payable monthly	120,000
Principal payment due on debt in March	140,000
Interest due in March	60,000
Dividend payable in March	200,000
Taxes payable in February	120,000
Addition to accumulated depreciation in March	20,000
Cash balance on January 1, 1997	200,000
Minimum desired cash balance	100,000

6. Continuing problem 5, Michigan Milling's income statement and balance sheet for December 31, 1996, follow. Additional information about the company's accounting methods and the treasurer's expectations for the first quarter of 1997 appear in the footnotes.

Michigan Milling
Income Statement
December 31, 1996 ($000)

Net sales	$4,000
Cost of goods sold[1]	2,600
Gross profits	1,400
Selling and administrative expenses[2]	1,080
Interest expense	60
Depreciation[3]	60
Net profit before tax	200
Tax at 33%	66
Net profit after tax	$ 134

Balance Sheet
December 31, 1996 ($000)

Assets

Cash	$ 200
Accounts receivable	640
Inventory	1,200
Total current assets	2,040
Gross fixed assets	600
Accumulated depreciation	100
Net fixed assets	500
Total assets	$2,540

Liabilities

Bank loan	$ 0
Accounts payable	1,060
Miscellaneous accruals[4]	40
Current portion long-term debt[5]	70
Taxes payable	200
Total current liabilities	1,540
Long-term debt	660
Shareholders' equity	340
Total liabilities and equity	$2,540

[1]Cost of goods sold consists entirely of purchase costs and is expected to continue to equal 65 percent of sales.

[2]Selling and administrative expenses consist entirely of wages.

[3]Depreciation is at the rate of $20,000 per quarter.

[4]Miscellaneous accruals are not expected to change in the first quarter.

[5]$140 due March 1997. No payments due in 1998.

a. Use this information and the information in problem 5 to construct a pro forma income statement for the first quarter of 1997 and a pro forma balance sheet for March 31, 1997. What is your estimated external financing need for March 31?

b. Does the March 31, 1997, estimated external financing equal your cash surplus (deficit) for this date from your cash budget in problem 5? Should it?

c. Do your pro forma forecasts tell you more than your cash budget does about Michigan Milling's financial prospects?

d. What do your pro forma income statement and balance sheet tell you about Michigan Milling's need for external financing on February 28, 1997?

7. Based on your answer to question 6, construct a first-quarter 1997 cash flow forecast for Michigan Milling.

CHAPTER 4

MANAGING GROWTH

Alas, the road to success is always under repair.

Anonymous

Growth and its management present special problems in financial planning, in part because many executives see growth as something to be maximized. They reason simply that as growth increases, the firm's market share and profits should rise as well. From a financial perspective, however, growth is not always a blessing. Rapid growth can put considerable strain on a company's resources, and unless management is aware of this effect and takes active steps to control it, rapid growth can lead to bankruptcy. Companies can literally grow broke. It is a sad truth that almost as many companies go bankrupt because they grew too fast as do those that grew too slowly. It is doubly sad to realize that those companies that grew too fast met the market test by providing a product people wanted and failed only because they lacked the financial acumen to manage their growth properly.

At the other end of the spectrum, companies growing too slowly have a different but no less pressing set of financial concerns. As will become apparent, if these companies fail to appreciate the financial implications of slow growth, they will become potential candidates for takeover by more perceptive raiders. In either case, the financial management of growth is a topic worthy of close inspection.

We begin our look at the financial dimensions of growth by defining a company's *sustainable growth rate*. This is the maximum rate at which company sales can increase without depleting financial resources. Then we look at the options open to management when a company's target

---

DELL GROWS UP

Even well-known, successful companies like $5 billion Dell Computer Corporation have experienced life-threatening growing pains. The company's young founder, Michael Dell, now admits that in 1993 Dell's growth spurt had come at the expense of a sound financial position. He says the company's cash reserves were down to $20 million at one point. "We could have used that up in a day or two. For a company our size, that was ridiculous. I realized we had to change the priorities."

Had Dell's priorities remained "growth, growth, growth," it might not be around today. Michael Dell founded Dell Computer before he was 20 years old. After several years of prodigious growth and with his company at the financial precipice, he lacked the expertise to manage the growth. Fortunately, he had the sense to hire more seasoned managers who could calm security analysts and steer Dell in a more conservative direction. Those managers urged Dell to focus on earnings and liquidity rather than sales growth. Slowing growth in 1994 cost the company market share, but it also helped convert a loss a year earlier into a $106.6 million profit. The company also instituted formal planning and budgeting processes. Today Dell is one of the world's largest computer manufacturers, with a healthy balance sheet and solid growth.

---

growth rate exceeds its sustainable growth rate and, conversely, when growth falls below sustainable levels. An important conclusion will be that growth is not necessarily something to be maximized. In many companies, it may be necessary to limit growth to conserve financial strength. In others, the money used to finance unprofitable growth might better be returned to owners. The need to limit growth is a hard lesson for operating managers used to thinking that more is better; it is a critical one, however, because operating executives bear major responsibility for managing growth.

SUSTAINABLE GROWTH

We can think of successful companies as passing through a predictable life cycle. The cycle begins with a start-up phase in which the company loses money while developing products and establishing a foothold in the market. This is followed by a rapid growth phase in which the company is profitable but is growing so rapidly that it needs regular infusions of outside financing. The third phase is maturity, characterized by a decline in growth and a switch from absorbing outside financing to generating more cash than the firm can profitably reinvest. The last phase is decline, during which the company is perhaps marginally profitable, generates more cash than it can reinvest internally, and suffers declining sales. Mature and declining companies frequently devote considerable time and money to seeking investment opportunities in new products or firms that are still in their growth phase.

We begin our discussion by looking at the growth phase, when financing needs are most pressing. Later we will consider the growth problems of mature and declining firms. Central to our discussion is the notion of sustainable growth. Intuitively, sustainable growth is merely a formalization of the old adage "It takes money to make money." Increased sales require more assets of all types, which must be paid for. Retained profits and the accompanying new borrowing generate some cash, but only limited amounts. Unless the company is prepared to sell common stock, this limit puts a ceiling on the growth it can achieve without straining its resources. This is the firm's sustainable growth rate.

The Sustainable Growth Equation

Let's begin by writing a simple equation to express the dependence of growth on financial resources. For this purpose, assume

1. The company wants to grow as rapidly as market conditions permit.
2. Management is unable or unwilling to sell new equity.
3. The company has a target capital structure and a target dividend policy that it wants to maintain.

We will say more about these assumptions shortly. For now it is enough to realize that although they certainly are not appropriate for all firms, the assumptions describe a great many.

Figure 4–1 shows the rapidly growing company's plight. It represents the firm's balance sheet as two rectangles, one for assets and the other for liabilities and owners' equity. The two long, unshaded rectangles represent the balance sheet at the beginning of the year. The rectangles are, of course, the same height because assets must equal liabilities plus owners' equity. Now, if the company wants to increase sales during the coming year, it must also increase assets such as inventory, accounts receivable, and productive capacity. The shaded area on the assets side of the figure represents the value of new assets necessary to support the increased sales. Because the company will not be selling equity by

FIGURE 4–1

New Sales Require New Assets, Which Must Be Financed

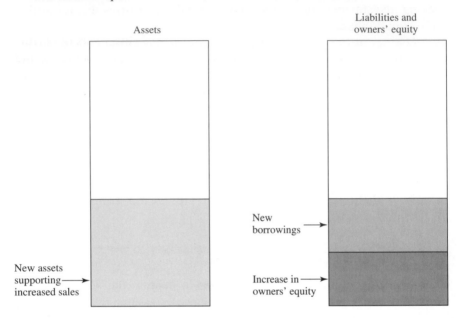

assumption, the cash required to pay for this increase in assets must come from retained profits and increased liabilities.

We want to know what limits the rate at which the company in Figure 4–1 can increase sales. Assuming, in effect, that all parts of a business expand in strict proportion like a balloon, what limits the rate of this expansion? To find out, start in the lower-right corner of the figure with owners' equity. As equity grows, liabilities can increase proportionately without altering the capital structure; together, the growth of liabilities and the growth of equity determine the rate at which assets expand. This, in turn, limits the growth rate in sales. So after all the dust settles, what limits the growth rate in sales is the rate at which owners' equity expands. A company's sustainable growth rate therefore is nothing more than its growth rate in equity.

Letting g^* represent the sustainable growth rate,

$$g^* = \frac{\text{Change in equity}}{\text{Beginning-of-period equity}}$$

With the help of a little algebra as shown below,[1] we can rewrite this expression more informatively as

$$g^* = PRA\hat{T}$$

where P, A, and $\hat{T}$ are our old friends from Chapter 2, the levers of performance. Recall that P is the profit margin, A is the asset turnover ratio, and $\hat{T}$ is the assets-to-equity ratio. The assets-to-equity ratio wears a hat here as a reminder that it is assets divided by *beginning-of-period* equity instead of end-of-period equity as defined in Chapter 2. The fourth ratio, R, is the firm's retention rate, defined as the fraction of earnings retained in the business. If a company distributes 30 percent of its earnings as dividends, its retention rate is 70 percent. Alternatively, the retention rate is 1 minus the firm's dividend payout ratio.

This is the sustainable growth equation.[2] Let's see what it tells us. Given the assumptions just noted, the equation says that a company's sustainable growth rate in sales, g^*, equals the product of four ratios, P, R, A, and $\hat{T}$. Two of these ratios, P and A, summarize the operating performance of the business, while the other two describe the firm's principal financial policies. Thus, the retention rate, R, captures management's attitudes toward the distribution of dividends, and the assets-to-equity ratio, $\hat{T}$, reflects its policies regarding financial leverage.

An important implication of the sustainable growth equation is that g^* *is the only growth rate in sales that is consistent with stable values of the four ratios.* If a company increases sales at any rate other than g^*, one

---

1 Assuming the firm issues no new equity, the numerator in the above equation equals R times earnings, where R is the firm's retention rate, defined as the proportion of earnings retained in the business. Thus,

$$g^* = \frac{(R)\ \text{Earnings}}{\text{Equity}_{\text{bop}}}$$

where bop denotes beginning-of-period equity. Representing Earnings/Equity$_{\text{bop}}$ as RO$\hat{\text{E}}$,

$$g^* = (R)\text{RO}\hat{\text{E}}$$

where the hat denotes beginning-of-period equity. Finally, recalling from Chapter 2 that

$$\text{ROE} = \frac{\text{Profit}}{\text{margin}} \times \frac{\text{Asset}}{\text{turnover}} \times \frac{\text{Financial}}{\text{leverage}}$$

$$g^* = PRA\hat{T}$$

where $\hat{T}$ is assets divided by beginning-of-period equity.

2 I shall refrain from admonishing you to avoid "prat" falls.

or more of the ratios *must* change. This means that when a company grows at a rate in excess of its sustainable growth rate, it had better improve operations (represented by an increase in the profit margin or the asset turnover ratio) or prepare to alter its financial policies (represented by increasing its retention rate or its financial leverage).

TOO MUCH GROWTH

This is the crux of the sustainable growth problem for rapidly expanding firms: Because increasing operating efficiency is not always possible and altering financial policies is not always wise, we see that it is entirely possible for a company to grow too fast for its own good. This is particularly true for smaller companies, which may do inadequate financial planning. Such companies see sales growth as something to be maximized and think too little of the financial consequences. They do not realize that rapid growth has them on a treadmill; the faster they grow, the more cash they need, even when they are profitable. They can meet this need for a time by increasing leverage, but eventually they will reach their debt capacity, lenders will refuse additional credit requests, and the companies will find themselves without the cash to pay their bills. All of this can be prevented if managers understand that growth above the company's sustainable rate creates financial problems that must be anticipated and solved.

Balanced Growth

Here is another way to think about sustainable growth. Recalling that a company's return on assets, ROA, can be expressed as the product of its profit margin times its asset turnover, we can rewrite the sustainable growth equation as[3]

$$g^* = R\hat{T} \times \text{ROA}$$

Here R and $\hat{T}$ reflect the company's financial policies, while ROA summarizes its operating performance. So if a company's retention ratio is 25

---

3 Strictly speaking, this equation should be expressed in terms of return on invested capital, not return on assets, but the gain in precision is too modest to justify the added mathematical complexity. See Gordon Donaldson, *Managing Corporate Wealth* (New York: Praeger, 1984), Chapter 4, for a more rigorous exposition.

F I G U R E   4–2

A Graphical Representation of Sustainable Growth

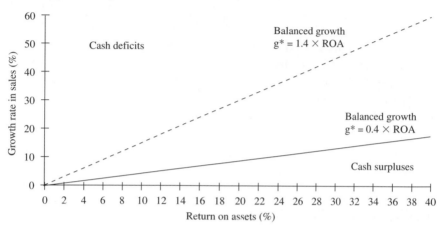

percent and its assets-to-equity ratio is 1.6, its sustainable growth equation becomes simply

$$g^* = 0.4 \times \text{ROA}$$

This equation says that given stable financial policies, sustainable growth varies linearly with return on assets. Figure 4–2 graphs this relationship with sales growth on the vertical axis, ROA on the horizontal axis, and the sustainable growth equation as the upward-sloping, solid, diagonal line. The line bears the label "Balanced growth" because the company can self-finance only the sales growth–ROA combinations lying on this line. All growth-return combinations lying off this line generate either cash deficits or cash surpluses. Thus, rapidly growing, marginally profitable companies will plot in the upper-left portion of the graph, implying cash deficits, while slowly expanding, highly profitable companies will plot in the lower-right portion, implying cash surpluses.

When a company experiences unbalanced growth of either the surplus or the deficit variety, it can move toward the balanced growth line in any of three ways: It can change its growth rate, alter its return on assets, or modify its financial policies. To illustrate the last option, suppose the company with the balanced growth line depicted in Figure 4–2 is in the deficit region of the graph and wants to reduce the deficit. One strategy would be to increase its retention ratio to, say, 50 percent and its assets-to-equity ratio to, say, 2.8 to 1, thereby changing its sustainable growth equation to

$$g^* = 1.4 \times \text{ROA}$$

In Figure 4–2, this is equivalent to rotating the balanced growth line upward to the left, as shown by the dotted line. Now any level of profitability will support a higher growth rate than before.

In this perspective, the sustainable growth rate is the nexus of all growth-return combinations yielding balanced growth, and the sustainable growth problem is that of managing the surpluses or deficits caused by unbalanced growth. We will return to strategies for managing growth after looking at a numerical example.

Analog Devices' Sustainable Growth Rate

To illustrate the growth management challenge a rapidly growing business faces, let's look again at Analog Devices, Inc., the firm highlighted in Chapters 1 and 2. Table 4–1 presents Analog Devices' actual and sustainable annual growth rates in sales for the period 1992 through 1995. For each year, I calculated ADI's sustainable growth rate by plugging the four required ratios for the relevant year into the sustainable growth equation. (ADI's financial statements for 1994 and 1995 appear in Tables 1–1 and 1–2 in Chapter 1; other relevant ratios are given in Table 2–2 in Chapter 2.) Table 4–1 shows two noteworthy trends: rapidly rising actual and sustainable growth rates and actual growth rates *above* sustainable rates in the first two years. How did ADI cope with actual growth above sustainable levels? A look at the four required ratios reveals that the company sharply increased its profit margin and modestly increased financial leverage. (At the same time, it allowed its asset turnover to decline, which worsened the problem.) Increasing profit margins were vital throughout the period because they enabled ADI to finance its accelerating growth without resorting to major increases in financial leverage or other, more extreme measures. Indeed, had ADI's profit margin not increased, the financial leverage required to generate the company's 1995 sustainable growth rate would have been an astronomical 9.4 times.[4]

---

[4] Assume ADI's 1995 profit margin equals 2.6 percent, and, in the following sustainable growth equation, let X equal the financial leverage ratio. $21.9\% = 2.6\% \times 100\% \times 0.9 \times X$. Solving for X, $X = 9.4$ times.

T A B L E   4-1

A Sustainable Growth Analysis for Analog Devices, Inc., 1992–1995

	1992	1993	1994	1995
Required ratios:				
Profit margin, P (%)	2.6	6.7	9.6	12.7
Retention ratio, R (%)	100	100	100	100
Asset turnover, A (times)	1.0	1.0	0.9	0.9
Financial leverage, $\hat{T}$ (times)	1.59	1.81	1.89	1.92
Analog Devices' sustainable growth rate, g^* (%)	4.1	12.1	16.3	21.9
Analog Devices' actual growth rate, g (%)	5.5	17.5	16.1	21.7

	What If?		
	Asset Turnover 1.1 Times	**Financial Leverage 2.20 Times**	**Both Occur**
Analog Devices' sustainable growth rate in 1995 (%)	26.8	25.1	30.7

Figure 4–3 says the same thing graphically. It shows Analog Devices' balanced growth lines in 1992 and 1995 and the growth-return combinations the company achieved each year. The increased slope of the balanced growth line is due to higher financial leverage, while the improving return on assets is attributable to improving margins. The generally close proximity of the yearly growth-return combinations to the balanced growth lines confirms that to date Analog Devices has done a superb job of managing its increasingly rapid growth.

"What If" Questions

When management faces sustainable growth problems, the sustainable growth equation can be useful in searching for solutions. This is done through a series of "what if" questions as shown in the bottom portion of Table 4–1. We see, for example, that if Analog Devices needs to increase its sustainable growth rate further in the coming years, it can raise it to 26.8 percent by speeding up its asset turnover from 0.9 to 1.1 times. Alternatively, it can boost its sustainable growth rate to 25.1 percent by

FIGURE 4-3

Analog Devices' Sustainable Growth Challenges, 1992–1995

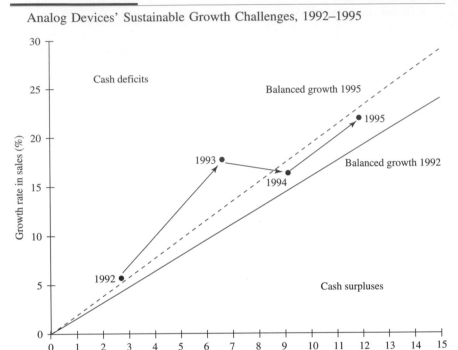

raising its financial leverage ratio to 2.2 times. Doing both simultaneously would raise sustainable growth to 30.7 percent.

WHAT TO DO WHEN ACTUAL GROWTH EXCEEDS SUSTAINABLE GROWTH

We have now developed the sustainable growth equation and illustrated its use for rapidly growing companies. The next question is: What should management do when actual growth exceeds sustainable growth? The first step is to determine how long the situation will continue. If the company's growth rate is likely to decline in the near future as the firm reaches maturity, the problem is only a transitory one that can probably be solved by further borrowing. Then, in the future, when the actual growth rate falls below the sustainable rate, the company will switch from being an absorber of cash to being a generator of cash and can repay the loans. For longer-term sustainable growth problems, some combination of the following strategies will be necessary: Sell new equity, increase financial leverage, reduce the dividend payout ratio, prune away marginal activities, outsource some or all of production, increase prices, or merge with a "cash cow." Let's consider each of these strategies in more detail.

Sell New Equity

If a company is willing and able to raise new equity capital by selling shares, its sustainable growth problems vanish. The increased equity, plus whatever added borrowing it makes possible, become sources of cash with which to finance further growth.

The problem with this strategy is that it is unavailable to many companies and unattractive to others. In most countries throughout the world, equity markets are poorly developed or nonexistent. To sell equity in these countries, companies must go through the laborious and expensive task of seeking out investors one by one to buy the new shares. This is a difficult undertaking because without active stock market trading of the shares, new investors will be minority owners of illiquid securities. Consequently, those investors interested in buying the new shares will be limited largely to family and friends of existing owners.

Even in countries with well-developed stock markets, such as the United States and Britain, many companies find it very difficult to raise new equity. This is particularly true of smaller concerns that, unless they have a glamorous product, find it difficult to secure the services of an investment banker to help them sell the shares. Without such help, the firms might just as well be in a country without developed markets, for a lack of trading in the stock will again restrict potential buyers largely to family and friends.

Finally, even many companies that are able to raise new equity prefer not to do so. This is evidenced in Table 4–2, which shows the sources of capital to U.S. nonfinancial corporations over the period 1965 through the first quarter of 1996. Observe that internal sources, depreciation and increases in retained earnings, were by far the most important sources of corporate capital, accounting for almost two-thirds of the total. At the other extreme, *new equity has been not a source of capital at all but a use*, meaning American corporations on average retired more stock than they issued over this period.

T A B L E 4–2

Sources of Capital to U.S. Nonfinancial Corporations, 1965 to First-
Quarter 1996

Internal	
Retained profits	15.2%
Depreciation	48.6%
Subtotal	63.7%
External	
Increased liabilities	39.0%
New equity issues	– 2.7%
Subtotal	36.3%
Total	100.0%

Sources: Federal Reserve System, *Flow of Funds Accounts, 1949–78*, and *Flow of Funds Accounts*, various issues.

Figure 4–4 shows the value of new equity issues, net of share repurchases and retirements, on a year-by-year basis for the United States from
1965 through the first quarter of 1996. Net new equity issues grew erratically to about $28 billion in 1983 and then plunged dramatically to a low
of *minus $130 billion* in 1988, meaning stock repurchases and retirements
by American companies exceeded new issues by this amount. Since then
the figure has bounced back positive and then turned sharply negative
again. Companies reduce common stock outstanding in two ways: by
repurchasing their own stock or acquiring the stock of another firm for
cash. Figure 4–4 attests to the huge wave of share repurchases and acquisitions on the part of U.S. companies in the last decade.

For comparison, the figure also includes the U.S. dollar value of net
new equity issues by nonfinancial companies in Germany, Japan, and the
United Kingdom from 1981 through 1994. These figures show quite
clearly that the dramatic reduction in equity outstanding achieved by
American companies has not occurred elsewhere. In fact, net new equity
issues in Japan were a whopping $71 billion in 1989, just about the time
the comparable U.S. figure was reaching an all-time low. The best available evidence suggests that the tremendous reduction in equity outstanding in the United States was triggered initially by the hostile takeover
battles that swept through the economy in the last half of the 1980s and
was less prevalent or nonexistent elsewhere around the globe. In more
recent years, the reduction in U.S. equity appears to be attributable to
the revival of merger activity and to the growing popularity of share

FIGURE 4-4

Net New Equity Issues, 1965 to First-Quarter 1996

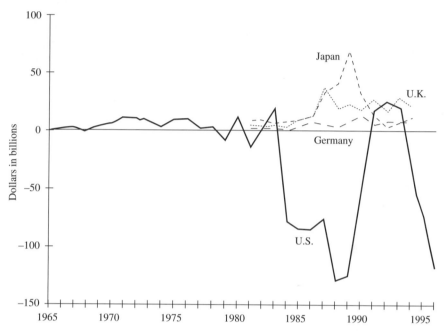

Sources: Federal Reserve System, *Flow of Funds Accounts, 1949–78*, and *Flow of Funds Accounts*, various issues; OECD, *Financial Statistics*, Part 2, *Financial Accounts of OECD Countries*, various issues.

repurchase as a way to distribute cash to shareholders and manage reported earnings per share.

These data on new equity capital as only a minor source of financing to American business are consistent with recent evidence showing that in an average year, only about 5 percent of publicly traded companies in the United States sell additional common stock. This means that a typical publicly traded company raises new equity capital only *once every 20 years*.[5]

Like the statistician who drowned crossing a stream because he had heard it was only five feet deep *on average*, we need to remember that the equity figures presented are the *net* result of new issues and retirements. Figure 4–5 shows the gross proceeds from new common stock sales for U.S. companies from 1970 to 1994. The 25-year average was $38.2

---

5 U.S. Securities and Exchange Commission, *Report of the Advisory Committee on the Capital Formation and Regulatory Process*, July 24, 1996, Figure 4.

F I G U R E 4-5

Gross New Equity Issues, 1970–1994

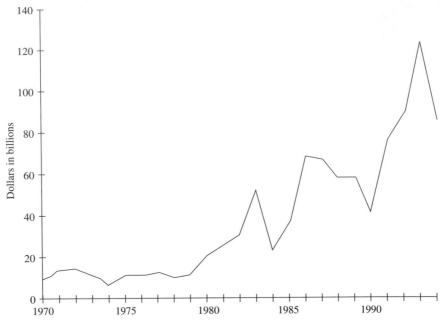

Note: New equity includes limited partnerships, preferred stock, and other equity

Source: Federal Reserve System, *Annual Statistical Digest*, various issues.

billion, and the peak was $122.4 billion in 1993. To put these numbers in perspective, *gross* proceeds from new stock issues equaled 6.4 percent of total sources of capital to corporations over the period.

The appropriate conclusion appears to be that *in the aggregate*, the stock market is not an important source of capital to corporate America, but it is critical to some companies. Companies making extensive use of the new equity market tend to be what brokers call "story paper," potentially high-growth enterprises with a particular product or concept that brokers can hype to receptive investors (the words *biotech* and *Internet* come most readily to mind).

Why Don't U.S. Corporations Issue More Equity?

There are a number of reasons U.S. firms have not raised more equity. We will consider several here and others in Chapter 6 when we review financing decisions in more detail.

First, it appears that in recent years companies in the aggregate simply have not needed new equity. Retained profits and new borrowing have been sufficient. Second, equity is expensive to issue. Issue costs commonly run in the neighborhood of 5 to 10 percent of the amount raised, and the percentage on small issues is even higher. This is at least twice as high as the issue costs for a comparable-size debt issue. (On the other hand, the equity can be outstanding forever, so its effective annualized cost is less onerous.) Third, many managers, especially U.S. managers, have a fixation with earnings per share (EPS). They translate a complicated world into the simple notion that whatever increases EPS must be good and whatever reduces EPS must be bad. In this view, a new equity issue is bad because, at least initially, the number of shares outstanding rises but earnings do not. EPS is said to have been *diluted*. Later, as the company makes productive use of the money raised, earnings should increase, but in the meantime EPS suffers. Moreover, as we will see in Chapter 6, EPS is almost always higher when debt financing is used in favor of equity.

A fourth reason companies do not raise more equity is what might be called the "market doesn't appreciate us" syndrome. When a company's stock is selling for $10 a share, management tends to think that the price will be a little higher in the future as soon as the current strategy begins to bear fruit. When the price rises to $15, management begins to believe this is just the beginning and the price will be even higher in the near future. Managers' inherent enthusiasm for their company's prospects produces a feeling that the firm's shares are undervalued at whatever price they currently command, and this view creates a bias toward forever postponing new equity issues. This syndrome is borne out by a 1984 Louis Harris poll of top executives from more than 600 firms. Fewer than one-third thought the stock market correctly valued their stock; only 2 percent believed their stock was overvalued; and fully 60 percent felt it was undervalued.[6]

A fifth reason managers appear to shy away from new equity issues is the feeling that the stock market is basically an unreliable funding source. In addition to uncertainty about the price a company can get for new shares, managers also face the possibility that during some future periods the stock market will not be receptive to new equity issues on any reasonable terms. In finance jargon, the "window" is said to be shut at these times. Naturally, executives are reluctant to develop a growth

---

6 As reported in Alfred Rappaport, "Stock Market Signals to Managers," *Harvard Business Review*, November–December 1987, p. 57.

strategy that depends on such an unreliable source of capital. Rather, the philosophy is to formulate growth plans that can be financed from retained profits and accompanying borrowing and relegate new equity financing to a minor, backup role. More on this topic in later chapters.

Increase Leverage

If selling new equity is not a solution to a company's sustainable growth problems, two other financial remedies are possible. One is to cut the dividend payout ratio, and the other is to increase leverage. A cut in the payout ratio raises sustainable growth by increasing the proportion of earnings retained in the business, while increasing leverage raises the amount of debt the company can add for each dollar of retained profits.

We will say considerably more about leverage in the next two chapters. It should be apparent already, however, that there are limits to the use of debt financing. As previously noted, all companies have a creditor-imposed debt capacity that restricts the amount of leverage they can employ. Moreover, as leverage increases, the risks borne by owners and creditors rise, as do the costs of securing additional capital.

Reduce the Payout Ratio

Just as there is an upper limit to leverage, there is a lower limit of zero to a company's dividend payout ratio. In general, owners' interest in dividend payments varies inversely with their perceptions of the company's investment opportunities. If owners believe the retained profits can be put to productive use earning attractive rates of return, they will happily forgo current dividends in favor of higher future ones. (There have been few complaints among Microsoft shareholders about the lack of dividends.) On the other hand, if company investment opportunities do not promise attractive returns, a dividend cut will anger shareholders, prompting a decline in stock price. An additional concern for closely held companies is the effect of dividend changes on owners' income and on their tax obligations.

Profitable Pruning

Beyond modifications in financial policy, a company can make several operating adjustments to manage rapid growth. One is called "profitable pruning." During much of the 1960s and early 1970s, some financial experts emphasized the merits of product diversification. The idea was that companies could reduce risk by combining the income streams of businesses in different product markets. The thought was that as long as these income streams were not affected in exactly the same way by economic events, the variability inherent in each stream would "average out" when combined with others. We now recognize two problems with this conglomerate diversification strategy. First, although it may reduce the risks seen by management, it does nothing for the shareholders. If shareholders want diversification, they can get it on their own by just purchasing shares of different independent companies. Second, because companies have limited resources, they cannot be important competitors in a large number of product markets at the same time. Instead, they are apt to be followers in many markets, unable to compete effectively with the dominant firms.

Profitable pruning is the opposite of conglomerate merger. This strategy recognizes that when a company spreads its resources across too many products, it may be unable to compete effectively in any. Better to sell off marginal operations and plow the money back into remaining businesses.

Profitable pruning reduces sustainable growth problems in two ways: It generates cash directly through the sale of marginal businesses, and it reduces actual sales growth by eliminating some of the sources of the growth. Many businesses have successfully employed this strategy in recent years, including Cooper Industries, a large Texas company. Beginning in the 1970s, Cooper sold several of its operations, not because they were unprofitable but because Cooper believed it lacked the resources to become a dominant factor in the markets involved.

Profitable pruning is also possible for a single-product company. Here the idea is to prune out slow-paying customers or slow-turning inventory. This lessens sustainable growth problems in three ways: It frees up cash, which can be used to support new growth; it increases asset turnover; and it reduces sales. Sales decline because tightening credit terms and reducing inventory selection drive away some customers.

Sourcing

Sourcing involves the decision of whether to perform an activity in-house or purchase it from an outside vendor. A company can increase its sustainable growth rate by sourcing more and doing less in-house. When a company sources, it releases assets that would otherwise be tied up in performing the activity, and it increases its asset turnover. Both results diminish growth problems. An extreme example of this strategy is a franchisor who sources out virtually all of the company's capital-intensive activities to franchisees and, as a result, has very little investment.

The key to effective sourcing is to determine where the company's unique abilities—or, as consultants would put it, "core competencies"—lie. If certain activities can be performed by others without jeopardizing the firm's core competencies, these activities are candidates for sourcing.

Pricing

An obvious inverse relationship exists between price and volume. When sales growth is too high relative to a company's financing capabilities, it may be necessary to raise prices to reduce growth. If higher prices increase the profit margin, the price increase will also raise the sustainable growth rate.

Is Merger the Answer?

When all else fails, it may be necessary to look for a partner with deep pockets. Two types of companies are capable of supplying the needed cash. One is a mature company, known in the trade as a "cash cow," looking for profitable investments for its excess cash flow. The other is a conservatively financed company that would bring liquidity and borrowing capacity to the marriage. Acquiring another company or being acquired is a drastic solution to growth problems, but it is better to make the move when a company is still financially strong than to wait until excessive growth forces the issue.

TOO LITTLE GROWTH

Slow-growth companies—those whose sustainable growth rate exceeds actual growth—have growth management problems too, but of a different kind. Rather than struggling continually for fresh cash to stoke the fires of growth, slow-growth companies face the dilemma of what to do with profits in excess of company needs. This might appear to be a trivial or even enviable problem, but to an increasing number of enterprises it is a very real and occasionally frightening one.

T A B L E   4–3

PCA International, Inc., Sustainable Growth Calculations, 1991–1995

	1991	1992	1993	1994	1995
Required ratios:					
Profit margin, P (%)	4.8	5.5	3.3	3.0	5.3
Retention ratio, R (%)	78.4	75.7	53.9	47.8	71.9
Asset turnover, A (times)	4.3	3.1	2.7	2.4	2.4
Financial leverage, $\hat{T}$ (times)	5.6	4.2	2.0	2.0	1.8
PCA's sustainable growth rate, g^* (%)	89.6	52.9	9.4	6.9	16.7
PCA's actual growth rate, g (%)	6.9	8.0	(6.2)	(2.9)	(0.1)

To give a closer look at the difficulties insufficient growth creates, Table 4–3 presents a five-year, sustainable growth analysis of PCA International, Inc., one of the largest color portrait photography chains in North America. PCA photographs, develops, and sells portrait packages through studios operated in Kmart stores. Recently the company teamed up with a leading pet supply superstore chain to test in-store studios specializing in pet photography. (I am not making this up.)

In every year shown, PCA's actual growth rate has been both mediocre and well below its sustainable growth rate. The predictable result of this mismatch has been under-used resources. PCA entered the period with a robust leverage ratio of 5.6 times, so devoting some excess operating cash to debt reduction made sense in the first few years. But by 1993 leverage was well under control, and PCA was still generating more cash than it could productively employ. Regrettably, from the shareholders' perspective, PCA did not distribute the excess cash to owners but instead appears to have frittered it away in an unproductive buildup of assets. Asset turnover fell by almost one-half over the period with little or no improvement in the profit margin. (It may appear from the reduced retention ratio in 1993 and 1994 that the company increased its dividend payout to owners in those years, but this is not the case. Instead the falling retention ratio resulted from a constant dividend in the face of declining earnings.) Looking forward, PCA International faces two problems: to generate some meaningful sales growth or, failing that, to find other productive uses for its under-used resources.

F I G U R E 4–6

PCA International's Sustainable Growth Problems, 1991–1995

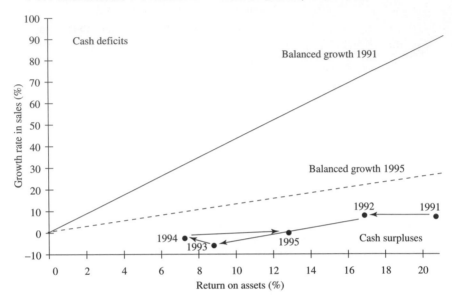

Figure 4–6 says the same thing graphically. PCA's reduced financial leverage sharply lowered the company's balanced growth line over the period. Nonetheless, the company consistently operated in the cash surplus region of the graph. The declining asset turnover pushed the company's return-on-assets ratio down from a stupendous 21 percent in 1991 to a still attractive 8 to 12 percent. But without some sales growth, the company continues to generate more cash than it needs.

WHAT TO DO WHEN SUSTAINABLE GROWTH EXCEEDS ACTUAL GROWTH

The first step in addressing problems of inadequate growth is to decide whether the situation is temporary or longer term. If temporary, management can simply continue accumulating resources in anticipation of future growth.

When the difficulty is longer term, the issue becomes whether the lack of growth is industrywide—the natural result of a maturing market— or unique to the company. If the latter, the reasons for inadequate growth and possible sources of new growth are to be found within the firm. In this event, management must look carefully at its own performance to identify and remove the internal constraints on company growth, a potentially painful process involving organizational changes as well as increased developmental expenses. The nerve-wracking aspect of such soul searching is that the strategies initiated to enhance growth must bear fruit within a few years or management will be forced to seek other, often more drastic solutions.

When a company is unable to generate sufficient growth from within, it has three options: ignore the problem, return the money to shareholders, or buy growth. Let us briefly consider each alternative.

Ignore the Problem

This response takes one of two forms: Management can continue investing in its core businesses despite the lack of attractive returns, or it can simply sit on an ever-larger pile of idle resources. The difficulty with either response is that, like dogs to a fire hydrant, underutilized resources attract unwelcome attention. Poorly utilized resources depress a company's stock price and make the firm a feasible and attractive target for a raider. If a raider has done its sums correctly, it can redeploy the target firm's resources more productively and earn a substantial profit in the process. And among the first resources to be redeployed in such a raid is incumbent managers, who find themselves suddenly reading help-wanted ads. Even if a hostile raid does not occur, boards of directors are increasingly likely to give the boot to underperforming managements.

Return the Money to Shareholders

The most direct solution to the problem of idle resources is to simply return the money to owners by increasing dividends or repurchasing shares. Although it is becoming more common, this solution is still not the strategy of choice among many executives, however, for several reasons. One is that, unlike the practice in many other countries, the U.S. tax code encourages earnings retention by fully taxing dividends at the corporate level and again at the personal level so that even mediocre investments by corporations can be more attractive to shareholders than increased dividends.

More important, many executives appear to have a bias in favor of growth, even when the growth creates little or no value for shareholders. At the personal level, many managers resist paying large dividends because the practice hints of failure. Shareholders entrust managers with the task of profitably investing their capital, and for management to return the money suggests an inability to perform a basic managerial function. A cruder way to say the same thing is that dividends reduce the size of management's empire, an act counter to basic human nature.

Gordon Donaldson and others also document a bias toward growth at the organizational level.[7] In a carefully researched review and synthesis of the decision-making behavior of senior executives in a dozen large companies, Donaldson noted that executives commonly opt for growth, even uneconomic growth, out of concern for the long-run viability of their organizations. As senior managers see it, size offers some protection against the vagaries of the marketplace, while growth contributes significantly to company morale by creating stimulating career opportunities for employees throughout the organization. And when growth slackens, the enterprise risks losing its best people.

After four straight years, going on five, of generating more cash than required to finance their business, PCA executives apparently began to take the threat of hostile takeover seriously. In March 1995, they announced a $7.5 million share repurchase, about equal in size to earnings for the year. Not surprisingly, shareholders responded enthusiastically to the announcement, bidding PCA's stock price up over 7 percent in the week following the announcement. Although surely lamenting the loss of a $7.5 million security blanket, PCA management also undoubtedly breathed a collective sigh of relief as the higher stock price calmed restive board members and reduced the threat of unwanted suitors.

Buy Growth

The third way to eliminate slow-growth problems is to buy growth. Motivated by pride in their ability as managers, concern for retaining key employees, and fear of raiders, managers often respond to excess cash flow by attempting to diversify into other businesses. Management systematically searches for worthwhile growth opportunities in other,

---

7 Donaldson, *Managing Corporate Wealth.*

more vibrant industries. And because time is a factor, this usually involves acquiring existing businesses rather than starting new ones from scratch.

The proper design and implementation of a corporate acquisition program is a challenging task that need not detain us here. Two points, however, are worth noting. First, in many important respects, the growth management problems of mature or declining companies are just the mirror image of those faced by rapidly growing firms. In particular, slow-growth businesses are generally seeking productive uses for their excess cash, while rapidly growing ones are in search of additional cash to finance their unsustainably rapid growth. It is natural, therefore, that high- and low-growth companies frequently solve their respective growth management problems by merging so that the excess cash generated by one organization can finance the rapid growth of the other. Second, after a flurry of optimism in the 1960s and early 1970s, accumulating evidence increasingly suggests that, from the shareholders' perspective, buying growth is distinctly inferior to returning the money to owners. More often than not, the superior growth prospects of potential acquisitions are fully reflected in the target's stock price, so that after paying a substantial premium to acquire another firm, the buyer is left with a mediocre investment or worse. The conflict between managers and owners in this regard is a topic of Chapter 9.

SUSTAINABLE GROWTH AND INFLATION

Growth comes from two sources: increasing volume and raising prices. Unfortunately, the amount of money a company must invest to support a dollar of inflationary growth is about the same as the investment required to support a dollar of real growth. Imagine a company that has no real growth—it makes and sells the same number of items every year—but is experiencing 10 percent inflationary growth. Then, even though it has the same number of units in inventory, each unit will cost more dollars to build, so the total investment in inventory will be higher. The same is true of accounts receivable. The same volume of customers will purchase the same number of units, but because each unit has a higher selling price, the total investment in accounts receivable will rise.

A company's investment in fixed assets behaves similarly under inflation, but with a delay. When the inflation rate increases, there is no immediate need for more fixed assets. The existing fixed assets can produce the same number of units. But as existing assets wear out and are replaced at higher prices, the company's investment in fixed assets rises.

This inflationary increase in assets must be financed just as if it were real growth. It is fair to say, then, that inflation worsens a rapidly expanding company's growth management problems. How much worse depends primarily on the extent to which management and creditors understand the impact of inflation on company financial statements.

Inflation does at least two things to company financial statements. First, as just noted, it increases the amount of external financing required. Second, in the absence of new equity financing, it increases the company's debt-to-equity ratio *when measured on its historical cost financial statements*. This combination can spell trouble. If management or creditors require that the company's historical-cost debt-to-equity ratio stay constant over time, inflation will lower the company's real sustainable growth rate. If the sustainable growth rate is 15 percent without inflation, the real sustainable growth rate will fall to about 5 percent when the inflation rate is 10 percent. Intuitively, under inflation, cash that would otherwise support real growth must be used to finance inflationary growth.

If managers and creditors understand the effects of inflation, this inverse relation between inflation and the sustainable growth rate need not exist. True, the amount of external financing required does rise with the inflation rate, but because the real value of liabilities declines as companies become able to repay their loans with depreciated dollars, the *net* increase in external financing may be little affected by inflation.

In sum, with historical-cost financial statements, inflationary growth appears to substitute for real growth on almost a one-for-one basis; each percentage point increase in inflation appears to reduce the real sustainable growth rate by the same amount. More accurate, inflation-adjusted financial statements show, however, that inflation turns out to have relatively little effect on sustainable growth. Let us hope that executives can convince their bankers of this fact. I have not been able to do so.

SUSTAINABLE GROWTH AND
PRO FORMA FORECASTS

It is important to keep the material presented here in perspective. I find that comparison of a company's actual and sustainable growth rates reveals a great deal about the principal financial concerns confronting senior management. When actual growth exceeds sustainable growth, management's focus will be on getting the cash to fund expansion; conversely, when actual growth falls below sustainable growth, the financial agenda will swing 180 degrees to one of productively spending the excess cash flow. The sustainable growth equation also appears to describe the way many top executives view their jobs: Avoid external equity financing and work to balance operating strategies, growth targets, and financial policies so that actual and sustainable growth are about equal. Finally, for nonfinancial types, the sustainable growth equation is a useful way to highlight the tie between a company's growth rate and its financial resources.

The sustainable growth equation, however, is essentially just a simplification of pro forma statements. If you really want to study a company's growth management problems in detail, therefore, I recommend that you take the time to construct pro forma financial statements. The sustainable growth equation may be great for looking at the forest but is considerably less helpful when studying individual trees.

C H A P T E R   S U M M A R Y

1. This chapter highlighted the financial management of growth and decline.
2. More growth is not always a blessing. Without careful financial planning, companies can literally grow broke.
3. A company's sustainable growth rate is the maximum rate at which it can grow without depleting financial resources. It equals the product of four ratios: the profit margin, the retention ratio, the asset turnover ratio, and financial leverage, defined here as assets divided by beginning-of-period equity. Alternatively, it equals the retention ratio times the return on beginning-of-period equity. If a company's sales expand at any rate other than the sustainable rate, one or some combination of the four ratios must change.
4. If a company's actual growth rate temporarily exceeds its sustainable rate, the required cash can probably be borrowed.
5. When actual growth exceeds sustainable growth for longer periods, management must formulate a financial strategy from among the following options: sell new equity, permanently increase financial leverage, reduce dividends, liquidate marginal operations, outsource more activities, increase prices, or find a merger partner with deep pockets.

6. For a variety of reasons, some of which are yet to be discussed, most businesses are reluctant to sell new equity. Indeed, since 1984 the market value of shares extinguished through repurchase or acquisition for cash by American corporations has far exceeded the value of shares issued.

7. When actual growth is less than the sustainable growth rate, management's principal financial problem is to find productive uses for the cash flows. Options are to increase dividends; reduce liabilities; increase assets; repurchase common shares; or buy growth; that is, acquire other companies for their growth potential.

8. If managers and creditors base decisions on historical-cost financial statements, inflation will reduce the company's sustainable growth rate. If they are more perceptive, inflation will have comparatively little effect on sustainable growth.

ADDITIONAL READING

Donaldson, Gordon. *Managing Corporate Wealth.* New York: Praeger, 1984. 199 pages.
   The result of an ambitious study undertaken by Donaldson and several colleagues at Harvard in which they reviewed the major resource allocation decisions of 12 large corporations over the course of a decade. The collaborators' synthesis of the behavior they observed provides a detailed portrait of how late-20th-century corporations really function, including the important role played by sustainable growth. Available in paperback.

Higgins, Robert C. "Sustainable Growth under Inflation." *Financial Management*, Autumn 1981, pp. 36–40.
   A look at the dependence of a company's sustainable growth rate on the inflation rate. The paper concludes that inflation will reduce sustainable growth only if an "inflation illusion" exists.

CHAPTER PROBLEMS

1. Table 3–1 in the last chapter presents R&E Supplies' financial statements for the period 1993 through 1996, and Table 3–5 presents a pro forma financial forecast for 1997. Use the information in these tables to answer the following questions.

    a. Calculate R&E Supplies' sustainable growth rate in each year from 1994 through 1997.

    b. Comparing the company's sustainable growth rate to its actual growth rate in sales over these years, what growth management problems does R&E Supplies appear to face in this period?

    c. How does the company appear to have coped with these problems? Do you see any difficulties with the way it has addressed its growth problems over this period? If so, what are they?

    d. What advice would you offer management regarding managing future growth?

2. Following are selected financial data for Lindsay Manufacturing Company, a manufacturer of farm machinery and irrigation equipment located in Lindsay, Nebraska.

	1991	1992	1993	1994	1995
Profit margin (%)	9.00	10.10	10.50	10.00	10.50
Retention ratio (%)	1.00	1.00	1.00	1.00	1.00
Asset turnover (×)	1.63	1.53	1.28	1.27	1.30
Financial leverage* (×)	2.51	2.18	1.80	1.59	1.26
Growth rate in sales (%)	−3.90	10.40	−6.30	10.40	−0.70

*Assets divided by beginning-of-period equity.

    a. Calculate Lindsay's sustainable growth rate in each year.

    b. Comparing the company's sustainable growth rate to its actual growth rate in sales, what growth problems does Lindsay appear to have faced over this period?

    c. How does the company appear to have coped with these problems?

    d. Lindsay's retention ratio indicates that the company did not distribute a dividend over the period. As a shareholder, would you support a no-dividends policy for Lindsay?

    e. In 1995, Lindsay repurchased some of its stock. From a growth management perspective, does this appear to have been a wise move?

3. Following are selected financial data for Williams-Sonoma, Inc., a chain of specialty retail stores and mail-order marketer of

fine-quality cooking and serving equipment headquartered in San Francisco.

	1991	1992	1993	1994	1995
Profit margin (%)	0.50	0.50	2.70	3.70	0.40
Retention ratio (%)	1.00	1.00	1.00	1.00	1.00
Asset turnover (×)	2.26	2.35	2.45	2.43	2.02
Financial leverage* (×)	1.85	1.85	2.01	2.29	2.70
Growth rate in sales (%)	8.90	10.30	18.90	28.90	22.00

*Assets divided by beginning-of-period equity.

a. Calculate Williams-Sonoma's sustainable growth rate in each year.
b. Comparing the company's sustainable growth rate to its actual growth rate in sales, what growth problems does Williams-Sonoma appear to have faced over this period?
c. How does the company appear to have coped with these problems?
d. Should the company's solution to its sustainable growth problems cause any concern for management and owners?

PART III

FINANCING OPERATIONS

CHAPTER 5

FINANCIAL INSTRUMENTS AND MARKETS

Don't tell mom I'm an investment banker. She still thinks I play piano in a brothel.

Bruce McKern

A major part of a financial executive's job is to raise money to finance current operations and future growth. In this capacity, the financial manager acts much as a marketing executive. He or she has a product—claims on the company's future cash flow—that must be packaged and sold to yield the highest price to the company. The financial manager's customers are creditors and investors who put money into the business in anticipation of future cash flows. In return these customers receive a *financial security*, such as a stock certificate or a bond, that describes the nature of their claim on the firm's future cash flow.

In packaging the product, the financial executive must select or design a financial security that meets the needs of the company and is attractive to potential creditors and investors. To do this effectively requires knowledge of financial instruments, the markets in which they trade, and the merits of each instrument to the issuing company. In this chapter, we consider the first two topics, financial instruments and markets. In the next chapter, we look at a company's choice of the proper financing instrument.

Operating executives seldom participate directly in company financing decisions. They are nonetheless better managers when they understand the logic on which these decisions rest. The importance of financing decisions to operating executives is apparent in the fact that financial leverage is one of the levers of performance by which managers seek to generate competitive returns, and it is a principal determinant of a company's sustainable growth rate. So failure to appreciate the logic driving an enterprise's financing decisions robs operating managers of a complete understanding of their company and its challenges.

FINANCIAL INSTRUMENTS

Fortunately, lawyers and regulators have not yet taken all of the fun and creativity out of raising money. When selecting a financial instrument for sale in securities markets, a company is *not* significantly constrained by law or regulation. The company is largely free to select or design any instrument, provided only that the instrument appeals to investors and meets the needs of the company. Securities markets in the United States are regulated by the Securities and Exchange Commission (SEC) and, to a lesser extent, by state authorities. SEC regulation can create red tape and delay, but the SEC does not pass judgment on the investment merits of a security. It requires only that investors have access to all information relevant to valuing the security and have adequate opportunity to evaluate it before purchase. This freedom has given rise to such unusual securities as Foote Minerals' $2.20 cumulative, if earned, convertible preferred stock and Sunshine Mining's silver-indexed bonds. My favorite is a 6 percent bond issued by Hungary in 1983 that, in addition to paying interest, included a firm promise of telephone service within three years. The usual wait for a phone at the time was said to run up to 20 years. A close second is a bond proposed by a group of Russian vodka distillers. Known as *Lial,* or "Liter" bonds, they were to pay annual interest of 20 percent in hard currency or 25 percent in vodka. According to one of the promoters, "Vodka has been currency for 1,000 years. We have just made the relationship formal."

But do not let the variety of securities obscure the underlying logic. When designing a financial instrument, the financial executive works with three variables: investors' claims on future cash flow, their right to participate in company decisions, and their claims on company assets in liquidation. We will now describe the more popular security types in terms of these three variables. In reading the descriptions, bear in mind that the characteristics of a specific financial instrument are determined by the terms of the contract between issuer and buyer, not by law or regulation. So the descriptions that follow should be thought of as indicating general security types rather than exact definitions of specific instruments.

Bonds

Economists like to distinguish between physical assets and financial assets. A *physical asset*, such as a home, a business or a painting, is one whose value depends on its physical properties. A *financial asset* is a piece of paper or, more formally, a security representing a legal claim to future cash payouts. The entity agreeing to make the payouts is the *issuer*, and the recipient is the *investor*. It is often useful to draw a further distinction among financial assets depending on whether the claim to future payments is *fixed* as to dollar amount and timing or *residual*, meaning the investor receives any cash remaining after all prior fixed claims have been paid. Debt instruments offer fixed claims, while equity, or common stock, offers residual claims. Human ingenuity being what it is, you should not be surprised to learn that some securities, such as convertible preferred stock, are neither fish nor fowl, offering neither purely fixed nor purely residual claims.

A bond, like any other form of indebtedness, is a *fixed-income* security. The holder receives a specified annual interest income and a specified amount at maturity—no more and no less (unless the company goes bankrupt). The difference between a bond and other forms of indebtedness such as trade credit, bank loans, and private placements is that bonds are sold to the public in small increments, usually $1,000 per bond. After issue, the bonds can be traded by investors on organized security exchanges. Aggregate data indicate that bonds constitute about one-third of the liabilities of American nonfinancial corporations and loans, including mortgage loans, equal about one-quarter of liabilities.

Three variables characterize a bond: its *par value,* its *coupon rate*, and its *maturity date*. For example, a bond might have a $1,000 par value, a 9 percent coupon rate, and a maturity date of December 31, 2005. The par value is the amount of money the holder will receive on the bond's maturity date. By custom, the par value of bonds issued in the United States is usually $1,000. The coupon rate is the percentage of par value the issuer promises to pay the investor annually as interest income. Our bond will pay $90 per year in interest (9% × $1,000), usually in two semiannual payments of $45 each. On the maturity date, the company will pay the bondholder $1,000 per bond and will cease further interest payments.

On the issue date, companies usually try to set the coupon rate on the new bond equal to the prevailing interest rate on other bonds of similar maturity and quality. This ensures that the bond's initial market price will about equal its par value. After issue, the market price of a bond can differ substantially from its par value as market interest rates change. As we will see in Chapter 7, when interest rates rise, bond prices fall, and vice versa.

Most forms of long-term indebtedness require periodic repayment of principal. This principal repayment is known as a *sinking fund*. Readers who have studied too much accounting will know that technically a sinking fund is a sum of money the company sets aside to meet a future obligation, and this is the way bonds used to work, but no more. Today a bond sinking fund is a direct payment to creditors that reduces principal. Depending on the indenture agreement, there are several ways a firm can meet its sinking-fund obligation. It can repurchase a certain number of bonds in securities markets, or it can retire a certain number of bonds by paying the holders par value. When a company has a choice, it will naturally repurchase bonds if the market price of the bonds is below par value, which occurs whenever interest rates rise after the bond is issued.

I have just described a fixed-interest-rate bond. An alternative more common to loans than bonds is floating-rate debt in which the interest rate is tied to a short-term interest rate such as the 90-day U.S. Treasury bill rate. If a floating-rate instrument promises to pay, say, one percentage point over the 90-day bill rate, the interest to be paid on each payment date will be calculated anew by adding one percentage point to the then prevailing 90-day bill rate. Because the interest paid on a floating-rate instrument varies in harmony with changing interest rates over time, the instrument's market value always approximates its principal value.

Call Provisions
Virtually all corporate bonds contain a clause giving the issuing company the option to retire the bonds prior to maturity. Frequently the call price for early retirement will be at a modest premium above par; or the bond may have a *delayed call*, meaning the issuer may not call the bond until it has been outstanding for a specified period, usually 5 or 10 years. An important difference between corporate and U.S. government bonds is that very few government bonds contain call options.

Companies want call options on bonds for two obvious reasons. One is that if interest rates fall, the company can pay off its existing bonds and issue new ones at a lower interest cost. The other is that the call option gives a company flexibility. If changing market conditions or changing company strategy requires it, the call option enables management to rearrange its capital structure.

At first glance, it may appear that a call option works entirely to the company's advantage. If interest rates fall, the company calls the bonds and refinances at a lower rate. But if rates rise, investors have no similar option. They must either accept the low interest income or sell their bonds at a loss. From the company's perspective, it looks like "heads I win, tails you lose," but investors are not so naive. As a general rule, the more attractive the call provisions to the issuer, the higher the coupon rate on the bond.

Covenants

Under normal circumstances, no creditors, including bondholders, have a direct voice in company decisions. Bondholders and other long-term creditors exercise control through *protective covenants* specified in the indenture agreement. Typical covenants include a lower limit on the company's current ratio, an upper limit on its debt-to-equity ratio, and perhaps a requirement that the company not acquire or sell major assets without prior creditor approval. Creditors have no say in company operations as long as the firm is current in its interest and sinking-fund payments and no covenants have been violated. If the company falls behind in its payments or violates a covenant, it is in *default*, and creditors gain considerable power. At the extreme, creditors can force the company into bankruptcy and possible liquidation. In liquidation, the courts supervise the sale of company assets and distribution of the proceeds to the various claimants.

Rights in Liquidation

The distribution of liquidation proceeds in bankruptcy is determined by what is known as the *rights of absolute priority*. First in line are, naturally, the government for past-due taxes and the bankruptcy lawyers who wrote the law. Among investors, the first to be repaid are *senior* creditors, then *general* creditors, and finally *subordinated* creditors. Preferred stockholders and common shareholders bring up the rear. Because each class of claimant is paid off in full before the next class receives anything, equity shareholders frequently get nothing in liquidation.

Secured Creditors

A *secured credit* is a form of senior credit in which the loan is collateralized by a specific company asset or group of assets. In liquidation, proceeds from the sale of this asset go only to the secured creditor. If the cash generated from the sale exceeds the debt to the secured creditor, the excess cash goes into the pot for distribution to general creditors. If the cash is insufficient, the lender becomes a general creditor for the remaining liability. Mortgages are a common example of a secured credit in which the asset securing the loan is land or buildings.

Bonds as an Investment

For many years, investors thought bonds to be very safe investments. After all, interest income is specified and the chances of bankruptcy are remote. However, this reasoning ignored the pernicious effects of inflation on fixed-income securities. For although the *nominal* return on fixed-interest-rate bonds is specified, the value of the resulting interest and principal payments to the investor is much less when inflation is high. This implies that investors need to concern themselves with the *real*, or inflation-adjusted, return on an asset, not the nominal return. And according to this yardstick, even default-free bonds can be quite risky in periods of high and volatile inflation.

Table 5–1 presents the nominal rate of return investors earned on selected securities over the period 1926 to 1995. Looking at long-term corporate bonds, you can see that had an investor purchased a representative portfolio of corporate bonds in 1926 and held them through 1995 (while reinvesting all interest income and principal payments in similar bonds), his annual return would have been 6.0 percent over the entire 70-year period. By comparison, the annual return on an investment in long-term U.S. government bonds would have been 5.5 percent over the same period. We can attribute the 0.5 percent difference to a "risk premium." This is the added return investors in corporate bonds earn over government bonds as compensation for the risk that the corporations will default on their liabilities or call their bonds prior to maturity.

The bottom entry in Table 5–1 contains the annual percentage change in the consumer price index over the period. Subtracting the annual inflation rate from 1926 through 1995 of 3.2 percent from these nominal returns yields real, or inflation-adjusted, returns of 2.8 percent for corporates and 2.3 percent for governments. Long-term bonds did little more than keep pace with inflation over this period.

Bond Ratings

Several companies analyze the investment qualities of many publicly traded bonds and publish their findings in the form of bond ratings. A bond rating is a letter grade, such as AA, assigned to an issue that reflects the

T A B L E   5–1

Rate of Return on Selected Securities, 1926–1995

Security	Return*
Large company common stocks	12.5%
Long-term corporate bonds	6.0
Long-term government bonds	5.5
Short-term government bills	3.8
Consumer price index	3.2

*Arithmetic mean of annual returns ignoring taxes and assuming reinvestment of all interest and dividend income.

Source: *SBBI, Stocks, Bonds, Bills, and Inflation, 1996 Yearbook*™, © Ibbotson Associates, Chicago, p. 33 (annually updates work by Roger G. Ibbotson and Rex A. Sinquefield). All rights reserved.

analyst's appraisal of the bond's default risk. Analysts determine these ratings using many of the techniques discussed in earlier chapters, including analysis of the company's balance sheet debt ratios and its coverage ratios relative to competitors. Table 5–2 contains selected debt-rating definitions of Standard & Poor's, a major rating firm. Table 6–6 in the next chapter shows the differences in key performance ratios by rating category.

Junk Bonds

A company's bond rating is important because it affects the interest rate the company must offer. Moreover, many institutional investors are prohibited from investing in bonds that are rated less than "investment" grade, usually defined as BBB– and above. As a result, there have been periods in the past when companies with lower-rated bonds had great difficulty raising debt in public markets. Below-investment-grade bonds are known variously as *speculative, high-yield*, or simply *junk* bonds.

An important recent development has been the rise of the original-issue, junk bond market. Starting from a base of little more than $10 billion in 1979, the market exploded to over $200 billion by late 1989. Then, after weathering a severe crisis that saw new-issue volume almost disappear in 1990, the market quickly righted itself, and by 1992 new-issue volume was again setting record highs.

Until the emergence of a vibrant market for speculative-grade bonds, public debt markets were largely the preserve of huge, blue-chip corporations. Excluded from public bond markets, smaller, less prominent

WHEN INVESTING INTERNATIONALLY, WHAT YOU SEE ISN'T ALWAYS WHAT YOU GET

A 10 percent interest rate on a dollar-denominated bond is not comparable to a 6 percent rate on a yen bond or a 14 percent rate on a British sterling bond. To see why, let's calculate the rate of return on $1,000 invested today in a one-year, British sterling bond yielding 14 percent interest. Suppose today's exchange rate is 1£ = $1.50 and the rate in one year is 1£ = $1.35.

$1,000 will buy £666.67 today ($1,000/1.50 = £666.67), and in one year interest and principal on the sterling bond will total £760 (£666.67[1 + .14] = £760). Converting this amount back into dollars yields $1,026 in one year (£760 × 1.35 = $1,026). So the investment's rate of return, measured in dollars, is only 2.6 percent ([$1,026 − $1,000]/$1,000 = 2.6%).

Why is the dollar return so low? Because investing in a foreign asset is really two investments: purchase of a foreign-currency asset and speculation on future changes in the dollar value of the foreign currency. Here the foreign asset yields a healthy 14 percent, but sterling depreciates 10 percent against the dollar ([$1.50 − $1.35]/$1.50); so the combined return is roughly the difference between the two. The exact relationship is

(1 + Return) = (1 + Interest rate)(1 + Change in exchange rate)
(1 + Return) = (1 + 14%)(1 − 10%)
       Return = 2.6%

Incidentally, we know that sterling depreciated relative to the dollar over the year because a pound costs less at the end of the year than at the start.

companies in need of debt financing were forced to rely on bank and insurance company loans. Although bond markets are still closed to most smaller businesses, the junk bond market has been a boon to many mid-size and emerging companies, which now find public debt an attractive alternative to traditional bank financing.

Common Stock

Common stock is a *residual income* security. The stockholder has a claim on any income remaining after the payment of all obligations, including interest on debt. *If the company prospers, stockholders are the chief beneficiaries; if it falters, they are the chief losers.* The amount of money a stockholder receives annually depends on the dividends the company chooses to pay, and the board of directors, which makes this decision quarterly, is under no obligation to pay any dividend at all.

T A B L E   5–2

Selected Standard & Poor's Debt-Rating Definitions

> A Standard & Poor's corporate or municipal debt rating is a current assessment of the credit worthiness of an obligor with respect to a specific obligation. This assessment may take into consideration obligors such as guarantors, insurers, or lessees.
>
> The debt rating is not a recommendation to purchase, sell, or hold a security, inasmuch as it does not comment as to market price or suitability for a particular investor.
>
> The ratings are based, in varying degrees, on the following considerations:
>
> (1) Likelihood of default capacity and willingness of the obligor as to the timely payment of interest and repayment of principal in accordance with the terms of the obligation.
>
> (2) Nature of and provisions of the obligation.
>
> (3) Protection afforded to, and relative position of, the obligation in the event of bankruptcy, reorganization, or other arrangement under the laws of bankruptcy and other laws affecting creditors' rights.
>
> **AAA** Debt rated 'AAA' has the highest rating assigned by Standard & Poor's. Capacity to pay interest and repay principal is extremely strong.
>
> •
> •
> •
>
> **BBB** Debt rated 'BBB' is regarded as having an adequate capacity to pay interest and repay principal. Whereas it normally exhibits adequate protection parameters, adverse economic conditions or changing circumstances are more likely to lead to a weakened capacity to pay interest and repay principal for debt in this category than in higher rated categories.
>
> Debt rated 'BB', 'B', 'CCC', 'CC' and 'C' is regarded as having predominantly speculative characteristics with respect to capacity to pay interest and repay principal. 'BB' indicates the least degree of speculation and 'C' the highest degree of speculation. While such debt will likely have some quality and protective characteristics, these are outweighed by large uncertainties or major risk exposures to adverse conditions.
>
> •
> •
> •
>
> **CCC** Debt rated 'CCC' has a current identifiable vulnerability to default, and is dependent upon favorable business, financial, and economic conditions to meet timely payment of interest and repayment of principal. In the event of adverse business, financial, or economic conditions, it is not likely to have the capacity to pay interest and repay principal.
>
> •
> •
> •
>
> **D** Debt rated 'D' is in default, or is expected to default upon maturity or payment date.
>
> Plus (+) or minus (–): The ratings from 'AA' to 'CCC' may be modified by the addition of a plus or minus sign to show relative standing within the major rating categories.

Source: Standard & Poor's, "Corporate and Municipal Rating Definitions," *Standard Corporation Descriptions*. New York, December 1990, p. 6938. Reprinted by permission of Standard & Poor's, a division of The McGraw-Hill Companies, Inc.

Shareholder Control

At least in theory, stockholders exercise control over company affairs through their ability to elect the board of directors. In the United States, the wide distribution of share ownership and the laws governing election of the board have frequently combined to greatly reduce this authority, although the winds of change may be blowing. In some companies, ownership of as little as 10 percent of the stock has been sufficient to control the entire board. In many others, there is no dominant shareholder group, and management has been able to control the board even if it owns little or none of the company's shares.

This does not imply that managers in such companies are free to ignore shareholder interests entirely, for they face at least two potential constraints on their actions. One is created by their need to compete in product markets. If management does not make a product or provide a service efficiently and sell it at a competitive price, the company will lose market share to more aggressive rivals and will eventually be driven from the industry. The actions managers take to compete effectively in product markets are consistent with shareholder interests.

Securities markets provide a second check on management discretion. If a company wants to raise debt or equity capital in future years, it must maintain its profitability to attract money from investors. Moreover, if managers ignore shareholder interests, stock price will suffer, and the firm may become the target of a hostile takeover. Even when not facing a takeover, a number of company boards, often prodded by large institutional shareholders, have become more diligent in monitoring management performance and replacing poor performers. Such corporate stalwarts as General Motors, IBM, and American Express, to name but a few, have experienced such palace revolts in recent years. We will have more to say about corporate takeovers and the evolving role of the board of directors in Chapter 9.

German and Japanese owners exercise much more direct control over company managements than do their U.S. or English counterparts. In Germany, the legal ability of banks to hold unlimited equity stakes in industrial companies, combined with the historical insignificance of public financial markets, has led to high concentrations of ownership in many companies. Banks are controlling shareholders of many German businesses, having representation on the board of directors and effective control over the business's access to debt and equity capital. German managers are thus inclined to think twice before ignoring shareholder interests.

Like their American counterparts, Japanese banks are prohibited from owning more than 5 percent of an industrial company's shares, and Japanese capital markets are more highly developed than German markets. Nonetheless, Japan's *keiretsu* form of organization produces results similar to those in Germany. A *keiretsu* is a group of companies, usually including a lead bank, that purchase sizable ownership interests in one another as a means of cementing important business relations. As noted in the appendix to Chapter 2, estimates are that cross-stock holdings of this type account for as much as half of total shares outstanding on Japanese markets.[1] When the majority of a company's stock is in the hands of business partners and associates through cross-share holdings, managers ignore shareholder interests only at their peril.

Whether the more direct control exercised by German and Japanese shareholders is any better economically than the more indirect American variety is open to question. For while the German and Japanese models may facilitate a direct shareholder voice in company affairs, they also tend to encourage a clubby, "old-boy" approach to corporate governance that can be inimical to necessary change and innovation. Moreover, evidence is accumulating that both the German and Japanese approaches to corporate governance are in decline. In Germany a growing interest on the part of companies in raising capital on public markets rather than from banks has undermined banks' authority, while in Japan an increasing emphasis on stock price performance as opposed to business relationships as the principal criterion for holding shares has led to declines in cross-share holdings.

Common Stock as an Investment

Common stockholders receive two types of investment return: dividends and possible share price appreciation. If d_0 is the dividends per share during the year and P_0 and P_1 are the beginning-of-year and end-of-year stock price, respectively, the *annual income* the stockholder earns is

$$d_0 + P_1 - P_0$$

Dividing by the beginning-of-year stock price, the *annual return* is

$$\frac{\text{Annual}}{\text{Return}} = \frac{\text{Dividend}}{\text{yield}} + \frac{\text{Percentage change}}{\text{in share price}}$$

$$= \frac{d_0}{P_0} + \frac{P_1 - P_0}{P_0}$$

---

1 Brian Bremner, "High-Water Mark?" *Business Week*, September 2, 1996, p.53.

DO DIVIDENDS INCREASE ANNUAL RETURN?

It may appear from the preceding equation that annual return rises when dividends rise. But the world is not so simple. An increase in current dividends means one of two things: The company will have less money to invest, or it will have to raise more money from external sources to make the same investments. Either way, an increase in current dividends reduces the stockholders' claim on future cash flow, which reduces share price appreciation. Depending on which effect dominates, annual returns may or may not increase as dividends rise.

Over the 1926–1995 period, equity investors in large-company common stocks received an average dividend yield of 4.6 percent and average capital appreciation of 5.7 percent.

Common stocks are an ownership claim against primarily real, or productive, assets. If companies can maintain profit margins during inflation, real, inflation-adjusted profits should be relatively unaffected by inflation. For years this reasoning led to the belief that common stocks are a hedge against inflation, but this did not prove to be the case during the bout of high inflation during the 1970s. Looking at Table 5–1 again, we see that had an investor purchased a representative portfolio of common stocks in 1926 and reinvested all dividends received in the same portfolio, his average annual return in 1995, over the entire 70 years, would have been 12.5 percent. However, from 1973 through 1981, a period when prices rose an average of 9.2 percent per annum, the average annual nominal return on common stocks was only 5.2 percent. This implies a negative *real* return of about 4 percent. The comparable figures for corporate bonds over this period were a nominal return of 2.5 percent and a negative real return of about 6.7 percent.

The common stock return of 12.5 percent from 1926 through 1995 compares with a return of 5.5 percent on government bonds over the same period. The difference between the two numbers of 7.0 percent can be thought of as a *risk premium*, the extra return common stockholders earned as compensation for the added risks they bore. Comparing the return on common stocks to the annual percentage change in consumer prices, we see that the *real* return to common stock investors over the period was 9.3 percent (12.5% − 3.2%).

Figure 5–1 presents much of the same information more dramatically. It shows an investor's wealth at year-end 1995 had she invested $1 in various assets at year-end 1925. Common stocks are the clear winners

F I G U R E 5–1

Wealth Indices of Investments in the U.S. Capital Markets, 1926–1995
(assumed initial investment of $1 at year-end 1925; includes reinvestment income)

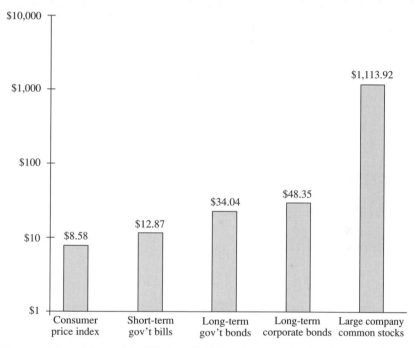

here. By 1995 the original $1 investment in the common stock of large companies would have grown to a whopping $1,113.92. In contrast, $1 invested in long-term government bonds would have been worth only $34.04 in 1995. Common stocks, however, have proven to be a much more volatile investment than bonds, as Figure 5–2 attests.

Preferred Stock

Preferred stock is a hybrid security: like debt in some ways, like equity in others. Like debt, preferred stock is a fixed-income security. It promises the investor an annual fixed dividend equal to the security's coupon rate times its par value. Like equity, the board of directors need not distribute this dividend unless it chooses. Also like equity, preferred

F I G U R E 5–2

Distribution of Annual Returns on Stocks and Bonds, 1926–1995

Monthly Total Returns in Percent

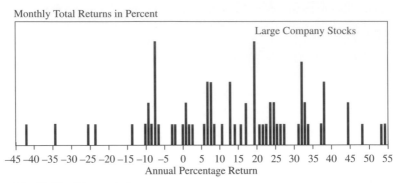

Monthly Total Returns in Percent

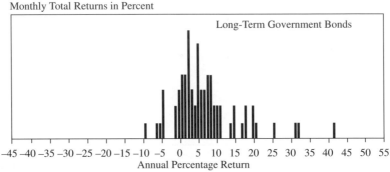

dividend payments are *not* a deductible expense for corporate tax purposes. For the same coupon rate, this makes the *aftertax* cost of bonds about two-thirds that of preferred shares. Another similarity with equity is that although preferred stock may have a call option, it frequently has no maturity. The preferred shares are outstanding indefinitely unless the company chooses to call them.

Cumulative Preferred

Company boards of directors have two strong incentives to pay preferred dividends. One is that preferred shareholders have priority over common shareholders with respect to dividend payments. Common shareholders receive no dividends unless preferred holders are paid in full. Second, virtually all preferred stocks are *cumulative*. If a firm passes a preferred dividend, the arrearage accumulates and must be paid in full before the company can resume common dividend payments.

The control preferred shareholders have over management decisions varies. In some instances, preferred shareholders' approval is routinely required for major decisions; in others, preferred shareholders have no voice in management unless dividend payments are in arrears.

Preferred stock is not a widely used form of financing. Some managers see preferred stock as *cheap equity*. They observe that preferred stock gives management much of the flexibility regarding dividend payments and maturity dates that common equity provides. Yet because preferred shareholders have no right to participate in future growth, they see preferred stock as less expensive than equity. The majority, however, see preferred stock as *debt with a tax disadvantage*. Because few companies would ever omit a preferred dividend payment unless absolutely forced to, most managers place little value on the flexibility of preferred stock. To them the important fact is that interest payments on bonds are tax deductible, whereas dividend payments on preferred stock are not.

FINANCIAL MARKETS

Having reviewed the basic security types, let us now turn to the markets in which these securities are issued and traded. Of particular interest is the provocative notion of market efficiency.

Private Placement or Public Issue?

Companies raise money in two broad ways: through private negotiations with banks, insurance companies, pension funds, or other financial institutions or by selling securities to the public. The former is known as a *private placement*; the latter is a *public issue*. Although private placements of equity are rather rare except among small businesses, private placements of debt account for a significant fraction of total corporate debt.

To sell securities to the public, a company must register the issue with the Securities and Exchange Commission. This has traditionally been an expensive, time-consuming, cumbersome task, but unless registered securities may not trade on public markets. This is a valuable privilege. It means the owner of registered securities can sell them simply by calling a stockbroker and placing an order. In contrast, when a financial institution

CURRENCY AND INTEREST RATE SWAPS

An innovative new security, known as a *swap*, has altered the way many financial executives think about issuing and managing company debt. Swaps are members of a class of securities known as *derivatives* because their value derives from the value of one or more underlying assets. Other common derivatives are options, futures, and forward contracts. Recent estimates put the total value of derivative contracts in existence at approximately $55 *trillion*.

A swap is a piece of paper documenting the trade of future cash flows between two parties in which each commits to pay or receive the other's cash flows. The market value of a swap at any time equals the difference in the value of the underlying cash flows exchanged. A *currency* swap involves the trade of liabilities denominated in different currencies, while an *interest rate* swap entails the trade of fixed-rate payments for floating-rate ones. Swaps do not appear on the participating companies' financial statements, and lenders typically are unaware a swap has occurred. Swaps have become so commonplace that an active market now exists in which standard swaps are bought and sold over the phone much like stocks and bonds. If your company has a 10-year, Swiss franc liability and would prefer one denominated in U.S. dollars, phone a swap dealer for a quote.

Swaps inevitably seem exotic and a bit pathological on first acquaintance, but the underlying concept is really an elementary one. Whenever each of two parties has something the other wants, a trade can benefit both. A swap is such a trade, in which the items exchanged are future interest and principal payments. Some swaps, denoted as asset swaps, involve rights to *receive* future payments, while more common liability swaps involve the obligation to *make* future payments.

Swaps have proven to be valuable financing tools for at least two reasons. First, swaps help solve a fundamental problem facing many companies when raising capital. Prior to the advent of swaps, a company's decision about what type of debt to issue often involved a compromise between what the company really wanted and what investors were willing to buy. An issuer might have wanted fixed-rate, French franc debt but settled for floating-rate, Canadian dollar debt because the terms were better. But with swaps, the issuer can have his cake and eat it too. Just issue floating-rate, Canadian dollar debt and immediately swap into fixed-rate, French franc debt. In effect, swaps enable the issuer to separate concerns about what type of debt the company needs from those regarding what type investors want to buy, thereby greatly simplifying the issuance decision and reducing borrowing costs.

A second virtue of swaps involves the management of certain company risks. Thanks to the growth of an active swap market, company treasurers have discovered that swaps are a slick tool for interest rate and currency risk management. Worried the Swiss franc will soon strengthen, increasing the dollar burden of your company's Swiss franc debt? No problem; Swap out of francs into dollars. Worried that interest rates are about to fall, saddling your company with a pile of high-cost, fixed-rate debt? Piece of cake: Swap into floating-rate debt and watch borrowing costs float down with the rates.

The appendix to this chapter offers a more detailed look at the use of other financial instruments, including forward contracts and options, to manage corporate risks. As you read the appendix, bear in mind that swaps are an honored member of the same family.

wants to liquidate some of its holdings of private placements, it must sell them to other institutions.

A company's choice of whether to raise money via private placement or public issue comes down to this: Private placements are simpler, are quicker, and can be tailored more closely to the particular needs of the issuer, but because buyers find them difficult to resell, private placements carry somewhat higher interest rates than public issues.

Exchanges and Over-the-Counter Markets

Public issues trade on two types of markets: organized exchanges and over-the-counter markets. Organized exchanges, such as the New York Stock Exchange and the American Stock Exchange, are centralized trading locations that maintain active markets in hundreds of stocks and bonds. Stockbroker members of the exchange transmit clients' buy-and-sell orders to specialists on the floor of the exchange, who attempt to match buyers with sellers. Specialists may buy or sell securities for their own accounts, but more often they act as agents, pairing buyers with sellers.

Over-the-counter (OTC) markets are much more informal. Any brokerage house anywhere in the country can create an OTC market for a stock or a bond by quoting a *bid* price at which it will buy the security and a higher *asked* price at which it will sell it. The spread between the bid and asked prices is the broker's revenue. In return, the broker must keep an inventory of the security and must frequently trade for her own account to maintain an active market. With a few notable exceptions, including Microsoft and Intel, most well-known equity securities trade on organized exchanges, whereas the shares of smaller, regional companies and a great many bonds trade over the counter.

International Financial Markets

From a global perspective, companies can raise money on any of three types of markets: *domestic, foreign,* or *international.* A domestic financial market is the market in the company's home country, while foreign markets are the domestic markets of other countries. U.S. financial markets are thus domestic to IBM and General Motors but foreign to Sony Corporation and British Petroleum; Japanese markets are domestic to Sony but foreign to IBM, General Motors, and British Petroleum.

Companies find it attractive to raise money in foreign markets for a variety of reasons. When the domestic market is small or poorly developed, a company may find that only foreign markets are large enough to absorb the contemplated issue. Companies may also want liabilities denominated in the foreign currency instead of their own. For example, when Walt Disney expanded into Japan, it sought yen-denominated liabilities to reduce the foreign exchange risk created by its yen-denominated revenues. Finally, issuers may believe foreign-denominated liabilities will prove cheaper than domestic ones in view of anticipated exchange rate changes.

Access to foreign financial markets has historically been a sometime thing. The Swiss and Japanese governments have frequently restricted access to their markets by limiting the aggregate amount of money foreigners may raise in a given time period or imposing firm size and credit quality constraints on foreign issuers. Even U.S. markets, the largest and traditionally most open markets in the world, have not always offered unrestricted access to foreigners. Beginning in the late 1960s and continuing for almost a decade, foreign borrowers in the United States were subject to a surcharge known as the interest equalization tax (IET). The tax was purportedly to compensate for low U.S. interest rates, but most observers saw it as an attempt to bolster a weak dollar in foreign exchange markets by constraining foreign borrowing.

The third type of market on which companies can raise money, international financial markets, are a free market response to domestic regulation. A transaction is said to occur in the international financial market whenever the currency employed is outside the control of the issuing monetary authority. A dollar-denominated loan to an American company in London, a German mark loan to a Japanese company in Singapore, and a French franc bond issue by a Dutch company underwritten in Frankfurt are all examples of international financial market transactions. In each instance, the transaction occurs in a locale that is beyond the direct regulatory reach of the issuing monetary authority. Thus, the U.S. Federal Reserve has trouble regulating banking activities in London even when the activities involve American companies and are denominated in dollars. Similarly, the Bundesbank has difficulty regulating German mark activities in Singapore.

International financial markets got their start in London shortly after World War II and were originally limited to dollar transactions in Europe. From this beginning, the markets have grown enormously to encompass most major currencies and trading centers around the globe. Today international financial markets give companies access to large pools of capital, at very competitive prices, with minimal regulatory or reporting requirements.

Two important reasons international markets have been able to offer lower-cost financing than domestic markets are the absence of reserve requirements on international bank deposits and the ability to issue bonds in what is known as *bearer form*. In the United States and many other domestic markets, banks must abide by reserve requirements stipulating that they place a portion of each deposit in a special, often non-interest-bearing account at the central bank. Because these reserves tie up resources without yielding a competitive return, domestic loans must carry a higher interest rate than international loans to yield the same profit.

The chief appeal of bearer bonds is that they make it easier for investors to avoid paying taxes on interest income. The company issuing a bearer bond never knows the bond's owners and simply makes interest and principal payments to anyone who presents the proper coupon at the appropriate time. In contrast, the issuer of a registered security maintains records of the owner and the payments made. Because bearer securities facilitate tax avoidance, they are illegal in the United States. Their use in international markets means international bonds can carry lower coupon rates than comparable domestic bonds and still yield the same aftertax returns.

The ability of international financial markets to draw business away from domestic markets has sharply accelerated the deregulation of domestic financial markets. As long as companies and investors can avoid onerous domestic regulations by simply migrating to international markets, regulators face a Hobson's choice: They can either remove the offending regulations or keep the regulations and watch international markets grow at the expense of domestic ones. The interest equalization tax is an apt example. When first imposed, the tax had the desired effect of restricting foreign companies' access to dollar financing. Over time, however, borrowers found they could avoid the tax by simply going to the international markets. The longer-run effect of the IET, therefore, was to shift business away from the United States without greatly affecting the total volume of dollar financing. Indeed, an avowed goal in repealing the IET was to make U.S. markets more competitive with international markets.

Not all regulations are bad, of course. Regulatory oversight of financial markets and the willingness of governments to combat financial panics have greatly stabilized markets and economies for over 50 years. The ongoing question is whether the deregulatory pressures created by international financial markets are improving efficiency by stripping away unwarranted restraints or dangerously destabilizing the world economy. Stay tuned.

Investment Banking

Investment bankers are the grease that keeps financial markets running smoothly. They are finance specialists who assist companies in raising money. Other activities include stock and bond brokerage, investment counseling, merger and acquisition analysis, and corporate consulting. Some investment banking companies, such as Merrill Lynch, employ thousands of brokers and have offices all over the world. Others, such as Morgan Stanley and Goldman Sachs, specialize in working with companies or trading securities and consequently are less in the public eye. As to the range of services provided, H. F. Saint said it best in his Wall Street thriller *Memoirs of an Invisible Man*: "[Investment bankers] perform all sorts of interesting services and acts—in fact any service or act that can be performed in a suit, this being the limitation imposed by their professional ethics."[2]

When a company is about to raise new capital, an investment banker's responsibilities are not unlike his fees: many and varied. (Capital-raising techniques vary from one country to another depending on custom and law. In the interest of space, and with apologies to non-American readers, I will confine my comments here to the American scene.) In a private placement, the investment banker customarily acts as an agent, bringing issuer and potential buyer together and helping them negotiate an agreement. In a public issue, the investment banker's responsibilities are much broader and vary depending on whether the company registers the securities with the SEC in the traditional manner or uses what is known as a *shelf registration*.

Traditional Registration
In a traditional registration, the investment banker begins working with the issuing company very early in the decision process. In most instances, the banker will have worked closely with management for some years and

---

2 H. F. Saint, *Memoirs of an Invisible Man* (New York: Dell, 1987), p. 290.

built up a working rapport. The first task is to help the company decide what type of security to sell. Then, if it is to be a public issue, the banker will help the company register the issue with the SEC. This usually takes 30 to 90 days and includes public disclosure of detailed information about the company's finances, officer compensation, plans, and so on—information some managements would prefer to keep confidential.

While a traditional registration wends its way toward approval, the investment banker puts together a *selling* and an *underwriting syndicate*. A syndicate is a team of as many as 100 or more investment banking houses that join forces for a brief time to sell the new securities. Each member of the selling syndicate accepts responsibility for selling a specified portion of the new securities to investors. Members of the underwriting syndicate in effect act as wholesalers, purchasing all of the securities from the company at a guaranteed price and attempting to sell them to the public at a higher price. The "Rules of Fair Practice" of the National Association of Securities Dealers prohibit underwriters from selling the securities to the public at a price above the original offer price quoted to the company. If necessary, however, the syndicate may sell them at a lower price.

Given the volatility of security prices and the length of time required to go through registration, it may appear that underwriters bear significant risks when they guarantee the company a fixed price. This is not the way the world works, however. Underwriters do not commit themselves to a firm price on a new security until just hours before the sale, and if all goes as planned, the entire issue will be sold to the public on the first day of offer. It is the company, not the underwriters, that bears the risk that the terms on which the securities can be sold will change during registration.

The life of a syndicate is brief. Syndicates form several months prior to an issue for the purpose of preselling and disband as soon as the securities are sold. Even on unsuccessful issues, the syndicate breaks up several weeks after the issue date, leaving the underwriters to dispose of their unsold shares on their own.

Shelf Registration

First authorized in 1982, a shelf registration allows frequent security issuers to file a general-purpose registration, good for up to two years, indicating in broad terms the securities the company may issue. Once the registration is approved by the SEC, and provided it is updated periodically, the company can put the registration on the "shelf," ready for use as desired. A shelf registration cuts the time lag between the decision to issue a security and receipt of the proceeds from several months to as little as 48 hours.

Because 48 hours is far too little time in which to throw a syndicate together, shelf registrations tend to be "bought deals" in which a single investment house buys the entire issue in the hope of reselling it piecemeal at a profit. Also, because it is just as easy for the issuer to get price quotes from two investment houses as from one, shelf registrations increase the likelihood of competitive bidding among investment banks. As a result, issue costs for shelf registrations are as much as 10 to 50 percent lower than for traditional registrations, depending on the type of security and other factors.[3]

Until now the benefits of shelf registration have been restricted to a select group of large, public companies, but this may soon change, for the SEC appears to be on the verge of expanding the notion of registering companies rather than securities to virtually all publicly traded companies. As this happens, look for declining issue costs, expanding volume, and continued consolidation in the investment banking industry.

Issue Costs

Financial securities impose two kinds of costs on the issuer: annual costs, such as interest expense, and issue costs. We will consider the more important annual costs later. Issue costs are the costs the issuer and its shareholders incur on initial sale. For a private placement, the only substantive cost is the fee charged by the investment banker in his or her capacity as agent. On a public issue, there are legal, accounting, and printing fees, plus those paid to the investment banker. The investment banker states his fee in the form of a *spread*. To illustrate, suppose ABC Corporation wants to sell 1 million new shares of common stock using traditional registration procedures and its shares presently trade at $20 on the American Stock Exchange. A few hours prior to public sale, the lead investment banker might inform ABC management that "Given the present tone of the markets, we can sell the new shares at an issue price of $19.00 and a spread of $1.50,

---

3 Robert J. Rogowski and Eric H. Sorensen, "Deregulation in Investment Banking, Shelf
Registrations, Structure, and Performance," *Financial Management*, Spring 1985,
pp. 5–15. See also Sanjai Bhagat, M. Wayne Marr, and G. Rodney Thompson, "The Rule
415 Experiment: Equity Markets," *Journal of Finance*, December 1985, pp. 1385–1402.

for a net to the company of $17.50." This means the investment banker intends to *underprice* the issue $1.00 per share ($20 market price less $19 issue price) and is charging a fee of $1.50 per share, or $1.5 million, for his services. This fee will be split among the managing underwriter, or lead bank, and the syndicate members by prior arrangement according to each bank's importance in the syndicates.

To underprice an issue means to offer the new shares at a price below that of existing shares. Investment bankers often underprice on the theory that the price of the new shares must be below that of existing shares to induce investors to hold more and because underpricing makes their own job easier. Selling something worth $20 for $19 is a lot easier than selling it for $20. Underpricing is not an out-of-pocket cost to the company, but it is a cost to shareholders. The greater the underpricing, the more new shares a company must issue to raise a given amount of money. And as the number of shares issued goes up, the percentage ownership of existing shareholders goes down.

Empirical studies of issue costs confirm two prominent patterns. First, equity is much more costly than debt. Representative costs of raising capital in public markets average about 2.2 percent of proceeds for straight debt, 3.8 percent for convertible bonds, and 7.1 percent for offerings of equity by publicly traded companies. The average cost of initial public offerings of equity, ignoring underpricing, is 11.0 percent. Second, issue costs for all security types rise rapidly as issue size declines. Issue costs as a percentage of gross proceeds for equity are as low as 3 percent for issues larger than $100 million but rise to *over 20 percent* for issues under $500,000. Comparable figures for debt financing are from below 0.9 percent for large issues to over 10 percent for very small ones.[4]

Regulatory Changes

Financial market deregulation has ignited a revolution among American financial institutions. In part, deregulation has been the outgrowth of a changing regulatory philosophy, but at least as important has been a wide

---

4 Wayne H. Mikkelson and M. Megan Partch, "Valuation Effects of Security Offerings and the Issuing Process," *Journal of Financial Economics*, January–February 1986; Inmoo Lee, Scott Lockhead, Jay Ritter, and Quanshui Zhao, "The Cost of Raising Capital," *Journal of Financial Research*, Spring 1996; Securities and Exchange Commission, "Report of the Advisory Committee on the Capital Formation and Regulatory Process" (Washington, DC: U.S. Government Printing Office, July 24, 1996).

array of technological and competitive innovations that have made regulation increasingly ineffective.

Prior to the Great Depression, U.S. banks were allowed to engage
in commercial and investment banking. In 1933, Congress passed the
Glass-Steagall Act to eliminate perceived conflicts of interest between
the two activities. Since then, commercial banks have been prohibited
from engaging in most securities-trading activity, while investment
banks have been prohibited from accepting deposits and making loans.
However, it has become increasingly difficult to clearly separate what
constitutes commercial banking versus investment banking; today we
see a steady encroachment of each type of bank on the other's turf. This
trend has prompted many observers to predict that the legal barriers
separating the two activities cannot be maintained long in the face of
heightening competition. Bank regulators have recognized this reality
and have done what they can to facilitate the inevitable integration.
Meanwhile, the U.S. Congress continues to dither over whether to further deregulate financial institutions or attempt to turn back the clock by
reregulating them. In many other countries, banks, including U.S. multinational banks, are free to engage in investment and commercial banking activities.

EFFICIENT MARKETS

A recurring issue in raising new capital is *timing*. Companies are naturally
anxious to sell new securities when prices are high. Toward this end,
managers routinely devote considerable time and money to predicting
future price trends in financial markets.

Concern for proper timing of security issues is natural, but there is a
perception among many academicians and market professionals that
attempts to forecast future prices in financial markets will be successful
only in exceptional circumstances and that unless these circumstances
exist, nothing is to be gained by forecasting. Such pessimism follows from
the notion of *efficient markets* a much-debated and controversial topic in
recent decades. A detailed discussion of efficient markets would take us
too far afield, but because the topic has far-reaching implications, it merits
some attention. Check the recommended readings at the end of the chapter
for more detailed treatments.

Market efficiency is controversial in large part because many pro-
ponents have overstated the evidence supporting efficiency and have

misrepresented its implications. To avoid this, let us agree on two things right now. First, market efficiency is a question not of black or white but of shades of gray. A market is not efficient or inefficient but *more* or *less* efficient. Moreover, the degree of efficiency is an empirical question that can be answered only by studying the particular market under consideration. Second, market efficiency is a matter of perspective. The New York Stock Exchange can be efficient to a dentist in Des Moines who doesn't know an underwriter from an undertaker; at the same time, it can be highly *in*efficient to a specialist on the floor of the exchange who has detailed information about buyers and sellers of each stock and up-to-the-second prices.

What Is an Efficient Market?

Market efficiency describes how prices in competitive markets respond to new information. The arrival of new information at a competitive market can be likened to the arrival of a lamb chop at a school of flesh-eating piranha, where investors are, plausibly enough, the piranha. The instant the lamb chop hits the water, turmoil erupts as the fish devour the meat. Very soon the meat is gone, leaving only the worthless bone behind, and the waters soon return to normal. Similarly, when new information reaches a competitive market, much turmoil erupts as investors buy and sell securities in response to the news, causing prices to change. Once prices adjust, all that is left of the information is the worthless bone. No amount of gnawing on the bone will yield any more meat, and no further study of old information will yield any more valuable intelligence.

An *efficient market, then, is one in which prices adjust rapidly to new information and current prices fully reflect available information about the assets traded.* "Fully reflect" means investors rapidly pounce on new information, analyze it, revise their expectations, and buy or sell securities accordingly. They continue to buy or sell securities until price changes eliminate the incentive for further trades. In such an environment, current prices reflect the cumulative judgment of investors. They *fully reflect* available information.

The degree of efficiency a particular market displays depends on the speed with which prices adjust to news and the type of news to which they respond. It is common to speak of three levels of informational efficiency:

1. A market is *weak-form* efficient if current prices fully reflect all information about past prices.
2. A market is *semistrong-form* efficient if current prices fully reflect all publicly available information.
3. A market is *strong-form* efficient if current prices fully reflect all information public or private.

Extensive tests of many financial markets suggest that with limited exceptions, most financial markets are semistrong-form efficient but not strong-form efficient. This statement needs to be qualified in two respects. First, there is the issue of perspective. The preceding statement applies to the typical investor, who is subject to brokerage fees and lacks special information-gathering equipment. It does *not* apply to market makers. Second, it is impossible to test every conceivable type and combination of public information for efficiency. All we can say is that the most plausible types of information tested with the most sophisticated techniques available indicate efficiency. This does not preclude the possibility that a market will be inefficient with respect to some as yet untested information source.

Implications of Efficiency

If financial markets are semistrong-form efficient, the following statements are true:

- Publicly available information is not helpful in forecasting future prices.
- In the absence of private information, the best forecast of future price is current price, perhaps adjusted for a long-run trend.
- Without private information, a company cannot improve the terms on which it sells securities by trying to select the optimal time to sell.
- Without private information or the willingness to accept above-average risk, investors should not expect to consistently earn above the market-average rate of return.

Individuals without private information have two choices: They can admit that markets are efficient and quit trying to forecast security prices, or they can attempt to make the market inefficient from their perspective.

HOW RAPIDLY DO STOCK PRICES ADJUST TO NEW INFORMATION?

Figure 5–3 gives an indication of the speed with which common stock prices adjust to new information. It is a result of what is known as an *event study*. In this instance the researcher, Michael Bradley, is studying the effect of acquisition offers on the stock price of the target firm. It is easiest to think of the graph initially as a plot of the daily prices of a single target firm's stock from a period beginning 40 days before the announcement of the acquisition offer and ending 40 days after. An acquisition offer is invariably good news to the target firm's shareholders, because the offer is at a price well above the prevailing market price of the firm's shares; so we expect to see the target company's stock price rise after the announcement. The question is: How rapidly? The answer evident from the graph is: Very rapidly. We see that the stock price drifts upward prior to the announcement, shoots up dramatically on the announcement day, and then drifts with little direction after the announcement. Clearly, if you read about the announcement in the evening paper and buy the stock the next morning, you will miss out on the major price move. The market will already have responded to the new information.

The upward drift in stock price prior to the announcement is consistent with three possible explanations: (1) Insiders are buying the stock in anticipation of the announcement, (2) security analysts are very good at anticipating which firms will be acquisition targets and when the offer will be made, or (3) acquiring firms tend to announce offers after the price of the target firm's stock has increased for several weeks. I have my own views, but will leave it to you to decide which explanation is most plausible.

An old Jewish proverb says, "For example is no proof." If the price pattern illustrated by the graph were for just one firm, it would be only a curiosity. To avoid this problem, Bradley studied the price patterns of 161 target firms involving successful acquisitions that occurred over 15 years ending in 1977. The prices you see are an index composed of the prices of the 161 firms, and the time scale is in "event time," not calendar time. Here the event is the acquisition announcement, defined as day 0, and all other dates are relative to this event date. The pattern observed therefore describes general experience, not an isolated event.

In recent years, academicians have performed a great number of event studies involving different markets and events, and the preponderance of these studies indicates that financial markets in the United States respond to new, publicly available information within one day or sooner.

This involves becoming a market insider by acquiring the best available information-gathering system in the hope of learning about events before others do. A variation, usually illegal, is to seek inside information. Advance knowledge that Hilton Hotels will make a hostile bid to acquire ITT, for example, would undoubtedly be useful in forecasting ITT's future stock price. A third strategy some investors use is to purchase the forecasts of prestigious consulting firms. The chief virtue of this approach appears

F I G U R E 5–3

Time Series of the Mean Price Index of the Shares of 161 Target Firms
Involved in Successful Tender Offers

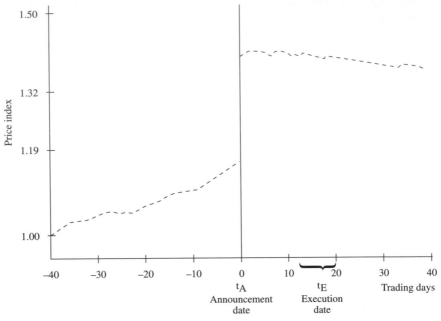

Source: Michael Bradley, "Interfirm Tender Offers and the Market for Corporate Control," *Journal of Business* 53, no. 4 (1980).

to be that there will be someone to blame if things go wrong. After all, if
the forecasts were really any good, the consulting firms could make money
by trading, thereby eliminating the need to be nice to potential customers.

As the preceding comments suggest, market efficiency is a subtle
and provocative notion with a number of important implications for investors as well as companies. Our treatment of the topic here has been necessarily brief, but it should be sufficient to suggest that unless executives
have inside information or superior information-gathering and analysis
systems, they may have little to gain from trying to forecast prices in
financial markets. This conclusion applies to many markets in which companies participate, including those for government and corporate securities, foreign currencies, and commodities.

There is, however, one important caveat to this conclusion. Because managers clearly possess private information about their own companies, they should have some ability to predict future prices of their own

securities. This means managers' efforts to time new security issues based on inside knowledge of their company and its prospects may in fact be appropriate. But notice the distinction. The decision to postpone an equity issue because the president believes the company will significantly outperform analysts' expectations in the coming year is fully defensible in a world of semistrong-form- efficient markets, but the decision to postpone an issue because the treasurer believes stocks in general will soon rise is not. The former decision is based on inside information; the latter is not.

Using Financial Markets to Manage Corporate Risks

In this chapter, we noted the growing popularity of currency and interest rate swaps for reducing borrowing costs and avoiding unwanted risks. This appendix looks briefly at two additional weapons in the manager's risk management arsenal: forward contracts and options. Risk management merits our consideration for several reasons. First, sharp increases in the volatility of foreign exchange rates, interest rates, and commodity prices beginning in the early 1970s have heightened corporate interest in controlling these risks. Second, the increasing globalization of commerce has increased the sensitivity of many companies to exchange rate movements. Third, as companies make increasing use of forward and option markets to manage risk, the need for all executives to appreciate what these markets can and *cannot* do to enhance company performance grows apace. Fourth, the popularity of forward and option trading has grown rapidly among stock and bond investors, sometimes as a means of controlling portfolio risks and other times as a potent alternative to a day at the track. The speculative appeal of the instruments discussed here has become painfully apparent to a growing list of otherwise sophisticated companies, including Procter & Gamble, as they have announced multi-million-dollar losses on what were originally intended to be risk-reducing activities.

In the interest of brevity, we will confine our attention here to the use of financial markets to manage foreign exchange risks. If you want to study the topic in more depth or to learn about similar techniques for managing interest rate and commodity price risks, take a look at the book referenced below.[1]

Forward Markets

Most markets are *spot* markets, in which a price is set today for immediate exchange. In a *forward* market, the price is set today but exchange occurs at some stipulated *future* date. Buying bread at the grocery store is a spot market transaction, while reserving a hotel room to be paid for later is a forward market transaction. Most assets trading in forward markets also trade spot. To illustrate these markets, as I write these words, the spot price of one German mark in currency markets is $0.6272, meaning payment of

---

1 Tim S. Campbell and William A. Kracaw, *Financial Risk Management* (New York: HarperCollins, 1993).

this amount will buy one mark for immediate delivery. In contrast, the 180-day forward rate is $0.6351, meaning payment of this slightly greater amount in 180 days will buy one mark for delivery at that time. A forward transaction typically involves a contract, most likely with a bank, in which the parties set the price today at which they agree to trade marks for dollars at a future date.

Speculating in Forward Markets

Although our focus in this appendix is on risk avoidance, we will begin at the opposite end of the spectrum by looking at forward market speculation. As you will see, speculation—especially the creative use of one speculation to counteract another—is the essence of the risk management techniques to be described. To demonstrate this important fact, imagine that an irresistible impulse has prompted you to remortgage your home and bet $100,000 on the New York Knicks to beat the Boston Celtics in an upcoming basketball game. Your spouse, however, is not amused to learn of your wager and threatens serious consequences unless you immediately cancel the bet. But, of course, bets are seldom canceled without a broken kneecap or two.

So what do you do? You hedge your bet. Acknowledging that your mother was wrong all those years ago—that two wrongs may indeed make one right—you place a second wager, but this time on the Celtics to beat the Knicks. Now, no matter who wins, the proceeds from your winning wager will cover the cost of your losing one, and except for the bookie's take, it's just as though you had never made the first bet. You have covered your bet. Companies use financial market "wagers" analogously to manage unavoidable commercial risks.

For a closer look at forward market speculation, suppose the treasurer of American Merchandising Inc. (AMI) believes the German mark will weaken dramatically over the next six months.[2] Forward currency markets offer a simple way for the treasurer to bet on his belief by executing a modest variation on the old "buy-low, sell-high" strategy. Here he will sell high first and buy low later: sell marks forward today at $0.6351, wait 180 days as the mark plummets, and then purchase marks in the spot market for delivery on the forward contract. If the treasurer is correct, the

---

2 My apologies to non-U.S. readers for making the United States the home country throughout this appendix. Please take solace in the fact that we Americans need all the help we can get when it comes to understanding exchange rates.

forward price at which he sells the marks today will exceed the spot price at which he buys them in six months, and he will profit from the difference. Of course, the reverse is also possible: If the mark strengthens relative to the dollar, the forward selling price could be below the spot buying price, and the treasurer will lose money.

Putting this into equation form, the treasurer's gain or loss on, say, a 1 million mark forward sale is

$$\text{Gain or loss} = (F - \tilde{S})\text{DM 1 million}$$

where F is the 180-day forward price and $\tilde{S}$ is the spot price 180 days hence. The spot price has a tilde over it as a reminder that it is unknown today.

A convenient way to represent such transactions is with a *position diagram* showing the transaction's gain or loss on the vertical axis as a function of the uncertain future spot rate. Figure 5A–1(a) shows, the treasurer's gamble is a winner when the future spot price is below today's forward rate and a loser when it is above that rate. We will refer to this and similar position diagrams throughout the appendix.

Hedging in Forward Markets

We are now ready to see how currency speculation can reduce the risk of loss on cross-border transactions. Set aside the treasurer's bet on the mark for a moment and suppose AMI has just booked a 1 million mark sale to a German buyer, with payment to be received in 180 days. The dollar value of this account receivable, of course, depends on the future exchange rate. In symbols,

$$\$ \text{ Value of AMI's receivable} = \tilde{S}(\text{DM 1 million})$$

where $\tilde{S}$ is again the spot exchange rate. AMI faces foreign exchange risk, or exposure, because the dollar value of its German receivable in six months depends on the uncertain, future spot rate.

Figure 5A–1(b) is a position diagram for AMI's account receivable. It shows the change in the dollar value of AMI's receivable as the exchange rate changes. If the spot rate remains at $0.6272, the receivable will show neither a gain nor a loss in value, but as the price of the mark changes, so does the value of the receivable. In particular, an unlucky fall in the mark in coming months could turn an expected profit on the German sale into a loss—not exactly a morale booster for the operating folks who worked so hard to make the sale.

F I G U R E 5A–1

Forward Market Hedge

(a) Forward Sale of DM 1 Million

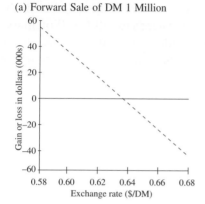

(b) DM Account Receivable

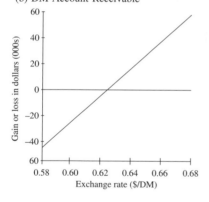

(c) Forward Market Hedge of Receivable

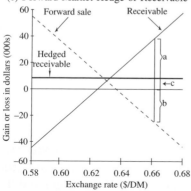

F I G U R E 5A–2

Option Market Hedge

(a) Put Option on DM 1 Million

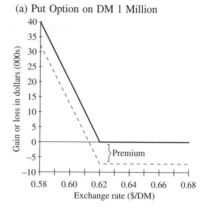

(b) Call Option on DM 1 Million

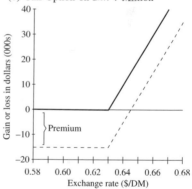

(c) Option Market Hedge of Receivable

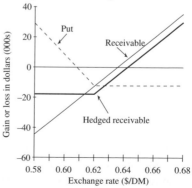

By generating the German account receivable, AMI has inadvertently bet that the mark will strengthen. If it wants to shed this risk, it can easily do so by instructing the treasurer to place an offsetting bet in the forward market. In this instance, the treasurer needs to sell 1 million marks 180 days forward, just as before. Upon adding the gain or loss on the forward sale to the dollar value of the account receivable, we find that AMI has "locked in" a value for the German receivable of $635,100:

$$\begin{array}{l} \text{Gain or loss on} \\ \text{forward sale} \end{array} + \begin{array}{l} \$ \text{ Value of} \\ \text{receivable} \end{array}$$

$(F - \tilde{S})\text{DM 1 million} + (\tilde{S})\text{DM 1 million}$
$= (F)\text{DM 1 million}$
$= (0.6351)\text{DM 1 million}$
$= \$635,100$

The elimination of $\tilde{S}$ from the equation indicates that the treasurer's judicious combination of two opposing bets eliminates AMI's currency exposure. Now, regardless of what happens to the spot rate, AMI will receive $635,100 in 180 days. The treasurer has executed a *forward market hedge*, the effect of which is to replace the unknown future spot rate with the known forward rate in determining the dollar value of the receivable. AMI has locked in the forward rate.

How does the forward market hedge differ from the forward market speculation described earlier? It doesn't; the transactions are identical. The only difference is one of intent. In the speculation, the treasurer intends to benefit from his belief that the mark will fall. In the hedge, the treasurer presumably has no opinion about the mark's future price and intends only to avoid the risk of losing money on the account receivable. When the same transaction can be either a risky speculation or a risk-reducing hedge depending only on the intent of the person rolling the dice, it should come as no surprise to learn that companies frequently have trouble controlling their risk management activities.

Figure 5A–1(c) shows the forward market hedge graphically. The solid, upward-sloping line is the gain or loss on the unhedged receivable from (b), while the dotted, downward-sloping line is the position diagram for the forward sale from (a). The horizontal line represents the combined effect of the receivable and the forward sale. When both are undertaken, the *net* outcome is independent of the future spot rate. The forward hedge eliminates risk just as opposing bets on the Celtics–Knicks game did.

Instead of manipulating equations to determine the net effect of hedging, it is usually simpler to do the same thing graphically by adding the position diagram from one bet to that of the other at each exchange rate. For instance, adding the gain on the receivable, denoted by *a* in Figure 5A–1(c), to the loss on the forward sale, *b*, yields the net result, *c*. The fact that the net result at each exchange rate lies on the horizontal line confirms that the hedge eliminates exchange risk.[3]

Hedging in Money and Capital Markets

The treasurer eliminated exchange risk on AMI's German asset by creating a German mark liability of precisely the same size and maturity. In the jargon of the trader, he *covered* the company's *long position* by creating an offsetting *short position*, where a long position refers to a foreign-currency asset and a short position corresponds to a foreign-currency liability. By offsetting one against the other, he *squared* the position. As you might expect in efficient markets, the costs of hedging in forward markets and those in money and capital markets are almost identical.

A second way to create a short position in marks is to borrow marks today, promising to repay 1 million marks in 180 days, and sell the marks immediately in the spot market for dollars. Then, in 180 days, the 1 million marks received in payment of the account receivable can be used to repay the loan. After the dust settles, such a *money market* hedge enables AMI to receive a known sum of dollars today in return for 1 million marks in 180 days.

Hedging with Options

Options are for those who tire of Russian roulette—unless, of course, the options are one leg of a hedge. An *option* is a security entitling the holder to either buy or sell an underlying asset at a specified price and for a specified time. Options come in two flavors: A *put* option conveys the right to sell the underlying asset, while a *call* is the right to buy it. To illustrate, for a payment of $8,400 today, you can purchase *put* options on

---

3 The hedged position in Figure 5A–1(c) appears to result in a gain. Strictly speaking, however, this is not necessarily the case. A hedge involves an expected gain only when the forward rate is above the treasurer's expected *future* spot rate. The figure implicitly assumes the treasurer's expected future spot rate equals the current spot, which clearly need not be true.

184 PART III Financing Operations

the German mark giving you the right to sell 1 million German marks for $0.6200 a mark at any time over the next 180 days. As a matter of semantics, $0.6200 is known as the option's *exercise*, or *strike*, price, and 180 days is its *maturity*. The $8,400 purchase price, payable today, is referred to as the *premium*.

Figure 5A–2(a) shows the position diagram for these put options at maturity for different exchange rates. The lower, dotted line includes the premium, while the solid line omits it. Concentrating first on the solid line, we see that the puts are worthless at maturity, when the spot exchange rate exceeds the option's strike price. The right to sell marks for 62 cents each obviously isn't very enticing when they command a higher price in the spot market. In this event, the options will expire worthless, and you will have spent the $8,400 premium for nothing. The outcome is very different, however, when the spot rate is below the strike price at maturity. If the spot exchange rate falls to 60 cents, for instance, the option to sell 1 million marks at 62 cents is worth $20,000, and this number rises rapidly as the mark sinks further toward zero. In the best of all possible worlds (provided you're not German), the mark will be worthless, and your puts will garner $620,000—not a bad return on an $8,400 bet.

The position diagram for call options is just the reverse of that for puts. According to today's closing prices, 180-day call options on 1 million marks with a strike price of 63 cents are available for a premium of $15,400. As shown in Figure 5A–2(b), these calls will expire worthless unless the spot price rises above the strike price; the right to buy something for more than its spot price has no value. But once above the strike price, the value of the calls rises penny for penny with the spot.

To understand why options appeal to serious speculators, imagine you believe the mark will rise to 66 cents within six months. Using the forward market to speculate on your belief, you can purchase 1 million marks forward today for 63.51 cents each and sell them in six months for 66 cents, thereby generating a return of less than 4 percent ([0.66 − 0.6351]/0.6351 = 3.9%). Alternatively, you can purchase the call options for $15,400, followed in six months by exercise of the call and immediate sale of the marks for 0.66 cents each, thereby producing a heart-skipping return of 95 percent ([(0.66 − 0.63) × 1 million − 15,400]/15,400 = 94.8%.)—almost a twenty-five-fold increase relative to the forward market speculation. Of course, the downside risks are equally stimulating; a fall in the mark to 60 cents would generate a loss of only 5.5 percent in the forward market compared to a 95 percent loss with options.

How might AMI use options to reduce exchange risk on the company's German receivable? Because the receivable makes the company long in marks, the treasurer will want to create an offsetting short position; that is, he will want to purchase put options. Calls would only add to AMI's currency risk.

Analyzing the hedge graphically, Figure 5A–2(c) shows the combined effect of AMI's German receivable and purchase of the described put options. As before, the upward-sloping, solid line represents the gain or loss in the dollar value of the receivable, and the bent, dotted line shows the payoff on the puts, including the premium. Adding the two together at each exchange rate yields the kinked solid line, portraying AMI's exchange risk after hedging with options.

Comparing the forward market hedge in Figure 5A–1 with the option hedge, we see that the option works much like an insurance policy, limiting AMI's loss when the mark weakens while still enabling the company to benefit when it strengthens. The cost of this policy is the option's premium.

Options are especially attractive hedging vehicles in two circumstances. One is when the hedger has a view about which way currencies will move but is too cowardly to speculate openly. Options enable the hedger to benefit when her views prove correct but limits losses when they are incorrect. Options are also attractive when the exposure is contingent. When a company bids on a foreign contract, its currency exposure obviously depends on whether the bid is accepted. Hedging this contingent exposure in forward markets results in unintended, and possibly costly, reverse exposure whenever the bid is rejected. The worst possible outcome with an option hedge, however, is loss of the premium.

Limitations of Financial Market Hedging

Because new initiates to the world of hedging frequently overestimate the technique's power, a few cautionary reflections on the severe limitations of financial market hedges are in order.

Two basic conditions must hold before commercial risks can be hedged effectively in financial markets. One is that the asset creating the risk, or one closely correlated with it, must trade in financial markets. In our example, this means German marks must be a traded currency. For this reason, an exposure in Indian rupiahs is much harder to manage than one in German marks.

The second necessary condition for effective foreign-currency hedging in financial markets is that the amount and the timing of the foreign cash flow be known with reasonable certainty. This is usually not a problem when the cash flow is a foreign receivable or payable, but when it is an operating cash flow, such as expected sales, cost of sales, or earnings, the story is quite different. For example, suppose the treasurer of an American exporter to Germany anticipates earnings next year of 1 million marks, and she wants to lock in the dollar value of these profits today. What should she do? At first glance, the answer is obvious: Sell 1 million marks forward for dollars. But further consideration will reveal severe problems with this strategy. First, the exporter's long position in German marks equals not next year's profits but next year's sales, a much larger number. Second, instead of hedging a known future cash flow as in our account receivable example, the exporter must hedge an unknown, expected amount. Moreover, because changes in the dollar-mark exchange rate will affect the competitiveness of the American exporter's products in Germany, we know that expected sales are themselves dependent on the future exchange rate. In terms of a position diagram, this means the foreign cash flow we seek to hedge cannot be represented by a straight line, which greatly complicates any hedging strategy. Third, if the American company expects to continue exporting to Germany into the foreseeable future, its exposure extends far beyond next year's sales. So even if it successfully hedges next year's sales, this represents only a small fraction of the company's total German mark exposure. We conclude that hedging the risks of individual transactions such as those generating accounts receivable is a straightforward task, but hedging the much larger risks inherent in operating cash flows in financial markets is a complex, nearly impossible undertaking.

Our final caveat about financial market hedging is more philosophical. Empirical studies suggest that foreign exchange, commodity, and debt markets are all "fair games," meaning the chance of benefiting from unexpected price changes in these markets about equals the chance of losing. If this is so, companies facing repeated exchange exposures, or those with a number of exposures in different currencies, might justifiably dispense with hedging altogether on the grounds that over the long run, losses will about equal gains anyway. According to this philosophy, financial market hedging is warranted only when the company seldom faces currency exposures, when the potential loss is too big for the company to absorb gracefully, or when the elimination of exchange exposure yields administrative benefits such as more accurate performance evaluation or improved employee morale.

C H A P T E R   S U M M A R Y

1. This chapter examined financial instruments and markets. When raising capital, the financial manager acts much like a marketing manager. The product is claims on the firm's cash flow and assets, and the manager's goal is to package and sell these claims in a manner that will yield the highest price to the company.

2. Companies are *not* greatly restricted by law or regulation in their ability to select or design a security. The key questions in designing a new security are: What does the investor want, and what meets the company's needs?

3. Fixed-income securities, such as bonds and most preferred stocks, generate a comparatively safe income stream but do not participate in the growth of the firm. Over the last 60-odd years, corporate bonds as an investment have done little more than keep up with inflation.

4. Common stock is a residual-income security with claim on all income after payment of prior fixed claims. Common stockholders are the principal beneficiaries of company growth. They receive income in the form of dividends and share price appreciation. Since 1926, the average *real* return on common stocks has been about 9 percent per year.

5. A transaction is said to take place in the international market when the currency employed is outside the control of the issuing monetary authority. International markets are a free market response to regulated domestic financial markets. Competition from international markets has pressured domestic markets to deregulate or lose business.

6. A large body of empirical evidence suggests that financial markets in the United States and other well-developed financial markets are quite efficient. To earn above-average returns, an investor in these markets must have access to private information, be among the first to act on newly available public information, or accept above-average risk.

ADDITIONAL READING AND RECOMMENDED WEB SITES

Fabozzi, Frank J., and Franco Modigliani. *Capital Markets: Institutions and Instruments.* 2nd ed. Englewood Cliffs, NJ: Prentice Hall, 1996.

> A thorough introduction to financial markets by two MIT economists, loaded with relevant concepts and institutional details. About $70.

Malkiel, Burton G. *A Random Walk Down Wall Street: Including a Life-Cycle Guide to Personal Investing.* 6th ed. New York: W. W. Norton, 1996. 522 pages.

> A best-selling introduction to personal investing by someone who knows both the academic and the professional sides of the story. No get-rich-quick schemes, but the straight stuff for the intelligent beginner. Available in paperback for about $16.

Stigum, Marcia. *The Money Market.* 3rd ed. Burr Ridge, IL.: Dow Jones-Irwin, 1990. 1,252 pages.

> The bible of the money markets. When you devote over 1,200 pages to financial instruments with maturities of one year or less, you can cover the topic in considerable depth. Very well written, especially considering the level of detail. About $85.

Van Horne, James C. *Financial Market Rates and Flows.* 4th ed. Englewood Cliffs, NJ: Prentice Hall, 1994.

> A well-written, informative look at the function of financial markets, the flow of funds through markets, market efficiency, interest rates, and interest rate differentials. An excellent summary of empirical studies of financial markets. Intended as a supplement for courses in financial markets and for practitioners interested in issuing or investing in fixed-income securities. Not a bedtime read. Available in paperback for about $40.

Robert's Option Pricer:http://www.intrepid.com/~robertl/option-pricer.html

> Lots of information on stock options and related topics. You give the option pricer the five pieces of information necessary to price an option, and it returns the estimated price. (Note: the symbol after robert is a lower case l, not a 1.)

Stockmaster: http://www.stockmaster.com/

> Stock and mutual fund quotes with a 15-minute delay. Sexy stock price and volume graphs.

CHAPTER PROBLEMS

1. Company A has 4 million shares of common stock outstanding trading at $5 a share. Company B has 1 million shares outstanding trading at $20 a share.

   a. Which company has the higher market value of equity?

    b. If you owned 400 shares of company A's stock, how many shares of company B's stock would someone have to offer you before you would trade your A shares for his B shares?

    c. If you owned 10 percent of A's equity, how many shares of B's stock would someone have to offer you before you would trade your A shares for his B shares?

    d. What is more important to investors: the number of a company's shares they own or the percentage of the company's equity they own? Why?

2. If the stock market in the United States is efficient, how do you explain the fact that some people make very high returns? Would it be more difficult to reconcile very high returns with efficient markets if the same people made extraordinary returns year after year?

3. The return an investor earns on a bond over a period of time is known as the *holding period return*, defined as interest income plus or minus the change in the bond's price, all divided by the beginning bond price.

    a. What is the holding period return on a bond with a par value of $1,000 and a coupon rate of 6 percent if its price at the beginning of the year was $940 and its price at the end was $1,050? Assume interest is paid annually.

    b. Can you give two reasons the price of the bond might have increased over the year?

4. You bought a yen-denominated bond at the beginning of the year for ¥100,000. The bond paid 3 percent annual interest and was trading for ¥110,000 at year end. The exchange rate was $1 = ¥100 at the beginning of the year and $1 = ¥94 at year-end.

    a. What holding period return, measured in yen, did you earn on the bond?

    b. What was your U.S. dollar holding period return on the bond?

    c. What portion of the dollar return was due to the yen return as opposed to changes in currency values?

5. A company wants to raise $200 million in a new stock issue. The company's investment banker indicates that a sale of new stock will require 5 percent underpricing and a 6 percent spread.

  a. Assuming the company's stock price does not change from its
      current price of $56 per share, how many shares must the
      company sell and at what price to the public?
  b. How much money will the investment banking syndicates earn
      on the sale?
  c. Is the 5 percent underpricing a cash flow? Is it a cost? If so, to
      whom?

CHAPTER 6

THE FINANCING DECISION

Equity Capital: The least amount of money owners can invest in a
business and still obtain credit.

Michael Sperry

In the last chapter, we began our inquiry into financing a business by
looking at financial instruments and the markets in which they trade. In this
chapter, we examine the company's choice of a proper financing instrument.

Selecting the proper financing instrument is a two-step process. The
first step is to decide how much external capital is required. Frequently
this is the straightforward outcome of the forecasting and budgeting process described in Chapter 3. Management estimates sales growth, the need
for new assets, and the money available internally. Any remaining monetary needs must be met from outside sources. Often, however, this is only
the start of the exercise. Next comes a careful consideration of financial
markets and the terms on which the company can raise capital. If management does not believe it can raise the required sums on agreeable terms, a
modification of operating plans to bring them within budgetary constraints
is initiated.

Once the amount of external capital to be raised has been determined, the second step is to select—or, more accurately, design—the instrument to be sold. This is the heart of the financing decision. As
indicated in the last chapter, an issuer can choose from a tremendous
variety of financial securities. The proper choice will provide the company
with needed cash on attractive terms. An improper choice will result in
excessive costs, undue risk, or an inability to sell the securities.

For simplicity, we will concentrate on a single financing choice:
XYZ Company needs to raise $200 million this year; should it sell bonds

or stock? But do not let this narrow focus obscure the complexity of the topic. First, bonds and stocks are just extreme examples of a whole spectrum of possible security types. Fortunately, the conclusions drawn regarding these extremes will apply to a modified degree to other instruments along the spectrum. Second, and more important, financing decisions are never one-time events. Instead, the raising of money at any point in time is just one event in an evolving financial strategy. Yes, XYZ Company needs $200 million today, but it will likely need $150 million in two years and an undetermined amount in future years. Consequently, a major element of XYZ's present financing decision is the effect today's choice will have on the company's future ability to raise capital. Ultimately, then, a company's financing strategy is closely intertwined with its long-run competitive goals and the way it intends to manage growth.

This chapter begins by considering a central topic in finance known as OPM: other people's money. We look at the advantages and disadvantages of OPM in financing operations and examine how the choice of a financing strategy affects company performance. This will involve a close look at *financial leverage* and at techniques for evaluating alternative financing options. The chapter will conclude by considering financing decisions in light of a company's growth objectives and its access to financial markets. The appendix to the chapter takes up the related topic of the financing decision and firm value.

FINANCIAL LEVERAGE

In physics, a lever is a device to increase force. In business, OPM, or what is commonly called *financial leverage*, is a device to increase owners' returns. It involves the prudent substitution of fixed-cost debt financing for owners' equity *in the hope* of increasing equity returns. The word *hope* is important here, because leverage does not always have the intended effect. If operating profits are below a critical value, financial leverage will reduce, not increase, equity returns. If we think of the increased variability in the return to owners as an increase in risk, we can say that financial leverage is the proverbial two-edged sword: It increases the expected return to owners but also increases their risk.

Financial leverage is a close cousin to *operating leverage*, defined as the substitution of fixed-cost methods of production for variable-cost methods. Replacing hourly workers with a robot increases operating leverage because the robot's initial cost pushes up fixed costs, while the robot's willingness to work longer hours without additional pay reduces variable costs. This produces two effects: Sales required to cover fixed costs rise, but once break-even is reached, profits grow more quickly with additional sales. Analogously, the substitution of debt for equity financing increases fixed costs in the form of higher interest and principal payments, but because creditors do not share in company profits, it also reduces variable costs. Increased financial leverage thus has two effects as well: More operating income is required to cover fixed financial costs, but once break-even is achieved, profits grow more quickly with additional operating income.

To see these effects more clearly, let's look at the influence of financial leverage on a company's return-on-equity ratio, ROE. Recall from Chapter 2 that despite some problems, ROE is the most widely used single measure of financial performance. It is defined as

$$\text{ROE} = \frac{\text{Profit after tax}}{\text{Equity}}$$

In Chapter 2, we said that an increase in financial leverage usually increases ROE. Here we want to explore this linkage more closely. To begin, write profit after tax as

$$\text{Profit after tax} = (\text{EBIT} - iD)(1 - t)$$

where EBIT is earnings before interest and tax, iD is interest expense—written as the interest rate, i, times interest-bearing debt outstanding, D—and t is the firm's tax rate. This equation reflects the steps an accountant goes through to calculate profit after tax from EBIT.

Then, with the help of a little algebra,[1] we can write ROE as

$$\text{ROE} = \text{ROIC} + (\text{ROIC} - i')D/E$$

where ROIC is the company's *return on invested capital* (defined in Chapter 2 as EBIT after tax divided by all sources of cash on which a return must be earned), i' is the aftertax interest rate, defined as $(1 - t)i$, and E is the book value of equity. You can think of ROIC as the return the company earns before the effects of financial leverage are considered. Looking at i',

---

[1] $$\text{ROE} = \frac{(\text{EBIT} - iD)(1 - t)}{E} = \frac{\text{EBIT}(1 - t)}{E} - \frac{iD(1 - t)}{E}$$

$$= \text{ROIC} \times \frac{D + E}{E} - i'\frac{D}{E} = \text{ROIC} + (\text{ROIC} - i')\frac{D}{E}$$

recall that because interest is a tax-deductible expense, a company's tax bill declines whenever its interest expense rises; i' takes this relationship into account.

To illustrate this equation, we can write Analog Devices' ROE in 1995 as

$$ROE = 16.6\% + (16.6\% - 3.9\%) \$82.4/\$656.0$$
$$18.2\% = 16.6\% + 1.6\%$$

where 3.9 percent is Analog Devices' aftertax borrowing rate, $82.4 million is its interest-bearing debt, and $656.0 million is its book value of equity. Analog Devices earned a basic return of 16.6 percent on its assets, which it levered into an 18.2 percent return on equity by substituting $82.4 million of debt for equity in its capital structure.

The revised expression for ROE is revealing. It shows clearly that the impact of financial leverage on ROE depends on the size of ROIC relative to i'. If ROIC exceeds i', financial leverage, as measured by D/E, increases ROE. The reverse is also true: If ROIC is less than i', leverage reduces ROE. Leverage improves financial performance when things are going well but worsens performance when things are going poorly. It is the classic fair-weather friend.

Figure 6–1 says the same thing graphically. It shows how ROE changes with leverage for three values of ROIC, corresponding to a boom of 28 percent, an expected outcome of 12 percent, and a bust of –4 percent. The aftertax interest rate is assumed to be 4 percent. Increasing leverage has two obvious effects: It increases expected ROE, *and* it increases the range of possible ROEs.

For at least two reasons, it is appropriate to think of the range of possible ROEs as a measure of risk. First, a larger range of possible outcomes means greater uncertainty about what ROE the company will earn. Second, a larger range of possible ROEs means a greater chance of bankruptcy. Look at the "bust" line in Figure 6–1. With zero leverage, the worst the company will do is earn a modest loss of 4 percent on equity, but with a debt-to-equity ratio of 4.00, the same level of operating income generates a *ninefold* increase in the loss to 36 percent. In this situation, operating income is not sufficient to cover interest expense, and a loss results. If the loss is large enough or persistent enough, bankruptcy can occur.

To summarize, *financial leverage increases both expected return to shareholders and risk.* The trick is to balance one against the other.

F I G U R E 6–1

Leverage Increases Risk and Expected Return

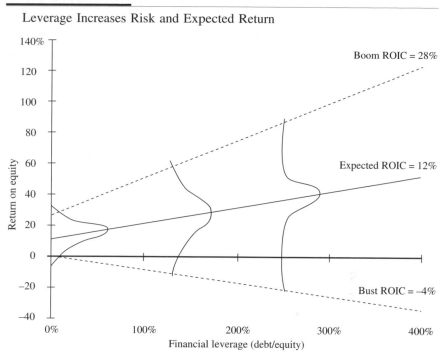

TECHNIQUES FOR EVALUATING
FINANCING ALTERNATIVES

If management knew its return on invested capital in advance, the financing decision would be easy: Whenever ROIC exceeds i', pile on the debt; whenever ROIC is less than i', finance with equity. What makes life exciting, of course, is that future values of ROIC are unknown and frequently highly uncertain. The financing decision therefore comes down to a comparison of the possible benefits of leverage against the possible costs.

Ideally, we would like to be able to calculate precisely what degree of financial leverage would yield a company the greatest net benefit, but presently this is not possible. The best we can do is measure in a rough way the increased returns and risks created by debt financing and offer some broad generalizations about what should be paramount in management's mind when contemplating the amount of financial leverage to employ.

For a practical look at the measurement of the risks and returns of debt financing, consider the problem faced by Clark Thompson, financial vice president of Harbridge Fabrics in early 1997. Harbridge Fabrics, a manufacturer of quality cotton and wool fabrics, was trying to decide how best to raise $30 million to finance the acquisition of a Spanish manufacturer of cotton materials. After considerable negotiation, a price of $35 million cash was agreed to. Thompson had determined that $5 million could be financed internally, leaving $30 million to be financed from outside sources. Harbridge's investment bankers indicated that the following two options were possible:

1. Sell 1.5 million new shares of common stock at a net price of $20 per share.
2. Sell $30 million, par value bonds at an interest rate of 12 percent. The maturity would be 20 years, and the bonds would carry an annual sinking fund of $1.5 million.

Looking to the future, Thompson expected that the addition of the Spanish manufacturer would increase Harbridge's earnings before interest and taxes (EBIT) to $30 million in 1997. Past EBIT levels had been as follows:

	1990	1991	1992	1993	1994	1995	1996	1997F
EBIT ($ millions)	15	10	30	26	5	15	21	30

F = forecast.

Thompson anticipated that Harbridge's need for outside capital in the coming years would be substantial, ranging from $5 million to $20 million annually. The company had paid annual dividends of 50 cents per share in recent years, and Thompson believed management intended to continue doing so. Tables 6–1 and 6–2 present Harbridge's recent financial statements.

Range of Earnings Chart

Thompson's first task in analyzing the financing options available to Harbridge should be to measure the effect of the decision on Harbridge's return to shareholders. He could do this by calculating the company's ROE under alternative financing plans. Instead, the common practice is to

T A B L E   6–1

Harbridge Fabrics Income Statement, 1996 ($ millions except earnings per share)

Sales	$200
Cost of goods sold	144
Gross profit	56
General and administrative expenses	36
Interest expense	4
Earnings before tax	16
Tax at 40%	7
Earnings after tax	9
Preferred dividends	1
Earnings available for common	$8
Number of common shares outstanding	5 million
Earnings per share	$1.60

simplify the procedure somewhat by looking at the decision's effect on earnings per share (EPS) rather than ROE. Because the analysis is virtually the same either way, I will adhere to this convention.

To see the effect of financial leverage on Harbridge's EPS, we need to look at the company's income statement under the two financing plans. We can save considerable effort by presuming, as is usually the case, that all of the income statement entries from sales down through EBIT are unaffected by the way the company is financed. Then we can ignore these items and begin our income statement with EBIT. Table 6–3 shows the bottom portion of a 1997 pro forma income statement for Harbridge under bust and boom conditions. Bust corresponds to a recessionary EBIT of only $10 million, while boom represents a very healthy EBIT of $40 million.

The accounting in Table 6–3 is straightforward. Interest expense under the stock financing alternative is 10 percent of the debt outstanding in 1997. Debt outstanding in 1997 equals existing short- and long-term debt of $40 million, less the $4 million sinking fund due during 1997, or $36 million. Interest expense under the bond alternative is higher by an amount equal to the interest on the new bonds. Preferred dividends are an aftertax expense, so they are subtracted from earnings after tax. Finally,

T A B L E   6–2

Harbridge Fabrics Balance Sheet, 1996 ($ millions)

Assets	
Cash and securities	$ 14
Accounts receivable	32
Inventories	22
Total current assets	68
Net fixed assets	70
Total assets	$138
Liabilities and Owners' Equity	
Accrued expenses	$ 15
Accounts payable	21
Short-term debt	2
Current portion long-term debt	4
Total current liabilities	42
Long-term debt*	34
Preferred stock†	8
Common stock	13
Retained earnings	41
Total liabilities and owners' equity	$138

*Average interest rate on debt in 1996 was 10 percent; annual sinking-fund requirements were $4 million. Both of these numbers will stay at this level through the year 2002.

†Dividend rate on preferred stock is 12 percent; there are no principal repayment requirements on the preferred.

selling stock increases the number of common shares outstanding from 5 million to 6.5 million.

Several noteworthy observations emerge from these figures. One involves the tax advantage of debt financing. Provided only that Harbridge has sufficient taxable income, its tax liability is always $1.5 million lower under bond financing than under stock financing. This figure equals 40 percent of the interest expense on the new debt. In effect, the government pays companies a subsidy, in the form of reduced taxes, to encourage the use of debt financing. Letting t be the company's tax rate and I its interest expense, the subsidy equals tI annually. Many believe this subsidy, frequently known as the *interest tax shield* from debt financing, is the chief benefit of debt financing.

A second observation is that common stock financing always produces higher earnings after tax simply because it involves no additional

T A B L E   6–3

Harbridge Fabrics Partial Pro Forma Income Statement, 1997 ($ millions except EPS)

	Bust		Boom	
	Bonds	**Stock**	**Bonds**	**Stock**
EBIT	$10.0	$10.0	$40.0	$40.0
Interest expense	7.2	3.6	7.2	3.6
Earnings before tax	2.8	6.4	32.8	36.4
Tax at 40%	1.1	2.6	13.1	14.6
Earnings after tax	1.7	3.8	19.7	21.8
Preferred dividends	1.0	1.0	1.0	1.0
Earnings available for common	0.7	2.8	18.7	20.8
Number of shares (millions)	5.0	6.5	5.0	6.5
EPS	$ 0.14	$ 0.44	$ 3.74	$ 3.21

interest expense. But the most important thing to observe is the impact of the financing decision on EPS. We concentrate on earnings per share here because it reflects the fact that equity financing will force current owners to share Harbridge's earnings with newcomers, while debt will not. Looking at the boom conditions, we see the expected impact of leverage: EPS with debt financing is a healthy 17 percent higher than with equity financing. Under bust conditions, the reverse is true: Stock financing produces a significantly higher EPS. This corresponds to our earlier example, where ROIC was less than i'.

To display this information more informatively, it is useful to construct a *range of earnings chart*. To do so, we need only plot the EBIT-EPS pairs calculated in Table 6–3 on a graph and connect the appropriate points with straight lines. Figure 6–2 shows the resulting range of earnings chart for Harbridge. It presents the EPS Harbridge will report for any level of EBIT under the two financing plans. Consistent with our boom-bust pro formas, note that the bond financing line passes through an EPS of $3.74 at $40 million EBIT and $0.14 at $10 million EBIT, while the corresponding figures for stock financing are $3.21 and $0.44, respectively.

F I G U R E   6–2

Range of Earnings Chart for Harbridge Fabrics

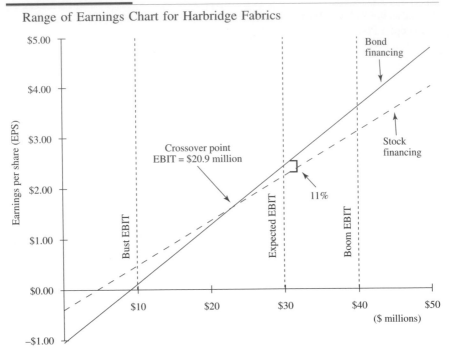

Earnings before interest and taxes (EBIT)

Thompson will be particularly interested in two aspects of the range of earnings chart. One is the increase in EPS Harbridge will report at the expected EBIT level if the company selects bond financing over stock financing. As the graph shows, this increase will be 11 percent at an expected EBIT of $30 million. Thompson will also observe that in addition to generating an immediate increase in EPS, bond financing puts Harbridge on a faster growth trajectory. This is represented by the steeper slope of the bond financing line. For each dollar Harbridge adds to EBIT, EPS will rise more with bond financing than with equity financing. Unfortunately, the reverse is also true: For each dollar EBIT declines, EPS will fall more with bond financing than with equity financing.

The second aspect of the range of earnings chart that will catch Thompson's eye is that bond financing does not always yield a higher

T A B L E 6–4

Harbridge Fabrics Financial Obligations ($ millions)

	Bonds		**Stock**	
	Aftertax	**Before-Tax**	**Aftertax**	**Before-Tax**
Interest expense		$7.2		$3.6
Principal payment	$5.5	9.2	4.0	6.7
Preferred dividends	1.0	1.7	1.0	1.7
Common dividends	2.5	4.2	3.3	5.5

EPS. If Harbridge's EBIT falls below a critical crossover value of about $21 million, EPS will actually be higher with stock financing than with bond financing. Harbridge's expected EBIT is well above the crossover value, but the historical record presented earlier indicates that EBIT has been quite volatile in past years. In fact, it has been below $21 million in four of the seven years for which we have data. A higher EPS with bond financing clearly is not guaranteed.

Coverage Ratios

The primary use of a range of earnings chart is to examine the return dimension of financial leverage: What EPS, or ROE, can a company antic- ipate at various levels of operating income for the financing plans under consideration? The risk dimension of leverage is best considered by calcu- lating a few coverage ratios. Because coverage ratios were treated in Chapter 2, our discussion here will be brief.

The before- and aftertax burdens of Harbridge Fabrics' financial obligations appear in Table 6–4. Recall that because we wish to compare these financial obligations to the company's EBIT, a before-tax number, we need to calculate their *before*-tax equivalents. Since Harbridge is in the 40 percent tax bracket, the before-tax burden is one and two-thirds times the aftertax burden for all obligations except interest, which is a tax- deductible expense ($1/[1 - .40] = 1.67$).

Four coverage ratios, corresponding to the progressive addition of each financial obligation listed in Table 6–4, appear below for an assumed EBIT of $30 million. To illustrate the calculation of these ratios, "times

common covered" equals $30 million EBIT divided by the sum of all four
financial burdens in before-tax dollars. (For bonds, $1.35 = 30/[7.2 + 9.2 + 1.7 + 4.2]$.)

	Bonds		Stocks	
	Coverage	Percentage EBIT Can Fall	Coverage	Percentage EBIT Can Fall
Times interest earned	4.17	76%	8.33	88%
Times burden covered	1.83	45	2.91	66
Times preferred covered	1.66	40	2.50	60
Times common covered	1.35	26	1.71	42

The column headed "Percentage EBIT Can Fall" presents a second
way to interpret coverage ratios. It is the percentage amount by which
EBIT can decline from its expected level before coverage equals 1.0. For
example, interest expense with bond financing is $7.2 million; thus, EBIT
can fall from $30 million to $7.2 million, or 76 percent, before times
interest earned for bond financing equals 1.0. A coverage of 1.0 is critical,
because any lower coverage indicates that the financial burden under examination cannot be covered out of operating income and another source
of cash must be available.

Harbridge's coverage ratios clearly illustrate the added risks inherent
in debt financing. For each ratio, coverage is significantly worse with bond
financing than with stock financing. Given the instability of Harbridge's
operating income over past years, debt financing implies a worrisome
increase in the possibility of default.

To put Harbridge's numbers into perspective and to see how coverage has changed in recent years, Table 6–5 presents interest-bearing
debt-to-total-asset ratios and times-interest-earned ratios for companies
comprising the Standard & Poor's 400 industrial stock averages and for
selected industries from 1990 to 1995. Note that the debt-to-assets ratio
has held steady at about 20 percent, while times interest earned has improved, due to declining interest rates and improving profits. Table 6–6
shows the variation in key performance ratios across Standard & Poor's
rating categories in the 1993–1995 period. Observe that the median times-
interest-earned ratio fell steadily from 13.50 for AAA corporations down
to 1.17 for B corporations.

T A B L E   6–5

Debt Ratios, 1990–1995 (numbers in parentheses are the number of companies in industry sample)

	1990	1991	1992	1993	1994	1995
Standard & Poor's 400 Industrials:						
Debt to total assets* (%)	21	21	20	19	20	20
Times interest earned	3.1	2.6	3.0	3.4	5.1	5.0
Aerospace/defense (8):						
Debt to total assets (%)	14	14	12	14	13	14
Times interest earned	4.3	4.4	5.8	7.1	6.2	4.4
Airlines (4):						
Debt to total assets (%)	22	30	35	34	36	32
Times interest earned	0.3	−0.5	−0.9	0.2	0.5	2.0
Broadcast media (4):						
Debt to total assets (%)	53	53	57	47	45	43
Times interest earned	1.4	1.2	1.7	2.1	2.4	1.1
Computer systems (13):						
Debt to total assets (%)	10	11	9	10	11	7
Times interest earned	3.4	−0.7	0.4	0.8	1.5	8.4
Electronics (semiconductors) (7):						
Debt to total assets (%)	9	10	9	7	6	7
Times interest earned	4.9	5.3	9.8	21.0	24.7	35.6
Hardware & tools (3)						
Debt to total assets (%)	38	38	32	31	27	26
Times interest earned	2.0	2.1	1.9	3.0	3.3	3.1

*Interest-bearing debt.

Source: *Standard & Poor's Analysts Handbook: Official Series, 1995.* Reprinted by permission of Standard & Poor's, a division of The McGraw-Hill Companies, Inc. Companies in selected industries are those firms represented in the Standard & Poor's 500 stock averages. Generally, they are among the largest companies in the industry.

SELECTING THE APPROPRIATE FINANCING INSTRUMENT

Thompson now has quantitative indicators of the risk and the return to Harbridge from each financing option, indicators that might be supplemented with some judicious computer-based sensitivity and scenario analysis of the company's financial projections. The next question is how best to use this information to pick the most appropriate financing

T A B L E   6–6

Median Values of Key Ratios by Standard & Poor's Rating Category
(industrial long-term debt, three-year figures, 1993–1995)

	AAA	AA	A	BBB	BB	B
Times interest earned	13.50	9.67	5.76	3.94	2.14	1.17
EBITDA interest coverage*	17.08	12.80	8.18	6.00	3.49	2.16
Funds from operations/total debt† (%)	98.2	69.1	45.5	33.3	17.7	12.8
Pretax return on permanent capital‡ (%)	29.3	21.4	19.1	13.9	12.0	9.0
Long-term debt/capital§ (%)	13.3	21.1	31.6	42.7	55.6	65.5

*EBITDA = Earnings before interest, taxes, depreciation, and amortization.

†Funds from operations = Net income from continuing operations plus depreciation, amortization, deferred income taxes, and other noncash charges.

‡Permanent capital = Average of beginning and ending current maturities, long-term debt, noncurrent deferred taxes, minority interest, and shareholders' equity plus average short-term borrowings.

§Capital = Long-term debt + equity.

Note: These figures are not meant to be minimum standards.

Source: "Key Industrial Ratios Show Improvement," *Standard & Poor's CreditWeek*, October 30, 1996, p. 25. Reprinted by permission of Standard & Poor's, a division of The McGraw-Hill Companies, Inc.

instrument. Unfortunately, the state of the art does not allow very specific answers to this question, so we must be content with some rather general advice. Let us begin by placing Harbridge's decision in the proper time frame.

Financial Flexibility

Up to now, we have looked at the financing decision as though it were a one-time event. Should Harbridge Fabrics raise $30 million today by selling bonds or stock? Realistically, such individual decisions are invariably part of a longer-run financing strategy that is shaped in large part by the firm's growth potential and its access to capital markets over time.

At one extreme, if Harbridge has the rare luxury of always being able to raise debt or equity capital on acceptable terms, the decision is straightforward. Thompson can simply select a target capital structure based on long-run risk-return considerations and then base specific debt-equity choices on the proximity of the company's present capital structure to its target. So if Harbridge's existing debt-to-equity ratio were below target, debt financing would be the obvious choice, unless equity were available on unusually attractive terms.

In the more realistic case where continuous access to capital markets is not ensured, the decision becomes more complex. For now Thompson must worry not only about long-run targets but also about how today's decision might affect Harbridge's future access to capital markets. This is the notion of *financial flexibility*: the concern that today's decision not jeopardize future financing options.

Looking at Harbridge, we know the company anticipates tapping the markets for from $5 million to $20 million annually in coming years. Also, given the company's volatile past earnings and comparatively low coverage ratios, it is possible that selling bonds now will "close off the top," meaning that over the next few years Harbridge may be unable to raise meaningful amounts of additional debt without a proportional increase in equity. (*Top* as used here refers to the top portion of the liabilities side of an American balance sheet. British and Australian balance sheets show equity on top of liabilities, but then they drive on the wrong side too.) Having thus reached its debt capacity, Harbridge would find itself dependent on the equity market for any additional external financing over the next few years. This is a precarious position, for if equity were unavailable at a reasonable price when needed, Harbridge would be forced to forgo attractive investment opportunities for lack of cash. This could prove very expensive, because the inability to make competitively mandated investments can result in a permanent loss of market position. On a more personal note, Thompson's admission that Harbridge must pass up lucrative investment opportunities because he cannot raise the money to finance them will not be greeted warmly by his colleagues. Consequently, a concern for financing future growth suggests that Harbridge issue equity now while it is available, thereby maintaining financial flexibility to meet future contingencies.

Market Signaling

Concern for future financial flexibility customarily favors equity financing today. A persuasive counterargument against equity financing, however, is the stock market's likely response. In Chapter 4, we mentioned that on balance, U.S. corporations do not make extensive use of new equity financing and suggested several possible explanations for this apparent bias. It is time now to discuss another.

REVERSE ENGINEERING THE CAPITAL
STRUCTURE DECISION

Most companies select or stumble into a particular capital structure and then pray the
rating agencies will treat them kindly when rating the debt. A growing number of businesses, however, are reverse engineering the process: first selecting the bond rating
they want and then working backward to estimate the maximum amount of debt consistent with the chosen rating. Several consulting companies facilitate this effort by
selling proprietary models—based on the observed pattern of past rating agency decisions—for predicting what bond rating a company will receive at differing debt levels.

   The appeal of reverse engineering the capital structure decision is twofold. First, it
reveals how much more debt a company can take on before suffering a rating down-
grade. This is important information to businesses concerned about overuse of debt
and to those interested in increasing the interest tax shields associated with debt
financing. Second, it eliminates all speculation about how creditors will respond to a
particular financing decision, enabling executives to focus instead on the more concrete question of what credit rating is appropriate for their company given its current
prospects and strategy.

   Academic researchers have recently explored the stock market's reaction to various company announcements regarding future financing, and
the results make fascinating reading. In one study, Paul Asquith and David
Mullins, then of Harvard, were interested in what happens to a company's
stock price when the firm announces a new equity sale.[2] To find out, they
performed an event study, similar to the one described in the last chapter,
on 531 common stock offerings over the period 1963 to 1981. Defining the
event date as the day of first public announcement, Asquith and Mullins
found that *over 80 percent* of the industrial firms sampled experienced a
decline in stock price on the event date and that for the sample as a whole,
the decline could not reasonably be attributed to random chance. Moreover, the observed decline did not appear to be recouped in subsequent
trading; rather, it remained as a permanent wealth loss to existing owners.

   The size of the announcement loss was startling, averaging *over 30
percent* of the size of the new issue. To put this number into perspective, a
30 percent loss means Harbridge Fabrics could expect to suffer a permanent
loss in the market value of existing equity of about $9 million the day it
announced a $30 million equity issue (.30 × $30 million = $9 million).
Alternatively, the announcement loss would equal 9 percent of Harbridge's

---

2 Paul Asquith and David W. Mullins, Jr., "Equity Issues and Offering Dilution," *Journal of
   Financial Economics*, January–February 1986, pps. 61–89.

preannouncement equity value ($9 million/5 million shares = $1.80 per share, or 9 percent of the current $20 share price). Asquith and Mullins found that the comparable number in their large sample was 3 percent, meaning that if shares sold for $100 before the equity announcement, they fell to $97 on average immediately after the announcement.

To complete the picture, similar studies of debt announcements have *not* observed the adverse price reactions found for equity financing. Further, it appears that equity announcements work both ways; that is, a company's announcement of its intention to repurchase some of its shares is greeted by a significant *increase* in stock price.

Why do these price reactions occur? No one is certain yet, but several tentative explanations exist. One, suggested most often by executives and market practitioners, attributes the observed price reactions to dilution. According to this reasoning, a new equity issue slices the corporate pie into more pieces and reduces the portion of the pie owned by existing shareholders. It is therefore natural that the shares existing shareholders own will be worth less. Conversely, when a company repurchases its shares each remaining share represents ownership of a larger portion of the company and hence is worth more.

Other observers, including yours truly, remain unconvinced by this reasoning, pointing out that while an equity issue may be analogous to slicing a pie into more pieces, the pie also grows by virtue of the equity issue. And there is no reason to expect that a smaller slice of a larger pie is necessarily worth less; nor is there any reason to expect remaining shareholders to necessarily gain from a share repurchase. True, each post-repurchase share represents a larger percentage ownership claim, but the repurchase also reduces the size of the company.

A more intriguing explanation involves what is known as *market signaling*. Suppose, plausibly enough, that Harbridge Fabrics' top managers know much more about their company than do outside investors, and consider again Harbridge's range of earnings chart, Figure 6–2. Begin by reflecting on which financing option you would recommend if, as Harbridge's financial vice president, you were highly optimistic about the company's future. After a thorough analysis of the market for Harbridge's products and its competitors, you are confident that EBIT can only grow over the next decade, most likely at a rapid rate. If you have been awake the last few pages, you will know that the logical choice in this circumstance is debt financing. Debt produces higher EPS today and puts the company on the steeper growth trajectory.

Now reverse the exercise and consider which financing option you would recommend if you were concerned about Harbridge's prospects, fearing that future EBIT might well decline. In this scenario, equity financing is the clear winner because of its superior coverage and higher EPS at low operating levels.

But if those who know the most about a company finance with debt when the future looks bright and with equity when it looks grim, what does an equity announcement tell investors? Right. It signals the market that management is concerned about the future and has opted for the safe financing choice. Is it any wonder, then, that stock price falls on the announcement and that many companies are thus reluctant to even mention the "E" word, much less sell it?

The market signal conveyed by a share repurchase announcement is just the reverse. Top management is optimistic about the company's future prospects and perceives that current stock price is inexplicably low, so low that share repurchase constitutes an irresistible bargain. A repurchase announcement therefore signals good news to investors, and stock price rises.

A more Machiavellian view, which nonetheless comes to the same conclusion, sees management as exploiting investors by opportunistically selling shares when they are overpriced and repurchasing them when they are underpriced. But regardless of whether management elects to sell new equity because it is concerned about the company's future or because it wants to gouge new investors, the signal is the same: New equity announcements are bad news and repurchase announcements are good news.

I find market signaling stories such as these highly plausible, but only time will tell whether they will stand up to further inquiry. But regardless of what explanation one favors, it does appear that the stock price reaction to new equity announcements is usually large and negative.

The Financing Decision and Sustainable Growth

We have suggested so far that when selecting a financing instrument, management should be cognizant of the need to maintain financial flexibility and of the decision's effect on stock price. Concern for financial flexibility customarily favors equity financing, while concern for stock price favors debt. How, then, does management strike a balance between these opposing concerns? The answer for many companies is to place the financing decision within the larger context of managing growth.

DON'T TALK TO DEERE & COMPANY ABOUT MARKET SIGNALING

The experiences of Deere & Company, the world's largest farm equipment manufacturer, in the late 1970s and early 1980s provide a vivid object lesson for much of this chapter. Among the lessons illustrated are the value of financial flexibility, the use of finance as a competitive weapon, and the power of market signaling.

Beginning in 1976, rising oil prices, high and increasing inflation rates, and record high interest rates sent the farm equipment industry into a severe tailspin. Much more conservative financially than its principal rivals, Massey Ferguson and International Harvester, Deere chose this moment to use its superior balance sheet strength as a competitive weapon. While competitors retrenched under the burden of high interest rates and heavy debt loads, Deere borrowed liberally to finance a major capital investment program and support financially distressed dealers. The strategy saw Deere's three-company market share rise from 38 percent in 1976 to 49 percent by 1980; such was the value of Deere's superior financial flexibility.

But by late 1980, with its borrowing capacity dwindling and the farm equipment market still depressed, Deere faced the difficult choice between curtailing its predatory expansion program and issuing new equity into the teeth of an industry depression. On January 5, 1981, the company announced a $172 million equity issue and watched the market value of its existing shares immediately fall by $241 million. So powerful was the announcement effect that Deere's existing shareholders lost more value than Deere stood to raise from the issue.

Despite the negative market response, Deere managers were so strongly convinced of the long-run virtues of their strategy that they gritted their teeth, issued the equity, and used the proceeds to reduce indebtedness. Deere thus regained the borrowing capacity and the financial flexibility it needed to continue expanding, while its rivals remained mired in financial distress.

Deere's predatory strategy largely accomplished its mission, allowing the company to increase its market dominance while both Massey Ferguson and International Harvester collapsed into bankruptcy. The victory may have been a pyrrhic one, however, for although Deere's return on equity has been over 20 percent for the past three years, its stock price performance since the early 1980s has significantly lagged market averages.

Recall from Chapter 4 that when a company is unable or unwilling to sell new equity, its sustainable growth rate is

$$g^* = PRA\hat{T}$$

where P, R, A, and $\hat{T}$ are profit margin, retention ratio, asset turnover, and financial leverage, respectively. In this equation, P and A are determined on the operating side of the business. The financial challenge is to develop dividend, financing, and growth strategies that will enable the firm to expand at the desired rate without resorting to common stock financing. This leads to two distinct financing strategies depending on whether the company's sustainable growth rate is above or below its desired growth rate.

Rapid Growth and the Virtues of Conservatism
Companies growing more rapidly than their sustainable growth rate face the dual challenge of maintaining financial flexibility and, insofar as possible, avoiding the negative signals of new equity announcements. The sustainable growth equation suggests that the best way to reconcile these partially conflicting objectives is to make financing the passive servant of growth. The logic is straightforward: The most powerful engine of value creation in a growing business is new investment, not interest tax shields or levered equity returns that might accompany debt financing. The appropriate financing strategy therefore is one that best facilitates growth. This suggests the following policies:

- Maintain a conservative leverage ratio with ample unused borrowing capacity to ensure continuous access to financial markets.
- Adopt a modest dividend payout ratio that will enable the company to finance most of its growth internally.
- Use cash, marketable securities, and unused borrowing capacity as temporary liquidity buffers to provide financing in years when investment needs exceed internal sources.
- If external financing is necessary, raise debt unless the resulting leverage ratio threatens financial flexibility.
- Sell equity or reduce growth only as a last resort after all other alternatives have been exhausted.

Stewart Myers of MIT has referred to these policies as a "pecking order." At the top of the pecking order, the most preferred means of financing is internal sources, composed of retained profits and excess cash accumulated from past profit retentions. External sources are second in order of preference, with debt financing dominating equity. The financing decision, then, essentially amounts to working progressively down this pecking order in search of the first feasible source. Myers also notes that the observed debt-to-equity ratios of such pecking-order companies are less a product of a rational balancing of advantages and disadvantages of debt relative to equity and more the aggregate result over time of the company's profitability relative to its investment needs. Thus, high-margin, modestly growing companies can get away with little or no debt, while lower-margin, more rapidly expanding businesses may be forced to live with much higher leverage ratios.

Low Growth and the Appeal of Aggressive Financing

Compared to their rapidly growing brethren, slow-growth companies have a much easier time with financing decisions. Because their chief financial problem is disposing of excess operating cash flow, concerns about financial flexibility and adverse market signaling are largely foreign to them. However, beyond merely eliminating a problem, this situation creates an opportunity that a number of companies have successfully exploited. The logic goes like this. Face the reality that the business has few attractive investment opportunities, and seek to create value for owners through aggressive use of debt financing. Use the company's healthy operating cash flow as the magnet for borrowing as much money as is feasible, and use the proceeds to repurchase shares.

Such a strategy promises at least three possible payoffs to owners. First, increased interest tax shields reduce income taxes, leaving more money for investors. Second, the share repurchase announcement should generate a positive market signal. Third, the high financial leverage may significantly improve management incentives. Thus, the burden high financial leverage imposes on management to make large, recurring interest and principal payments or face bankruptcy may be just the elixir needed to encourage them to squeeze more cash flow out of the business. More on this topic in Chapter 9.

In summary, an old saw among bank borrowers is that the only companies banks are willing to lend money to are those that don't need it. We see now that much the same dynamic may be at work on the borrowers' side. Slow-growth businesses that don't need external financing may find it attractive to finance aggressively, while rapidly growing businesses in need of external cash find it appealing to maintain conservative capital structures.

Recent empirical work supports the wisdom of this perspective. In their study of the ties between company value and the use of debt financing, John McConnell and Henri Servaes have found that for high-growth businesses increasing leverage reduces firm value, while precisely the reverse is true for slow-growth businesses.[3]

---

3 John J. McConnell and Henri Servaes, "Equity Ownership and the Two Faces of Debt," *Journal of Financial Economics*, September 1995, pp. 131–57.

COLT INDUSTRIES' EXPERIENCE WITH AGGRESSIVE FINANCING

Colt Industries' late 1986 recapitalization illustrates the potential of aggressive financing in mature businesses. Facing increasing cash flows from its aerospace and automotive operations and a dearth of attractive investment opportunities, Colt decided to recapitalize its business by offering shareholders $85 in cash plus one share of stock in the newly recapitalized company in exchange for each old share held.

To finance the $85 cash payment, Colt borrowed $1.4 billion, raising total long-term debt to $1.6 billion and reducing the book value of shareholders' equity to *minus* $157 million. In other words, after the recapitalization, Colt's liabilities exceeded the book value of its assets by $157 million, yielding a negative book value of equity. We are talking serious leverage here. But book values are of secondary importance to lenders when the borrower has the cash flow to service its obligations, and this is where Colt's healthy operating cash flows were critical. Management's willingness to commit virtually all of its future cash flow to debt service enabled the company to secure the needed financing.

How did the shareholders make out? Quite well, thank you. Just prior to the announcement of the exchange offer, Colt's shares were trading at $67, and immediately after the exchange was completed, shares in the newly recapitalized company were trading for $10. So the offer came down to this: $85 cash plus one new share of stock worth $10 in exchange for each old share worth $67. This works out to a windfall gain to owners of $28 a share, or 42 percent ($85 + $10 − $67 = $28).

FRICTO

To conclude our discussion of company financing decisions, it may be useful to introduce an acronym long used by students and executives to remember the key elements of financing decisions. FRICTO stands for *flexibility, risk, income, control, timing*, and *other*. (In my student days the acronym was FRIC, but several decades of diligent research have led to the addition of T and O.) Here are brief summaries of each element:

- *Flexibility*: The need to worry about the extent to which today's financing decision affects the company's ability to raise money on acceptable terms in the future. This is especially important for rapidly growing businesses.
- *Risk*: The adverse effect of financial leverage on the risk of bankruptcy and on the volatility of shareholders' income.
- *Income*: The effect of leverage on the level of shareholder income as reflected in earnings per share and return on equity.

- *Control*: The interplay between company financing and the distribution of decision rights among old and new owners, creditors, and managers.
- *Timing*: The need to decide the time at which new securities are to be sold as well as the type to sell. Efficient financial markets suggest that the timing of security issues based on general market conditions is probably a fruitless exercise, but the same is not true when it is based on privileged, inside information about the company.
- *Other*: Who could argue against the possibility of other factors? One key other element, in my mind, is the incentive effects of high financial leverage on incumbent managers.

SELECTING A MATURITY STRUCTURE

When a company decides to raise debt, the next question is: What maturity should the debt have? Should the company take out a 1-year loan, sell 7-year notes, or market 30-year bonds? Looking at the firm's entire capital structure, *the minimum-risk maturity structure occurs when the maturity of liabilities equals that of assets*, for in this configuration, cash generated from operations over coming years should be sufficient to repay existing liabilities as they mature. In other words, the liabilities will be self-liquidating. If the maturity of liabilities is less than that of assets, the company incurs a refinancing risk because some maturing liabilities will have to be paid off from the proceeds of newly raised capital. Also, as noted in Chapter 5, the rollover of maturing debt is not an automatic feature of capital markets. When the maturity of liabilities is greater than that of assets, cash provided by operations should be more than sufficient to repay existing liabilities as they mature. This provides an extra margin of safety, but it also means the firm may have excess cash in some periods.

If maturity matching is minimum risk, why do anything else? Why allow the maturity of liabilities to be less than that of assets? Companies mismatch either because long-term debt is unavailable on acceptable terms or because management anticipates that mismatching will reduce total borrowing costs. For example, if the treasurer believes interest rates will decline in the future, an obvious strategy is to use short-term debt now and hope to roll it over into longer-term debt at lower rates in the future. Of

ACADEMIC VIEWS OF THE DEBT-EQUITY CHOICE

Rather than study the impact of financial leverage on shareholder risk and return as we have done, the usual academic approach is to examine the effect of leverage on the market value of the firm. Fundamentally, these are not conflicting approaches, because a capital structure that effectively balances risk against return in the long-run interests of the company should also maximize firm value.

Academicians usually begin by demonstrating that in properly functioning markets with no taxes and no bankruptcy costs, the increased risk to equity from debt financing just counterbalances the increased expected return so that leverage has no effect on firm value. Financial economists then relax the no-taxes, no-bankruptcy assumptions to demonstrate that the capital structure decision ultimately involves a prudent balancing of the tax advantage of debt financing against the increased chance of bankruptcy. At low levels of indebtedness, the tax advantage predominates, so increases in leverage produce higher market values. But beyond some prudent range, the increasing probability of bankruptcy begins to outweigh the tax advantage, and firm value falls with further increases in leverage.

To date, academic research has yielded two benefits: It has greatly clarified our thinking about the financing decision, and it has encouraged a reassessment of the role debt can play in financing businesses. Gone are the depression-era beliefs that debt is at best a necessary evil, replaced by a more holistic view that in the right circumstances and in the right proportions, debt can enhance firm value. However, until quite recently, academic research has been of only modest help to financial executives charged with developing practical financing strategies. The principal difficulty has been that by assuming continuous availability of debt and equity capital to firms and ignoring incentive and market signaling effects, academicians have too often assumed away a major part of the problem as it really exists. See the appendix to this chapter for more on the ties between the financing decision and firm value.

course, efficient markets advocates criticize this strategy on the grounds that the treasurer has no basis for believing he can forecast future interest rates.

Inflation and Financing Strategy

An old adage in finance is that it's good to be a debtor during inflation because the debtor repays the loan with depreciated dollars. It is important to understand, however, that this saying is correct only when the inflation is *unexpected*. When creditors expect inflation, the interest rate they charge rises to compensate for the expected decline in the purchasing power of the loan principal. This means it is not necessarily advantageous to borrow during inflation. In fact, if inflation unexpectedly declines during the life of a loan, it can work to the disadvantage of the borrower.

APPENDIX

The Financing Decision and Firm Value

Our purpose here is to study the relation between a company's capital structure and its market value. As noted in Chapter 2, many academicians and consultants recommend that managers work to increase the market value of their firms. With this in mind, we are interested in whether financial leverage affects firm value and, if so, what capital structure maximizes value.

Our strategy will be to begin with an idealized world of no taxes and no bankruptcy. Once this foundation is firmly established, we will add progressive doses of reality in the form of taxes and bankruptcy. While other potentially influential forces might also be considered, taxes and bankruptcy are thought to be among the more pervasive, and their review will provide a useful overview of the subject.[1] Although this line of inquiry will not enable us to specify precisely how much debt a particular company should have, it will allow us to identify several important factors management should consider when making financing decisions.

No Taxes or Bankruptcy

When once asked into how many slices he would like his pizza cut, Yogi Berra is said to have replied, "You'd better make it six; I don't think I'm hungry enough to eat eight." Absent taxes and bankruptcy, a company's financing decision can be likened to slicing Yogi's pizza: No matter how you slice up claims to the firm's earnings, it is still the same firm with the same earning power and hence the same market value. In this world, the benefits of increased return to shareholders from higher leverage are precisely offset by the increased risks so that market value is unaffected by leverage.

Here is an example demonstrating this apparently extreme position. You have an extra $1,000 in your pocket (clearly a hypothetical example) and plan to start a small business that you believe will generate earnings before interest and tax of $400 per year into the indefinite future. To keep things simple, we will suppose your company plans to distribute all of its earnings every year as a dividend. Column 1 of Table 6A–1 shows the bottom portion of a pro forma income statement for the enterprise. Note that the company's earnings and your total income both equal $400.

---

1 See Thomas E. Copeland and J. Fred Weston, *Financial Theory and Corporate Policy*, 3rd ed. (Reading, MA: Addison-Wesley, 1988, Chapters 13 and 14, for a more complete review of the possible links between capital structure and firm value.

T A B L E 6A–1

In the Absence of Taxes, Debt Financing Affects Neither Income nor Firm Value; in the Presence of Taxes, Prudent Debt Financing Increases Income and Firm Value

	No Taxes		Corporate Taxes at 40%	
	No Debt Financing	80% Debt Financing	No Debt Financing	80% Debt Financing
Corporate Income				
EBIT	$400	$400	$400	$400
Interest expense	0	120	0	120
Earnings before tax	400	280	400	280
Corporate tax	0	0	160	112
Earnings after tax	400	280	240	168
Personal Income				
Dividends received	400	280	240	168
Interest received	0	120	0	120
Total income	$400	$400	$240	$288
Personal Taxes at 33%				
Total income	400	400	240	288
Personal tax	0	0	80	96
Income after tax	$400	$400	$160	$192

A $400 annual income on a $1,000 investment implies a 40 percent annual return. Not bad. But your brother-in-law, the real estate broker, has sung the praises of debt financing for years. So just to see what difference it might make, you talk to a local banker. She affirms that an interest-only loan for $800 can be arranged, but that in view of such high leverage, a 15 percent interest rate will be required. A revised pro forma assuming debt financing appears in column 2 of Table 6A–1. Your company's earnings are down with debt financing, but so is your investment. With an $800 loan, you need to invest only $200 in equity, and a $280 annual income on a $200 investment produces an expected return of 140 percent ($280/$200 = 140%). Wow!

But you have studied enough finance to know that the expected return to equity almost always rises with debt financing, so this result is not especially surprising. Moreover, a moment's reflection should convince you that it is incorrect to compare returns on two investments with different risk. If the return on investment A is greater than the return on investment B *and* they have the same risk, A is the better choice. But if A has a higher return *and* higher risk, as in the present case, all bets are off. Poker players and fighter pilots might prefer investment A despite its higher risk, while we more timid souls might reach the opposite conclusion.

To make a fair comparison of the two financing schemes, we need to set their risks equal. We can do this by concentrating on the $800 remaining in your pocket when you take advantage of the bank loan. In particular, let us assume you will lend this $800 to some worthy borrower at an interest rate of 15 percent. (The fact that your $800 loan and the bank's loan bear the same interest rate confirms that the two loans are equally risky.)

If you prefer, another way to think about equalizing the risks is to imagine you deposit the $800 left in your pocket in the bank at a 15 percent interest rate and the bank loans the same $800 to your company. This way the entire $1,000 invested in the business is yours, as in the all-equity case, except now you are calling $800 of your investment debt.

With the risks now equal, we can decide which financing scheme is better by looking only at their prospective returns. Recall that with all-equity financing, your annual return is 40 percent. If you opt for debt financing, you will receive a $280 annual dividend from the business and $120 in interest on your loan, for a total of $400 (0.15 × $800 = $120). This, of course, is precisely the same total income you would receive with all-equity financing and the same 40 percent return on your $1,000 investment.

So what have we proven? We have shown that with risks held equal and ignoring taxes and bankruptcy costs, the way a business is financed does not affect the total return to owners. And if total return is unaffected, so is the value of the business. Firm value is independent of financing. (If the logic here still seems a bit obtuse, you will be heartened to learn that Franco Modigliani and Merton Miller won a Nobel prize for originally explaining it. This is also why it is often referred to as the M&M theory.)

Here is a more intuitive way to say the same thing. Companies typically *own* physical assets, such as trucks and buildings, and *owe* paper liabilities, such as stocks and bonds. Our argument is essentially that a company's physical assets are the real creators of value and that simply reshuffling paper claims to the income produced by these assets does not add value. The company is worth no more with one set of paper claims than with another. The only exception to this proposition would occur if the reshuffling of claims somehow changed the income produced by the assets, and in the absence of taxes and bankruptcy, this does not occur. Firm value in this hypothetical world is therefore independent of financial leverage.

Corporate Taxes but Still No Bankruptcy

Let us now repeat our saga in a more interesting world that includes corporate taxes. Suppose you finance your new business entirely with your own money; column 3 in Table 6A–1 shows your firm's pro forma income statement assuming a 40 percent corporate tax rate. Your company's income and your total personal income are now $240, which implies a 24 percent return on investment.

Finally, column 4 of Table 6A–1 shows your business's pro forma income statement and your total personal income when you use 80 percent debt financing at 15 percent interest. The return on your $200 investment in the business is now 84 percent ($168/$200 = 84%), but we know this is not comparable to the "all-equity" return of 24 percent because it is much riskier. Assuming as before that you set the risks equal by lending your remaining $800 at 15 percent interest, your total income will be $288 ($168 + $120), yielding an expected return of 28.8 percent. Contrary to the no-taxes case, use of financial leverage now increases your total income by $48 annually and your risk-equivalent return from 24.0 to 28.8 percent. The business is now a better investment, and hence more valuable, when financed with debt.

Why does debt financing increase the value of the business? Look at the tax bill. When financed solely with equity, the company owes $160 in taxes, but with 80 percent debt financing, taxes fall to only $112, a reduction of $48. Three parties share the fruits of your company's success: creditors, owners, and the tax collector. Our example shows that debt financing, with its tax-deductible interest expense, reduces the tax collector's take in favor of the owners'. Or, as Warren Buffett so deftly put it back in the days of a 48 percent corporate tax rate, "If you can eliminate the federal government as a 48 percent partner in your business, it's got to be worth more."

The bottom portion of Table 6A–1 is for suspicious readers who think these results might hinge on the omission of personal taxes. There you will note that imposition of a 33 percent personal tax on income reduces the annual aftertax advantage of debt financing from $48 to $32, but does not eliminate it. Because many investors, such as mutual funds and pension funds, do not pay personal taxes, the convention is to dodge the problem of defining an appropriate personal tax rate by concentrating on earnings after corporate, but before personal, taxes. We will gratefully follow that convention here.

I should note that our finding of a tax law bias in favor of debt financing is largely an American result. In most other industrialized countries, corporate and personal taxes are at least partially integrated, meaning dividend recipients receive at least partial credit on their personal tax bills for corporate taxes paid on distributed profits. As in our no-tax example, financial leverage does not affect firm value when corporate and personal taxes are fully integrated.

In the presence of American-style corporate taxes, then, the reshuffling of paper claims to include more debt *does* create value—at least from the shareholders' perspective, if not from that of the U.S. Treasury— because it increases the income available to private investors. The amount of the increase in annual income to shareholders created by debt financing equals the corporate tax rate times the interest expense, or what we referred to earlier as the *interest tax shield*. In our example, annual company earnings increase $48 per year, which equals the tax rate of 40 percent times the interest expense of $120.

To say the same thing in symbols, if V_L is the value of your company when levered and V_U is the value of the company unlevered, our example says that

$$V_L = V_U + \text{Value } [tI]$$

where t is the corporate tax rate, I is annual interest expense in dollars, and Value $[tI]$ represents the value today of all future interest tax shields. In the next chapter, we will refer to this last term as the *present value* of future tax shields. In words, then, our equation says the value of a levered company equals the value of the same company unlevered plus the present value of the interest tax shields.

Taken at face value, this equation and our example suggest a disquieting conclusion: The value of a business is maximized when the firm is financed entirely with debt. Fortunately, there is more to our story. But before proceeding, it is worth reflecting for a moment on the practical implications of our example and the preceding equation for company financing. The equation tells us that not all companies can benefit from interest tax shields. Certainly, if a company is losing money, it has no taxable income to shield and hence sees no benefit from debt financing. Similarly, a company that is in danger of incurring losses over the life of the debt financing will find the tax benefits of leverage less appealing than will a company with robust profits. A similarly disposed group of companies are those that, although profitable, already shield all or most of their income from taxes through the use of various tax credits, accelerated depreciation, and other legitimate tax reduction or deferral techniques. We should thus expect companies such as these to use less debt financing than other enterprises facing predictable future tax liabilities.

Taxes and Bankruptcy

We have seen that the tax deductibility of interest increases after tax income to owners and thereby increases firm value. Corporate bankruptcy creates a second link between the financing decision and income that works in opposition to interest tax shields.

A number of events can push a company into bankruptcy. For present purposes, let us agree that a company is bankrupt when the market value of its assets is equal to or less than its liabilities or, equivalently, when the market value of equity falls to zero. Once in bankruptcy, the economic logic of what should occur is straightforward. The court should first determine whether the bankrupt company is worth more dead than alive. If worth more dead, the court should oversee the company's liquidation and distribution of the cash proceeds to creditors according to the rights of absolute priority, which require that the most senior class of claimants be paid in full before junior claimants receive anything. If the company is worth more alive than dead, the court should oversee a reorganization of the business for the benefit of creditors. In most instances, this means equity investors would be wiped out, or at least forced to suffer large losses, and creditors would have to accept some common stock in the reorganized company in trade for their claims on the bankrupt business.

This is what *should* happen. What *actually* happens is something else again. Over the past two decades, the fundamental purpose of bankruptcy laws in the United States has gradually shifted from protecting the rights of creditors toward saving the jobs of workers in the distressed business by

---

CHANGING ATTITUDES TOWARD BANKRUPTCY

As the public purpose of the bankruptcy process in the United States has shifted from protecting the rights of creditors toward protecting those of workers, communities, and society at large, managers' attitudes toward bankruptcy have changed. Bankruptcy used to be seen as a black hole in which companies were clumsily dismembered for the benefit of creditors and shareholders lost everything. Today many executives view it as a quiet refuge where the courts keep creditors at bay while management works on its problems. Manville Corporation was the first company to see the virtues of bankruptcy in August 1982, when, although solvent by any conventional definition, it declared bankruptcy in anticipation of massive product liability suits involving asbestos. Continental Airlines followed in September 1983, using bankruptcy protection to abrogate what it considered ruinous labor contracts. Subsequently A. H. Robbins and Texaco, among others, have found bankruptcy an inviting haven while wrestling with product liability suits and a massive legal judgment, respectively. In all of these instances, the companies expected to emerge from bankruptcy healthier and more valuable than when they entered.

---

helping it to recover. While this is a meritorious objective, its pursuit has made it impossible to predict with any confidence what will befall a bankrupt firm. For once in bankruptcy, a company's fate rests in the hands of a bankruptcy judge and a multitude of attorneys, each representing an aggrieved party and each determined to pursue the best interests of his or her client until justice is done or the money runs out. Bankruptcy in the United States today is thus akin to a high-stakes poker game in which the only certain winners are attorneys. And, depending on their luck, managers and owners could come away with a strengthened firm or with nothing, in which case managers will suddenly find themselves with ample free time to polish their résumés.

   Whether the growing chorus of criticism of American bankruptcy laws and procedures will soon prompt a congressional overhaul of the system is open to question at this date. However, when so many members of Congress are lawyers, and when lawyers are also the chief beneficiaries of the current system, it is hard to be very optimistic.

The Probability of Bankruptcy

Presuming bankruptcy is something most companies would just as soon avoid, we can say that the expected cost of bankruptcy depends on two things: the probability that bankruptcy will occur and the cost to the company if it does occur. Looking first at the probability of occurrence, it should come as no surprise that increasing financial leverage also increases the probability of bankruptcy. To illustrate, suppose some unforeseen economic event causes the market value of a company's assets to fall from $10 billion to $5 billion. If the firm has $4 billion of debt outstanding, equity will fall from $6 billion to $1 billion, but because it is still positive, bankruptcy will not occur. If instead the company has $6 billion in debt, equity will fall from $4 billion to − $1 billion, and bankruptcy awaits.

Because companies in volatile, unpredictable economic environments are more likely to suffer such unanticipated declines in value, an obvious inference is that high-risk companies are wise to use less debt financing than low-risk ones. This is a major reason high-technology companies, such as Hewlett-Packard, Intel, and Analog Devices, employ comparatively little debt financing, while public utilities use much more.

The Cost of Bankruptcy
To some companies, bankruptcy is little more than a pothole along the road of corporate life; to others, it is an abyss. A key factor determining the cost of bankruptcy to an individual company is what can be called the "resale value" of its assets. Two simple examples will illustrate the concept.

First, suppose ACE Corporation's principal asset is an apartment complex and, due to local overbuilding and overly aggressive use of debt financing, ACE has been forced into bankruptcy. Because apartment complexes are readily salable, the likely outcome will be the sale of the complex to a new owner and distribution of the proceeds to creditors. The cost of bankruptcy in this instance will be correspondingly modest, consisting of the obvious legal, appraisal, and court costs, plus whatever price concessions are necessary to sell the apartments. In substance, because bankruptcy will have little effect on the operating income generated by the apartment complex, bankruptcy costs will be relatively low.

Note that the cost of bankruptcy does *not* include the difference between what ACE and its creditors originally thought the apartments were worth and their value just prior to bankruptcy. This loss is due to overbuilding, not bankruptcy, and is incurred by the firm regardless of how it is financed or whether or not it declares bankruptcy. Even all-equity financing, while it may prevent bankruptcy, will not eliminate this loss.

At the other extreme, consider Moletek, a genetic engineering firm, whose chief assets are a brilliant research team and attractive growth opportunities. If Moletek stumbles into bankruptcy, the costs are likely to be very high. Selling the company's assets individually in a liquidation will generate little cash, because most of the assets are intangible. It will also be difficult to realize value by keeping the company intact, either as an independent company or in the hands of a new owner, for in such an unsettled environment it will be hard to retain key employees and raise the funds needed to exploit growth opportunities. In essence, because bankruptcy will adversely affect Moletek's operating income, bankruptcy costs are likely to be high.

In addition to bankruptcy costs themselves, companies may incur costs of *financial distress* as the probability of bankruptcy increases. Internally these costs include lost profit opportunities as the company cuts back investment, research and development, and advertising to conserve cash. Externally they include lost sales as potential customers become concerned about future parts and service availability and increased costs as suppliers become reluctant to make long-run commitments and provide trade credit.

In sum, our brief review of bankruptcy costs suggests that they vary with the nature of a company's assets. If the resale value of the assets is high either in liquidation or when sold intact to new owners, bankruptcy costs are correspondingly modest. Such firms should be expected to make liberal use of debt financing. Conversely, when resale value is low because the assets are largely intangible and would be difficult to sell intact, bankruptcy costs are comparatively high. Companies matching this profile should use more conservative financing.

Concluding Comments

Figure 6A–1 summarizes the results of our musings about debt financing and firm value. It shows the value of a typical company as a function of financial leverage, denoted by the ratio of debt to firm value. At modest debt levels, the tax shield benefits outweigh the expected cost of bankruptcy, and value rises with leverage. But at higher debt levels, bankruptcy costs predominate, and value declines with further increases in leverage. The object of the exercise is to position the firm at the optimal capital structure, $(D/V)^*$, where value is maximized.

Beyond identifying the main costs and benefits of debt financing, our present line of inquiry is not especially helpful in pinpointing the precise location of $(D/V)^*$ for an individual firm. It does, however, suggest that

F I G U R E   6A–1

The Market Value of a Company Increases and Then Decreases as
Financial Leverage Rises

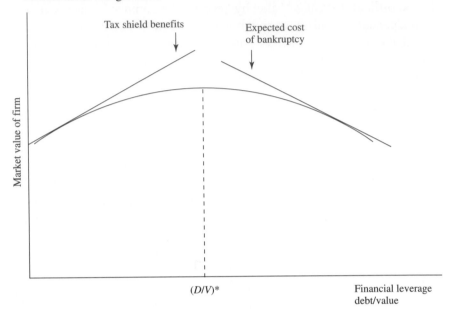

managers should consider the following three firm-specific issues when
making financing choices:

1. The ability of the company to utilize additional interest tax
   shields over the life of the debt.
2. The increased risk of bankruptcy created by added leverage.
3. The cost to the firm if bankruptcy occurs.

A final observation: Our perspective throughout this appendix has
been that of shareholders; yet it is ultimately managers, not shareholders,
who make financing decisions. This distinction is important because there
is reason to believe that the costs and benefits of leverage to managers
differ systematically from those to shareholders. In particular, managers
appear to incur much higher costs in bankruptcy, in the form of disrupted
lives and careers, than do shareholders. They probably see fewer benefits
of debt financing as well. Indeed, because the tax shield advantages of

debt accrue to shareholders rather than to managers, the chief benefit of leverage to managers may be nothing more than a higher sustainable growth rate. As a result, managers, unless burdened by sustainable growth problems, may be much more conservative in their use of debt financing than shareholders would prefer.

CHAPTER SUMMARY

1. This chapter studied the corporate financing decision, in particular the advantages and disadvantages of financial leverage.
2. The chief benefits of debt financing are increased expected return on equity, increased interest tax shields, and possibly improved management performance incentives.
3. The chief costs of debt financing are increased variability of income and return on equity and increased bankruptcy risk.
4. Coverage ratios are useful for evaluating the added risk of debt financing, while a range of earnings chart is useful for looking at the return dimensions of the decision.
5. The announcement that a company intends to sell new equity appears to signal investors that management is concerned about the company's future prospects or that management believes its shares are overpriced. Either way, the result is an average stock price decline equal to about 30 percent of the new issue. Repurchase announcements have a positive effect on stock price, while debt announcements have little or no impact.
6. Because money from external sources is not always available on agreeable terms, a major concern in most financing decisions is the impact of today's choice on tomorrow's options. Decisions that constrain a company's future ability to raise capital reduce financial flexibility.
7. Many companies view their financing decision as part of the larger problem of managing growth. Growing businesses, which are dependent on financial markets for funding, find modest dividend payout ratios and conservative leverage ratios attractive. Conversely, mature, slow-growth businesses may find aggressive leverage ratios appealing.

ADDITIONAL READING

Asquith, Paul, and David W. Mullins, Jr. "Signaling with Dividends, Stock Repurchases, and Equity Issues." *Financial Management*, Autumn 1986, pp. 27–44.
  A well-written summary of empirical work on measuring the capital market's reaction to major equity-related decisions. An excellent introduction to and overview of market signaling.
Myers, Stewart C. "The Capital Structure Puzzle." *Journal of Finance*, July 1984, pp. 575–92.
  An accessible overview of alternative explanations of company financing decisions with emphasis on the pecking-order theory, written by one of the leading contributors to capital structure research.
Myers, Stewart C. "The Search for Optimal Capital Structure." *Midland Corporate Finance Journal* (since renamed *Bank of America Journal of Applied Corporate Finance*), Spring 1983, pp. 6–16.
  A nontechnical review of what we think we know about the effect of financial leverage on firm value and its implications for corporate decision making.

CHAPTER PROBLEMS

1. Explain how each of the following changes will affect Harbridge Fabrics' range of earnings chart (Figure 6–2). Which changes would make debt financing more attractive? Which would make it less attractive?

   a. An increase in the interest rate on debt.

   b. An increase in Harbridge Fabrics' stock price.

   c. Increased uncertainty about Harbridge's future earnings.

   d. Increased common stock dividends.

   e. An increase in the amount of debt Harbridge already has outstanding.

2. As the financial vice president for Suntone Enterprises, you have the following information:

Expected net income after tax next year before effects of new financing	$40 million
Sinking-fund payments due next year on existing debt	$14 million
Interest due next year on existing debt	$10 million
Company tax rate	40%
Common stock price per share	$25
Common shares outstanding	16 million

a. Calculate Suntone's times-interest-earned ratio for next year assuming the firm raises $40 million of new debt at an interest rate of 6 percent.

b. Calculate Suntone's times-burden-covered ratio for next year assuming annual sinking-fund payments on the new debt will equal $8 million.

c. Calculate next year's earnings per share assuming Suntone raises the $40 million of new debt.

d. Calculate next year's times-interest-earned ratio, times-burden-covered ratio, and earnings per share if Suntone sells 1.6 million new shares at $25 a share instead of raising new debt.

e. Looking at your results, what do you think Suntone should do? Why?

3. Plasteel Devices has 100 million shares outstanding trading at $5 a share. The company announces its intention to raise $50 million by selling new shares.

a. What do market signaling studies suggest will happen to Plasteel's stock price on the announcement date? Why?

b. How large a gain or loss, in aggregate dollar terms, do market signaling studies suggest existing Plasteel shareholders will experience on the announcement date?

c. What percentage of the amount of money Plasteel intends to raise is this expected gain or loss?

d. What percentage of the value of Plasteel's existing equity prior to the announcement is this expected gain or loss?

e. At what price should Plasteel expect its existing shares to sell immediately after the announcement?

4. This is a more difficult but informative problem. James Brodrick & Sons, Inc., is growing rapidly and, if at all possible, would like to finance its growth without selling new equity. Selected information from the company's five-year financial forecast follows.

Year	1	2	3	4	5
Earnings after tax (millions)	$100	$130	$170	$230	$300
Investment (millions)	$175	$300	$300	$350	$440
Debt-to-equity ratio (%)	120	120	120	120	120
Dividend payout ratio (%)					
Marketable securities (millions)	$200	$200	$200	$200	$200

a. According to this forecast, what dividends will the company be able to distribute annually without raising new equity? What will the annual dividend payout ratio be?

b. Assume the company wants a stable payout ratio over time and plans to use its marketable securities portfolio as a buffer to absorb year-to-year variations in earnings and investments. Set the annual payout ratio equal to the five-year sum of total dividends paid in question *a* divided by total earnings. Then solve for the size of the company's marketable securities portfolio each year.

c. Suppose earnings fall below forecast every year. What options does the company have for continuing to fund its investments?

d. What does the pecking-order theory say about how management will rank these options?

e. Why might management be inclined to follow this pecking order?

EVALUATING INVESTMENT OPPORTUNITIES

CHAPTER 7

DISCOUNTED CASH FLOW TECHNIQUES

A nearby penny is worth a distant dollar.

Anonymous

$\mathbf{T}$he chief determinant of what a company will become is the investments it makes today. The generation and evaluation of creative investment proposals is far too important a task to be left to finance specialists; instead, it is the ongoing responsibility of all managers throughout the organization. In well-managed companies, the process starts at a strategic level with senior management specifying the businesses in which the company will compete and determining the means of competition. Operating managers then translate these strategic goals into concrete action plans involving specific investment proposals. A key aspect of this process is the financial evaluation of investment proposals, or what is frequently called *capital budgeting.* The achievement of an objective requires the outlay of money today in expectation of increased future benefits. It is necessary to decide, first, whether the anticipated future benefits are large enough, given the risks, to justify the current expenditure, and second, whether the proposed investment is the most cost-effective way to achieve the objective. This and the following chapter address these questions.

Viewed broadly, the discounted cash flow techniques considered here and in the following chapters are relevant whenever a company contemplates an action entailing costs or benefits that extend beyond the current period. This covers a lot of ground, including such disparate topics as valuing stocks and bonds, analyzing equipment acquisitions or sales, choosing among competing production technologies, deciding whether to launch a new product, valuing divisions or whole companies for purchase or sale, assessing marketing campaigns and R&D programs, and even designing a corporate strategy. Indeed, it is not an exaggeration to say that discounted cash flow analysis is the backbone of modern finance and even modern business.

FIGURES OF MERIT

The financial evaluation of any investment opportunity involves three discrete steps:

1. Estimate the relevant cash flows.
2. Calculate a figure of merit for the investment.
3. Compare the figure of merit to an acceptance criterion.

A *figure of merit* is a number summarizing an investment's economic worth. A common figure of merit is the rate of return. Like the other figures of merit to be discussed, the rate of return translates the complicated cash inflows and outflows associated with an investment into a single number summarizing its economic worth. An *acceptance criterion*, on the other hand, is a standard of comparison that helps the analyst determine whether an investment's figure of merit is attractive enough to warrant acceptance. It's like a fisher who can keep only fish longer than 10 inches. To the fisher, the length of the fish is the relevant figure of merit, and 10 inches is the acceptance criterion.

Although determining figures of merit and acceptance criteria appears to be difficult on first exposure, the first step, estimating the relevant cash flows, is the most challenging in practice. Unlike the basically mechanical problems encountered in calculating figures of merit and acceptance criteria, estimating relevant cash flows is more of an art form, often requiring thorough understanding of a company's markets, competitive position, and long-run intentions. Difficulties range from commonplace concerns with depreciation, financing costs, and working capital investments to more arcane questions of shared resources, excess capacity, and contingent opportunities. And pervading the whole topic is the fact that many important costs and benefits cannot be measured in monetary terms and so must be evaluated qualitatively.

In this chapter, we will initially set aside questions of relevant cash flows and acceptance criteria to concentrate on figures of merit. Later we

T A B L E 7–1

Cash Flows for Container-Loading Pier ($ millions)

Year	0	1	2	3	4	5	6	7	8	9	10
Cash flow	($40)	7.5	7.5	7.5	7.5	7.5	7.5	7.5	7.5	7.5	17

F I G U R E 7–1

Cash Flow Diagram for Container-Loading Pier

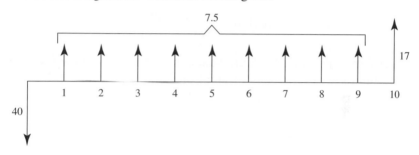

will return to the estimation of relevant cash flows. Acceptance criteria will be addressed in the following chapter under the general heading, "Risk Analysis in Investment Decisions."

To begin our discussion of figures of merit, let's consider a simple numerical example. Pacific Rim Resources, Inc., is contemplating construction of a container-loading pier in Seattle. The company's best estimate of the cash flows associated with constructing and operating the pier for a 10-year period appears in Table 7–1.

Figure 7–1 presents the same information in the form of a *cash flow diagram*, which is simply a graphical display of the pier's costs and benefits distributed along a time line. Despite its simplicity, I find that many common mistakes can be avoided by preparing such a diagram for even the most elementary investment opportunities. We see that the pier will cost $40 million to construct and is expected to generate cash inflows of $7.5 million annually for 10 years. In addition, the company expects to salvage the pier for $9.5 million at the end of its useful life, bringing the 10th-year cash flow to $17 million.

The Payback Period and the Accounting Rate of Return

Pacific's management wants to know whether the anticipated benefits from the pier justify the $40 million cost. As we will see shortly, a proper answer to this question must reflect *the time value of money*. But before addressing this topic, let's consider two commonly used, back-of-the-envelope-type figures of merit that, despite their popularity, suffer from some glaring weaknesses. One, known as the *payback period*, is defined as the time the company must wait before recouping its original investment. For an investment with a single cash outflow followed by uniform annual inflows,

$$\text{Payback period} = \frac{\text{Investment}}{\text{Annual cash inflow}}$$

The pier's payback period is 5 1/3 years, meaning the company will have to wait this long to recoup its original investment (5 1/3 = 40/7.5).

The second widely used, but nonetheless deficient, figure of merit is the *accounting rate of return*, defined as

$$\text{Account rate of return} = \frac{\text{Annual average cash inflow}}{\text{Total cash outflow}}$$

The pier's accounting rate of return is 21.1 percent ([(7.5 × 9 + 17) /10]/40).

The problem with the accounting rate of return is its insensitivity to the timing of cash flows. For example, a postponement of all of the cash inflows from Pacific's container-loading pier to year 10 obviously reduces the value of the investment but does not affect the accounting rate of return. In addition to ignoring the timing of cash flows, the payback period is insensitive to all cash flows occurring beyond the payback date. Thus, an increase in the salvage value of the pier from $9.5 million to $90.5 million clearly makes the investment more attractive. Yet it has no effect on the payback period, nor does any other change in cash flows in years 6 through 10.

In fairness to the payback period, I should add that although it is clearly an inadequate figure of investment merit, it has proven to be useful as a rough measure of investment risk. In most settings, the longer it takes to recoup an original investment, the greater the risk. This is especially true in high-technology environments where management can forecast only a few years into the future. Under these circumstances, an investment that does not promise to pay back within the forecasting horizon is equivalent to a night in Las Vegas without the floor show.

The Time Value of Money

An accurate figure of merit must reflect the fact that a dollar today is worth more than a dollar in the future. This is the notion of the time value of money, and it exists for at least three reasons. One is that inflation reduces the purchasing power of future dollars relative to current ones; another is that in most instances, the uncertainty surrounding the receipt of a dollar increases as the date of receipt recedes into the future. Thus, the promise of $1 in 30 days is usually worth more than the promise of $1 in 30 months, simply because it is customarily more certain.

A third reason money has a time value involves the important notion of *opportunity costs*. By definition, the opportunity cost of any investment is the return one could earn on the next best alternative. A dollar today is worth more than a dollar in one year because the dollar today can be productively invested and will grow into more than a dollar in one year. Waiting to receive the dollar until next year carries an opportunity cost equal to the return on the forgone investment. Because there are always productive opportunities for investment dollars, all investments involve opportunity costs.

Compounding and Discounting
Because money has a time value, we cannot simply combine cash flows occurring at different dates as we do in calculating the payback period and the accounting rate of return. To adjust investment cash flows for their differing time value, we need to use the ideas of compounding and discounting. Anyone who has ever had a bank account knows intuitively what compounding is. Suppose you have a bank account paying 10 percent annual interest, and you deposit $1 at the start of the year. What will it be worth at the end of the year? Obviously, $1.10. Now suppose you leave the dollar in the account for two years. What will it be worth then? This is a little harder, but most of us realize that because you earn interest on your interest, the answer is $1.21. *Compounding* is the process of determining

the future value of a present sum. The following simple cash flow diagrams summarize the exercise.

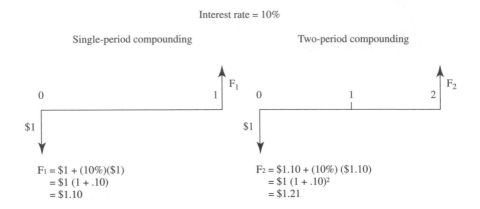

Interest rate = 10%

Single-period compounding

$F_1 = \$1 + (10\%)(\$1)$
$\quad = \$1 (1 + .10)$
$\quad = \$1.10$

Two-period compounding

$F_2 = \$1.10 + (10\%)(\$1.10)$
$\quad = \$1 (1 + .10)^2$
$\quad = \$1.21$

Discounting is simply compounding turned on its head: It is the process of finding the present value of a future sum. Yet despite the obvious similarities, many people find discounting somehow mysterious. And as luck would have it, the convention has become to use discounting rather than compounding to analyze investment opportunities.

Here is how discounting works. Suppose you can invest money to earn a 10 percent annual return and you are promised $1 in one year. What is the value of this promise today? Clearly, it is worth less than $1, but the exact figure is probably not something that pops immediately to mind. In fact, the answer is $0.909. This is the *present value* of $1 to be received in one year, because if you had $0.909 today, you could invest it at 10 percent interest, and it would grow into $1 in one year ($1.00 = 0.909[1 + 0.10]).

Now, if we complicate matters further and ask what is the value of one dollar to be received in two years, intuition fails most of us completely. We know the answer must be less than $0.909, but beyond that things are a fog. In fact, the answer is $0.826. This sum, invested for two years at 10 percent interest, will grow, or compound, into $1 in two years. The following cash flow diagrams illustrate these discounting problems. Note the formal similarity to compounding. The only difference is that in compounding we know the present amount and seek the future sum, whereas in discounting we know the future sum and seek the present amount.

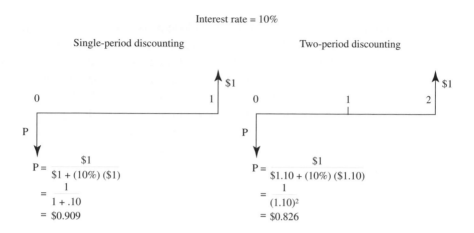

Interest rate = 10%

Single-period discounting

Two-period discounting

$$P = \frac{\$1}{\$1 + (10\%)\,(\$1)}$$
$$= \frac{1}{1 + .10}$$
$$= \$0.909$$

$$P = \frac{\$1}{\$1.10 + (10\%)\,(\$1.10)}$$
$$= \frac{1}{(1.10)^2}$$
$$= \$0.826$$

Present Value Tables

How did I know the answers to the discounting problems? I could have used the formulas appearing below the cash flow diagrams, or I could have used one of several brands of pocket calculators or a computer spreadsheet, but I did none of these. I looked up the answers in Appendix A at the end of the book. I undoubtedly would have used a calculator or a computer if my sole purpose were to solve the problems posed, but because I also want to offer an intuitive explanation of compounding and discounting, I used the less elegant Appendix A. Appendix A, known as a *present value table*, shows the present value of $1 to be received at the end of any number of periods from 1 to 50 and at interest rates ranging from 1 to 50 percent per period. The present values appearing in the table are generated from repeated application of the above formulas for differing time periods and interest rates. It might be useful to consult Appendix A for a moment to confirm the present values just mentioned.

As a matter of semantics, the interest rate in present value calculations is frequently called the *discount rate*. It can be interpreted two ways. If a company already has cash in hand, the discount rate is the rate of return it could earn on alternative investments. In other words, it is the company's *opportunity cost of the capital*. If a firm must raise the cash by selling securities, the discount rate is the rate of return expected by buyers of the securities. In other words, it is the investors' *opportunity cost of capital*. As we will see in the next chapter, the discount rate is frequently used to adjust the investment cash flows for risk and hence is also known as a *risk-adjusted* discount rate.

Appendix B at the end of the book is a close cousin to Appendix A. It shows the present value of $1 to be received at the end of *each period* for anywhere from 1 to 50 periods and at discount rates ranging from 1 to 50 percent per period. To illustrate both appendixes, suppose the Cincinnati Reds sign a new, young catcher to a contract promising $500,000 per year for four years. Let us calculate what the contract is worth today if the ballplayer has investment opportunities yielding 15 percent per year.

The cash flow diagram for the contract is as follows:

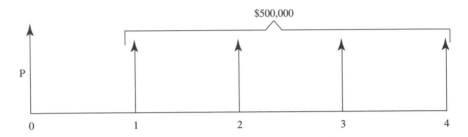

To find the present value, P, using Appendix A, we must find the present value at 15 percent of each individual payment. The arithmetic is

$$\begin{aligned}\text{Present value of contract} &= 0.870 \times \$500,000 + 0.756 \times \$500,000 \\ &\quad + 0.658 \times \$500,000 + 0.572 \times \$500,000 \\ &= \$1,428,000\end{aligned}$$

A much simpler approach is to recognize that since the dollar amount is the same each year, Appendix B can be used. Consulting Appendix B, we learn that the present value of $1 per period for four periods at a 15 percent discount rate is $2.855. Thus, the present value of $500,000 per period is

$$\text{Present value of contract} = 2.855 \times \$500,000 = \$1,428,000$$

Although the baseball player will receive a total of $2 million over the next four years, the present value of these payments is barely over $1.4 million. Such is the power of compound interest.

Equivalence

The important fact about the present value of future cash flows is that the present sum is *equivalent* in value to the future cash flows. It is equivalent because if you had the present value today, you could transform it into the future cash flows simply by investing it at the discount rate. To confirm this important fact, the following table shows the cash flows involved in transforming $1,428,000 today into the baseball player's contract of $500,000 per year for four years. We begin by investing the present value at 15 percent interest. At the end of the first year, the investment has grown to over $1.6 million, but the first $500,000 salary payment reduces the principal to just over $1.1 million. In the second year, the investment grows to over $1.3 million, but the second salary installment brings the principal down to just over $800,000. And so it goes until at the end of four years, the $500,000 salary payments just exhaust the account. Hence, from the baseball player's perspective, $1,428,000 today is equivalent in value to $500,000 per year for four years because he can readily convert the former into the latter by investing it at 15 percent.

Year	Beginning-of-Period Principal	Interest at 15%	End-of-Period Principal	Withdrawal
1	$1,428,000	$214,200	$1,642,200	$500,000
2	1,142,200	171,330	1,313,530	500,000
3	813,530	122,030	935,560	500,000
4	435,560	65,334	500,894	500,000

Note: The $894 remaining in the account after the last withdrawal is due to round-off error in the present value tables.

The Net Present Value

Now that you have mastered compounding, discounting, and equivalence, let's use these concepts to analyze the container pier investment. More specifically, let us use Appendixes A and B to replace the future cash flows appearing in Figure 7–1 with a single cash flow of equivalent worth occurring today. Because all cash flows will then be in current dollars, we will have eliminated the time dimension from the decision and can proceed to a direct comparison of present value cash inflows against present value outflows.

Here is how it works in practice. Assuming Pacific Rim Resources, Inc., has other investment opportunities yielding 10 percent annual interest, the present value of the cash inflows for the pier investment is

$$\frac{\text{Present value}}{\text{of cash inflows}} = 5.759 \times \$7.5 + 0.386 \times \$17$$

$$= \$49.755 \text{ million}$$

In this calculation, 5.759 is the present value of $1 per year for nine years at a discount rate of 10 percent, and 0.386 is the present value of $1 in year 10 at the same discount rate.

The cash flow diagrams that follow provide a schematic representation of this calculation. The present value calculation transforms the messy original cash flows on the left into two cash flows of equivalent worth on the right, each occurring at time zero. And our decision becomes elementary. Should Pacific invest $40 million today for a stream of future cash flows with a value today of $49.755 million? Yes, obviously. Paying $40 million for something worth $49.755 million makes sense.

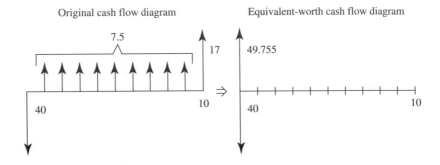

What we have just done is calculate the pier's *net present value*, or NPV, an important figure of investment merit:

$$\text{NPV} = \frac{\text{Present value of}}{\text{cash inflows}} - \frac{\text{Present value of}}{\text{cash outflows}}$$

The NPV for the container pier is $9.755 million.

NPV and Value Creation

The declaration that an investment's NPV is $9.755 million may not generate a lot of enthusiasm around the water cooler; so it is important to provide a more compelling definition of the concept. An investment's NPV is nothing less than a measure of how much richer you will become by undertaking the investment. Thus, Pacific's wealth rises $9.755 million when it builds the pier because it pays $40 million for an asset worth $49.755 million.

This is an important insight. For years, a common mantra among academics, management gurus, and an increasing number of senior executives has been that managers' purpose in life should be to create value for owners. A crowning achievement of finance has been to transform value creation from a catchy management slogan into a practical decision-making tool that not only indicates which activities create value but also estimates the amount of value created. Want to create value for owners? Here's how: Embrace positive-NPV activities—the higher the NPV, the better—and eschew negative-NPV activities. Treat zero-NPV activities as marginal because they neither create nor destroy wealth.

In symbols, when

NPV > 0, accept the investment.

NPV < 0, reject the investment.

NPV = 0, the investment is marginal.

The Benefit-Cost Ratio

The net present value is a perfectly respectable figure of investment merit, and if all you want is one way to analyze investment opportunities, feel free to skip ahead to the section "Determining Relevant Cash Flows." On the other hand, if you want to be able to communicate with people who use different but equally acceptable figures of merit, and if you want to reduce the work involved in analyzing certain types of investments, you will need to slog though a few more pages.

A second time-adjusted figure of investment merit popular in government circles is the *benefit-cost ratio (BCR)*, defined as

$$BCR = \frac{\text{Present value of cash inflows}}{\text{Present value of cash outflows}}$$

The container pier's BCR is 1.24 ($49.755/$40). Obviously, an investment is attractive when its BCR exceeds 1.0 and is unattractive when its BCR is less than 1.0.

The Internal Rate of Return

Without doubt the most popular figure of merit among executives is a close cousin to the NPV known as the investment's *internal rate of return*, or IRR. To illustrate the IRR and show its relation to the NPV, let's follow the fanciful exploits of the Seattle area manager of Pacific Rim Resources as he tries to win approval for the container pier investment. After determining that the pier's NPV is positive at a 10

T A B L E 7–2

NPV of Container Pier at Different Discount Rates

Discount Rate	NPV
10%	$9.755 million
12	5.434
	← IRR = 15%
18	−4.481

percent discount rate, the manager forwards his analysis to the company treasurer with a request for approval. The treasurer responds that she is favorably impressed with the manager's methodology but believes that in today's interest rate environment, a discount rate of 12 percent is more appropriate. So the Seattle manager calculates a second NPV at a 12 percent discount rate and finds it to be $5.434 million—still positive but considerably lower than the original $9.7 million ($5.434 million = 5.328 × $7.5 million + 0.322 × $17 million − $40 million). Confronted with this evidence, the treasurer reluctantly agrees that the project is acceptable and forwards the proposal to the chief financial officer. (That the NPV falls as the discount rises here should come as no surprise, for all of the pier's cash inflows occur in the future, and a higher discount rate reduces the present value of future flows.)

The chief financial officer, who is even more conservative than the treasurer, also praises the methodology but argues that with all the risks involved and the difficulty in raising money, an 18 percent discount rate is called for. After doing his calculations a third time, the dejected Seattle manager now finds that at an 18 percent discount rate, the NPV is − $4.481 million. Because the NPV is now negative, the chief financial officer, betraying his former career as a bank loan offer, gleefully rejects the proposal. The manager's efforts prove unproductive, but in the process he has helped us to understand the IRR.

Table 7–2 summarizes the manager's calculations. From these figures, it is apparent that something critical happens to the investment merit of the container pier as the discount rate increases from 12 to 18 percent. Somewhere within this range, the NPV changes from positive to negative and the investment changes from acceptable to unacceptable. The critical discount rate at which this change occurs is the investment's IRR.

Formally, an investment's IRR is defined as

IRR = Discount rate at which the investment's NPV equals zero

The IRR is yet another figure of merit. The corresponding acceptance criterion against which to compare the IRR is the opportunity cost of capital to the firm. If the investment's IRR exceeds the opportunity cost of capital, the investment is attractive, and vice versa. If the IRR equals the cost of capital, the investment is marginal.

In symbols, if K is the percentage cost of capital, then if

IRR > K, accept the investment.

IRR < K, reject the investment.

IRR = K, the investment is marginal.

You will be relieved to learn that in most, but regrettably not all, instances, the IRR and the NPV yield the same investment recommendations. That is, in most instances, if an investment is attractive based on its IRR, it will also have a positive NPV, and vice versa. Figure 7–2 illustrates the relation between the container pier's NPV and its IRR by plotting the information in Table 7–2. Note that the pier's NPV = 0 at a discount rate of about 15 percent, so this by definition is the project's IRR. At capital costs below 15 percent, the NPV is positive and the IRR also exceeds the cost of capital, so the investment is acceptable on both counts. When the cost of capital exceeds 15 percent, the reverse is true, and the investment is unacceptable according to both criteria.

Figure 7–2 suggests several informative ways to interpret an investment's IRR. One is that the IRR is a break-even return in the sense that at capital costs below the IRR the investment is attractive, but at capital costs greater than the IRR it is unattractive. A second, more important interpretation is that the IRR is the rate at which money remaining in an investment grows, or compounds. As such, an IRR is comparable in all respects to the interest rate on a bank loan or a savings deposit. This means you can compare the IRR of an investment directly to the annual percentage cost of the capital to be invested. We cannot say the same thing about other, simpler measures of return, such as the accounting rate of return, because they do not properly incorporate the time value of money.

Calculating an Investment's IRR

The IRR has considerably more intuitive appeal to most executives than the NPV or the BCR. The statement that an investment's IRR is 45 percent is more likely to get the juices flowing than one indicating the

F I G U R E 7–2

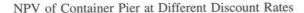

NPV of Container Pier at Different Discount Rates

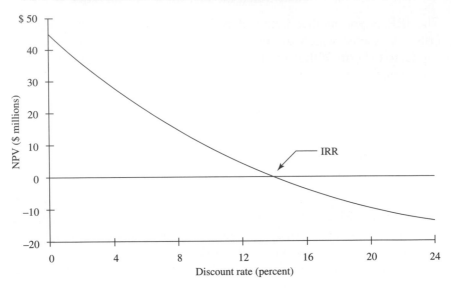

investment's NPV is $12 million or its BCR is 1.41. The IRR is, however, usually harder to calculate; it is frequently necessary to search for the IRR by trial and error or, as computer people would say, iteratively.

The first step in this trial-and-error process is to pick a likely IRR, selected in any fashion you like, and test it by calculating the investment's NPV at the chosen rate. If the resulting NPV is zero, you're through. If it is positive, this is usually a signal that you need to try a higher discount rate. Conversely, if the NPV is negative, you need to try a lower one. This trial-and-error process continues until you find a discount rate for which the NPV equals zero.

To see how this works in practice, let's calculate the container pier's IRR. From Table 7–2 and Figure 7–2, we know that the IRR must be somewhere between 12 and 18 percent because 12 percent yields a positive NPV and 18 percent a negative one. So let's try 15 percent. Using Appendixes A and B,

$$NPV = 4.772 \times \$7.5 + 0.247 \times \$17 - \$40 \overset{?}{=} 0$$

$$- 0.01 \overset{?}{=} 0$$

THE CONTAINER PIER INVESTMENT IS ECONOMICALLY
EQUIVALENT TO A BANK ACCOUNT PAYING 15 PERCENT
ANNUAL INTEREST

To confirm that an investment's IRR is equivalent to the interest rate on a bank account, suppose that instead of building the pier, Pacific Rim Resources puts the $40
million cost of the pier in a bank account earning 15 percent annual interest. The table
below demonstrates that Pacific can then use this bank account to replicate precisely
the cash flows from the pier and that, just like the investment, the account will run dry in
10 years. In other words, ignoring any differences in risk, the fact that the pier's IRR is
15 percent means the investment is economically equivalent to a bank savings account yielding this rate.

($ millions)

Year	Beginning-of-Period Principal	Interest Earned at 15%	End-of-Period Principal	Withdrawals = Investment Cash Flows
1	$40.0	$6.0	$46.0	$ 7.5
2	38.5	5.8	44.3	7.5
3	36.8	5.5	42.3	7.5
4	34.8	5.2	40.0	7.5
5	32.5	4.9	37.4	7.5
6	29.9	4.5	34.4	7.5
7	26.9	4.0	30.9	7.5
8	23.4	3.5	26.9	7.5
9	19.4	2.9	22.3	7.5
10	14.8	2.2	17.0	17.0

For practical purposes, the NPV is zero at a discount rate of 15 percent;
therefore, this is the project's IRR. Further, if Pacific's opportunity cost of
capital is less than 15 percent, we know the pier is acceptable; otherwise, it
is not. The need to solve for an investment's IRR iteratively was a meaningful limitation before the advent of computers and pocket calculators, but this
is no longer a significant barrier to its use. Today you simply punch in the
appropriate cash flows and let the electronics do the searching.

Calculating NPVs, IRRs, and BCRs with a
Computer Spreadsheet

To demonstrate how easy it is to calculate figures of investment merit with
a computer spreadsheet, the simulated spreadsheet in Table 7–3 contains
the estimated cash flows for the container pier project and the pier's NPV,

TABLE 7-3

Calculating NPVs, IRRs, and BCRs with a Computer Spreadsheet

	A	B	C	D	E	F	G	H	I	J	K	L
1	**ESTIMATED ANNUAL CASH FLOWS ($ millions)**											
2	*Year*	*0*	*1*	*2*	*3*	*4*	*5*	*6*	*7*	*8*	*9*	*10*
3	Cash flow	($40)	7.5	7.5	7.5	7.5	7.5	7.5	7.5	7.5	7.5	17
4												
5	Discount rate:	10%										
6						Equation				**Answer**		
7	Net present value (NPV):					= npv(B5, C3:L3) + B3				$9.75		
8	Benefit Cost Ratio (BCR):					= npv(B5, C3: L3)/– B3				1.24		
9	Internal Rate of Return (IRR):					= irr(B3: L3, B5)				15%		

246

IRR, and BCR. The three entries in the column labeled *"Equation"* would not normally appear on a computer spreadsheet. They are the equations I entered to coax the computer into calculating the figures of merit shown in the *"Answer"* column. Each equation takes advantage of the fact that all computer spreadsheets contain a number of built-in functions for performing various financial calculations. The NPV function calculates the net present value, at the specified interest rate appearing in cell B5, of the cash flows appearing in the range C3 through L3. From this present value, I have subtracted the initial $40 million expense in cell B3 to calculate the desired net present value.

The IRR function calculates the internal rate of return of the numbers appearing in cells B3 through L3. To aid in the iterative search for the IRR, the function requests an initial guess of what the IRR might be. I have used the 10 percent figure located in B5. The equations in Table 7–3 are appropriate for an Excel® spreadsheet. Lotus 1-2-3® has a very similar protocol.

A common mistake to avoid: The NPV function calculates the net present value of an indicated range of numbers *as of one period before the first cash flow occurs.* Consequently, if I had entered =npv(B5,B3:L3), the computer would have calculated the NPV as of time − 1. Because I want the NPV at time 0, I added the time 0 cash flow of ($40) to the net present value, at time 0, of the annual cash flows in years 1 through 10.

Bond Valuation: An Example of NPV and IRR Calculations

Investors regularly use discounted cash flow techniques to value bond investments. Here is an example. Suppose ABC Corporation bonds have an 8 percent coupon rate paid annually, a par value of $1,000, and nine years to maturity. What is the most an investor should pay for an ABC bond if she wants a return of at least 14 percent on her investment? The cash flow diagram is as follows:

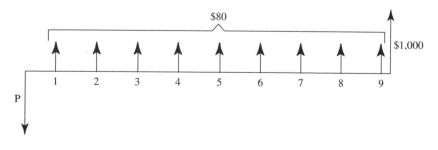

We want to find P such that it is equivalent in value to the future cash receipts discounted at 14 percent. Taking the present value of the receipts,

$$P = \$80 \times 4.946 + \$1,000 \times 0.308$$
$$= \$703.68$$

Thus, we know that when the investor pays $703.68 for the bond, her return over nine years will be 14 percent. When she pays more, her return will fall below 14 percent.

Suppose now that we know a bond's price and want to learn the return we will earn by holding the bond to maturity. In the jargon of the trade, we want to know the bond's *yield to maturity*. Specifically, suppose a $1,000 par value bond pays a 10 percent annual coupon, matures in seven years, and is presently selling for $639.54. What is its yield to maturity or, equivalently, its IRR? Let's begin by trying a discount rate of 12 percent:

$$NPV = 4.564 \times \$100 + 0.452 \times \$1,000 - \$639.54 \stackrel{?}{=} 0$$
$$268.85 \neq 0$$

Clearly, 12 percent is too low a discount rate. Suppose we try 25 percent:

$$NPV = 3.161 \times \$100 + 0.210 \times \$1,000 - \$639.54 \stackrel{?}{=} 0$$
$$- \ 113.44 \neq 0$$

The NPV is now negative, so 25 percent is too high. Let's try 20 percent:

$$NPV = 3.605 \times \$100 + 0.279 \times \$1,000 - \$639.54 \stackrel{?}{=} 0$$
$$-0.04 \cong 0$$

Because NPV is approximately zero, we know the bond's yield to maturity, or IRR, is a bit under 20 percent.

Mutually Exclusive Alternatives and Capital Rationing

Before turning to the determination of relevant cash flows in investment analysis, we should consider briefly two common occurrences that often complicate investment selection. We begin by looking at *mutually exclusive alternatives*.

THE IRR OF A PERPETUITY

An *annuity* is a stream of cash flows having the same value each year. A *perpetuity* is an annuity that lasts forever. Many preferred stocks are perpetuities, as are some British and French government bonds. They have no maturity date and promise the holder a constant annual dividend or interest payment forever. Let us use Appendix B to calculate the approximate present value of a perpetuity yielding $1 per year forever. Begin by noting that at a discount rate of, say, 15 percent, the present value of $1 per year for 50 years is $6.661. Think of it: Although the holder will receive a total of $50, the present value of this stream is less than $7. Why? Because if the investor put $6.661 in a bank account today yielding 15 percent per year, he could withdraw approximately $1 in interest each year *forever* without touching the principal. (15% × $6.661 = $0.999). Consequently, $6.661 today is approximately equivalent in value to $1 per year forever.

This suggests the following very simple formula for the present value of a perpetuity. Letting A equal the annual receipt, r the discount rate, and P the present value,

$$P = \frac{A}{r}$$

and

$$r = \frac{A}{P}$$

As an example, suppose a share of preferred stock sells for $480 and promises an annual dividend of $82 forever. Then its IRR is 17.1 percent (82/480). Because the equations are so simple, perpetuities are often used to value long-lived assets.

Frequently there is more than one way to accomplish an objective, and the investment problem is to select the best alternative. In this case, the investments are said to be mutually exclusive. Examples of mutually exclusive alternatives abound, including the choice of whether to build a concrete or a wooden structure, whether to drive to work or take the bus, and whether to build a 40-story or a 30-story building. Even though each option gets the job done and may be attractive individually, it does not make economic sense to do more than one. If you decide to take the bus to work, driving to work as well could prove a difficult feat. When confronted with mutually exclusive alternatives, then, it is not enough to decide if each option is attractive individually; you must determine which is best. Mutually exclusive investments are in contrast to independent investments, where the capital budgeting problem is simply to accept or reject a single investment.

When investments are independent, all three figures of merit introduced earlier—the NPV, BCR, and IRR—will generate the same investment decision, but this is no longer true when the investments are mutually exclusive. In all of the preceding examples, we implicitly assumed independence.

A second complicating factor in many investment appraisals is known as *capital rationing*. So far we have implicitly assumed that sufficient money is available to enable the company to undertake all attractive opportunities. In contrast, under capital rationing, the decision maker has a fixed investment budget that may not be exceeded. Such a limit on investment capital may be imposed externally by investors' unwillingness to supply more money, or it may be imposed internally by senior management on operating units within the company as a way to control the amount of investment dollars each unit spends. In either case, the investment decision under capital rationing requires the analyst to *rank* the opportunities according to their investment merit and accept only the best.

Both mutually exclusive alternatives and capital rationing require a ranking of investments, but here the similarity ends. With mutually exclusive investments, money is available, but for technological reasons only certain investments can be accepted; under capital rationing, a lack of money is the complicating factor. Moreover, even the criteria used to rank the investments differ in the two cases, so the best investment among mutually exclusive alternatives may not be best under conditions of capital rationing. The appendix to this chapter discusses these technicalities and indicates which figures of merit are appropriate under which conditions.

DETERMINING THE RELEVANT CASH FLOWS

Calculating a figure of merit requires an understanding of the time value of money and equivalence, and it necessitates a modicum of algebra. But these difficulties pale to insignificance compared to those arising in the estimation of an investment's relevant cash flows; the former requires only technical competence, whereas the latter calls for the exercise of judgment and perspective.

Two principles govern the determination of relevant cash flows. Both are obvious when stated in the abstract but can be devilishly difficult to apply in practice:

  1. *The cash flow principle*: Because money has a time value,
     record investment cash flows when the money actually moves,

not when the accountant using accrual concepts says they occur.

2. *The with-without principle*: Imagine two worlds, one in which the investment is made and one in which it is rejected. All cash flows that are different in these two worlds are relevant to the decision, and all those that are the same are irrelevant.

The following examples illustrate the practical application of these principles to commonly recurring cash flow estimation problems.

Depreciation

Accountants' treatment of depreciation is reminiscent of the Swiss method of counting cows: Count the legs and divide by four. It gets the job done, but not always in the most direct manner.

The physical deterioration of assets over time is an economic fact of life that must be included in investment evaluation. And we do so whenever we forecast that an asset's salvage value will be less than its original cost. Thus, an asset acquired for $1 million and salvaged 10 years later for $10,000 is clearly forecasted to depreciate over its life. Having included depreciation by using a salvage value below initial cost, it would clearly be double-counting to also subtract an annual amount from operating income as the accountant would have us do.

And here our story would end were it not for the tax collector. Although annual depreciation is a noncash charge and hence irrelevant for investment analysis, annual depreciation does affect a company's tax bill, and taxes *are* relevant. So we need to use the following two-step procedure: (1) Use standard accrual accounting techniques, including the treatment of depreciation as a cost, to calculate taxes due; then (2) add depreciation back to income after tax to calculate the investment's aftertax cash flow (ATCF). ATCF is the correct measure of an investment's operating cash flow. To illustrate, assume the container-loading pier considered earlier in the chapter will generate an annual income before depreciation and taxes of $10.3 million, annual depreciation will be $3 million, and Pacific Rim Resources is in the 38 percent tax bracket. Then aftertax cash flow is $7.5 million, as shown in the following table:

DEPRECIATION AS A TAX SHIELD

Here is yet another way to view the relation between depreciation and aftertax cash flows.

The recommended way to calculate an investment's aftertax cash flow is to add depreciation to profit after tax. In symbols,

$$ATCF = (R - C - D)(1 - T) + D$$

where R is revenue, C is cash costs of operations, D is depreciation, and T is the firm's tax rate. Combining the depreciation terms, this expression can also be written as

$$ATCF = (R - C)(1 - T) + TD$$

where the last term is known as the *tax shield from depreciation*.

This expression is interesting in several respects. First, it shows unambiguously that were it not for taxes, annual depreciation would be irrelevant for estimating an investment's aftertax cash flow. Thus, if T is zero in the expression, depreciation disappears entirely.

Second, the expression demonstrates that aftertax cash flow rises with depreciation. The more depreciation a profitable company can claim, the higher its aftertax cash flow. On the other hand, if a company is not paying taxes, added depreciation has no value.

Third, the expression is useful for evaluating a class of investments known as *replacement decisions*, in which a new piece of equipment is being considered as a replacement for an old one. In these instances, cash operating costs and depreciation may vary among equipment options, but not revenues. Setting R equal to zero above, it is apparent that the relevant aftertax cash flows for replacement decisions equal differences in operating costs after taxes plus differences in depreciation tax shields.

Aftertax Cash Flow = Earnings after Tax + Depreciation

Operating income	$10.3 million
Less: Depreciation	3.0
Earnings before tax	7.3
Less: Tax at 38%	2.8
Earnings after tax	4.5
Plus: Depreciation	3.0 ◀
Aftertax cash flow	7.5

Another way to say the same thing is

$$\text{Aftertax cash flow} = \text{Operating income} - \text{Taxes}$$
$$\$7.5 = \$10.3 - \$2.8$$

This formulation shows clearly that aftertax cash flow treats depreciation as irrelevant except for its role in determining taxes.

Working Capital and Spontaneous Sources

In addition to increases in fixed assets, many investments, especially those for new products, require increases in working-capital items, such as inventories and receivables. According to the with-without principle, changes in working capital that are the result of an investment decision are relevant to the decision. In some instances, they are the largest cash flows involved.

Working-capital investments have two unique features. One is that such investments are reversible in the sense that at the end of the project's life, the liquidation of working capital generates cash inflows approximately as large as the original outflows. The second unique feature is that many investments requiring working-capital increases also generate *spontaneous sources of cash* in the form of sources of cash to the company that arise in the natural course of business and have no explicit cost. Examples include increases in virtually all noninterest-bearing short-term liabilities such as accounts payable, accrued wages, and accrued taxes. The proper treatment of these spontaneous sources is to subtract them from the increases in current assets when calculating the project's working-capital investment.

To illustrate, suppose XYZ Corporation is considering a new-product investment that, in addition to an increase in plant and equipment, will require a $3 million investment in inventories and accounts receivable. Partially offsetting this buildup in current assets, management also anticipates that accounts payable, accrued wages, and accrued taxes will rise by $1 million as a result of the new product. So the *net* increase in working capital is $2 million. Management has agreed to analyze the proposed investment over a 10-year horizon and believes all of the working-capital investment will be recovered at the end of 10 years as the company sells off inventory, collects receivables, and pays off trade creditors. The cash flow associated only with the working-capital portion of this investment appears in the following diagram.

If money had no time value, these offsetting cash flows would cancel one another out, but because money does have a time value, we need to include them in our analysis.

Allocated Costs

The proper treatment of depreciation and working capital in investment evaluation is comparatively straightforward. Now things get a bit trickier. According to the with-without principle, those cash flows that do not change as a result of an investment are irrelevant to the decision. To illustrate, many companies allocate overhead costs to departments or divisions in proportion to the amount of direct labor expense the department incurs. Suppose a department manager in such an environment has the opportunity to invest in a labor-saving asset. From the department's narrow perspective, such an asset offers two benefits: (1) a reduction in direct labor expense and (2) a reduction in the overhead costs allocated to the department. Yet from the total-company perspective and from the correct economic perspective, only the reduction in direct labor is a benefit because total-company overhead costs are unaffected by the decision. They are simply reallocated from one cost center to another.

　　　Now consider a subtler example. Suppose a company is considering a new-product investment that, if undertaken, will increase sales by 5 percent over the next 10 years. The point at issue is whether corporate expenses not directly associated with the new product, such as the president's salary, legal department expenses, and accounting department expenses, are relevant to the decision. A narrow interpretation of the with-without principle suggests that if the president's salary will not change as a result of the investment, it is not relevant; nor are legal and accounting department expenses, if they will not change. That seems clear enough. Yet we observe that over time, as companies grow, presidents' salaries tend to increase while legal and accounting departments expand. This suggests that although we may be unable to see a direct cause-effect tie between such expenses and increasing sales, a longer-run relation exists between the two. Consequently, such costs may well be relevant to the decision.

Sunk Costs

A *sunk cost* is one that has already been incurred and that, according to the with-without principle, is not relevant to present decisions. This seems easy enough, but consider some examples. Suppose you purchased some common stock a year ago at $100 per share and it is presently trading at $70. Even though you believe the stock is fairly priced at $70, would you be prepared to admit your mistake and sell it now, or would you be tempted to hold it in the hope of recouping your original investment? The with-without principle says the $100 price is sunk and hence irrelevant, except for possible tax effects, so sell the stock. Yet natural human reluctance to admit a mistake and the daunting prospect of having to justify the mistake to a skeptical spouse frequently muddy our thinking.

As another example, suppose the R&D department of a company has devoted 10 years and $10 million to perfecting a new, long-lasting light bulb. Its original estimate was a development time of two years at a cost of $1 million, and every year since R&D has progressively extended the development time and increased the cost. Now it is estimating only one more year and an added expenditure of only $1 million. Since the present value of the benefits from such a light bulb is only $4 million, there is a strong feeling in the company that the project should be killed and whoever had been approving the budget increases throughout the years should be fired.

In retrospect, it is clear the company should never have begun work on the light bulb. Even if successful, the cost will be well in excess of the benefits. Yet at any point along the development process, including the current decision, it may have been perfectly rational to continue work. Past expenditures are sunk, so the only question at issue is whether the anticipated benefits exceed the *remaining* costs required to complete development. Past expenditures are relevant only to the extent that they influence one's assessment of whether the remaining costs are properly estimated. So if you believe the current estimates, the light bulb project should be continued for yet another year.

Excess Capacity

For technological reasons, it is frequently necessary to acquire more capacity than required to accomplish an objective, and a question arises of how to handle the excess. For example, suppose a company is considering the acquisition of a hydrofoil boat to provide passenger service across a lake, but effective use of the hydrofoil will require construction of two very expensive special-purpose piers. Each pier will be capable of handling 10 hydrofoils, and for technical reasons it is impractical to construct smaller piers. If the full cost of the two piers must be borne by the one boat presently under consideration, the boat's NPV will be large and negative, suggesting rejection of the proposal; yet if only 1/10 of the pier costs is assigned to the boat, its NPV will be positive. How should the pier costs be treated?

The proper treatment of the pier costs depends on the company's future plans. If the company does not anticipate acquiring any additional hydrofoils in the future, the full cost of the piers is relevant to the present decision. On the other hand, if this boat is but the first of a contemplated fleet of hydrofoils, it is appropriate to consider only a fraction of the pier's costs. More generally, the problem the company faces is that of defining the investment. The relevant question is not whether the company should acquire a boat but whether it should enter the hydrofoil transportation business. The broader question forces the company to look at the investment over a longer time span and consider explicitly the number of boats to be acquired.

The reverse situation also arises. A company has excess capacity of some sort and is considering an investment that will utilize the unused resources. In this case, the question is what cost, if any, to assign to the excess capacity. As an example, a prominent producer of canned foods was considering the addition of a new product line that would utilize some presently underemployed canning facilities. Some company executives argued that since the facilities had already been paid for, their cost was sunk and consequently irrelevant. Others argued that the canning capacity was a scarce resource and should be assigned a cost. What cost should be assigned to the excess capacity?

The answer again depends on future plans. If there are no alternative uses for the canning facilities now or in the future, no costs are involved in their use. On the other hand, if the company is likely to need the facilities in the future, there is an opportunity cost associated with their use by the new product line.

Financing Costs

Financing costs refer to any dividend, interest, and principal repayments associated with the particular means by which a company intends to finance an investment. There is no doubt that in the spirit of the with-without principle, financing costs of some nature are relevant to investment decisions; money is seldom free. But care must be taken not to double-count them. As the next chapter will clarify, the most common discount rate used in calculating any of the recommended figures of merit equals the annual percentage cost of capital to the company. It would obviously be double-counting to subtract financing costs from an investment's annual cash inflows *and* expect an investment to generate a return greater than the cost of the capital. The standard procedure, therefore, is to reflect the cost of money in the discount rate and ignore all financing costs when estimating an investment's cash flows. We will revisit this problem in the next chapter.

Mutually Exclusive Alternatives and Capital Rationing

We noted briefly in the chapter that the presence of mutually exclusive alternatives or capital rationing complicates investment analysis. This appendix explains how investments should be analyzed in these cases.

Two investments are mutually exclusive if accepting one precludes further consideration of the other. The choices between building a steel or a concrete bridge, laying a 12-inch pipeline instead of an 8-inch one, or driving to Boston instead of flying are all mutually exclusive alternatives. In each case, there is more than one way to accomplish a task, and the objective is to choose the best way. Mutually exclusive investments stand in contrast to independent investments, where each opportunity can be analyzed on its own without regard to other investments.

When investments are independent and the decision is simply to accept or reject, the NPV, the BCR, and the IRR are equally satisfactory figures of merit. You will reach the same investment decision regardless of the figure of merit used. When investments are mutually exclusive, the world is not so simple. Let's consider an example. Suppose Petro Oil and Gas Company is considering two alternative designs for new service stations and wants to evaluate them using a 10 percent discount rate. As the cash flow diagrams in Figure 7A–1 show, the inexpensive option involves a present investment of $522,000 in return for an anticipated $100,000 per year for 10 years; the expensive option costs $1.1 million but, because of its greater customer appeal, is expected to return $195,000 per year for 10 years.

Table 7A–1 presents the three figures of merit for each investment. All of the figures of merit signal that both options are attractive, the NPVs are positive, the BCRs are greater than 1.0, and the IRRs exceed Petro's opportunity cost of capital. If it were possible, Petro should make both investments, but because they are mutually exclusive, this does not make technological sense. So rather than just accepting or rejecting the investments, Petro must rank them and select the better. When it comes to ranking the alternatives, however, the three figures of merit no longer give the same signal, for although the inexpensive option has a higher BCR and a higher IRR, it has a lower NPV than the expensive one.

To decide which figure of merit is appropriate for mutually exclusive alternatives, we need only remember that the NPV is a direct measure of the anticipated increase in wealth created by the investment. Since the expensive option will increase wealth by $98,275, as opposed to only

F I G U R E   7A-1

Cash Flow Diagrams for Alternative Service Station Designs

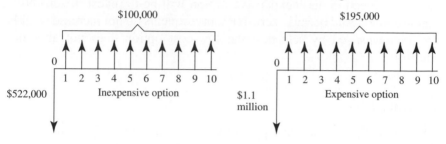

$92,500 for the inexpensive option, the expensive option is clearly superior.

The problem with the BCR and the IRR for mutually exclusive alternatives is that they are insensitive to the scale of the investment. As an extreme example, would you rather have an 80 percent return on a $1 investment or a 50 percent return on a $1 million investment? Clearly, when investments are mutually exclusive, scale is relevant, and this leads to the use of the NPV as the appropriate figure of merit.

What Happened to the Other $578,000?

Some readers may think the preceding reasoning is incomplete because we have said nothing about what Petro can do with the $578,000 it would save by choosing the inexpensive option. It would seem that if this saving could be invested at a sufficiently attractive return, the inexpensive option might prove to be superior after all. We will address this concern in the section titled "Capital Rationing." For now, it is sufficient to say that the problem arises only when there are fixed limits on the amount of money Petro has

T A B L E   7A-1

Figures of Merit for Service Station Designs

	NPV at 10%	BCR at 10%t	IRR
Inexpensive option	$92,500	1.18	14%
Expensive option	98,275	1.09	12

available for investment. When the company can raise enough money to make all investments promising positive NPVs, the best use of any money saved by selecting the inexpensive option will be to invest in zero-NPV opportunities. And because zero-NPV investments do not increase wealth, any money saved by selecting the low-cost option does not alter our decision.

Unequal Lives

The Petro Oil and Gas example conveniently assumed that both service station options had the same 10-year life. This, of course, is not always the case. When the alternatives have different lives, a simple comparison of NPVs is usually inappropriate. Consider the problem faced by a company trying to decide whether to build a wooden bridge or a steel one:

- The wooden bridge has an initial cost of $125,000, requires annual maintenance expenditures of $15,000, and will last 10 years.
- The steel bridge costs $200,000, requires $5,000 annual maintenance, and will last 40 years.

Which is the better buy? At a discount rate of, say, 15 percent, the present value cost of the wooden bridge over its expected life of 10 years is $150,190 ($125,000 + 5.019 × $15,000). This compares to a figure for the steel bridge over its 40-year life expectancy of $233,210 ($200,000 + 6.642 × $5,000). So if the object is to minimize the cost of the bridge, a simple comparison of present values would suggest that the wooden structure is a clear winner. However, this obviously overlooks the difference in the life expectancy of the two bridges, implicitly assuming that if the company builds the wooden bridge, it will not need a bridge after 10 years.

When comparing mutually exclusive alternatives having different service lives, it is necessary to examine each over the same *common investment horizon*. For example, suppose our company believes it will need a bridge for 20 years; due to inflation, the wooden bridge will cost $200,000 to reconstruct at the end of 10 years; and the salvage value of the steel bridge in 20 years will be $90,000. The cash flow diagrams for the two options are thus as follows:

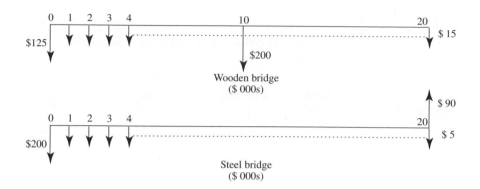

Now the present value cost of the wooden bridge is $268,285 ($125,000 + 6.259 × $15,000 + 0.247 × $200,000), and that of the steel bridge is $225,805 ($200,000 + 6.259 × $5,000 − 0.061 × $90,000). Compared over a common 20-year horizon, the steel bridge has the lower present value cost.

Capital Rationing

Implicit in our discussion to this point has been the assumption that money is readily available to companies at a cost equal to the discount rate. The other extreme is *capital rationing*. Under capital rationing, the company has a fixed investment budget, which it may not exceed. As was true with mutually exclusive alternatives, capital rationing requires us to rank investments rather than simply accept or reject them. Despite this similarity, however, you should understand that the two conditions are fundamentally different. With mutually exclusive alternatives, the money is available but, for technological reasons, the company cannot make all investments. Under capital rationing, it may be technologically possible to make all investments, but there is not enough money. This difference is more than semantic, for, as the following example illustrates, the nature of the ranking process differs fundamentally in the two cases.

Suppose Sullivan Electronics Company has a limited investment budget of $200,000 and management has identified the four independent investment opportunities appearing in Table 7A–2. According to the three figures of merit, all investments should be undertaken, but this is impossible because the total cost of the four investments exceeds Sullivan's budget. Looking at the investment rankings, the NPV criterion ranks A as the

T A B L E 7A–2

Four Independent Investment Opportunities under Capital Rationing
(capital budget = $200,000)

Investment	Initial Cost	NPV at 12%	BCR at 12%	IRR
A	$200,000	$ 10,000	1.05	14.4%
B	120,000	8,000	1.07	15.1
C	50,000	6,000	1.12	17.6
D	80,000	6,000	1.08	15.5

best investment, followed by B, C, and D in that order, while the BCR and IRR rank C best, followed by D, B, and A. So we know that A is either the best investment or the worst.

To make sense of these rankings, we need to remember that the underlying objective in evaluating investment opportunities is to increase wealth. Under capital rationing, this means the company should undertake that *bundle* of investments generating the highest *total* NPV. How is this to be done? One way is to look at every possible bundle of investments having a total cost less than the budget constraint and select the bundle with the highest *total* NPV. A short cut is to rank the investments by their BCRs and work down the list, accepting investments until either the money runs out or the BCR drops below 1.0. This suggests that Sullivan should accept projects C, D, and 7/12 of B, for a total NPV of $16,670 [(6,000 + 6,000 + 7/12 × 8,000)]. Only 7/12 of B should be undertaken because the company has only $70,000 remaining after accepting C and D.

Why is it incorrect to rank investments by their NPVs under capital rationing? Because under capital rationing, we are interested in the payoff per dollar invested—bang per buck—not just the payoff itself. The Sullivan example illustrates the point. Investment A has the largest NPV, equal to $10,000, but it has the smallest NPV per dollar invested. Since investment dollars are limited under capital rationing, we must look at the benefit per dollar invested when ranking investments. This is what the BCR does.

Two other details warrant mention. In the preceding example, the IRR provides the same ranking as the BCR, and although this is usually the case, it is not always so. It turns out that when the two rankings differ, the BCR ranking is the correct one. Why the rankings differ and why the BCR is superior are not worth explaining here. It is sufficient to remember that if you rank by IRR rather than BCR, you might occasionally be in error, but in the grand sweep of life, it probably doesn't matter much. A second detail is that when fractional investments are not possible—when it does not make sense for Sullivan Electronics to invest in 7/12 of project B—rankings according to any figure of merit are unreliable, and one must resort to the tedious method of looking at each possible bundle of investments in search of the highest total NPV.

The Problem of Future Opportunities

Implicit in the preceding discussion is the assumption that as long as an investment has a positive NPV, it is better to make the investment than to let the money sit idle. However, under capital rationing, this may not be true. To illustrate, suppose the financial executive of Sullivan Electronics believes that within six months, company scientists will develop a new product costing $200,000 and having an NPV of $60,000. In this event, the company's best strategy is to forgo all of the investments presently under consideration and save its money for the new product.

This example illustrates that investment evaluation under capital rationing involves more than a simple appraisal of current opportunities; it also involves a comparison between current opportunities and future prospects. The difficulty with this comparison, at a practical level, is that it is unreasonable to expect a manager to have anything more than a vague impression of what investments are likely to arise in the future. Consequently, it is impossible to decide with any assurance whether it is better to invest in current projects or wait for brighter future opportunities. This means practical investment evaluation under capital rationing necessarily involves a high degree of subjective judgment.

A Decision Tree

Mutually exclusive investment alternatives and capital rationing complicate an already confusing topic. To provide a summary and an overview, Figure 7A–2 presents a capital budgeting decision tree. It indicates the figure or figures of merit that are appropriate under the various conditions discussed in the chapter. For example, following the lowest branch in the tree, we see that when evaluating investments under capital rationing that

F I G U R E   7A–2

Capital Budgeting Decision Tree

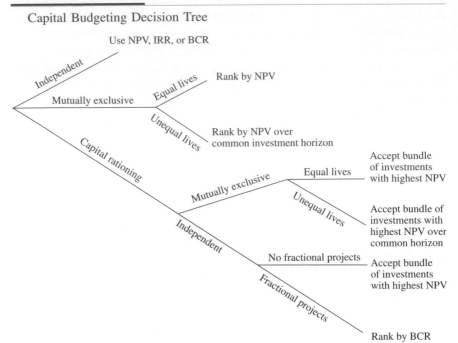

are independent and can be acquired fractionally, ranking by the BCR is the appropriate technique. To review your understanding of the material, see if you can explain why the recommended figures of merit are appropriate under the various conditions indicated, whereas the others are not.

C H A P T E R   S U M M A R Y

1. This chapter examined the use of discounted cash flow techniques in investment appraisal.

2. The three steps in financial evaluation of investment opportunities are (*a*) estimate the relevant cash flows, (*b*) calculate a figure of merit, and (*c*) compare it with an acceptance criterion. The first step is the hardest in practice.

3. Money has a time value because risk customarily increases with the futurity of an event, because inflation reduces the purchasing power of future cash flows, and because waiting for future cash flows involves a lost opportunity to make interim investments.

4. The payback period and the accounting rate of return ignore the time value of money and hence are inferior figures of merit. The payback period, however, is a useful indicator of investment risk.

5. Cash flows at two dates are equivalent if it is possible to transform the near-term cash flow into the later cash flow by investing it at the prevailing interest rate. Discounting uses equivalence to convert a messy stream of future receipts and disbursements into equal-value cash flows occurring today.

6. A valid figure of merit is the net present value, defined as the difference between the present value of cash inflows and that of outflows. Projects with a positive net present value are acceptable. They increase the decision maker's wealth by an amount equal to the opportunity's NPV. NPV transforms the value creation slogan into a practical guide for decision making.

7. A second popular, valid figure of merit is the internal rate of return, defined as the discount rate that makes the investment's NPV equal to zero. It is also the rate at which money left in a project is compounding and is therefore comparable to the interest rate on a bank loan. Investments with an internal rate of return greater than the cost of capital are acceptable.

8. The guiding principles in deciding what cash flows are relevant for an investment decision are the with-without principle and the cash flow principle.

9. Recurring problems in determining relevant cash flows involve depreciation, working-capital changes, allocated costs, sunk costs, temporary excess capacity, and financing costs.

A D D I T I O N A L   R E A D I N G

Bierman, Harold, Jr., and Seymour Smidt. *The Capital Budgeting Decision: Economic Analysis of Investment Projects.* 8th ed. New York: Macmillan, 1992. 608 pages.
   This textbook has more of a finance orientation than *Principles of Engineering Economy*, described below, and is somewhat harder to follow. About $65.
Grant, Eugene L., et al. *Principles of Engineering Economy.* 8th ed. New York: John Wiley & Sons, 1990. 591 pages.
   Everything you ever wanted to know about discounted cash flow techniques and more. A very solid, understandable treatment containing many practical examples. About $85.

CHAPTER PROBLEMS

1. Answer the following questions assuming the interest rate is 10 percent.

   a. What is the present value of $100 in six years?

   b. What is the present value of $100 in 10 years? Why does the present value fall as the number of years increases?

   c. How much would you pay for the right to receive $500 at the end of year 1, $300 at the end of year 2, and $1,000 at the end of year 5?

   d. How much would you pay to receive a 15-year bond with a par value of $1,000 and a 12 percent coupon rate? Assume interest is paid annually.

   e. How much would you pay for a share of preferred stock paying an $8-per-share annual dividend forever?

   f. What will be the value in 10 years of $5 invested today? (Hint: Present value = PVF times the future value, where PVF is the present value factor from the appendix for the appropriate interest rate and time period. Thus, future value = [1/PVF] times the present value.)

   g. About how long will it take for a $10 investment to double in value?

   h. What will be the value in 10 years of $5 invested at the end of each year for the next 10 years?

   i. A couple wishes to save $100,000 over the next 15 years for their child's college education. What uniform annual amount must they deposit at the end of each year to accomplish their objective?

   j. What return will you earn if you pay $342 for a stream of $100 payments lasting six years? What does it mean if you paid less than $342 for the stream? More than $342?

   k. How long must a stream of $50 payments last to justify a purchase price of $500? Suppose the stream lasted only seven years. How large would the salvage value (liquidating payment) have to be to justify the investment of $500?

   l. An investment of $100 today returns $433 in 30 years. What is the internal rate of return on this investment?

2. An investment costing $50,000 promises an aftertax cash flow of $18,000 per year for six years.

   a. Find the investment's accounting rate of return and its payback period.

   b. Find the investment's net present value at a 15 percent discount rate.

   c. Find the investment's benefit-cost ratio at a 15 percent discount rate.

   d. Find the investment's internal rate of return.

   e. Assuming the required rate of return on the investment is 15 percent, which of the above figures of merit indicate the investment is attractive? Which indicate it is unattractive?

3. An individual wants to borrow $10,000 from a bank and repay it in five equal annual end-of-year payments, including interest. If the bank wants to earn a 14 percent rate of return on the loan, what should the payments be? You may ignore taxes and default risk.

4. If ABC Company reported earnings per share of $10.00 in 1990 and $15.50 in 1999, at what rate did earnings per share grow over this period?

5. Times are tough for Microdyne. If it engages in a new, one-time promotional campaign costing $10 million, its annual aftertax cash flow over the next five years will be only $100,000. If it does not undertake the campaign, it expects its aftertax cash flow to be *minus* $3 million annually for the same period. Assuming the company has decided to stay in its chosen business, is this campaign worthwhile when the discount rate is 10 percent? Why or why not?

6. One year ago, Baffle Bag and Box Company (BB&B) purchased a new folder for $11,000. The company now finds that a new box folder is available that may offer significant advantages. The new machine can be purchased for $15,000, has an economic life of 10 years, and has no salvage value. It is expected that the new machine will produce a gross margin of $4,000 per year; thus, using straight-line depreciation, the annual taxable income will be $2,500.

   The current machine is expected to produce a gross margin of $2,000 per year and, assuming a total economic life of 11 years and straight-line depreciation, a profit before tax of $1,000. The current market value of the old machine is $5,000. BB&B's tax rate is 45 percent, and its cost of capital after tax is 10 percent.

Ignoring possible capital gains taxes and assuming zero salvage values at the end of the machines' economic lives, should BB&B replace its year-old box folder?

7. (Read the chapter appendix before attempting this problem.) A company is considering the following investment opportunities.

Investment	A	B	C
Initial cost	$550,000	$300,000	$200,000
Expected life	10 years	10 years	10 years
NPV @ 10%	$34,000	$30,000	$20,000
IRR	20%	30%	40%

a. If the company can raise large amounts of money at an annual cost of 10 percent and the investments above are independent of one another, which should it undertake?

b. If the company can raise large amounts of money at an annual cost of 10 percent and the investments are mutually exclusive, which should it undertake?

c. If the company has a fixed capital budget of $550,000 and the investments are independent of one another, which should it undertake?

8. (You will need a business calculator or a computer to answer this question.) In 1987, a Van Gogh painting, *Sunflowers* (not reputed to be one of his best), sold at auction, net of fees, for $36 million. Ninety-eight years earlier, in 1889, the same painting sold for $125. Calculate the rate of return to the seller on this investment. What does this suggest about the merits of fine art as an investment?

RISK ANALYSIS IN INVESTMENT DECISIONS

A man's gotta make at least one bet a day, else he could be walking around lucky and never know it.

Jimmy Jones, horse trainer

$\mathbf{M}$ ost thoughtful individuals and some investment bankers know that all interesting financial decisions involve risk as well as return. By their nature, business investments require the expenditure of a known sum of money today in anticipation of uncertain future benefits. Consequently, if the discounted cash flow techniques discussed in the last chapter are to be useful in evaluating realistic investments, they must incorporate considerations of risk as well as return. Two such considerations are relevant. At an applied level, risk increases the difficulty of estimating relevant cash flows. More important at a conceptual level, risk itself enters as a fundamental determinant of investment value. Thus, if two investments promise the same expected return but have differing risks, most of us will prefer the low-risk alternative. In the jargon of economics, we are *risk averse*, and as a result, risk reduces investment value.

Risk aversion among individuals and corporations creates the recognizable pattern of investment risk and return shown in Figure 8–1. The figure shows that for low-risk investments, such as government bonds, expected return is modest, but as risk increases, so too must the anticipated return. I say "must" because the risk-return pattern shown is more than wishful thinking. Unless higher-risk investments promise higher returns, you and I, as risk-averse investors, will not hold them.

This risk-return trade-off is fundamental to much of finance. Over the past three decades, researchers have demonstrated that under idealized conditions, and with risk defined in a specific way, the risk-return trade-off

F I G U R E   8-1

The Risk-Return Trade-Off

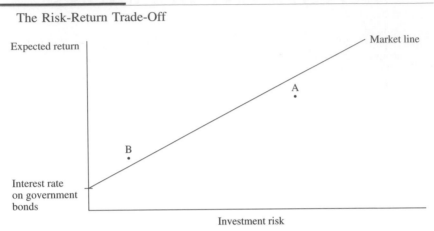

is a straight-line one as depicted in the figure. The line is known as the *market line* and represents the combinations of risk and expected return one can anticipate in a properly functioning economy.

The details of the market line need not detain us here. What is important is the realization that knowledge of an investment's expected return is not enough to determine its worth. Instead, investment evaluation is a two-dimensional task involving a balancing of risk against return. The appropriate question when evaluating investment opportunities is not "What's the rate of return?" but "Is the return sufficient to justify the risk?" The investments represented by A and B in Figure 8–1 illustrate this point. Investment A has a higher expected return than B; nonetheless, B is the better investment. Despite its modest return, B lies above the market line, meaning it promises a higher expected return for its risk than available alternatives, whereas investment A lies below the market line, meaning alternative investments are available promising a higher expected return for the same risk.

This chapter examines the incorporation of risk into investment evaluation, with particular emphasis on risk-adjusted discount rates and the cost of capital. After defining terms, we will estimate the cost of capital to Analog Devices, Inc., the high-tech semiconductor manufacturer profiled in earlier chapters, and we will examine the strengths and limitations of the cost of capital as a risk adjustment mechanism. The chapter concludes with a look at several important pitfalls to avoid when evaluating investment opportunities and at economic value added, a hot new topic in the world of performance appraisal. The appendix to the chapter considers diversification and what is known as β-risk as they affect investment appraisal.

You should know at the outset that the topics in this chapter are not simple, for the addition of a whole second dimension to investment analysis in the form of risk introduces a number of complexities and ambiguities. The chapter therefore will offer a general road map for how to proceed and an appreciation of available techniques rather than a detailed set of answers. But look on the bright side: If investment decisions were simple, there would be less demand for well-educated managers and aspiring financial writers.

RISK DEFINED

Intuitively, investment risk is concerned with the range of possible outcomes from an investment; the greater this range, the greater the risk. Figure 8–2 extends this intuitive notion. It shows the possible rates of return that might be earned on two investments in the form of bell-shaped curves. According to the figure, the expected return on investment A is about 12 percent, and the corresponding figure for investment B is about 20 percent.

A statistician would define *expected return* as the probability-weighted average of possible returns. To take a simple example, if three returns are possible—8, 12, and 18 percent—and if the chance of each occurring is 40, 30, and 30 percent, respectively, the investment's expected return is

Expected return = 0.40 × 8% + 0.30 × 12% + 0.30 × 18% = 12.2%

Risk refers to the bunching of possible returns about an investment's expected return. If there is considerable bunching, as with investment A, the investment is low risk. With investment B there is considerably less clustering of returns about the expected return, so it has higher risk. Borrowing again from statistics, one way to measure this clustering tendency is to calculate a probability-weighted average of the deviations of possible returns from the expected return. One such average is the standard deviation of returns. The details of calculating an

F I G U R E   8–2

Illustration of Investment Risk: Investment A Has a Lower Expected
Return and a Lower Risk Than B

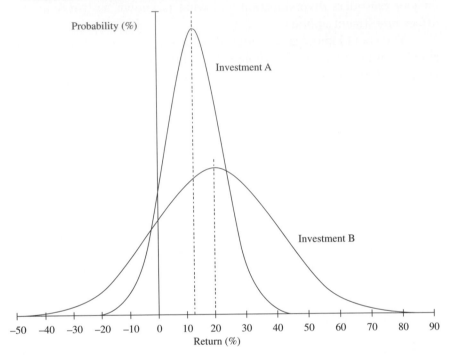

investment's standard deviation of returns need not concern us here.[1]
It is sufficient to know that risk corresponds to the dispersion, or

---

1 To illustrate calculation of the standard deviation of returns, the differences between the
possible returns and the expected return in the above example are (8% − 12.2%), (12% −
12.2%), and (18% − 12.2%). Because some of these differences are positive and others
are negative, they would tend to cancel one another out if we added them directly. So we
square them to ensure the same sign, calculate the probability-weighted average of the
squared deviations, and then find the square root.

$$\text{Standard deviation} = [0.4(8\% - 12.2\%)^2 + 0.3(12\% - 12.2\%)^2 + 0.3(18\% - 12.2\%)^2]^{1/2}$$
$$= 4.1\%$$

The probability-weighted average difference between the investment's possible returns and its
expected return is 4.1 percentage points. In symbols, the standard deviation of returns is

$$\sigma_i = \left[\sum_{i=1}^{n} p_i \, (r_i - \bar{r})^2 \right]^{1/2}$$

ARE YOU RISK AVERSE?

Here is a simple test to find out. Which of the following investment opportunities do you prefer?

1. You pay $10,000 today and flip a coin in one year to determine whether you will receive $50,000 or *pay* another $20,000.
2. You pay $10,000 today and receive $15,000 in one year.

If investment 2 sounds better than 1, join the crowd; you are risk averse. Even though both investments cost $10,000 and promise an expected one-year payoff of $15,000, studies indicate that most people, when sober and not in a casino, prefer the certainty of option 2 to the uncertainty of option 1. The presence of risk reduces the value of 1 relative to 2.

---

uncertainty, in possible outcomes and that techniques exist to measure this dispersion.

ESTIMATING INVESTMENT RISK

Having defined risk and risk aversion in at least a general way, let us next consider how we might estimate the amount of risk present in a particular investment opportunity. In some business situations, an investment's risk can be calculated objectively from scientific or historical evidence. This is true, for instance, of oil and gas development wells. Once an exploration company has found a field and mapped out its general configuration, the probability that a development well drilled within the boundaries of the field will be commercially successful can be determined with reasonable accuracy.

Sometimes history can be a guide. A company that has opened 1,000 fast-food restaurants around the world should have a good idea about the expected return and risk of opening the 1,001st. Similarly, if you are thinking about buying AT&T stock, the historical record of the past variability of annual returns to AT&T shareholders is an important starting point when estimating the risk of AT&T shares.

---

where σ_i is the investment's standard deviation of returns, p_i is the probability that the ith return will occur, r_i is the ith return, $\bar{r}$ is the expected return, n is the number of different returns that might occur, and Σ indicates that the n-squared deviations should be added together.

These are the easy situations. More often, business ventures are one-of-a-kind investments for which the estimation of risk must be largely subjective. When a company is contemplating a new-product investment, for example, there is frequently little technical or historical experience on which to base an estimate of investment risk. In this situation, risk appraisal depends on the perceptions of the managers participating in the decision, their knowledge of the economics of the industry, and their understanding of the investment's ramifications.

Three Techniques for Estimating Investment Risk

Three previously mentioned techniques—sensitivity analysis, scenario analysis, and simulation—are useful for making subjective estimates of investment risk. Although none of the techniques provides an objective measure of investment risk, they all help the executive to think systematically about the sources of risk and their effect on project return. Reviewing briefly, an investment's IRR or NPV depends on a number of uncertain economic factors, such as selling price, quantity sold, useful life, and so on. Sensitivity analysis involves an estimation of how the investment's figure of merit varies with changes in one of these uncertain factors. One commonly used approach is to calculate three returns corresponding to an optimistic, a pessimistic, and a most likely forecast of the uncertain variables. This provides some indication of the range of possible outcomes. Scenario analysis is a modest extension that changes several of the uncertain variables in a mutually consistent way to describe a particular event.

Simulation is an extension of sensitivity and scenario analysis in which the analyst assigns a probability distribution to each uncertain factor, specifies any interdependence among the factors, and asks a computer repeatedly to select values for the factors according to their probability of occurring. For each set of values chosen, the computer calculates the investment's return. The result is a graph, such as Figure 8–2, plotting project return against frequency of occurrence. The chief benefits of sensitivity analysis, scenario analysis, and simulation are that they force the analyst to think systematically about the individual economic determinants of investment risk, indicate the sensitivity of the investment's return to each of these determinants, and provide information about the range of possible returns.

AN EXAMPLE OF SENSITIVITY ANALYSIS

A number of commercially available software programs make it possible to analyze investment opportunities on a personal computer. A standard option in many is the ability to analyze the sensitivity of the results to changes in key assumptions. Below is representative output from such an analysis.

Relative Impact of Key Variables on Net Present Value
(Investment NPV = $212,597)

A 1% Increase in:	Increases NPV by:	Percent Increase
Sales growth rate	$2,240	1.33%
Operating profit margin	3,462	2.05
Capital investment	−1,249	−0.74
Working-capital investment	−1,143	−0.68
Discount rate	−4,996	−2.96

INCLUDING RISK IN INVESTMENT EVALUATION

Once you have an idea of the degree of risk inherent in an investment, the second step is to incorporate this information into your evaluation of the opportunity.

Risk-Adjusted Discount Rates

The most common way to do this is to add an increment to the discount rate; that is, discount the expected value of the risky cash flows at a discount rate that includes a premium for risk. Alternatively, you can compare an investment's IRR, based on expected cash flows, to a required rate of return that again includes a risk premium. The size of the premium naturally increases with the perceived risk of the investment.

To illustrate the use of such risk-adjusted discount rates, consider a $10 million investment promising risky cash flows with an expected value of $2 million annually for 10 years. What is the investment's NPV when the risk-free interest rate is 8 percent and management has decided to use a 6 percent risk premium to compensate for the uncertainty of the cash flows?

The cash flow diagram for the investment follows. At a 14 percent risk-adjusted discount rate, the project's NPV is

$$NPV = - \$10 \text{ million} + \$2 \text{ million } (5.216)$$
$$= \$432,000$$

where 5.216, from Appendix B, equals the present value of $1 per year for 10 years at 14 percent interest. Because the investment's NPV is positive, the investment is attractive even after adjusting for risk. An equivalent approach is to calculate the investment's IRR, using expected cash flows, and compare it to the risk-adjusted rate. Because the project's IRR of 15.1 percent exceeds 14 percent, we again conclude that the investment is attractive despite its risk.

Note how the risk-adjusted discount rate reduces the investment's appeal. If the investment were riskless, its NPV at an 8 percent discount rate would be $3.4 million, but because a higher risk-adjusted rate is deemed appropriate, NPV falls by almost $3 million. In essence, management requires an inducement of at least this amount before it is willing to make the investment.

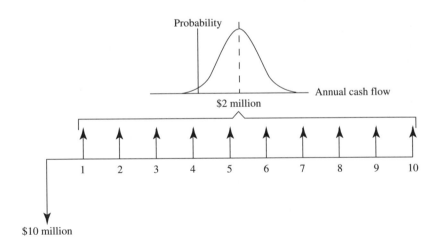

Two things make risk-adjusted discount rates appealing in practical application. One is that most executives have at least a rough idea of how an investment's required rate of return should vary with risk. Stated differently, they have a basic idea of the position of the market line in Figure 8–1. For instance, they know from the historical data in Table 5–1 of

Chapter 5 that over many years, common stocks have yielded an average annual return about 7 percentage points higher than the return on government bonds. If the present return on government bonds is 8 percent, it is plausible to expect an investment that is about as risky as common stocks to yield a return of about 15 percent. Similarly, executives know that an investment promising a return of 40 percent is attractive unless its risk is extraordinarily high. Granted, such reasoning is imprecise; nonetheless, it does lend some objectivity to risk assessment.

THE COST OF CAPITAL

The second attraction of risk-adjusted discount rates involves the cost of capital. When creditors and owners invest money in a company, they incur an opportunity cost equal to the return they could have earned on alternative, similar-risk investments. This opportunity cost is the firm's cost of capital; it is the minimum rate of return the company can earn on existing assets and still meet the expectations of its capital providers. The cost of capital is a risk-adjusted discount rate, and because we can at least estimate the cost of capital to individual companies, it introduces a welcome degree of objectivity into the risk-adjustment process. Rather than relying on managers' "gut feelings" about risk, we can look to financial markets for information about appropriate risk-adjusted discount rates. In the following paragraphs we will define the cost of capital more precisely, estimate Analog Devices' cost of capital, and discuss its use as a risk adjustment factor.

The Cost of Capital Defined

Suppose we want to estimate the cost of capital to XYZ Corporation and we have the following information:

	XYZ Liabilities and Owners' Equity	Opportunity Cost of Capital
Debt	$100	10%
Equity	200	20

We will discuss the origins of the opportunity costs of capital in a few pages. For now just assume we know that given alternative investment opportunities, creditors expect to earn at least 10 percent on their loans and shareholders expect to earn at least 20 percent on their ownership of XYZ shares. With this information, we need answer only two simple questions to calculate XYZ's cost of capital:

1. *How much money must XYZ earn annually on existing assets to meet the expectations of creditors and owners?*

The creditors expect a 10 percent return on their $100 loan, or $10. However, because interest payments are tax deductible, the effective after-tax cost to a profitable company in, say, the 50 percent tax bracket is only $5. The owners expect 20 percent on their $200 investment, or $40. So in total, XYZ must earn $45 ($45 = [1 − 0.5][10%] $100 +[20%]$200).

2. *What rate of return must the company earn on existing assets to meet the expectations of creditors and owners?*

A total of $300 is invested in XYZ on which the company must earn $45, so the required rate of return is 15 percent ($45/$300). This is XYZ's cost of capital.

Let's repeat the above reasoning using symbols. The money XYZ must earn annually on existing capital is

$$(1 − t)K_D D + K_E E$$

where t is the tax rate, K_D is the expected return on debt or the cost of debt, D is the amount of interest-bearing debt in XYZ's capital structure, K_E is the expected return on equity or the cost of equity, and E is the amount of equity in XYZ's capital structure. Similarly, the annual return XYZ must earn on existing capital is

$$K_W = \frac{(1 − t)K_D D + K_E E}{D + E} \tag{8–1}$$

where K_W is the cost of capital.

From the preceding example,

$$15\% = \frac{(1 − 50\%)10\% \times \$100 + 20\% \times \$200}{\$100 + \$200}$$

In words, a company's cost of capital is the cost of the individual sources of capital, weighted according to their importance in the firm's capital structure. The subscript W appears in the cost of capital expression to denote that the cost of capital is a weighted-average cost. To demonstrate that K_W is the weighted average of the costs of individual sources of capital to the business, note that one-third of XYZ's capital is debt and two-thirds is equity, so its cost of capital is one-third the cost of debt plus two-thirds the cost of equity:

$$15\% = (1/3 \times 5\%) + (2/3 \times 20\%)$$

The Cost of Capital and Stock Price

An important tie exists between a company's cost of capital and its stock price. To see the linkage, ask yourself what happens when XYZ Corporation earns a return on existing assets greater than its cost of capital. Because the return to creditors is fixed by contract, the excess return accrues entirely to shareholders. And because the company can earn more than shareholders' opportunity cost of capital, XYZ's stock price will rise as new investors are attracted by the excess return. Conversely, if XYZ earns a return below its cost of capital on existing assets, shareholders will not receive their expected return, and stock price will fall. The price will continue falling until the prospective return to new buyers again equals equity investors' opportunity cost of capital. Another definition of the cost of capital, therefore, is *the return a firm must earn on existing assets to keep its stock price constant.* Finally, from a shareholder value perspective, we can say that management creates value when it earns returns above the firm's cost of capital and destroys value when it earns returns below this target.

Analog Devices' Cost of Capital

To use the cost of capital as a risk-adjusted discount rate in investment evaluation, we must be able to measure it. This involves assigning values to all of the quantities on the right side of equation 8–1. To illustrate the process, let's estimate Analog Devices' cost of capital at fiscal year-end 1995.

The Weights

We begin by measuring the weights, D and E. There are two common ways to do this, only one of which is correct: Use the *book values* of debt and equity appearing on the company's balance sheet, or use the *market values*. By *market value*, I mean the price of the company's bonds and common shares in securities markets multiplied by the number of each security type outstanding. As Table 8–1 shows, the book values of Analog Devices' debt and equity at the end of fiscal 1995 were $82.4 million and $656.0 million, respectively. The figure for debt includes only interest-bearing debt because

TABLE 8–1

Book and Market Values of Analog Devices' Debt and Equity
(October 30, 1995)

	Book Value		Market Value	
Source	Amount ($ millions)	Percentage of Total	Amount ($ millions)	Percentage of Total
Debt	$ 82.4	11.2%	$ 82.4	2.8%
Equity	656.0	88.8	2,848.0	97.2
Total	$230.0	100.0%	$2,930.4	100.0%

other liabilities are either the result of tax accruals that are subsumed in the estimation of aftertax cash flow or spontaneous sources of cash that are part of working capital in the investment's cash flows. The table also indicates that the market values of Analog Devices' debt and equity on the same date were $82.4 million and $2,848.0 million, respectively.

Consistent with common practice, I have assumed here that the market value of Analog Devices' debt equals its book value. This assumption is almost certainly incorrect, but just as certainly the difference between the book and market values of debt is quite small compared to that for equity. The market value of Analog Devices' equity is its price per share at year-end of $24.88 times 114.5 million common shares outstanding. The market value of equity exceeds the book value by a ratio of 4.3 to 1 because investors are quite optimistic about ADI's future prospects.

To decide whether book weights or market weights are appropriate for measuring the cost of capital, consider the following analogy. Suppose that 10 years ago you invested $20,000 in a portfolio of common stocks that, through no doing of your own, is now worth $50,000. After talking to stockbrokers and investment consultants, you believe a reasonable return on the portfolio, given present market conditions, is 10 percent a year. Would you be satisfied with a 10 percent return on the original $20,000 cost of the portfolio, or would you expect to earn 10 percent on the current $50,000 market value? Obviously, the current market value is relevant for decision making; the original cost is sunk and therefore irrelevant. Similarly, Analog Devices' owners and creditors have investments worth $2,848 million and $82.4 million, respectively, on which they expect to earn competitive returns. Thus, the market values of debt and equity are appropriate for measuring the cost of capital.

The Cost of Debt

This is an easy one. Bonds and short-term loans of a maturity similar to Analog Devices' were yielding a return of approximately 7.5 percent in October 1995, and the company's marginal tax rate is about 34 percent. Consequently, the aftertax cost of debt to Analog Devices was 5.0 percent ([1 − 34%] × 7.5%). Some financial neophytes are tempted to use the coupon rate on the debt rather than the prevailing market rate in this calculation. But the coupon rate is, of course, a sunk cost. Moreover, because we want to use the cost of capital to evaluate new investments, we want the cost of new debt.

The Cost of Equity

Estimating the cost of equity is as hard as estimating debt was easy. With debt, or preferred stock, the company promises the holder a specified stream of future payments. Knowing these promised payments and the current price of the security, it is a simple matter to calculate the expected return. This is what we did in the last chapter when we calculated the yield to maturity on a bond. With common stock, the situation is more complex. Because the company makes no promises about future payments to shareholders, there is no simple way to calculate the return expected.

The following cash flow diagrams illustrate the problem, displaying the cash flows first to a bond investor and then to a stock investor. Finding K_D is a simple discounted cash flow problem. Finding K_E would be just as simple, except we do not know the future cash receipts shareholders expect. This calls for some ingenuity.

Investor's Cash Flow Diagram for a Bond

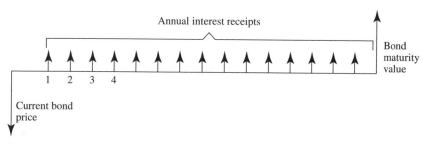

K_D = Discount rate that makes present value of cash inflows equal to current price.

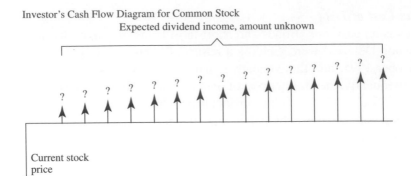

Investor's Cash Flow Diagram for Common Stock
Expected dividend income, amount unknown

Current stock price

K_E = Discount rate that makes present value of unknown expected dividend income equal current price.

Assume a Perpetuity

One way out of this dilemma recalls the story of the physicist, the chemist, and the economist trapped at the bottom of a 40-foot pit. After failing with a number of schemes based on their knowledge of physics and chemistry to extract themselves from the pit, the two finally turn to the economist in desperation and ask if there isn't anything in his professional training that might help them devise a means of escape. "Why, yes," he replies. "The problem is really quite elementary. Simply assume a ladder." Here our "ladder" is an assumption about the future payments shareholders expect. From this heroic beginning, the problem really does become quite elementary. To illustrate, suppose equity investors expect to receive an annual dividend of $d per share forever. The cash flow diagram then becomes

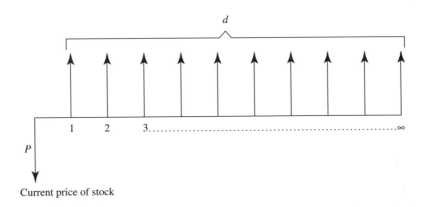

d

1   2   3..∞

P

Current price of stock

Because we know P and have assumed a future payment stream, all that remains is to find the discount rate that makes the present value of the payment stream equal the current price. From the last chapter, we know that the present value of such a perpetuity at a discount rate of K_E is

$$P = \frac{d}{K_E}$$

and solving for the discount rate,

$$K_E = \frac{d}{P}$$

In words, if you are willing to assume investors expect a company's stock to behave like a perpetuity, the cost of equity capital is simply the dividend yield.

Perpetual Growth
A somewhat more plausible but still tractable assumption is that shareholders expect a per share dividend next year of d, and expect this dividend to grow at the rate of g percent per annum forever. In this case, the cash flow diagram becomes

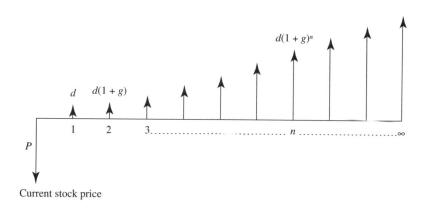

Fortunately, it turns out that this discounted cash flow problem also has an unusually simple solution. Without boring you with the arithmetic details, the present value of the assumed payment stream at a discount rate of K_E is

$$P = \frac{d}{K_E - g}$$

and solving for the discount rate,

$$K_E = \frac{d}{P} + g$$

This equation says that if the perpetual growth assumption is correct, the cost of equity capital equals the company's dividend yield (d/P), plus the growth rate in dividends. This is known as the *perpetual growth equation* for K_E.

The problem with the perpetual growth estimate of K_E is that it is only as good as the assumption on which it is based. For *mature* companies such as railroads, electric utilities, and steel mills, it may be reasonable to assume that observed growth rates will continue indefinitely. And in these cases, the perpetual growth equation yields a plausible estimate of the cost of equity capital. The equation is not applicable to Analog Devices, however, because ADI's growth rate is well above one that could be sustained in perpetuity.

Let History Be Your Guide

A second, and generally more fruitful, approach to estimating the cost of equity capital looks at the structure of expected returns on risky investments. In general, the expected return on any risky asset is composed of three factors:

$$\text{Expected return on risky asset} = \text{Risk-free interest rate} + \text{Inflation premium} + \text{Risk premium}$$

The equation says that the owner of a risky asset should expect to earn a return from three sources. The first is compensation for the opportunity cost incurred in holding the asset. This is the risk-free interest rate. The second is compensation for the declining purchasing power of the investment over time. This is the inflation premium. The third is compensation for bearing risk. This is the risk premium. Fortunately, we do not need to treat the first two terms as separate factors because together they equal the expected return on a default-free bond such as a government bond. In other words, owners of government bonds expect a return from the first two sources but not the third. Consequently,

$$\text{Expected return on risky asset} = \text{Interest rate on government bond} + \text{Risk premium}$$

Since we can readily determine the government bond interest rate, the only challenge is to estimate the risk premium.

When the risky asset is a common stock, it is useful to let history be our guide and recall from Table 5–1 that on average over the period 1926 to 1995, the annual return on common stocks exceeded that on government bonds by 7 percentage points. As a reward for bearing the added risk, common stockholders earned a 7 percentage point higher annual return than government bondholders. Treating this as a risk premium and adding it to a 1995 long-term government bond rate of 6.4 percent yields an estimate of 13.4 percent as the cost of equity capital for a typical company.

What is the logic of treating the 7 percentage point historical excess return as a risk premium? Essentially it is that over a long enough time, the return investors receive and what they expect to receive should approximate each other. For example, suppose investors expect a 20 percentage point excess return on common stocks but the actual return keeps turning out to be 3 percentage points. Then two things should happen: Investors should lower their expectations, and selling by disappointed investors should increase subsequent realized returns. Eventually expectations and reality should come into rough parity.

We now have an estimate of the cost of equity capital to an "average-risk" company, but of course few companies are precisely average-risk. How, then, can we customize our average cost expression to reflect the risk of a specific firm? The answer is to insert a "fudge factor," known as the company's *equity beta*, into the expression so that it becomes

$$\begin{array}{c}\text{Cost of equity}\\\text{capital}\end{array} = \begin{array}{c}\text{Interest rate on}\\\text{government bond}\end{array} + \beta_e \left(\begin{array}{c}\text{Historical excess return}\\\text{on common stock}\end{array} \right)$$

where β_e is the equity beta of the target company. Think of β_e as a scale factor reflecting the risk of the particular company's shares. For average-risk shares, β_e simply equals 1.0, and the historical risk premium applies directly. But for riskier shares, β_e exceeds 1.0, and the risk premium grows accordingly. Conversely, for safer shares, β_e is below 1.0, and only a fraction of the historical risk premium applies.

The appendix to this chapter offers a closer look at equity beta, including its conceptual underpinnings, a simple way to estimate beta, and examples of company and industry betas. Using methods described in the appendix, one source estimates that Analog Devices' equity beta in late 1995 was 1.60, implying well-above-average risk for the company's shares. This result should come as no surprise, for although ADI is very

T A B L E 8-2

Calculation of Analog Devices' Cost of Capital

Source	Amount ($ millions)	Percentage of Total	Cost after Tax	Weighted Cost
Debt	$ 82.4	2.8%	5.0%	0.1%
Equity	2,848.0	97.2	17.6	17.1%
			Cost of capital =	17.2%

conservatively financed, the volatile, unpredictable nature of its product markets suggests high equity risk. Inserting ADI's estimated equity beta into the preceding equation yields the following cost of equity capital:

$$\text{ADI's cost of equity capital} = 6.4\% + 1.60 \times 7.0\% = 17.6\%$$

Calculation of Analog Devices' Weighted-Average Cost of Capital

All that remains now is the figure work. Table 8–2 presents my estimate of Analog Devices' cost of capital in tabular form. ADI's weighted-average cost of capital is 17.2 percent. This means that in 1995, ADI had to earn at least this percentage return on the market value of existing assets to meet the expectations of creditors and shareholders and, by inference, to maintain share price.

In equation form:

$$K_W = \frac{(1 - 0.34)(7.5\%)(\$82.4 \text{ million}) + (17.6\%)(\$2,848.0 \text{ million})}{\$82.4 \text{ million} + \$2,848.0 \text{ million}}$$

$$= 17.2\%$$

The Cost of Capital in Investment Appraisal

The fact that the cost of capital is the return a company must earn on *existing assets* to meet creditor and shareholder expectations is an interesting detail, but we are after bigger game here: We want to use the cost of capital as an acceptance criterion for *new investments*.

Are there any problems in applying a concept derived for existing assets to new investments? Not if one critical assumption holds: The new investment must have the same risk existing assets do. If it does, the new

F I G U R E 8-3

An Investment's Risk-Adjusted Discount Rate Increases with Risk

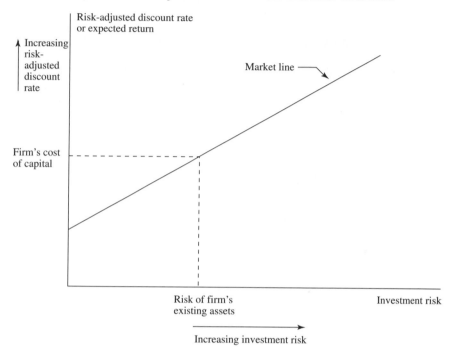

investment is essentially a "carbon copy" of existing assets, and the cost of capital is the appropriate risk-adjusted discount rate. If it does not, we must proceed more carefully.

The market line in Figure 8–3 clearly illustrates the importance of the equal-risk assumption. It emphasizes that the rate of return risk-averse individuals anticipate rises with risk. This means, for example, that management should demand a higher expected return when introducing a new product than when replacing aged equipment, because the new product is presumably riskier and therefore warrants a higher return. The figure also shows that a company's cost of capital is but one of many possible risk-adjusted discount rates, the one corresponding to the risk of the firm's existing assets. We conclude that the cost of capital is an appropriate acceptance criterion only when the risk of the new investment equals that of existing assets. For other investments, the cost of capital is inappropriate; but even when inappropriate itself, the cost of capital frequently serves as an important, practical keystone about which further adjustments are made.

Multiple Hurdle Rates

Many companies adjust for differing levels of investment risk by using multiple hurdle rates, with each rate applying to a different level of risk. For example, Analog Devices might use the following array:

Type of Investment	Discount Rate (%)
Replacement or repair	10.0
Cost reduction	13.0
Expansion	17.2
New product	23.0

Investments to expand capacity in existing products are essentially carbon-copy investments, so their hurdle rates equal Analog Devices' cost of capital. Other types of investments have a higher or lower hurdle rate, depending on their risk relative to expansion investments. Replacement or repair investments are the safest because virtually all of the cash flows are well known from past experience. Cost reduction investments are somewhat riskier because the magnitude of potential savings is uncertain. New-product investments are the riskiest type of all, because both revenues and costs are uncertain.

Multiple hurdle rates are consistent with risk aversion and with the market line, but the amount by which the hurdle rate should be adjusted for each level of risk is largely arbitrary. Whether the hurdle rate for cost reduction investments should be 3 or 5 percentage points below ADI's cost of capital cannot be determined objectively without a lot more work.

Rather than assign a different discount rate to each type of investment, some multidivision companies assign a different discount rate to each division. A potential advantage of this approach is that if a division competes against one or several single-product firms, the cost of capital of these competitors can be used as the division's hurdle rate for new investment. An offsetting disadvantage of divisional hurdle rates is the implicit assumption that all investments a division makes have the same business risk.

THE FALLACY OF THE MARGINAL COST OF CAPITAL

Some readers, especially engineers, look at equation 8–1 and naively conclude that it is possible to reduce a company's weighted-average cost of capital by using more of the cheap source of financing, debt, and less of the expensive source, equity. In other words, they conclude that increasing leverage will reduce the cost of capital. This reasoning, however, evidences an incomplete understanding of leverage. As we observed in the last chapter, increasing leverage increases the risk borne by shareholders. Because they are risk averse, shareholders react by demanding a higher return on their investment. Thus, K_E and, to a lesser extent, K_D rise as leverage increases. This means that increasing leverage affects a company's cost of capital in two opposing ways: Increasing use of cheap debt reduces K_W, but the rise in K_E and K_D that accompanies leverage added increases it.

To review this reasoning, ask yourself how you would respond to a subordinate who made the following argument in favor of an investment: "I know the company's cost of capital is 12 percent and the IRR of this carbon-copy investment is only 10 percent. But at the last directors' meeting, we decided to finance this year's investments with new debt. Since new debt has a cost of only about 4 percent after tax, it is clearly in our shareholders' interest to invest 4 percent money to earn a 10 percent return."

The subordinate's reasoning is incorrect. Financing with debt means increasing leverage and increasing K_E. Adding the change in K_E to the 4 percent interest cost means the true *marginal* cost of the debt is well above the interest cost. In fact, it is probably quite close to K_W.

FOUR PITFALLS IN THE USE OF DISCOUNTED CASH FLOW TECHNIQUES

You now know the basics of investment appraisal: Estimate the opportunity's annual, expected aftertax cash flows and discount them to the present at a risk-adjusted discount rate appropriate to the risk of the cash flows. When the opportunity is a "carbon-copy" investment, the firm's weighted-average cost of capital is the appropriate discount rate. In other instances, an upward or downward adjustment to the firm's cost of capital is necessary.

This brings us to a moment of truth. Having convinced you of the power of discounted cash flow techniques and illustrated in at least a general way how to incorporate risk into decision making, should I quit while ahead, or should I risk undermining your enthusiasm for the subject by acknowledging the existence of several pitfalls in the practical application of these techniques? In the interest of full disclosure, I will gingerly mention four such pitfalls. The first two are easily avoided once you are aware of them; the last two highlight important limitations of discounted cash flow techniques as conventionally applied. Collectively these pitfalls mean you need to master several more topics before attempting to pass as an expert.

The Entity Perspective versus the Equity Perspective

Any corporate investment partially financed with debt can be analyzed from either of two perspectives: that of the company, commonly known as the *entity* perspective, or that of its owners, often referred to as the *equity* perspective. As the following example demonstrates, these two perspectives are functionally equivalent in the sense that when properly applied they yield the same investment decision—but woe be to him who confuses the two.

Suppose ABC Enterprises has a capital structure composed of 40 percent debt, costing 5 percent after tax, and 60 percent equity, costing 20 percent. Its weighted-average cost of capital is therefore

$$K_W = 5\% \times 0.40 + 20\% \times 0.60 = 14\%$$

The company is considering an average-risk investment costing $100 million and promising an aftertax cash flow of $14 million a year in perpetuity. If undertaken, ABC plans to finance the investment with $40 million in new borrowings and $60 million in equity. Should ABC make the investment?

The Entity Perspective
The left-hand side of the following diagram shows the investment's cash flows from the entity perspective. Applying our now standard approach, the investment is a perpetuity with a 14 percent internal rate of return. Comparing this return to ABC's weighted-average cost of capital, also 14 percent, we conclude that the investment is marginal. Undertaking it will neither create nor destroy shareholder value.

The Equity Perspective
The right-hand side of the diagram shows the same investment from the owners' viewpoint, or the *equity* perspective. Because $40 million of the initial cost will be financed by debt, the equity outlay is only $60 million. Similarly, because $2 million after tax must be paid to creditors each year as interest, the residual cash flow to equity will be only $12 million. The

investment's internal rate of return from the equity perspective is therefore 20 percent.

Cash Flow Diagrams for ABC Enterprises' Investment

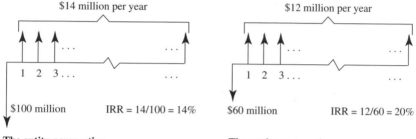

The entity perspective   The equity perspective

Does the fact that the return is now 20 percent mean the investment is suddenly an attractive one? Clearly, no. Because the equity cash flows are levered, they are riskier than the original cash flows and hence require a higher risk-adjusted discount rate. Indeed, the appropriate acceptance criterion for these equity cash flows is ABC's cost of equity capital, or 20 percent. (Remember, the discount rate should reflect the risk of the cash flows to be discounted.) Comparing the project's 20 percent IRR to equity with ABC's cost of equity, we again conclude that the investment is only marginal.

It is not an accident that the entity and equity perspectives yield the same result. Because the weighted-average cost of capital is defined to ensure that each supplier of capital receives a return equal to her opportunity cost, we know that an investment by ABC earning 14 percent, from the entity perspective, will earn just enough to service the debt and generate a 20 percent IRR on invested equity. Problems arise only when you mix the two perspectives, using K_E to discount entity cash flows or, more commonly, using K_W to discount equity cash flows.

Which perspective is better? Some of my best friends use the equity perspective, but I believe the entity perspective is easier to apply in practice. The problem with the equity perspective is that both the IRR to equity and the appropriate risk-adjusted discount rate vary with the amount of leverage used. The IRR to equity on ABC Enterprises' investment is 20 percent with $40 million of debt financing but jumps to 95 percent with $90 million of debt and rises to *infinity* with all-debt financing.

The interdependency between the means of financing and the risk-adjusted discount rate is easily handled in a classroom, but when real money is on the line, we often become so enthralled by the return-enhancing aspect of debt that we forget the required rate of return rises as well. Moreover, even when we remember that leverage increases risk as well as return, it is devilishly hard to estimate exactly how much the cost of equity should change with leverage.

Life is short. I recommend that you avoid unnecessary complications by using the entity perspective whenever possible. Assess the economic merit of the investment without regard to how it will be financed or how you will divvy up the spoils. If the investment meets this fundamental test, you can then turn to the nuances of how best to finance it.

Inflation

The second pitfall involves the improper handling of inflation. Too often managers ignore inflation when estimating an investment's cash flows but inadvertently include it in their discount rate. The effect of this mismatch is to make companies overly conservative in their investment appraisal, especially with regard to long-lived assets. Table 8–3 illustrates the point. A company with a 15 percent cost of capital is considering a $10 million, carbon-copy investment. The investment has a four-year life and is expected to increase production capacity by 10,000 units annually. Because the product sells for $900, the company estimates that annual revenues will rise $9 million ($900 × 10,000 units), which, after subtracting production costs, yields an increase in annual aftertax cash flows of $3.3 million. The IRR of the investment is calculated to be 12.1 percent, which is below the firm's cost of capital.

Did you spot the error? By assuming a constant selling price and constant production costs over four years, management has implicitly estimated real, or constant-dollar, cash flows, whereas the cost of capital as calculated earlier in the chapter is a nominal one. It is nominal because both the cost of debt and the cost of equity include a premium for expected inflation.

The key to capital budgeting under inflation is to always compare like to like. When cash flows are in nominal dollars, use a nominal discount rate. When cash flows are in real, or constant, dollars, use a real discount rate. The bottom portion of Table 8–3 illustrates a proper evaluation of the investment. After including a 5 percent annual increase in

T A B L E   8–3

When Evaluating Investments under Inflation, Always Compare Nominal
Cash Flows to a Nominal Discount Rate or Real Cash Flows to a Real
Discount Rate ($ millions)

*(a) Incorrect Investment Evaluation Comparing Real Cash Flows to a Nominal
Discount Rate*

	1998	1999	2000	2001	2002
Aftertax cash flow	($10.0)	$3.3	$3.3	$3.3	$3.3

IRR = 12.1%

K_W = 15%

Decision: Reject

*(b) Correct Investment Evaluation Comparing Nominal Cash Flows to Nominal
Discount Rate*

	1998	1999	2000	2001	2002
Aftertax cash flow	($10.0)	$3.5	$3.8	$4.0	$4.3

IRR = 20.0%

K_W = 15%

Decision: Accept

selling price and in variable production costs, the expected nominal cash
flows from the investment are as shown. As one would expect, the nominal
cash flows exceed the constant-dollar cash flows by a growing amount in
each year. The IRR of these flows is 20 percent, which now exceeds the
firm's cost of capital.[2]

Real Options

The third pitfall involves the possible omission of important managerial
options inherent in many corporate investment opportunities. These options seldom arise in simple textbook illustrations because most textbooks,

---

2 An alternative approach would have been to calculate the firm's real cost of capital and
  compare it to a real IRR. But because this approach is more work and is fraught with
  potential errors, I recommend working with nominal cash flows and a nominal discount
  rate instead.

in their emphasis on the mechanical dimensions of investment appraisal, implicitly assume investments are now-or-never opportunities and, once undertaken, management has no control over the outcome of an investment. Instead, simple textbook examples implicitly assume that, after having selected their favorite investments, managers stand idly by as Dame Fate rolls the dice.

Such passivity may be an appropriate assumption when the investments under review are stocks and bonds, but it can be dangerously inappropriate in other instances when managers have the ability to alter a project during its life. Examples of what are often called *real options*, in recognition of their formal equivalence to traded financial options, include the option to defer the investment to a later date, the option to abandon an investment if cash flows do not meet expectations, the option to modify the scale of operations as demand varies, the option to alter the mix of inputs as raw materials prices change, and the option to make follow-on investments if the initial investment is successful. In each case, management can change the nature or the scope of the investment in response to information not known at the time of the original decision. Such options enhance investment value because they give management the right, but not the obligation, to undertake a future activity. The importance of real options in valuing certain investments can be appreciated by noting that a pure R&D investment could never be justified were it not for the option such expenditures give management to exploit positive research results with follow-on investments.

Here is an example of how real options can affect the value of an investment.[3] General Design Corporation is considering investing $100 million to develop a new line of high-speed semiconductors based on an emerging diamond film technology. Part *a* of Table 8–4 shows that the investment's anticipated life is five years and annual cash flows are expected to be $60 million if the project succeeds and − $40 million if it fails. Management pegs the chance of success at only 50 percent. If General Design requires an 8 percent return on low-risk investments, 15 percent on moderate-risk investments, and 25 percent on high-risk investments, what should it do?

---

3 Strictly speaking, the discounted cash flow approach used in this example is only approximately correct. The correct approach relies on option pricing theory, which is beyond the scope of this book. See Avinash K. Dixit and Robert S. Pindyck, *Investment under Uncertainty* (Princeton, NJ: Princeton University Press, 1994), for a more rigorous exposition.

T A B L E   8–4

General Design's Diamond Film Project ($ millions)

(a) Stage 1: Ignoring Option to Abandon, Probability of Success = 50%

		Expected Aftertax Cash Flows in Year				
	0	**1**	**2**	**3**	**4**	**5**
Success	($100)	$ 60	$ 60	$ 60	$ 60	$ 60
Failure	($100)	–40	–40	–40	–40	–40
Expected	($100)	$ 10	$ 10	$ 10	$ 10	$ 10
NPV at 25% =	($ 73)					

(b) Stage 1: Including Option to Abandon, Probability of Success = 50%

		Expected Aftertax Cash Flows in Year				
	0	**1**	**2**	**3**	**4**	**5**
Success	($100)	$ 60	$ 60	$ 60	$ 60	$ 60
Failure	($100)	–40	–40	20	0	0
Expected	($100)	$ 10	$ 10	$ 40	$ 30	$ 30
NPV at 25% =	($ 43)					

(c) Stage 2: Option to Expand, Probability of Success (Assuming Stage 1 Successful) = 90%

			Expected Aftertax Cash Flows in Year				
	0	**1**	**2**	**3**	**4**	**5**	**6**	**7**
Success			($500)	$300	$300	$300	$300	$300
Failure			($500)	–200	–200	100	0	0
Expected			($500)	$250	$250	$280	$270	$270
NPV at 25% =		$130						
Total NPV at 25% (Stage 1 + 0.50 × Stage 2) = $22								

The Option to Abandon

Calculating expected cash flows and discounting at a 25 percent rate reflecting the venture's high risk, the net present value is large and negative, – $73 million. The diamond film project is clearly unacceptable. But on reflection, is it likely that General Design will passively incur losses for five years if the technology is found to be unworkable early on? Having once shot themselves in the foot, will managers continue shooting for another four years, or have they the sense to quit?

Assuming more realistically that management has the option to abandon the venture after two years at a salvage value of, say, $20 million, the revised cash flows appear in part *b* of Table 8–4. Note that the abandonment option is worth $30 million, bringing the NPV up to − $43 million.

The Option to Grow

A chief attraction of many new-technology investments is that success today creates the option to make highly profitable follow-on investments tomorrow, investments that are possible only because management took an intelligent gamble today. In this vein, suppose General Design believes initial success in diamond films will open the door to a stage 2, follow-on investment in two years that is precisely five times the size of today's stage 1 investment.

The probability assigned to a stage 2 success is critical. In management's eyes, if the stage 2 investment were made today, it would probably be no more likely to succeed than would stage 1; after all, stage 2 is the same technology, only five times as large. Consequently if made today, stage 2's NPV would just be five times as negative as stage 1's. But management does not have to make a decision on stage 2 today. It has the option to defer the decision until the initial results from stage 1 are in, and will thus be able to make a more informed choice. Supposing stage 2 will be undertaken only if stage 1 succeeds and that the chance of a stage 2 success given that stage 1 succeeded is 90 percent, part c in Table 8–4 shows that the NPV of the stage 2 investment at time zero is $130 million. Because General Design stands only a 50 percent chance of making the stage 2 investment, its expected NPV is half this amount, or $65 million. Adding the expected NPVs of both stages, the total NPV is now a healthy $22 million, and this ignores any stage 3 or stage 4 investments that might logically follow a stage 2 success. Proper consideration of the options embedded in General Design's investment transforms it from a clunker into a winner.

The moral should be clear: Failure to recognize and value these and other real options implicit in many corporate investments will make executives inappropriately timid in the face of high-risk, high-payoff opportunities.

Excessive Risk Adjustment

Our last pitfall is a subtle one concerning the proper use of risk-adjusted discount rates. Adding an increment to the discount rate to adjust for an investment's risk makes intuitive sense. You need to be aware, however,

T A B L E 8–5

Use of a Constant Risk-Adjusted Discount Rate Implies That Risk Increases with the Remoteness of a Cash Flow (risk-free rate = 5%; risk-adjusted rate = 10%)

| | Present Value of $1 | |
	Received in 1 Year	Received in 10 Years
Risk-free	$0.952	$0.614
Risk-adjusted	0.909	0.386
Reduction in present value due to risk	0.043	0.228

that as you apply this discount rate to more distant cash flows, the arithmetic of the discounting process compounds the risk adjustment. Table 8–5 illustrates the effect. It shows the present value of $1 in one year and in 10 years, first at a risk-free discount rate of 5 percent and then at a risk-adjusted rate of 10 percent. Comparing these present values, note that addition of the risk premium knocks a modest 4.3 cents off the value of a dollar in one year but a sizable 22.8 cents off in 10 years. Clearly, use of a constant risk-adjusted discount rate is appropriate only when the risk of a cash flow grows as the cash flow recedes farther into the future.

For many, if not most, business investments, the assumption that risk increases with the remoteness of a cash flow is quite appropriate, but as we will see by looking again at General Design's diamond film project, this is not always the case.

Recall that General Design is contemplating a possible two-stage investment. The first stage, costing $100 million, is attractive chiefly because it gives management the option to make a much more lucrative follow-on investment. Because both stages depend on a new, untested diamond film technology, the discount rate used throughout the analysis was General Design's high-risk hurdle rate of 25 percent.

Given the speculative nature of this investment, many executives would argue that it is entirely appropriate to use a high risk-adjusted discount rate throughout. But is it really? The investment clearly involves high risk, but because most of the risk will be resolved in the first two years, use of a constant risk-adjusted discount rate is overly conservative.

To see the logic, suppose you are at time 2, stage 1 has been successful, and the company is about to launch stage 2. Because the stage 2 cash
flows are now relatively certain, their value *at time 2* is their expected
values, as shown in part *c* of Table 8–4, *discounted at 15 percent*, the rate
applicable to moderate-risk investments. This amounts to $330 million.

As seen from the present, therefore, General Design's decision to
invest in stage 1 gives it a 50 percent chance at a follow-on investment
worth $330 million in two years. And because the next two years are high
risk, we can find the present value of stage 2 today by discounting the $330
million time 2 value to the present at 25 percent:

$$\text{Expected present value of stage 2 investment} = 0.50 \times \$330 \text{ million} \times 0.640$$
$$= \$106 \text{ million}$$

Adding this sum to the stage 1 NPV of – $43 million yields a total NPV of
$63 million. Explicit recognition of the two risk phases in General De-
sign's investment adds another $41 million to its present worth.

To recap, whenever you encounter an investment with two or more
distinct risk phases, be careful about using a constant risk-adjusted discount rate, for although such investments may be comparatively rare, they
are also frequently the type of opportunities companies can ill afford to
waste.

ECONOMIC VALUE ADDED

In late 1993, *Fortune* ran a cover story entitled "The Real Key to Creating
Wealth," which trumpeted, "Rewarded by knockout results, managers
and investors are peering into the heart of what makes businesses valuable
by using a tool called Economic Value Added."[4] With publicity like this
and a steady stream of laudatory articles since, it is little wonder that many
otherwise placid executives and investors are suddenly interested in what
Fortune calls "today's hottest financial idea and getting hotter."

Having mastered the intricacies of the cost of capital, you will find
economic value added, or EVA, to be little more than a restatement of
what you already know. The central message of this and the preceding
chapter has been that an investment creates value for its owners only
when its expected return exceeds its cost of capital. In essence, EVA

---

4 Shawn Tully, "The Real Key to Creating Wealth," *Fortune*, September 20, 1993, p. 38.

simply extends the cost of capital imperative to performance appraisal. It says that a company or a business unit creates value for owners only when its operating income exceeds the cost of capital employed. In symbols

$$EVA = EBIT(1 - \text{Tax rate}) - K_w C$$

where $EBIT(1 - \text{Tax rate})$ is the unit's aftertax operating income, K_w is its weighted-average cost of capital, and C is the capital employed by the unit. $K_w C$, then, represents an annual capital charge. The capital-employed variable, C, represents the money invested in the unit over time by creditors and owners. It can be approximated by making a number of technical accounting adjustments to the sum of interest-bearing debt plus the book value of equity.[5]

EVA and Investment Analysis

As we will see shortly, an important attribute of economic value added is that the present value of an investment's annual EVA stream equals the investment's NPV. This makes it possible to talk about investment appraisal in terms of EVA rather than NPV—provided, of course, there is something to be gained by doing so. The numerical example in Table 8–6 demonstrates this equality. Part *a* of the table is a conventional net present value analysis of a very simple investment. The investment requires an initial outlay of $100, which will be depreciated on a straight-line basis to zero over four years. Adding depreciation to prospective income after tax and discounting the resulting aftertax cash flow at 10 percent yields an NPV of $58.50.

Part *b* of the table presents a discounted EVA treatment of the same investment. To calculate EVA, we need a figure for the annual opportunity cost of capital employed. This equals the cost of capital times the book value of the investment at the beginning of each year. Subtracting this quantity from EBIT after tax yields annual project EVA, which, discounted at 10 percent, yields a discounted EVA of $58.50—precisely the NPV calculated in part *a*. Thus, another way to evaluate investment opportunities, which is equivalent to NPV analysis, is to calculate the present value of the investment's annual EVA.

---

5 For details, see G. Bennett Stewart III, *The Quest for Value* (New York: HarperBusiness. 1991).

T A B L E 8–6

Discounting an Investment's Annual EVA Stream Is Equivalent to
Calculating the Investment's NPV

(a) Standard NPV Analysis

	Year				
	0	1	2	3	4
Initial investment	−$100.00				
Revenue		$80.00	$80.00	$80.00	$80.00
Cash expenses		13.33	13.33	13.33	13.33
Depreciation		25.00	25.00	25.00	25.00
Income before tax		41.67	41.67	41.67	41.67
Tax at 40%		16.67	16.67	16.67	16.67
Income after tax		25.00	25.00	25.00	25.00
Depreciation		25.00	25.00	25.00	25.00
Aftertax cash flow	−$100.00	$50.00	$50.00	$50.00	$50.00
NPV at 10%	$58.50				

(b) Discounted EVA Analysis

	Year				
	0	1	2	3	4
Capital employed		$100.00	$75.00	$50.00	$25.00
K_W		0.10	0.10	0.10	0.10
$K_W \times$ Capital		10.00	7.50	5.00	2.50
EBIT$(1 - t)$		25.00	25.00	25.00	25.00
$- K_W \times$ Capital		10.00	7.50	5.00	2.50
EVA		$15.00	$17.50	$20.00	$22.50
EVA discounted at 10%	$58.50				

EVA's Appeal

If EVA looks vaguely familiar, it should. The fact that capital provided by
creditors and owners is costly and this cost is relevant for measuring
economic performance has been recognized for many years. Indeed, we
made the point in Chapter 1 when we noted that accounting income overstates true, economic income because it ignores the cost of equity. So

novelty cannot explain EVA's sudden appeal, nor can EVA's superiority to return on investment, ROI, as a measure of business unit performance. For the problems with ROI, generally defined as operating income divided by operating assets, have been widely known for decades without convincing many companies to abandon ROI in favor of EVA or, indeed, without creating a stir of any kind outside of academe.[6] So why the sudden appeal of EVA after all these years?

The answer, I think, is that EVA, in its present incarnation, addresses a pervasive business problem, one that has greatly undermined many managers' acceptance of modern finance. EVA's appeal is that it promises to integrate three crucial management functions: capital budgeting, performance appraisal, and incentive compensation. Together these functions are intended to positively shape management behavior, but too often they work at cross purposes, giving managers apparently confusing and often conflicting signals as to the best course of action. Thus, in the absence of EVA, operating managers often must contend with a welter of seemingly unrelated and sometimes contradictory performance indicators and decision aids—including ROI, EPS, NPV, IRR, and so on—and all the while the managers' bonus plan changes more often than the Italian government. A natural response on the part of operating managers to this apparent confusion has been to take none of it very seriously and rely instead on common sense to muddle through.

Contrast this with EVA-based management. The business goal is to create EVA. Capital budgeting decisions are based on discounted EVA at an appropriate cost of capital. Unit EVA, or change in EVA, measures business unit performance, and incentive compensation depends on unit EVA relative to an appropriate target—clean, simple, and straightforward. Consultants Stern Stewart & Company have even developed a clever method of distributing a manager's bonus over several periods that puts middle managers at risk much as though they were owners and also helps to discourage myopic, single-period decision making.[7]

---

6 Here is one problem with ROI. Imagine a division with an ROI of only 2 percent and ask what type of investments the division manager is apt to favor. Charged with the task of raising division ROI, the manager will naturally look favorably on any investment promising an ROI above 2 percent regardless of the investment's NPV. Conversely, managers in divisions with high ROIs will be quite conservative in their investment decisions for fear of lowering ROI. A company in which unsuccessful divisions invest aggressively while successful ones invest conservatively is probably not what shareholders want to see.

7 See Stewart, *The Quest for Value*, Chapter 6.

EVA certainly has its own problems, and some of its virtues are more cosmetic than real. But it does address an important barrier to the acceptance of the financial way of thinking in many companies, and for this reason alone deserves our attention. Or, as *Fortune* might put it, "EVA promises to complete the transformation of value creation from a mere slogan into a powerful management tool, one that may at last move modern finance out of the classroom and into the boardroom—perhaps even onto the shop floor!"

A CAUTIONARY NOTE

An always present danger when using analytic or numerical techniques in business decision making is that the "hard facts" will assume exaggerated importance compared to more qualitative issues and that the manipulation of these facts will become a substitute for creative effort. It is important to bear in mind that numbers and theories don't get things done; people do. And the best of investments will fail unless capable workers are committed to their success. As Barbara Tuchman put it in another context, "In military as in other human affairs will is what makes things happen. There are circumstances that can modify or nullify it, but for offense or defense its presence is essential and its absence fatal."[8]

---

8 Barbara W. Tuchman, *Stilwell and the American Experience in China 1911–1945* (New York: Bantam Books, 1971), pp. 561–62.

Diversification and β-Risk

In the chapter, we observed that the expected rate of return on a risky asset can be written as

$$\text{Expected return on risky asset} = \text{Interest rate on government bonds} + \text{Risk premium}$$

where the interest rate on government bonds is itself the sum of a risk-free interest rate and an inflation premium. We noted too that when the risky asset in question is a typical company's common stock, one measure of the risk premium is the *excess* return earned by common shareholders relative to government bondholders over a long period. Here we want to discuss the risk premium in more detail and relate it to risk measures that include the effects of diversification.

We can repeat the above equation in symbols by letting i equal the prevailing interest rate on government bonds, R_m the average annual return on a well-diversified portfolio of common stocks over a long period, and i_b the average annual return on government bonds over the same period.

$$\text{Expected return on typical company's common stock} = i + (R_m - i_b)$$

In late 1995, the interest rate on 10-year government bonds was 5.7 percent. Using the figures in Table 5–1, the average annual return investors earned in the 500 stocks comprising the Standard & Poor's 500 stock index over the period 1926 to 1995 was 12.5 percent, whereas the average annual return on government bonds over the same period was 5.5 percent. This suggests a risk premium, $(R_m - i_b)$, of 7.0 percent and an expected return on a typical company's stock, given prevailing interest rates of 12.7 percent (5.7% + 7.0%).

The preceding equation provides an estimate of a typical company's cost of equity capital, where by *typical* I mean a company having average risk.[1] However, if we want to use this equation to estimate the cost of capital of an *atypical* company, or if we want to estimate the expected return on any other kind of risky asset, we must modify the equation to

---

1 Careful study of this topic will reveal that estimating an equity risk premium is not quite as simple as implied here. The most complete discussion of the topic of which I am aware is Chapter 8 in *SBBI, Stocks, Bonds, Bills and Inflation, 1994 Yearbook* (Chicago: Ibbotson Associates, 1994), where, among other things, it is observed that the equity risk premium should vary with the expected life of the investment under consideration. As above, a "long-horizon" equity risk premium is the excess realized return on common stocks relative to long-term government bonds. A short-horizon equity risk premium would substitute the short-term government bill rate for the long-term bond rate.

reflect the particular risk of the company or asset in question. The following equation includes the necessary modification. Letting R_j equal the expected rate of return on risky asset j,

$$\begin{matrix} \text{Expected} \\ \text{return on} \\ \text{risky asset } j \end{matrix} = \begin{matrix} \text{Interest rate} \\ \text{on government} \\ \text{bonds} \end{matrix} + \begin{matrix} \beta\text{-risk} \\ \text{asset } j \end{matrix} \times \begin{matrix} \text{Risk} \\ \text{premium} \end{matrix}$$

$$R_j = \qquad i + \beta_j(R_m - i_b) \qquad\qquad\qquad (8A\text{--}1)$$

β_j is known as the asset's β-*risk*, or its *volatility*. We will talk more about the calculation of β_j in a few paragraphs. For now, think of it as simply the risk of asset j relative to that of the common stock portfolio, m:

$$\beta_j = \frac{\text{Risk of asset } j}{\text{Risk of portfolio } m}$$

If the risk of asset j is equal to that of a typical company's common stock, $\beta_j = 1.0$ and the equation is just as before. If the asset is of above-average risk, β_j exceeds 1.0, and if it is of below-average risk, β_j is less than 1.0.

In recent decades, β-risk has become an important factor in security analysis, so important that many stockbrokerage companies and investment advisers regularly publish the βs for virtually all publicly traded common stocks. Table 8A–1 presents year-end 1995 βs for a representative sample of firms, as well as industry-average βs. Recalling that a β of 1.0 is typical, or average, note that the range for company βs in the table is from a high of 1.70 for Dell Computer to a low of 0.39 for Allegheny Power.

With knowledge of a company's β, it becomes easy to use equation 8A–1 to estimate a company's cost of equity capital. For example, Dell Computer's cost of equity in 1995 according to this equation was

$$\begin{aligned} R_j &= i + \beta_j(R_m - i_b) \\ &= 5.7\% + 1.70(12.5\% - 5.5\%) \\ &= 17.6\% \end{aligned}$$

In contrast, Allegheny Power's was

$$5.7\% + 0.39(12.5\% - 5.5\%) = 8.4\%$$

At a conceptual level, equation 8A–1 is quite important, for it tells us the rate of return we should expect on any risky asset and how that return varies with the asset's β-risk. Looking at Figure 8–1, another way to say the same thing is that equation 8A–1 is the equation of the market line. To

T A B L E   8A–1

Representative Industry and Company Betas

Industry Median Betas		Company Betas	
Industry*	**Beta**	**Company**	**Beta**
Air transportation (11)	1.38	Advanced Micro Devices	1.51
Aircraft (7)	0.89	Alaska Air	1.42
Apparel (28)	1.29	Allegheny Power	0.39
Banks (98)	1.02	American Brands	0.85
Capital equipment (33)	1.13	Analog Devices	1.59
Communications equipment (40)	1.36	Apple Computer	1.66
Computers—micro (9)	1.66	AT&T	0.83
Electronic components (50)	1.46	Baltimore Gas & Electric	0.43
Farm machinery (5)	0.86	BankAmerica Corp.	1.11
Food and related (40)	0.83	Biogen	1.56
Gold & precious metals (4)	0.56	Boeing	0.98
Health care, general (60)	1.17	Campbell Soup	0.87
Hospital supply & mgt. (62)	1.42	Deere	0.77
Motion pictures (2)	1.28	Dell Computer	1.70
Motor vehicles (10)	1.13	Duke Power	0.44
Petroleum—international (5)	0.73	General Electric	1.05
Retail—food stores (20)	0.92	Hewlett-Packard	1.42
Utilities—electric (82)	0.42	Microsoft	1.27
Utilities—telephone (17)	0.72	Wal-Mart Stores	1.17

*Numbers in parentheses are number of firms in industry.

Source: Reprinted by permission of Vestek Systems, San Francisco, from *Investment Data Book*, January 1996.

determine the appropriate risk-adjusted discount rate for any risky asset, all we need to do is calculate the asset's β, plug this value into equation 8A–1, and calculate the expected return on the asset. This expected return, denoted by R_j, is the correct risk-adjusted discount rate for investment evaluation.

Diversification

To understand β-risk more fully, we need to take a slight detour and talk about risk in general. Table 8A–2 presents information about two very simple risky investments: purchase of an ice cream stand and an umbrella shop. For simplicity, we will consider only two possible states for

T A B L E 8A–2

Diversification Reduces Risk

Investment	Weather	Probability	Outcome	Weighted Outcome
Ice cream stand	Sun	0.40	$600	$240
	Rain	0.60	−200	−120
			Expected outcome	$120
Umbrella shop	Sun	0.40	−$300	−$120
	Rain	0.60	500	300
			Expected outcome	$180
Portfolio:	Sun	0.40	$300	$120
Ice cream stand				
and umbrella shop	Rain	0.60	300	180
			Expected outcome	$300

tomorrow's weather: sun or rain. Purchase of an ice cream stand is clearly a risky undertaking, since the investor stands to make $600 if it is sunny tomorrow but lose $200 if it rains. The umbrella shop is also risky, since the investor will lose $300 if tomorrow is sunny but will make $500 if it rains.

Yet despite the fact that these two investments are risky when viewed in isolation, they are not risky when viewed as members of a portfolio containing both investments. In a portfolio, the losses and gains from the two investments counterbalance each other in each state so that regardless of tomorrow's weather, the outcome is a riskless $300. The expected outcome from the portfolio is the sum of the expected outcomes from each investment in the portfolio, but the risk of the portfolio is zero.

This is an extreme example, but it does illustrate an important fact: When you own a portfolio of assets, the relevant measure of risk is not the asset's risk in isolation but its risk as part of the portfolio. And, as the example demonstrates, the difference between these two perspectives can be substantial.

An asset's risk in isolation is greater than its portfolio risk whenever the asset's cash flows and the portfolio's cash flows are less than perfectly correlated. In this commonplace situation, some of the asset's cash flow variability is offset by variability in the portfolio's cash flows, and the effective risk the investor bears is reduced. Look again at Table 8–2A. The ice cream stand cash flows are highly variable, but because they are perfectly inversely correlated with those from the umbrella shop, cash flow variability for the two investments disappears. An "averaging out" process occurs when assets are added to a portfolio that reduces risk.

Because most business investments are dependent to some extent on the same underlying business cycle, it is highly unusual to find investment opportunities with perfectly inversely correlated cash flows as in the ice cream stand–umbrella shop example. However, the described diversification effect still exists. Whenever investment cash flows are less than perfectly positively correlated—whenever individual investments are unique in some respects—an investment's risk in a portfolio context is less than its risk in isolation.

Let us refer to an asset's risk in isolation as its *total risk* and to its risk as part of a portfolio as its *nondiversifiable risk*. This is the risk remaining after the rest has been diversified away in the portfolio. The part that is diversified away is known as the asset's *diversifiable risk* (surprise!). Then, for any risky asset j,

$$\frac{\text{Total risk}}{\text{of asset } j} = \frac{\text{Nondiversifiable}}{\text{risk of asset } j} + \frac{\text{Diversifiable}}{\text{risk of asset } j}$$

From the preceding discussion, we know that the portion of an asset's total risk that is nondiversifiable depends on the correlation of the returns on the asset and on the portfolio. When the correlation is high, nondiversifiable risk is a large fraction of total risk, and vice versa. To say the same thing in symbols, let σ_j equal asset j's total risk and ρ_{jm} equal a scale factor reflecting the degree to which asset j's returns correlate with those of portfolio m. Then

$$\text{Nondiversifiable risk of asset } j = \rho_{jm}\sigma_j$$

(ρ and σ are lowercase Greek symbols for rho and sigma, respectively. The equation would perhaps appear less daunting had I used a and b instead, but ρ and σ have become standard notation in the literature.)

Studying this expression, the scale factor, ρ_{jm}, can have any value between $+1.00$ and -1.00. At one extreme, when the returns on asset j and portfolio m are perfectly positively correlated, $\rho_{jm} = 1.00$ and nondiversifiable risk equals total risk. In this case, no benefits occur from diversification. At the other extreme, when the returns on asset j and portfolio m are perfectly negatively correlated, as in the ice cream stand–umbrella shop example, $\rho_{jm} = -1.00$, and nondiversifiable risk is negative. This means that addition of an appropriate amount of asset j to the portfolio will eliminate risk entirely. For most business investments, ρ_{jm} is in the range 0.5 to 0.8, meaning 20 to 50 percent of an investment's total risk can be diversified away.

Measuring Beta

We are now ready to reconsider beta risk. Recall that β_j was described as the ratio of two risks and defined as

$$\beta_j = \frac{\text{Risk of asset } j}{\text{Risk of portfolio } m}$$

We now know that when diversification is possible, the relevant measure of asset j's risk is its nondiversifiable risk. Consequently,

$$\beta_j = \frac{\rho_{jm}\sigma_j}{\rho_{mm}\sigma_m}$$

This expression says that the beta risk of asset j is the ratio of j's nondiversifiable risk to the nondiversifiable risk of the analyst's portfolio. However, a moment's reflection should convince you that ρ_{mm} equals 1.00 because any asset's or any portfolio's return must be perfectly positively correlated with itself. Thus,

$$\beta_j = \frac{\rho_{jm}\sigma_j}{\sigma_m} \tag{8A–2}$$

If you have studied a little statistics, it will come as no surprise to learn that σ_j and σ_m are commonly defined as the *standard deviation* of returns for asset j and portfolio m, respectively, and ρ_{jm} is the *correlation coefficient* between these returns. Using these definitions and equation 8A–2, the betas appearing in Table 8A–1 were calculated as follows. First, for each stock calculate the monthly return to investors, including price appreciation and dividends, over the past five years. Then calculate the average monthly return and the standard deviation of returns about this average. The latter is σ_j. Second, go through the same exercise for a broad portfolio of common stocks such as the Standard & Poor's 500 stock averages. This generates σ_m. Third, calculate the correlation coefficient, ρ_{jm}, between the monthly returns for stock j and the portfolio.

Fourth, plug these numbers into equation 8A–2 to calculate the stock's β. Or, if you know a little regression analysis, simply regress r_j on r_m. The slope of this line is β_j.

Using Beta in Investment Evaluation

Beta can be used two ways in investment evaluation. As already suggested, one way is to use the beta of the company's common stock to calculate the firm's cost of equity and its weighted average cost of capital.

A more direct approach is to calculate the beta of an individual investment and plug it into equation 8A–1 to calculate the investment's risk-adjusted discount rate. This reduces risk adjustment to a totally mechanical, objective exercise. The approach has obvious conceptual appeal, but a number of problems must be solved before it can be applied in practice. The most serious is that there is usually no objective way to estimate an investment's beta. Some researchers have experimented with using the betas of publicly traded, single-product companies engaged in the same business as the proposed investment as surrogates for the investment's beta. But this has proven to be a complicated, imprecise exercise. One difficulty is that a company's beta depends on leverage as well as on business risk. So before using a company beta as a surrogate for an investment's beta, it is necessary to eliminate the effect of leverage. This can be done, but it's not easy. A second difficulty pervading all applications is that the real object of interest is the beta that will prevail in future years. But because this is unknown, we must calculate a historical beta and assume it will hold in the future. Empirical studies of beta over time suggest that this is a reasonable, but not infallible, assumption.

The bottom line in practice is that beta is useful for estimating a company's cost of equity capital. However, the calculation of project betas is still more a glimmer in the eyes of Ph.D. students.

Beta Risk and Conglomerate Diversification

Some executives have seized on the idea that diversification reduces risk as a justification for conglomerate diversification. Even when merger promises no increase in profitability, it is said to be beneficial because the resulting diversification reduces the risk of company cash flows. Because shareholders are risk averse, this reduction in risk is said to increase the value of the firm.

Such reasoning is at best incomplete. If shareholders wanted the risk reduction benefits of such a conglomerate merger, they could achieve them much more simply by just owning shares of the two independent companies in their own portfolios. Shareholders are not dependent on company management for such benefits. Executives intent on acquiring other firms must look elsewhere to find a rationale for their actions.

C H A P T E R   S U M M A R Y

1. This chapter incorporated risk into investment evaluation, with particular emphasis on risk-adjusted discount rates and the cost of capital.

2. Investments involve a trade-off between risk and return. The appropriate question when evaluating investment opportunities is not "What's the rate of return?" but "Is the return sufficient to justify the risk?"

3. *Risk* refers to the range of possible outcomes for an investment. Sometimes risk can be calculated objectively, but usually risk estimation must be subjective.

4. The most popular, practical technique for incorporating risk into investment decisions uses a risk-adjusted discount rate in which the analyst adds a premium to the discount rate that reflects the perceived risk of the project.

5. The cost of capital is a risk-adjusted discount rate suitable for a firm's average-risk, or carbon-copy, investments. It is the average cost of individual capital sources, weighted by their relative importance in the firm's capital structure. Average-risk investments yielding returns above the cost of capital create value and increase stock price.

6. Estimating the cost of equity is the most difficult step in measuring the cost of capital. For most businesses, the best estimate is the current cost of government borrowing plus the company's equity beta times a risk premium based on historical experience of about 7 percentage points. If the equity is above or below average risk, it is necessary to adjust the risk premium accordingly.

7. It is also necessary to raise or lower the discount rate relative to the cost of capital, depending on whether a specific project is above or below average risk for the business.

8. Leveraged investments can be analyzed from the perspective of the firm making the investment (the entity perspective) or from that of the equity owner (the equity perspective). Used properly, the two perspectives yield the same investment decisions, but for practical reasons, I recommend use of the entity perspective whenever possible.

9. Under inflation, one must always use nominal cash flows and a nominal discount rate or real cash flows and a real discount rate. Never mix the two.

10. Do not overlook real options, such as the option to abandon or the option to expand, when evaluating corporate investment opportunities.

11. A constant risk-adjusted discount rate should not be used to evaluate investments with two or more distinct risk phases. To evaluate such investments, begin with the most distant phase and use a risk-adjusted rate that is appropriate to each phase.

12. Economic value added equals a business unit's operating income after tax less a charge for the opportunity cost of the capital employed. EVA has the potential to integrate capital budgeting, performance appraisal, and incentive compensation.

13. Proper technique is never a substitute for thought, work, or leadership. People, not analysis, get things done.

ADDITIONAL READING

Brealey, Richard, and Stewart Myers. *Principles of Corporate Finance*. 5th ed. New York: McGraw-Hill, 1996.
   A leading graduate text. Very well written, almost lively. Part two, "Risk," is especially good. About $75.00.

Dixit, Avinash K., and Robert S. Pindyck. "The Options Approach to Capital Investment." *Harvard Business Review*, May–June 1995, pp. 105–15.
   A thought-provoking introduction to the importance of real options in capital investment and a critique of conventional discounted cash flow analysis.

Hodder, James E., and Henry E. Riggs. "Pitfalls in Evaluating Risky Projects." *Harvard Business Review*, January–February 1985, pp. 128–35.
   A thorough discussion of inflation and excessive risk adjustment in capital budgeting.

Myers, Stewart C. "Finance Theory and Financial Strategy." *Midland Corporate Finance Journal* (renamed *Bank of America Journal of Applied Corporate Finance*), Spring 1987, pp. 6–13.
   A nontechnical look at the integration, or lack thereof, of strategic planning and finance theory. Especially good on challenges to the use of discounted cash flow techniques in strategic decision making. Covers the four pitfalls mentioned in this chapter.
Stewart, G. Bennett, III. *The Quest for Value*. New York: HarperBusiness, 1991. 781 pages.
   A stimulating and provocative discussion of the implications of modern finance for corporations. Analyzes finance-driven company strategies, with particular emphasis on economic value added. An insightful translation of finance theory into practice.

CHAPTER PROBLEMS

1. Your company's weighted-average cost of capital is 12 percent. You believe the company should make a particular investment, but its internal rate of return is only 10 percent. What logical arguments would you use to convince your boss to make the investment despite its low rate of return? Is it possible that making investments with returns below capital costs will create value? If so, how?

2. How will a decrease in financial leverage affect a company's cost of equity capital, if at all? How will it affect a company's equity beta? Looking at equation 8A–2, which term, if any, on the right-hand side varies with leverage?

3. Looking at Figure 8–1, explain why a company should reject investment opportunities lying below the market line and accept those lying above it.

4. You have the following information about Surelock Homes, a lock manufacturer:

Stock price per share	$20.00
Equity shares outstanding	5 million
Yield to maturity on debt	8%
Book value of interest-bearing debt	$125 million
Coupon interest rate on debt	9%
Market value of debt	$130 million
Market value of equity	$100 million
Book value of equity	$55 million
Cost of equity capital	14%
Tax rate	40%

Surelock is contemplating what for the company is an average-risk investment costing $20 million and promising an annual aftertax cash flow of $2 million in perpetuity.
a. What is the internal rate of return on the investment?
b. What is Surelock's weighted-average cost of capital?
c. If this investment were undertaken, would you expect it to benefit shareholders? Why or why not?

5. What is the present value of a cash flow stream of $50 per year annually for 12 years that then grows at 7 percent per year forever when the discount rate is 14 percent?

6. An investment opportunity costs $100 million, will last 10 years, and promises an annual aftertax cash flow equal to $20.7 million. It will be financed with 80 percent debt yielding 8 percent. The debt will be repaid in 10 equal, end-of-year payments.
a. What is the IRR of this investment from the *entity* perspective?
b. What is the IRR of this investment from an *equity* perspective?
c. Assuming the investment is average risk and the decision maker's weighted-average cost of capital is 18 percent, is this an attractive opportunity? Why or why not?

7. The following information is available about an investment opportunity:

Initial cost	$10 million
Annual sales (in units)	100,000
Selling price per unit, this year	$50.00
Variable cost per unit, this year	$20.00
Life expectancy	10 years
Salvage value	$0
Depreciation	Straight line
Tax rate	34%
Nominal discount rate	18%
Real discount rate	10%

Assuming a uniform inflation rate of 8 percent throughout the economy over the next 10 years, calculate the investment's net present value.

8. Last year Backstage Enterprises had earnings before interest and tax of $5 million, its weighted-average cost of capital was 12 percent, it

employed capital of $40 million (interest-bearing debt plus book value of equity), and had a marginal tax rate of 40 percent.

a. What was Backstage's return on investment?

b. What was Backstage's economic value added?

c. As a shareholder, would you have been pleased with the company's performance last year? Why or why not?

d. Suppose you expect Backstage's operating profits to rise dramatically over the next few years without any additional investment. Would your answer to question *c* change? Why or why not?

CHAPTER 9

BUSINESS VALUATION AND CORPORATE RESTRUCTURING

Morality is all right, but what about dividends?

Kaiser Wilhelm II

In mid-August 1993, after a year of increasingly intimate courtship, American Telephone and Telegraph announced its intention to acquire McCaw Cellular Communications in a friendly, exchange-of-shares merger. Valued at $12.6 billion, the takeover was the second largest in U.S. corporate history.

Although it will be years and perhaps decades before we can say categorically whether AT&T's buy was a wise one, there can be little doubt about the initial response. Among the early winners were the McCaw family and other shareholders. Just prior to commencement of negotiations in late 1992, McCaw's stock was trading in the mid-20s and going nowhere fast. Two years later, when the deal closed, McCaw shareholders received one share of $55 AT&T stock for each McCaw share, implying an acquisition premium of over 100 percent.[1] Moreover, company founder Craig O. McCaw became an overnight billionaire and the largest holder of AT&T stock. AT&T shareholders, on the other hand, received no such largesse. In fact, their stock sagged $2.2 billion, or about 3 percent, on the announcement. The stock market's clear initial verdict was that AT&T had overpaid for McCaw.

The AT&T takeover of McCaw Communications aptly illustrates an important phenomenon in American business known broadly as *corporate*

---

1 A more conservative calculation incorporating only McCaw stock price increases immediately surrounding significant announcements about the pending merger puts the premium at 50 percent.

restructuring. Guided presumably by the financial principles examined in earlier chapters, senior executives make major, episodic changes in their company's asset mix, capital structure, or ownership composition in pursuit of increased value. In addition to friendly mergers of the AT&T–McCaw variety, corporate restructuring encompasses hostile acquisitions, purchases or sales of operating divisions, large repurchases of common stock, major changes in financial leverage, and leveraged buyouts, or LBOs. (An LBO is characterized by extensive use of the acquired entity's excess cash and borrowing capacity to help finance the acquisition.)

The AT&T–McCaw deal and many other restructurings pose several important questions to students of finance, and indeed to all executives. In terms of the McCaw purchase, they include the following:

1. What led AT&T chairman and CEO Robert Allen to believe that McCaw was worth as much as $55 a share? What analysis led to this conclusion?

2. If Allen was willing to pay as much as $55 a share for McCaw stock, why was the market price only $24? Does the stock market misprice companies this drastically, or is something else at work?

3. If McCaw stock really was worth $55, why didn't McCaw executives, who certainly knew more about their company than Allen did, realize this fact and do something to ensure that the value was reflected in McCaw's stock price?

4. Ultimately, who should decide the merits of corporate restructurings, management or owners? In the AT&T–McCaw merger, McCaw shareholders voted on the deal, but due to some fancy legal maneuvering, AT&T shareholders did not. More broadly, who *really* controls America's corporations, and who *should* control them? Is it shareholders, who collectively bear the financial risk, or is it the managers, who at least nominally work for the shareholders?

This chapter addresses these questions and, in the process, examines the principal financial dimensions of corporate restructuring. We begin by looking at business valuation, a family of techniques for estimating the value of a company or division. Attention then turns to what is known as "the market for corporate control," where we consider why one company might rationally pay a premium to acquire another and how to estimate an aspiring buyer's maximum acquisition price. Next, we examine three primarily financial motives for business restructuring predicated on the virtues of increased tax shields, enhanced management incentives, and shareholder control of free cash flow. The chapter closes with a brief review of the evidence on the economic merits of mergers and leveraged buyouts and a closer look at the AT&T–McCaw marriage.

VALUING A BUSINESS

Business valuation merits our serious attention because it is the underlying discipline for a wide variety of important financial activities. In addition to their use in structuring mergers and leveraged buyouts, business valuation principles guide security analysts in their search for undervalued stocks. Investment bankers use the same concepts to price initial public stock offerings, and venture capitalists rely on them to evaluate new investment opportunities. Companies intent on repurchasing their stock also frequently use valuation skills to time their purchases. Business valuation principles are even creeping into corporate strategy under the banner of value-based management, a consultant-spawned philosophy urging executives to evaluate alternative business strategies according to their predicted effect on the market value of the firm. It is thus not an exaggeration to say that although the details and the vocabulary differ from one setting to another, the principles of business valuation are integral to much of modern finance.

The first step in valuing any business is to decide precisely what is to be valued. This requires answering three basic questions:

- Do we want the value of the company's assets or its equity?
- Will the business be valued as a going concern or in liquidation?
- Are we to value a minority interest in the business or controlling interest?

Let us briefly consider each question in turn.

Assets or Equity?

When one company acquires another, it can do so by purchasing either the seller's assets or its equity. When the buyer purchases the seller's equity, it must then assume the seller's liabilities. Thus, when AT&T acquired

McCaw Communications, it paid $12.6 billion for McCaw's *equity* and assumed another $5.5 billion in McCaw liabilities, making the total purchase price for McCaw's assets $18.1 billion. Although it is common to speak of AT&T paying $12.6 billion for McCaw, this is incorrect, or at best misleading. For the true economic cost of the acquisition to AT&T shareholders is $18.1 billion, $12.6 billion incurred in the form of newly printed stock certificates and $5.5 billion in the form of a legal commitment to honor McCaw's existing liabilities. The effect on AT&T shareholders of assuming McCaw's debt is the same as paying $18.1 billion for McCaw's assets and financing $5.5 billion of the purchase price with new debt. In both cases, McCaw's assets had better generate future cash flows worth at least $18.1 billion or AT&T shareholders will have made a bad investment.

Most acquisitions involving companies of any size are structured as an equity purchase; so the ultimate objective of the valuation, and the focus of negotiations, is the value of the seller's equity. However, never lose sight of the fact that the true cost of the acquisition to the buyer is the cost of the equity *plus* the value of all liabilities assumed.

Dead or Alive?

Companies can generate value for owners in either of two states: in liquidation or as going-concerns. *Liquidation value* is the cash generated by terminating a business and selling its assets individually, while *going-concern value* is the present worth of expected future cash flows generated by a business. In most instances, we will naturally be interested in a business's going-concern value.

It will be helpful at this point to define an asset's *fair market value* (*FMV*) as the price at which the asset would trade between two rational individuals, each in command of all of the information necessary to value the asset and neither under any pressure to trade. Usually the FMV of a business is the *higher* of its liquidation value and its going-concern value. Figure 9–1 illustrates the relationship. When the present value of expected future cash flows is low, the business is worth more dead than alive, and FMV equals the company's liquidation value. At higher levels of expected future cash flows, liquidation value becomes increasingly irrelevant, and FMV depends almost entirely on going-concern value. It can also be the case that some of a company's assets, or divisions, are worth more in liquidation, while others are more valuable as going concerns. In this

F I G U R E   9-1

The Fair Market Value of a Business Is Usually the Higher of Its
Liquidation Value and Its Going-Concern Value

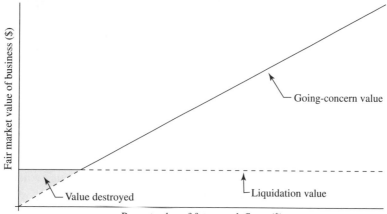

Present value of future cash flows ($)

instance, the firm's FMV is a combination of liquidation and going-concern values as they apply to individual assets.

An exception to the general rule that FMV is the higher of a company's liquidation value and going-concern value occurs when the individuals controlling the company—perhaps after reflecting on their alternative employment opportunities and the pleasures afforded by the corporate yacht—choose not to liquidate, even though the business is worth more dead than alive. Then, because minority investors cannot force liquidation, the FMV of a minority interest can fall below the liquidation value. This is represented in the figure by the shaded triangle labeled "value destroyed." Additional latent value exists, but because minority owners cannot get their hands on it, the value has no effect on the price they are willing to pay for the shares. As minority shareholders see it, the individuals controlling the business are destroying value by refusing to liquidate. Later in the chapter, we will consider other instances in which price, as determined by minority investors, does not reflect full value.

When speaking of control, it is important to note that ownership of a company's shares and control of the company are two vastly different things. Unless a shareholder owns or can influence at least 51 percent of a company's voting stock, there is no assurance he or she will have any say at all in company affairs. Moreover, in most large American public companies, no shareholder or cohesive group of shareholders owns enough stock to exercise voting control, and effective control devolves to the board of directors and incumbent management. In these instances, shareholders are just along for the ride.

Minority Interest or Control?

George Bernard Shaw once observed that "Economists know the price of everything and the value of nothing." And in a very real sense he is correct, since to an economist the value of an asset is nothing more or less than the price at which informed buyers and sellers are willing to trade it. The question of whether an asset has value beyond its selling price is one economists are content to leave to philosophers.

If value is synonymous with selling price, one obvious indicator of the worth of a business is its market value, the aggregate price at which its equity and debt trade in financial markets. Thus, when AT&T and McCaw first began their courtship in late 1992, McCaw had almost 200 million shares outstanding, each selling for about $24, and approximately $5.5 billion in debt; so its market value was $10.3 billion ($10.3 billion = 200 million × $24 + $5.5 billion).

As noted in earlier chapters, the market value of a business is an important indicator of company performance and a central determinant of a company's cost of capital. However, you need to realize that market value measures the worth of the business to *minority* investors. The stock price used to calculate the market value of a business is the price at which small numbers of shares have traded and is thus an unreliable indicator of the price at which a controlling interest might trade. The distinction between minority interest and controlling interest is vividly apparent in McCaw's case, where the market value of the firm was only $10.3 billion, yet controlling interest fetched a price of $18.1 billion.

Other instances in which market value is inadequate to the business valuation task include the following. The target is privately held, so market value does not exist. The target's stock trades so infrequently or in such modest volume that price is not a reliable indicator of value. The target's stock trades actively, but the analyst wants to compare market value to an independent estimate of value in search of mispriced stocks.

In sum, we can say that market value is directly relevant in business valuation only when the goal is to value a minority interest in a public company. In all other instances, market value may provide a useful frame of reference, but cannot by itself answer most interesting valuation questions. For this we need to think more carefully about the determinants of business value.

DISCOUNTED CASH FLOW VALUATION

Having examined business valuation in the large, we turn now to the specific task of estimating a company's going-concern value. For simplicity, we will begin by considering the value of a minority interest in a privately held firm.

Absent market prices, the most direct way to estimate going-concern value, if not always the most practical, is to think of the target company as if it were nothing more than a giant capital expenditure opportunity. Just as with any piece of capital equipment, investing in a company requires the expenditure of money today in anticipation of future benefits, and the central issue is whether tomorrow's benefits justify today's costs.

Equity Valuation

As noted earlier, the objective in most business valuations is to value the equity of the target company. Building on our earlier discussion of evaluating investment opportunities in Chapters 7 and 8, the most direct way to do this is to calculate the present value of expected future cash flows to the target firm's owners. In equation form,

FMV of equity = PV {Expected future cash flows to equity}

This formula says that the maximum price a minority investor should pay for the equity of a business equals the present value of expected future cash flows accruing to owners, discounted at an appropriate risk-adjusted discount rate. No surprises here, I trust. Moreover, as in any other application of risk-adjusted discount rates, we know the discount rate should match the risk of the cash flows being discounted. Because the cash flows here are to equity investors of the target firm, it follows that the discount rate should be the target company's cost of equity capital.

Firm Valuation

The equity valuation approach just described has it virtues, but it also has a significant weakness. One conclusion from our earlier discussion of investment analysis is that the investment decision should be separated from the financing decision whenever possible. First, decide if the investment makes economic sense regardless of how it is financed; then decide how best to finance it. Techniques that treat the two decisions simultaneously unnecessarily complicate the issue. Unfortunately, the equity approach to business valuation does precisely this, for both the cash flows to equity and the cost of equity depend on the way the business is financed. Thus, the calculated FMV reflects both the value of the business and its financing.

A second, back-door approach to valuing a business's equity neatly circumvents this problem by estimating the FMV of the firm and then simply subtracting interest-bearing liabilities. In equation form, we have our old friend

Value of equity = Value of firm − Value of liabilities

Moreover, because the market value and the book value of a company's liabilities are usually about equal to each other, estimating the value of the target's liabilities amounts to nothing more than grabbing a few numbers off the company's balance sheet.[2]

Applying the capital budgeting analogy again, except this time to the whole firm, we have

FMV of firm = PV {Expected aftertax cash flows to owners and creditors}

where the appropriate risk-adjusted discount rate is now the target's *weighted-average* cost of capital. As in the evaluation of investment opportunities, this approach reflects the benefits of the particular capital structure used by the target in the discount rate, not the cash flows. That is, use of the *aftertax* cost of interest in the weighted-average cost of capital calculation reflects the tax shield benefits of the firm's existing capital structure, and no further adjustments are necessary.

Free Cash Flow

In Chapter 7, we referred to the annual cash flows generated by an investment as the investment's aftertax cash flows (ATCF). When valuing a company, the relevant cash flows are a straightforward extension of ATCF commonly known as *free cash flow*, or *FCF*, defined as

---

2 We ignore noninterest-bearing liabilities such as accounts receivable and deferred taxes here
  because they are treated as part of free cash flow, to be described momentarily.

$$\frac{\text{Free cash}}{\text{flow}} = \text{EBIT}(1 - \text{Tax rate}) + \text{Depreciation} - \frac{\text{Capital}}{\text{expenditures}} \pm \frac{\text{Changes in net}}{\text{working capital}}$$

where EBIT is *e*arnings *b*efore *i*nterest and *t*ax.

The rationale for using free cash flow goes like this. EBIT is the income the company earns without regard to how the business is financed; so EBIT(1 − Tax rate) is income after tax excluding any effects of debt financing. Adding depreciation and any other significant noncash items yields the standard ATCF used in capital expenditure analysis. If management were prepared to run the company into the ground, it could distribute this cash flow to owners and creditors, and that would be the end of it. But in most companies, management retains some of this cash flow in the business to pay for new capital expenditures and possibly to increase net working capital. The cash available for distribution to owners and creditors is thus ATCF less capital expenditures and increases in net working capital. Reductions in net working capital are also possible, and they add to free cash flow.

The Terminal Value

We now come to a serious practical problem. Our equation says that the FMV of a business equals the present value of all future free cash flows. Yet because companies typically have an indefinitely long life expectancy, the literal application of this equation would have us estimating free cash flows for perhaps hundreds of years into the far distant future—a clearly unreasonable task.

The standard way around this impasse is to think of the target company's future as composed of two discrete periods. During the first period, of some 5 to 15 years, we presume the company has a unique cash flow pattern and growth trajectory that we seek to capture by estimating individual, annual free cash flows just as the equation suggests. However, by the end of this forecast period, we assume the company has lost its individuality—has grown up, if you will—and become a stable, slow-growth business. From this date forward, we cease worrying about annual cash flows and instead estimate a single *terminal value* representing the worth of all subsequent free cash flows. If the initial forecast period is, say, 10 years, our valuation equation becomes

FMV of firm = PV{FCF years 1–10 + Terminal value at year 10}

Introduction of a terminal value, of course, only trades one problem for another, for now we need to know how to estimate a company's terminal value. I wish I could assure you that financial economists have solved this problem and present a simple, accurate expression for a company's terminal value, but I can't. Instead, the best I can offer are several plausible alternative estimates and some general advice on how to proceed.

Following are five alternative ways to estimate a company's terminal value with accompanying explanatory comments and observations. To use these estimates effectively, note first that no single estimate is always best; rather each is more or less appropriate depending on circumstances. Thus, liquidation value may be highly relevant when valuing a mining operation with 10 years of reserves but quite irrelevant when valuing a rapidly growing software company. Second, resist the natural temptation to pick what appears to be the best technique for the situation at hand, ignoring all others. Avoid too the simple averaging of several estimates. Instead, calculate a number of terminal value estimates and begin by asking why they differ. In some instances, the differences will be readily explainable; in others, you may find it necessary to revise your assumptions to reconcile the differing values. Then, once you understand why remaining differences exist and feel comfortable with the magnitude of the differences, select a terminal value based on your assessment of the relative merits of each estimate for the target company.

Five Terminal Value Estimates

Liquidation Value   Highly relevant when liquidation at the end of the forecast period is under consideration, liquidation value usually grossly *understates* a healthy business's terminal value.

Book Value   Popular perhaps among accountants, book value usually yields a quite conservative terminal value estimate.

Warranted Price-to-Earnings Multiple   To implement this approach, multiply the target firm's estimated earnings to common stock at the end of the forecast horizon by a "warranted" price-to-earnings ratio; then add projected interest-bearing liabilities to estimate the firm's terminal value. As a warranted price-to-earnings ratio, consider the multiples of publicly traded firms that you believe represent what the target will become by the end of the forecast period. If, for example, the target company is a start-up but you believe it will be representative of other, mature companies in its industry by the end of the forecast period, the industry's current price-to-earnings multiple may be a suitable ratio. Another strategy is to bracket the value by trying multiples of, say, 10 and 20 times. The approach generalizes easily to other "warranted" ratios, such as market value to book value, price to cash flow, or price to sales.

No-Growth Perpetuity   We saw in Chapter 7 that the present value of a no-growth perpetuity is the annual cash flow divided by the discount rate. This suggests the following terminal value estimate:

$$\text{Terminal value of no-growth firm} = \frac{FCF_{T+1}}{K_W}$$

where FCF_{T+1} is free cash flow in the first year beyond the forecast horizon and K_W is the target's weighted-average cost of capital. As further refinement, we might note that when a company is not growing, its capital expenditures should about equal its annual depreciation charges and its net working capital should neither increase nor decrease over time, all of which imply that free cash flow should simplify to EBIT(1 − Tax rate).

Because most businesses expand over time, if due only to inflation, many analysts believe this equation understates the terminal value of a typical business. I am more skeptical. For, as noted repeatedly in earlier chapters, growth creates value only when it generates returns above capital costs; and in competitive product markets over the very long run, such performance is more the exception than the rule. Hence, even if many companies are capable of expanding, they may be worth no more than their no-growth brethren.

Perpetual Growth   In Chapter 8, we saw that the present value of a perpetually growing stream of cash equals next year's cash flow divided by the difference between the discount rate and the growth rate. Thus another terminal value estimate is

$$\text{Terminal value of perpetually growing firm} = \frac{FCF_{T+1}}{K_W - g}$$

where g is the perpetual-growth rate of free cash flow.

A few words of caution are in order about this popular expression. It is a simple arithmetic fact that any business growing faster than the economy *forever* must eventually become the economy. (When I made this point recently at a Microsoft seminar, the immediate response was "Yeah! Yeah!") The intended conclusion for mere mortal firms is that the absolute upper limit on g must be the long-run growth rate of the economy, or about 2 to 3 percent a year, plus expected inflation. Moreover, because even inflationary growth invariably requires higher capital expenditures and increases in working capital, free cash flow falls as g rises. This implies that the above expression may well overstate a company's terminal value even when the perpetual-growth rate is kept to a low figure.[3]

The Forecast Horizon

Terminal values of growing businesses can easily exceed 60 percent of firm value, so it goes without saying that proper selection of the forecast horizon and terminal value are critical to the successful application of discounted cash flow approaches to business valuation. Because most tractable terminal value estimates implicitly assume the firm is a mature, slow-growth, or no-growth perpetuity from that date forward, it is important to extend the forecast horizon far enough into the future that this assumption plausibly applies. When valuing a rapidly growing business, this perspective suggests estimating how long the company can be expected to sustain its supernormal growth before reaching maturity and setting the forecast horizon at or beyond this date.

A Numerical Example

Suppose you have the opportunity to purchase 100,000 shares of AT&P Railroad common stock and you want to estimate an appropriate price. AT&P has 1 million shares of common stock outstanding. You have already concluded that AT&P's weighted-average cost of capital is 12 percent and its interest-bearing liabilities are $500 million.

---

3 Here is a modestly more complex version of the perpetual-growth expression, to which I am
   partial:

$$\text{Terminal value} = \frac{\text{EBIT}(1 - \text{Tax rate})(1 - g/r)}{K_w - g}$$

where r is the rate of return on new investment. One virtue of this expression is that growth does not add value unless returns exceed capital cost. To confirm this, set $r = K_w$ and note that the expression collapses to the no-growth equation. A second virtue is that growth is not free, for as growth rises, so must capital expenditures and net working capital. In the equation, higher g reduces the numerator, which is equivalent to reducing free cash flow. See Appendix A in the Copeland, Koller, and Murrin book referenced at the end of this chapter for a demonstration that this expression is mathematically equivalent to the perpetual-growth equation above.

T A B L E 9–1

Free Cash Flow for AT&P Railroad ($ millions)

Year	(1 − Tax rate) EBIT	+ Depreciation	− Capital Expenditures	± Changes in NWC	= FCF
1	64	165	50	5	184
2	63	175	50	5	193
3	61	170	60	0	171
4	61	160	100	0	121
5	62	145	130	−5	71
6	62	140	140	−6	56
		Present value of FCF in years 1–6 @ 12% =			$586
7*	65	140	145	−2	59

*$59 = 56(1 + 5%)

Railroading, at least as practiced by AT&P, appears to be a declining business, for although the company has large annual depreciation charges, investment is quite modest. You believe this situation will continue for the next six years and have estimated the free cash flows appearing in Table 9–1. As the table notes, the present value of these free cash flows is $586 million.

You believe that beginning in the seventh year, free cash flow will grow into the indefinite future at 5 percent a year; the figure for year 7 will thus be $59 million. Free cash flow is less than EBIT after tax because capital expenditures will need to exceed depreciation charges and net working capital will have to increase to support the anticipated growth. You also think that by the end of the forecast horizon, AT&P will command a price-to-earnings multiple representative of other railroads. The industry multiple today is 15 times when earnings are defined as EBIT(1 − tax rate). Finally, you estimate that AT&P's book value at the end of the forecast period will be $750 million.

Using the perpetual-growth equation to estimate AT&P's terminal value at the end of year 6,

$$\text{Terminal value} = \frac{\text{FCF in year 7}}{K_W - g}$$
$$= \frac{\$59}{0.12 - 0.05}$$
$$= \$843 \text{ million}$$

A warranted price-to-earnings ratio estimate of the company's terminal value based on the current industry multiple is

$$\text{Terminal value} = 15 \times \$62$$
$$= \$930 \text{ million}$$

Finally, the projected asset book value of $775 million may have some relevance.

Considering the relative merits of these estimates, it appears that a terminal value of about $850 million is appropriate:

$$\text{Terminal value at year } 0 = \$850 \, (0.507)$$
$$= \$431 \text{ million}$$

Adding the present value of the free cash flows for the first six years to that of the terminal value and subtracting the value of interest-bearing liabilities, we get

$$\text{FMV}_{\text{equity}} = \$586 \text{ million} + \$431 \text{ million} - \$500 \text{ million}$$
$$= \$517 \text{ million}$$

Finally, if AT&P's equity is worth $517 million and it has 1 million shares outstanding, its value per share is $517. Thus, your 100,000-share purchase should cost $51.7 million ($51.7 × 100,000).

Problems with Present Value Approaches to Valuation

If you are a little hesitant at this point about your ability to apply these discounted cash flow techniques to anything but simple textbook examples, welcome to the club. While DCF approaches to business valuation are conceptually correct, and even rather elegant, they are devilishly difficult to apply in practice. Valuing a business may be conceptually equivalent to any other capital expenditure decision, but there are several fundamental differences in practice:

1. The typical investment opportunity has a finite—usually brief—life, while the life expectancy of a company is indefinite.
2. The typical investment opportunity promises stable or perhaps declining cash flows over time, while the ability of a company to reinvest earnings customarily produces a growing cash flow.

3. The cash flows from a typical investment belong to the owner, while the cash flows generated by the company go to the owner only when management chooses to distribute them. If management decides to invest in Mexican diamond mines rather than pay dividends, a minority owner can do little other than sell out.

As the problems in the accompanying boxes illustrate, these practical differences introduce potentially large errors into the valuation process and can make the resulting FMV estimates quite sensitive to small changes in the discount rate and the growth rate employed.

VALUATION BASED ON COMPARABLE TRADES

Granting that discounted cash flow approaches to business valuation are conceptually correct but difficult to apply, are there alternatives? One popular technique involves comparing the target company to similar, publicly traded firms. Imagine shopping for a used car. The moment of truth comes when the buyer finds an interesting car, looks at the asking price, and ponders what to offer the dealer. One strategy, analogous to a discounted cash flow approach, is to estimate the value of labor and raw materials in the car, add a markup for overhead and profit, and subtract an amount for depreciation. A more productive approach is comparison shopping: Develop an estimate of fair market value by comparing the subject car to similar autos that have recently sold or are presently available. If three similar-quality 1982 T-Birds have sold recently for $3,000 to $3,500, the buyer has reason to believe the target T-Bird has a similar value. Of course, comparison shopping provides no information about whether 1982 T-Birds are really worth $3,000 to $3,500 in any fundamental sense; it indicates only the going rate. However, in many instances this is sufficient. (Another tactic recommended by some is to skip the valuation process altogether and proceed directly to bargaining by asking the dealer what he wants for the car and responding, "B————t, I'll give you half of that." This probably works better for cars than for companies, but don't rule it out entirely.)

Use of comparable trades to value businesses requires equal parts art and science. First, it is necessary to decide which publicly traded companies are most similar to the target and then to determine what the share prices of the publicly traded companies imply for the FMV of the firm in

THE PROBLEM OF GROWTH AND LONG LIFE

In many investment decisions involving long-lived assets, it is common to finesse the problem of forecasting far distant cash flows by ignoring all flows beyond some distant horizon. The justification for this practice is that the present value of far distant cash flows will be quite small. When the cash flow stream is a growing one, however, growth offsets the discounting effect, and even far distant cash flows can contribute significantly to present value. Here is an example.

The present value of $1 a year in perpetuity discounted at 10 percent is $10 ($1/0.10). The present value of $1 a year for 20 years at the same discount rate is $8.51. Hence, ignoring all of the perpetuity cash flows beyond the 20th year reduces the calculated present value by only about 15 percent ($8.51 versus $10.00).

But things change when the income stream is a growing one. Using the perpetual-growth equation, the present value of $1 a year, growing at 6 percent per annum forever, is $25 ($1/[0.10 − 0.06]), while the present value of the same stream for 20 years is only $13.08. Thus, ignoring growing cash flows beyond the 20th year reduces the present value by almost half ($13.08 versus $25.00).

THE SENSITIVITY PROBLEM

At a 10 percent discount rate, the fair market value of a company promising free cash flows next year of $1 million, growing at 5 percent a year forever, is $20 million ($1 million/[0.10 − 0.05]).

Assuming the discount rate and the growth rate could each be in error by as much as 1 percentage point, what are the maximum and minimum possible FMVs for the company? What do you conclude from this?

Answer: The maximum is $33.3 million ($1 million/[0.09 − 0.06]), and the minimum is $14.3 million ($1 million/[0.11 − 0.04]). It is difficult to charge a client very high fees for advising that a business is worth somewhere between $14.3 and $33.3 million.

question. The discounted cash flow valuation equations just considered offer a useful starting point. They suggest that comparable companies should offer similar future cash flow patterns and similar business and financial risks. The risks should be similar so that roughly the same discount rate would apply to all of the firms.

In practice, these guidelines suggest we begin our search for comparable companies by considering firms in the same, or closely related, industries with similar growth prospects and capital structures. With luck, the outcome of this exercise will be several more or less comparable publicly traded companies. Considerable judgment will then be required to decide what the comparable firms as a group imply for the fair market value of the target.

Table 9–2 offers a quick look at the use of comparable trades to value our friend from earlier chapters, Analog Devices, Inc. It goes without saying that if I were being paid by the hour to value Analog Devices and you were being similarly compensated to read about it, we would both proceed much more thoroughly and deliberately; nonetheless, the table should give you a general idea of how the comparable trades approach is applied in practice.

The valuation date is December 31, 1995, and the chosen comparable companies are five businesses mentioned in ADI's annual report as direct competitors. Four of the companies are considerably smaller than ADI, while the fifth, Motorola, is about 25 times larger. Of course, Analog Devices itself is publicly traded, so at the end of this exercise we will be able to compare my estimated value with the actual market price to get some idea of the accuracy of the comparable-trades approach.

The first set of numbers in Table 9–2 looks at Analog Devices' returns, risk, and growth relative to the comparable firms. The numbers indicate that ADI is in the middle of the pack but a bit below the mean on return on equity, return on invested capital, and five-year growth rate in sales. All of the companies have modest financial leverage, and again ADI is representative of the other companies.

The second set of numbers in the table shows four possible indicators of value for the comparable firms. Broadly speaking, each indicator expresses how much investors are paying per dollar of current income, or per dollar of invested capital, for each comparable. Thus, the first indicator says that one dollar of Burr-Brown's income costs $14.20, while one dollar of Motorola's income is priced at $18.90. Similarly, the last indicator tells us that the market value of Maxim Integrated Products is 5.7 times its book value, while the same ratio for Siliconix is only 2.3 times. Indicators 1 and 3 focus on equity values, while the other two indicators concentrate on the value of the firm.

Reflecting on how Analog Devices stacks up against the other firms in terms of returns, risk, and growth, the valuation challenge is to decide what indicators of value are appropriate for ADI. The third set of numbers in Table 9–2 are my necessarily subjective estimates. In coming to these estimates, I considered several factors. First, I believe the first two indicators of value are generally better than the last two because they relate market value to income as opposed to assets. With rare exception,

T A B L E 9–2

Using Comparable Public Companies to Value Analog Devices, Inc. (December 31, 1995)

	Analog Devices	Burr-Brown	Linear Technology	Maxim Integrated Products	Siliconix	Motorola	Excluding Analog Devices: Median	Mean
	Comparison of Analog Devices with Comparable Companies: Returns, Risks, and Growth Rates							
Return on invested capital	16.6%	15.0%	25.5%	23.4%	27.4%	12.9%	23.4%	20.8%
Return on equity	18.2	16.3	25.5	23.4	26.8	16.1	23.4	21.6
Total liabilities to assets	34.5	29.0	16.9	22.1	56.6	51.5	29.0	35.2
5-year growth in sales	14.3	9.9	32.2	43.1	14.0	20.3	20.3	23.9
	Indicators of Value							
Price/earnings		14.2×	25.8×	30.3×	15.2×	18.9×	18.9×	20.9×
MV firm/EBIT(1 – Tax rate)	16.3	16.3	26.6	30.3	18.3	24.2	24.2	23.1
MV equity/BV equity	2.3	2.3	6.6	7.1	4.1	3.0	4.1	4.6
MV firm/BV firm	1.9	1.9	5.6	5.7	2.3	2.0	2.3	3.5

T A B L E 9–2 (concluded)

Using Comparable Public Companies to Value Analog Devices, Inc. (December 31, 1995)

My Estimated Indicators of Value for Analog Devices

Price/earnings	18.0×
MV firm/EBIT(1 – Tax rate)	22.0×
MV equity/BV equity	4.2×
MV firm/BV firm	3.2×

Implied Value of Analog Devices' Common Stock per Share

Price/earnings	$18.75	($18.75 = 18 × Net income / # of shares)
MV firm/EBIT(1 – Tax rate)	20.49	($20.49 = [22 × EBIT(1 – Tax rate) – Liabilities] / # of shares)
MV equity/BV equity	24.06	($24.06 = 4.2 × Book value of equity / # of shares)
MV firm/BV firm	24.98	($24.98 = [3.2 × (Book value of equity + Liabilities) – Liabilities] / # of shares)
My best guess	$20.50	
Actual stock price	$24.88	

MV = Market value

BV = Book value

Market value of firm estimated as book value of interest-bearing debt + market value of equity.

Earnings are calendar 1995 earnings.

333

investors are interested in a company's income potential when they buy its shares, not the assets it owns. Between the first two indicators of value, I prefer the second because the earnings measure used there is unaffected by the way the business is financed.

Second, it makes sense to assign more importance to those indicators of value that are relatively more stable across comparable companies. If the calculated value of one indicator were 10.0 for every comparable, I would deem it a more reliable indicator of value than if it varied from 1.0 to 30.0. Here the first two indicators, those relating market value to earnings, vary within a range of about 2 to 1, while the other two indicators vary within a range of about 3 to 1. This lends additional credence to the first two indicators as more reliable.

Third, Analog Devices' below-average earnings growth suggests to me that its indicator of value for the two income-based ratios should be somewhat below the average value for the comparable firms. I have selected values about 5 to 15 percent below the sample average.

Fourth, ADI's somewhat below-par return on invested capital and return on equity numbers suggest that its indicator of value for the last two asset-based ratios should again be somewhat below the comparable firms' average. I have chosen numbers about 10 percent below the sample mean.

The bottom set of numbers in the table presents the price of Analog Devices' stock implied by each chosen indicator of value. To the right of each stock price is an equation illustrating how I translated the chosen indicator of value into an implied stock price. To illustrate the second equation, I estimated that ADI's market value should equal 22 times its EBIT after tax. ADI's EBIT after tax in 1995 was $122.5 million, so its implied market value is $2.7 billion (22 × $122.5 million). Subtracting liabilities of $345.7 million and dividing by 114.5 million common shares yields an implied stock price of $20.49. The other three share prices are calculated similarly. The results fall within a range of $18.75 to $24.98 a share. Reflecting on the observations made above, my best guess of a fair price for Analog Devices' shares at year-end 1995 is $20.50. This compares to an actual price on the valuation date of $24.88, so my estimate is about 18 percent low. Before dumping my ADI stock (as if I owned any), I would want to investigate whether there exists some more recent information about ADI's prospects that would explain the apparent anomaly.

Lack of Marketability

An important difference between owning stock in a publicly traded company and stock in a private one is that the publicly traded shares are more liquid; they can be sold quickly for cash without significant loss of value. Because liquidity is a valued attribute of any asset, it is necessary to reduce the FMV of a private company estimated by reference to publicly traded comparable firms. Without boring you with details, a representative lack of marketability discount is on the order of 25 percent.[4] Of course, if the purpose of the valuation is to price an initial public offering of common stock, the shares will soon be liquid, and no discount is required.

A second possible adjustment when using the comparable-trades approach to valuation is a premium for control. Quoted prices for public companies are invariably for a minority interest in the firm, while valuations of private companies often involve transactions in which operating control passes from seller to buyer. Because control is valuable, it is necessary in these instances to add a premium to the estimated value of the target firm to reflect the value of control. Estimating the size of this control premium is our next task.

THE MARKET FOR CONTROL

We have noted on several occasions that buying a minority interest in a company differs fundamentally from buying control. With a minority interest, the investor is a passive observer; with control, she has complete freedom to change the way the company does business and perhaps increase its value significantly. Indeed, the two situations are so disparate that it is appropriate to speak of stock as selling in two separate markets: the market in which you and I trade minority claims on future cash flows and the market in which AT&T and other acquirers trade the right to control the firm. The latter, the *market for control*, involves a two-in-one sale. In addition to claims on future cash flows, the buyer in this market also gains the privilege of structuring the company as he or she wishes. Because shares trading in the two markets are really different assets, they naturally sell at different prices.

---

4 Shannon P. Pratt, *Valuing a Business: The Analysis and Appraisal of Closely Held Companies*, 2nd ed. (Burr Ridge, IL: Dow Jones-Irwin, 1988).

F I G U R E   9–2

FMV of a Corporation to Investors Seeking Control May Exceed FMV to Minority Investors

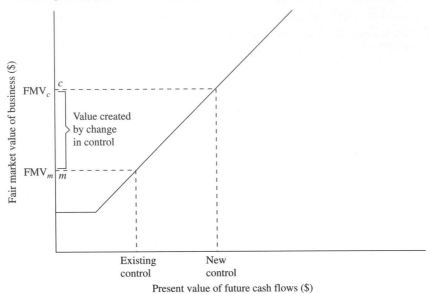

The Premium for Control

Figure 9–2 illustrates this two-tier market. From the perspective of minority investors, the fair market value of a company's equity, represented in the figure by m, is the present value of cash flows to equity given current management and strategy. To a corporation or an individual seeking control, however, the FMV is c, which may be well above m. The difference, $(c - m)$, is the value of control. It is the maximum premium over the minority fair market value an acquirer should pay to gain control. It is also the expected increase in shareholder value created by acquisition. When an acquirer pays FMV_c for a target, all of the increased value will be realized by the seller's shareholders, while at any lower price, part of the increased value will accrue to the acquirer's shareholders. FMV_c is therefore the maximum acquisition price a buyer can justify paying. Said differently, it is the price at which the net present value of the acquisition to the buyer is zero.

What Price Control?

There are two ways to determine how large a control premium an acquirer can afford to pay. The brute force approach values the business first assuming the merger takes place and then assuming it does not. The difference between these values is the maximum premium an acquirer can justify paying. The second, more practical approach focuses on the anticipated gains from the merger. In equation form,

$$FMV_c = FMV_m + \text{Enhancements}$$

where c and m again denote controlling and minority interest, respectively. This expression says the value of controlling interest in a business equals the business's FMV under the present stewardship, or what is often called the business's *stand-alone value*, plus whatever enhancements to value the new buyer envisions. If the buyer intends to make no changes in the business now or in the future, the enhancements are zero, and no premium over stand-alone value can be justified. On the other hand, if the buyer believes the merging of two businesses will create vast new profit opportunities, enhancements can be quite large.

Putting a price tag on the value of enhancements resulting from an acquisition is a straightforward undertaking conceptually: Make a detailed list of all the ways the acquisition will increase free cash flows or reduce risk, estimate the magnitude and timing of the cash flows involved, calculate their present values, and sum:

$$\text{Enhancements} = PV\{\text{All value-increasing changes due to acquisition}\}$$

Controlling Interest in a Publicly Traded Company

An important simplification of our expression for FMV_c is possible when the seller is publicly traded. If we are willing to assume that the preacquisition stock price of the target company reasonably approximates its FMV_m, or at least that we are unable to detect when the approximation is unreasonable, the expression reduces to

$$FMV_c = \text{Market value of business} + \text{Enhancements}$$

where the market value of the business is our old friend the stock market value of equity plus debt. A particular virtue of this formula for valuing acquisition candidates is that it forces attention on the specific improvements anticipated from the acquisition and the maximum price one should

T A B L E   9–3

Number of Mergers and Median Acquisition Premiums, 1990–1995

Year	Number of Transactions	Number over $1 Billion	Median 5-Day Premium*
1990	2,074	21	32.0%
1991	1,877	13	29.4
1992	2,574	18	34.7
1993	2,663	27	33.0
1994	2,997	51	35.0
1995	3,510	74	29.2

*Five-day premiums paid are only for those transactions revealing sufficient information to calculate the premium. This is usually about 10 percent of all transactions.

Source: *1996 Mergerstat Review*, Houlihan, Lokey, Howard and Zukin, Los Angeles, 1996.

pay to get them, a perspective that reduces the possibility that an exuberant buyer will become carried away during spirited bidding and overpay. In other words, it helps to keep animal spirits in check during the negotiation process.

That animal spirits might need an occasional reigning in is suggested by Table 9–3. It shows the number of mergers in the United States from 1990 through 1995 and the median premiums paid. Note that the number of acquisitions rose from a cyclical low in 1991 to over 3,500 in 1995, a 20-year high. The number of big-ticket purchases of more than $1 billion jumped over fivefold to 74. Preliminary data for 1996 indicate that this number climbed to over 100 transactions and that the total volume of mergers completed worldwide approximated $1 trillion.[5] Looking at the acquisition premiums, we see that the median purchase price was 30 to 35 percent above the seller's share price five days before the announcement. Acquirers are evidently quite confident of their ability to wring large enhancements out of their acquisitions.

---

5 Steven Lipin, "Corporations' Dreams Converge in One Idea: It's Time to Deal," *The Wall Street Journal*, February 26, 1997, p. 1.

KISSING TOADS

The Oracle of Omaha, Warren Buffett, deftly attributes corporate executives' willingness to pay large control premiums to three very human factors: an abundance of
animal spirits, an unwarranted emphasis on company size as opposed to profitability,
and overexposure during youth to "the story in which the imprisoned handsome prince
is released from a toad's body by a kiss from a beautiful princess. [From this tale,
executives] are certain their managerial kiss will do wonders for the profitability of
Company T(arget)." Why else, Buffett asks, would an acquiring company pay a premium to control another business when it could avoid the premium altogether by simply
purchasing a minority interest?

"In other words, investors can always buy toads at the going price for toads. If
investors instead bankroll princesses who wish to pay double for the right to kiss the
toad, those kisses had better pack some real dynamite. We've observed many kisses
but very few miracles. Nontheles, many managerial princesses remain serenely confident about the future potency of their kisses—even after their corporate backyards
are knee-deep in unresponsive toads."

Source: Warren Buffett, Berkshire Hathaway, Inc. 1981 annual report.

Financial Reasons for Restructuring

We conclude (or at least I conclude) that the best way to value a public
company for acquisition purposes is to add the present value of all benefits
attributable to the acquisition to the target's current market value. "So,"
you ask perceptively, "what types of benefits might motivate an acquisition or other form of restructuring?" The list is truly lengthy, ranging from
anticipated savings in manufacturing, marketing, distribution, or overhead
to better access to financial markets to enhanced investment opportunities;
and the perceived sources of value vary from merger to merger. So instead
of trying to catalog the myriad possible benefits to a restructuring, I will
concentrate on three finance-driven potential enhancements that are sufficiently common and controversial to warrant inquiry. I will refer to them
as *tax shields*, *incentive effects*, and *controlling free cash flow*.

Tax Shields
A number of takeovers and restructurings in recent years, especially those
involving mature, slow-growth businesses, appear to be driven primarily
by the desire to make more extensive use of depreciation and interest tax

AVOIDING DILUTION IN EARNINGS PER SHARE

An all-too-popular alternative approach to determining how much one company can afford to bid for another looks at the impact of the acquisition on the acquirer's earnings per share (EPS). Popularity is about all this approach has to recommend it, for it grossly oversimplifies the financial effects of an acquisition, and it rests on an inappropriate decision criterion.

Suppose the following data apply to an acquiring firm, A, and its target, T, in an exchange-of-shares merger; that is, A will give T's shareholders newly printed shares of A in exchange for their shares of T.

	Company A	Company T	Merged Company
Earnings ($ millions)	$ 100	$ 20	$130
Number of shares (millions)	20	40	26
Earnings per share	$ 5	$ 0.50	$ 5 (minimum)
Stock price	$ 70	$ 5	
Market value of equity (millions)	$1,400	$ 200	

The suggested decision criterion is that A should avoid dilution in EPS. If earnings of the merged firm are forecasted to be $130 million, the figures above indicate that A can issue as many as 6 million shares without suffering dilution (6 million shares = [$130 million/$5] − 20 million). At $70 a share, this implies a maximum price of $420 million for T ($70 × 6 million), or a 110 percent premium ([420 − 200]/200). It also suggests a maximum exchange ratio of 0.15 shares of A for each share of T (6 million/ 40 million).

The obvious shortcomings of this simplistic approach are, first, that earnings are not the cash flows that determine value and, second, that it is grossly inappropriate to base an acquisition decision on only one year's results. Doing so is comparable to making investments because they promise to increase next year's profits. If T's growth prospects are sufficiently bright, it may be perfectly reasonable to sacrifice near-term EPS in anticipation of long-run gains. Business valuation is tough in practice, but there is no reason to use flawed techniques just because they are tractable.

shields. As noted in Chapter 6, the tax deductibility of depreciation and interest expenses reduces a company's tax bill and hence may add value.

To illustrate the appeal of tax shields, consider the following restructuring of Mature Manufacturing, Inc. (2M). Pertinent data for 2M, a mature, publicly traded company, follow.

Mature Manufacturing, Inc. ($ millions)	
Annual EBIT	$ 25
Market value of equity	200
Long-term debt	0
Fixed plant and equipment	100
Annual depreciation	10

   Global Investing Corporation believes 2M's management may be interested in a leveraged buyout (LBO) and has approached it with a proposal to form a new corporation, invariably called NEWCO, to purchase all of 2M's equity. Because 2M's cash flows are very stable, Global figures it can finance most of the purchase price by borrowing $190 million on a 10-year loan at 10 percent interest. The loan will be interest only for the first five years. In addition, Global believes its auditors will allow NEWCO to write up the book value of 2M's fixed plant and equipment to a fair market value of $160 million on acquisition. This will generate an additional $6 million in annual depreciation for the next 10 years. The value of the anticipated tax shields to NEWCO, discounted at a 12 percent rate, is as follows:

Year	Increase in Interest Expense	Increase in Depreciation	Tax Shield @ 40% Tax Rate
1	$19.00	$6.00	$10.00
2	19.00	6.00	10.00
3	19.00	6.00	10.00
4	19.00	6.00	10.00
5	19.00	6.00	10.00
6	19.00	6.00	10.00
7	15.89	6.00	8.76
8	12.46	6.00	7.38
9	8.70	6.00	5.88
10	4.56	6.00	4.22
		PV @ 12% =	$51.54 million

   The figures suggest that NEWCO can bid up to $251.54 million, a 26 percent premium, to purchase 2M ($251.54 million = $200 million stand-alone value + $51.54 million of enhancements). Global's required equity investment will thus be as high as $61.54 million ($251.54 million value of firm − $190 million value of liabilities), implying a postacquisition debt-to-assets ratio of 76 percent. This, believe it or not, is representative financing by LBO standards. LBOs are indeed aptly named.

Note that if increased interest tax shields are the objective, an LBO is not the only way to obtain them. 2M can generate much the same effect by simply issuing debt and distributing the proceeds to owners as a large dividend or by a share repurchase. This was Colt Industries' strategy (described in Chapter 6) when it floated a huge debt issue to finance distribution of a special dividend and ended up with $1.6 billion in long-term debt and a *negative* net worth of $1 billion. But what's to fear from a mountain of debt as long as you have the cash flow to service it? And if you don't, your creditors have so much at stake in your company that they are more likely to behave like partners than like police.

Nor must a leveraged buyout necessarily involve a takeover. Many LBOs are initiated by incumbent management who teams up with outside investors to purchase all of the company's stock and take it private. Management risks its own money in return for a sizable equity position in the restructured company.

Incentive Effects

Tax shield enhancements are clearly just a game: To the extent that shareholders win, "we, the people" (in the form of the U.S. Treasury) lose. If this were the only financial gain to takeovers and restructurings, the phenomena would not command serious public attention. Best that we eliminate the tax benefits and get back to producing goods and services instead of stocks and bonds.

The other two potential enhancements are not so easily dismissed. Both involve free cash flow, and both are premised on the belief that restructuring powerfully affects the performance incentives confronting senior management. To examine the incentive effects of restructuring in more detail, let's return to Mature Manufacturing, Inc.

Before restructuring, the life of a senior manager at Mature Manufacturing Inc. may well have been an enviable one. With very stable cash flows, a mature business, and no debt, managers had no pressing reason to improve performance. They could pay themselves and their employees generously, make sizable corporate contributions to charity, and, if the president was so inclined, sponsor an Indy race car or an unlimited hydroplane. Alternatively, if they wanted 2M to grow, the company could acquire other firms. This might involve some uneconomical investments, but hey—as long as cash flows are strong, almost anything is possible.

Samuel Johnson once observed, "The certainty of hanging in a fortnight focuses the mind wonderfully." Restructuring can have a similar effect, for it fundamentally changes the world of 2M senior executives. Because they have probably invested much of their own resources in the equity of the newly restructured company, their own material well-being is closely tied to that of the business. Moreover, the huge debt service burden restructuring frequently creates forces management to generate healthy cash flows or face bankruptcy—no more "corpocracy" at 2M. The carrot of ownership and the stick of possible financial ruin create significant incentives for management to maximize free cash flow and spend it for the benefit of owners.

Controlling Free Cash Flow

This enhancement rests on the perception that in many public corporations, there is an ongoing tug-of-war between shareholders and incumbent management for control of the company. When shareholders have the upper hand, companies are run to maximize shareholder value; but when management is in the driver's seat, increasing value is only one of a number of competing corporate goals. After over 50 years on the losing end of this tug-of-war, the emergence of the hostile raider in the mid-1980s enabled shareholders to gain the ascendancy and force companies to restructure. According to this view, the hostile acquisitions and restructurings during the latter half of the 1980s were a boon not only to shareholders but to the entire economy; for to the extent that shareholders can force management to increase firm value, the economy's resources are allocated more efficiently.

Consistent with this adversarial view of corporate governance, many of the past decade's hostile takeovers occurred in mature or declining industries. Because investment opportunities in these industries were low, affected businesses often had large free cash flows. At the same time, industry decline created real concern in the minds of executives about the continued survival of their organization. And although the proper strategy from a purely financial perspective was to shrink or terminate the business, management often took another tack. Out of a deep commitment to the business and concern for employees, the community, and their own welfare, some managers continued to fight the good fight by reinvesting in the business despite its poor returns. The purpose of restructuring in these instances is brutally basic: Wrest control of free cash flow away from management and put it in the hands of owners.

How, you might ask, does incumbent management ever gain control of a business in the first place? In theory, managers should be incapable of acting in opposition to owners for at least two reasons. First, if a company operates in highly competitive markets, management has very little discretion; it must maximize value or the firm will be driven from the industry. Second, all corporations have boards of directors with the power to hire and fire management and the responsibility to represent owners' interests.

Theory, however, often differs from reality. Many corporations operate in less than perfectly competitive markets, and many corporate boards are not an effective, independent shareholder voice. Indeed, a common view among executives and the judges is that a board's primary responsibility is to help incumbent management run the business, not to safeguard shareholder interests. As a result, boards are often more closely affiliated with management than with owners. Directors are often company insiders; other directors have important ties to the enterprise other than ownership and are more beholden to the chief executive than to shareholders for their seat on the board. Consequently, while such boards may help keep the shelves stocked, they are not about to recommend selling the store. Or, in the words of one professional director, "The most important skill a board member can have is the ability to yawn with his mouth shut."

But change is in the wind. Having tasted the fruits of control in the form of unusually high investment returns during the hostile takeover era, a growing number of institutional investors are choosing to fight rather than switch. Led by Calpers, the California Public Employees Retirement System, institutional investors have lobbied the SEC for liberalization of rules governing voting and shareholder communications, commissioned and publicized studies identifying underperforming managements, and insisted on meeting with underperformers to discuss their recovery plans. And although company boards have generally opposed these public assaults, a growing number have elected to meet their critics halfway by initiating several basic procedural reforms intended to increase the board's independence from the chief executive. These include a written job description for the chief executive, regular performance reviews of the chief executive conducted by outside directors, regular meetings of outside directors, a requirement that the chief executive officer not also be the chair of the board, a board nominating committee controlled by outside directors, and full board access to all employees without necessary approval or knowledge of the chief executive.

As debate topics go, the question of whether management should have broader social responsibilities than simply creating shareholder value is among the more intriguing. Like many important societal questions, however, the issue has tended to be resolved more on the basis of power than of logic. Throughout most of this century, incumbent management retained the power to interpret its responsibilities broadly and to treat shareholders as only one of several constituencies possessing a claim on the corporation. The balance of power shifted abruptly in shareholders' favor during the era of the hostile takeover. And although corporations have largely neutralized the threat of hostile takeover, the rise of the activist shareholder and his ally, the activist board member, suggests that the battle is far from over. Stay tuned.

The Empirical Evidence

A final question remains: Do corporate restructurings create value? Do they provide any benefit to society? In the aggregate, the answer is yes. Looking first at mergers, the median five-day acquisition premiums of 30 to 35 percent reported in Table 9–3 leave no doubt that owners of acquired firms benefit handsomely from mergers. Whether the owners of acquiring firms also benefit is more problematic. Using the event study methodology described in Chapter 5, one academic study found that on average the price of an acquiring firm's shares rises a statistically significant 2.8 percent on the merger announcement.[6] A more recent study of all successful acquisitions involving public tender offers in the period 1963 to 1984 reports similar findings.[7] Investigators found that the combined market value of buyers' and sellers' shares rose an average of 7.4 percent on the announcement. However, they also found that virtually all of the increased stock market value flowed to selling shareholders, who saw their stock rise just over 30 percent on average. Buyers' shares, on the other hand, rose only about 1 percent. Moreover, most of the buyers' gains occurred in the early years of the study when tender offers were largely unregulated. In the last four years of the study, the price of acquiring firms' shares *fell* some 3 percent on the announcement.

---

6 Paul Asquith, Robert F. Bruner, and David W. Mullins, Jr., "The Gains to Bidding Firms from Merger," *Journal of Financial Economics*, April 1983, pp. 121–39.
7 Michael Bradley, Anand Desai, and E. Han Kim, "Synergistic Gains from Corporate Acquisitions and Their Division Between the Stockholders of Target and Acquiring Firms," *Journal of Financial Economics*, May 1988, pp.3–40.

Michael Porter looked at the same issue from a different perspective when he tracked the acquisition activity of 33 diversified companies over a 35-year period ending in 1986.[8] He found that these active acquirers divested or shuttered more than half of their acquisitions in following years and that the more unrelated the seller's business was to that of the buyer, the greater the chance of failure. He concluded quite naturally from these findings that many, if not most, acquisitions are unsuccessful from the buyer's perspective.

The best study to date on whether leveraged buyouts create value is by Steven Kaplan of the University of Chicago, who examined 48 large management buyouts executed between 1980 and 1986.[9] (A management buyout, or MBO, is an LBO in which prebuyout management plays an active role in taking the company private.)

Looking first at return on operating assets, Kaplan found that relative to overall industry performance, the median buyout firm increased return on operating assets a healthy 36.1 percent in the two years following the buyout. A similar look at capital expenditures revealed that on an industry-adjusted basis, the typical buyout firm reduced its ratio of capital expenditures to assets by a statistically *in*significant 5.7 percent over the same period. Reflecting both improved operating performance and reduced investment, Kaplan found that the typical buyout firm increased an industry-adjusted measure of free cash flow to total assets an enormous 85.4 percent in the two years following the buyout. Evidently the carrot of increased ownership and the stick of heavy debt service really do focus management's attention.

Realized returns to investors were equally impressive. Of the 48 firms in his sample, Kaplan was able to find postbuyout valuation data on 25 because they either issued stock to the public, repurchased stock, were liquidated, or were sold. Recognizing that these 25 may be the cream of the crop, he nonetheless observed impressive performance. The median, market-adjusted return to all sources of capital over the 2.6 years from the buyout date to the valuation date was 28 percent. Moreover, the median

8 Michael E. Porter, "From Competitive Advantage to Corporate Strategy," *Harvard Business Review*, May–June 1987, pp. 43–59. For a more optimistic view of the attractiveness of mergers, see Patricia L. Anslinger and Thomas E. Copeland, "Growth Through Acquisitions: A Fresh Look," *Harvard Business Review*, January–February 1996, pp. 126–35.

9 Steven Kaplan, "The Effects of Management Buyouts on Operating Performance and Value," *Journal of Financial Economics*, October 1989, pp. 217–54.

internal rate of return to equity on these firms was a staggering 785.6 percent; such is the power of extensive financial leverage when things go well. Is it any wonder that LBO investment firms continue to attract large piles of investment capital?

Kaplan's study tracks LBO performance during one of the longest business expansions in American economic history, so there is no guarantee that such performance could be repeated today. However, the data do suggest that LBOs are not just tax gimmicks. Rather, the increased managerial incentives that accompany LBO restructurings were apparently strong enough to stimulate sharp improvements in operating performance and in shareholder value. The data also pose a stark challenge to those who argue that management alone should control America's corporations.

The AT&T–McCaw Merger

AT&T's takeover of McCaw should no longer hold much mystery. McCaw's $24 premerger stock price was the value to minority investors given McCaw's potential as a stand-alone entity, while the $55 price paid by AT&T included a large premium for control. Clearly neither price was necessarily incorrect or irrational. Although one might wonder whether AT&T might have paid too much for McCaw, I can assure you that having paid over $40 million in fees to three investment banks, both companies had numerous valuation studies of the type described here supporting the acquisition pricing. Whether the assumptions and forecasts underlying those studies were accurate, of course, remains to be seen.

AT&T and McCaw came to the altar by way of two decidedly different paths and with decidedly different needs.

McCaw was the brash, decade-old creation of its visionary founder, Craig O. McCaw, who from the company's inception had maniacally driven it toward the single goal of creating a national, wireless communications network. By late 1992, he had all but reached his goal, but had so overextended the company in the process that his ability to ever capitalize on his creation was in serious doubt. The company had never made an operating profit, was losing money at the rate of over $350 million a year, faced a debt burden of $5.5 billion, and had a debt-to-total-capital ratio of 67 percent. Moreover, as part of its hostile acquisition of controlling interest in LIN Broadcasting in 1990, McCaw had agreed to either buy the 48 percent of LIN it didn't already own or sell what it did own by 1995. Purchasing the rest of LIN would cost several billion dollars, but selling the company would leave McCaw without a presence in New York or Los Angeles, its two most important markets. And if this were not enough, the company faced multibillion-dollar expenditures to upgrade its technology from analog to digital. McCaw needed some deep pockets fast.

Meanwhile, AT&T sat ponderously at the other end of the corporate spectrum. The epitome of a staid, blue-chip corporation, AT&T had tremendous financial and marketing muscle but little idea about how to capitalize on its strengths. AT&T's lucrative monopoly of the American telephone industry ended abruptly in 1984 when, as the result of an antitrust action filed by the U.S. Department of Justice, the courts carved AT&T up into a single long-distance telephone provider and seven independent, local providers. In addition, the courts threw the long-distance market open to new competition and required AT&T to provide competitors with access to its lines and switches at a fair price. Similarly, the seven local telephone companies, known colloquially as the Baby Bells, were required to provide AT&T with access to their lines at fair prices.

Since the breakup, AT&T had appeared to be running in three directions at once. It was fighting tenaciously to defend its eroding share of the long distance market against the likes of MCI and Sprint; it had attempted to capitalize on the anticipated coalescence of computer, entertainment, and communication technologies by acquiring computer manufacturer NCR; and through its interest in McCaw, it was seeking to reenter the local telephone market.

Ironically, AT&T's merger talks with McCaw marked its third chance to break into the cellular business. Indeed, AT&T engineers originally developed wireless technology in the 1950s but had not chosen to exploit it. Then, in the 1980s, when the federal government started granting regional cellular operating licenses and Craig McCaw began feverishly building his network, AT&T again chose to sit on the sidelines. Not until 1992, with cellular use apparently about to take off and growing evidence that wireless might supplant, not merely supplement, fixed wire telephony, did AT&T decide to act. It had missed the opportunity twice before, and with a market value of approximately $70 billion, AT&T was determined not to strike out.

AT&T's takeover of McCaw promised to create value in at least three ways. First, McCaw could use AT&T's cash and marketing prowess to further develop and exploit its cellular network. As one indication of AT&T's market presence, an informal McCaw survey of customers shortly after merger talks began revealed that the second most recognized name in the cellular industry, right behind McCaw, was AT&T, despite the fact that AT&T had no cellular service at the time. Second, the AT&T connection gave McCaw access to international opportunities where poorly developed traditional telephone service made wireless communications an enticing alternative. Third, control of McCaw's cellular network might enable AT&T to get back into the local telephone market and circumvent onerous local access charges. Although AT&T would not comment publicly, simple arithmetic suggested that if AT&T could move even a small fraction of its long-distance call originations from local Baby Bells to its own cellular network, large savings would result. Whether these admittedly attractive potential sources of increased value warranted a 100 percent control premium is, of course, the ultimate question.

A brief postscript: In early 1993, just as merger talks were getting serious, Nicholas Kauser, McCaw's chief technologist, began research on a new, fixed wireless telephone system intended to deliver better quality and faster data speeds than copper wire. Afraid that AT&T might steal the technology if the talks fell through, McCaw kept the research secret until after the deal closed in late 1994. Within a month, AT&T realized what it might inadvertently have purchased: the long-sought high-quality, low-investment alternative to the traditional home phone. If exploited properly, the technology might enable AT&T to realize its long-held dream of reentering the $100-billion-a-year local-calling market. It thus appears that what may ultimately prove to be the crown jewel of the McCaw acquisition was completely unknown to AT&T negotiators at the time of purchase. The moral is clear: Careful valuation and disciplined negotiation are vital to successful acquisitions, but in business as in life, it is sometimes more important to be lucky than smart.

CHAPTER SUMMARY

1. This chapter examined corporate restructuring, broadly defined as any episodic change in a company's asset mix, capital structure, or ownership composition.

2. The central discipline underlying all corporate restructurings is business valuation, the art of pricing all or part of a business.

3. Before valuing a business, it is necessary to decide whether to value the company's assets or its equity, whether to value it in

liquidation or as a going concern, and whether to value a minority or a controlling interest.

4. The discounted cash flow approach to business valuation estimates the present value of the target's free cash flows discounted at the target's weighted-average cost of capital.

5. Major challenges in discounted cash flow valuation are to estimate a forecast horizon and a terminal value for the target firm. The forecast horizon should be at or beyond the date when the target becomes a mature, slow-growth business. Common terminal value estimates include a warranted multiple of the target's earnings or assets and present value calculations presuming slow, perpetual growth.

6. The comparable-trades approach to business valuation infers the value of the target's equity from the prices at which the shares of comparable, publicly traded firms trade. The resulting value estimate must frequently be adjusted to reflect a lack of marketability or the fact that the buyer is acquiring control of the business.

7. It is often appropriate for a buyer to pay a premium above the minority value of a business to gain control. The maximum justifiable premium equals the present value of all value-increasing changes contemplated by the buyer.

8. Three controversial, finance-driven, potential benefits from restructuring are increased interest tax shields, enhanced management incentives, and owner control of free cash flow.

9. Empirical evidence suggests that acquisitions typically create value, but the great preponderance of it flows to selling shareholders. Leveraged buyouts appear to create substantial value.

10. Shareholder advocates argue that an active market for corporate control is good for the economy because the threat of takeover disciplines managers to pay more attention to shareholder value.

ADDITIONAL READING

Copeland, Tom; Tim Koller; and Jack Murrin. *Valuation: Measuring and Managing the Value of Companies.* 2nd ed. New York: John Wiley & Sons, 1995. 576 pages. Written by three McKinsey & Company consultants, this is a well-written, practical, how-to discussion of business valuation. Part III, "Applying Valuation," is especially well done, with whole chapters devoted to multinational business valuation and valuing banks. You can spend $60,000 and let McKinsey do a valuation for you or spend $65 for the paperback edition of this book and learn how to do it yourself.

Hickman, Kent, and Glenn H. Petry. "A Comparison of Stock Price Predictions Using Court Accepted Formulas, Dividend Discount, and P/E Models." *Financial Management*, Summer 1990, pp. 74–85.

One of the few studies I know of that attempts to assess the empirical accuracy of alternative valuation models. The authors conclude that the comparable-trades approaches they tested provided much more reliable estimates of value than the discounted cash flow models did.

Jensen, Michael C. "The Corporate Takeover Controversy: Analysis and Evidence." *Midland Corporate Finance Journal*, Summer 1986, pp. 6–32.

Harry Truman's proverbial "one-armed economist"; none of this "on the one hand but then on the other hand" from Mike Jensen. This article is a cogent, tightly reasoned, provocative review of the empirical literature on corporate takeovers and a strong statement in support of the virtues of an unfettered market for corporate control.

Kaplan, Steven N., and Richard S. Ruback. "The Valuation of Cash Flow Forecasts: An Empirical Analysis." *Journal of Finance*, September 1995, pp. 1059–93.

Empirical support for the discounted cash flow approach to business valuation. The authors compare present values of projected cash flows to subsequent market values of 51 highly levered transactions between 1983 and 1989. Discounted cash flow valuations are within 10 percent, on average, of market values. The DCF valuations prove at least as accurate as those based on comparable trades.

Pratt, Shannon P.; Robert F. Reilly; and Robert P. Schweihs. *Valuing a Business: The Analysis and Appraisal of Closely Held Companies.* 3rd. ed. Burr Ridge, IL: Irwin Professional Publishing, 1995. 850 pages.

A detailed road map of how to value a closely held company. A wealth of practical detail on sources of data and applied valuation approaches. Far less sophisticated than Tom Copeland's book described above. Relevant primarily for valuing small firms. Check your local library; it sells for $95.

C H A P T E R   P R O B L E M S

1. Why should the fair market value of a company be the higher of its liquidation value and its going-concern value? What would you expect to happen if a company's market value were the lower of its liquidation value and going-concern value?

2. Flatbush Marine is a no-growth company paying a $100-per-share annual dividend. Its cost of equity capital is 15 percent. The new president abhors the no-growth image and proposes to halve next year's dividend to $50 per share and use the savings to acquire another firm. The president maintains that this strategy will boost sales, earnings, and assets. Moreover, he is confident that after acquisition, dividends in year 2 and beyond can be increased to $105 per share.

a. Do you agree that the acquisition will likely increase sales, earnings, and assets?

b. Estimate the per share value of Flatbush's stock immediately prior to the president's proposal.

c. Estimate the per share value immediately after the proposal.

d. As an owner of Flatbush, would you support the president's proposal? Why or why not?

3. Timberland Company is a designer, manufacturer, and marketer of better-quality footwear and apparel headquartered in Hampton, New Hampshire. Like millions of others, you have probably been tempted to express your rugged individuality, concern for the environment, and fashion savvy in a pair of waterproof Timberland boots. Use the following information on Timberland and four other footwear manufacturers to value Timberland as of December 31, 1993.

Timberland Company, 1993 ($ millions)

Net income	$ 22.4
Number of common shares	10.85
Earnings before interest and tax	$ 46.9
Tax rate	34%
Book value of equity	$128.4
Book value interest-bearing debt	$101.6

Using Comparable Public Companies to Value Timberland Company (December 31, 1993)

	Timberland Company	Nike Inc.	Reebok Int'l.	Stride Rite	Wolvervine World Wide
Comparisons of Timberland with Comparable Companies: Returns, Risks, and Growth Rates					
Return on invested capital	11.6%	20.9%	23.7%	19.8%	9.2%
Return on equity	17.5	22.2	26.4	19.3	10.2
Liabilities to total capital	72.1	31.2	54.1	35.3	55.5
5-year growth in earnings	18.0	15.4	12.8	0.7	11.6
Indicators of Value					
Price/earnings		9.8 ×	11.9 ×	14.2 ×	18.1 ×
MV firm/EBIT(1 − Tax rate)		6.5	11.3	13.6	17.1
MV equity/BV equity		1.4	3.0	2.7	1.8
MV firm/BV firm		1.4	2.7	2.7	1.6

4. Following is a four-year forecast for Mayfair Modes.

	($ millions)			
	1999	2000	2001	2002
Earnings before interest and taxes	$100	$130	$ 170	$210
Capital expenditures	150	90	100	110
Changes in working capital	20	50	(10)	10
Depreciation	25	30	50	60

a. Calculate Mayfair Modes' projected free cash flow in each year.

b. What does a negative free cash flow imply? Does it mean the company is destroying value in that year, or might another interpretation be possible?

c. Estimate the fair market value of Mayfair Modes at the end of 1998. Assume that after 2002, earnings before interest and tax will remain constant at $210 million, depreciation will equal capital expenditures in each year, and working capital will not change. Mayfair Modes' weighted-average cost of capital is 14 percent.

d. Estimate the fair market value per share of Mayfair Modes' equity at the end of 1998 if the company has 50 million shares outstanding and the market value of its interest-bearing liabilities on the valuation date equals $300 million.

e. Now let's try a different terminal value. Estimate the fair market value of Mayfair Modes' equity per share at the end of 1998 under the following assumptions:

(*1*) Free cash flows in years 1999 through 2002 remain as above.

(*2*) EBIT after year 2002 grows at 4 percent per year forever.

(*3*) To support the perpetual growth in EBIT, capital expenditures in year 2003 exceed depreciation by $20 million, and this difference grows 4 percent per year forever.

(*4*) Similarly, working capital increases $10 million in 2003, and this amount grows 4 percent per year forever.

f. Finally, let's try a third terminal value. Estimate the fair market value of Mayfair Modes' equity per share at the end of 1998 under the following assumptions:

(*1*) Free cash flows in years 1999 through 2002 remain as above.

(*2*) At year-end 2002, Mayfair Modes has reached maturity, and its equity sells for a "typical" multiple of year 2002 net income. Use 8 as a typical multiple.

(*3*) At year-end 2002, Mayfair Modes has $200 million of interest-bearing liabilities outstanding at an average interest rate of 10 percent.

APPENDIX A
Present Value of $1 in Year *n*, Discounted at Discount Rate *k*

							Discount Rate (k)					
Period (*n*)	1%	2%	3%	4%	5%	6%	7%	8%	9%	10%	11%	12%
1	0.990	0.980	0.971	0.962	0.952	0.943	0.935	0.926	0.917	0.909	0.901	0.893
2	0.980	0.961	0.943	0.925	0.907	0.890	0.873	0.857	0.842	0.826	0.812	0.797
3	0.971	0.942	0.915	0.889	0.864	0.840	0.816	0.794	0.772	0.751	0.731	0.712
4	0.961	0.924	0.885	0.855	0.823	0.792	0.763	0.735	0.708	0.683	0.659	0.636
5	0.951	0.906	0.863	0.822	0.784	0.747	0.713	0.681	0.650	0.621	0.593	0.567
6	0.942	0.888	0.837	0.790	0.746	0.705	0.666	0.630	0.596	0.564	0.535	0.507
7	0.933	0.871	0.813	0.760	0.711	0.665	0.623	0.583	0.547	0.513	0.482	0.452
8	0.923	0.853	0.789	0.731	0.677	0.627	0.582	0.540	0.502	0.467	0.434	0.404
9	0.914	0.837	0.766	0.703	0.645	0.592	0.544	0.500	0.460	0.424	0.391	0.361
10	0.905	0.820	0.744	0.676	0.614	0.558	0.508	0.463	0.422	0.386	0.352	0.322
11	0.896	0.804	0.722	0.650	0.585	0.527	0.475	0.429	0.388	0.350	0.317	0.287
12	0.887	0.788	0.701	0.625	0.557	0.497	0.444	0.397	0.356	0.319	0.286	0.257
13	0.879	0.773	0.631	0.601	0.530	0.469	0.415	0.368	0.326	0.290	0.258	0.229
14	0.870	0.758	0.661	0.577	0.505	0.442	0.388	0.340	0.299	0.263	0.232	0.205
15	0.861	0.743	0.642	0.555	0.481	0.417	0.362	0.315	0.275	0.239	0.209	0.183
16	0.853	0.728	0.623	0.534	0.458	0.394	0.339	0.292	0.252	0.218	0.188	0.163
17	0.844	0.714	0.605	0.513	0.436	0.371	0.317	0.270	0.231	0.198	0.170	0.146
18	0.836	0.700	0.587	0.494	0.416	0.350	0.296	0.250	0.212	0.180	0.153	0.130
19	0.828	0.686	0.570	0.475	0.396	0.331	0.277	0.232	0.194	0.164	0.138	0.116
20	0.820	0.673	0.554	0.456	0.377	0.312	0.258	0.215	0.178	0.149	0.124	0.104
25	0.780	0.610	0.478	0.375	0.295	0.233	0.184	0.146	0.116	0.092	0.074	0.059
30	0.742	0.552	0.412	0.308	0.231	0.174	0.131	0.099	0.075	0.057	0.044	0.033
40	0.672	0.453	0.307	0.208	0.142	0.097	0.067	0.046	0.032	0.022	0.015	0.011
50	0.608	0.372	0.228	0.141	0.087	0.054	0.034	0.021	0.013	0.009	0.005	0.003

APPENDIX A (concluded)

Discount Rate (k)

Period (n)	13%	14%	15%	16%	17%	18%	19%	20%	25%	30%	35%	40%	50%
1	0.885	0.877	0.870	0.862	0.855	0.847	0.840	0.833	0.800	0.769	0.741	0.714	0.667
2	0.783	0.769	0.756	0.743	0.731	0.718	0.706	0.694	0.640	0.592	0.549	0.510	0.444
3	0.693	0.675	0.658	0.641	0.624	0.609	0.593	0.579	0.512	0.455	0.406	0.364	0.296
4	0.613	0.592	0.572	0.552	0.534	0.515	0.499	0.482	0.410	0.350	0.301	0.260	0.198
5	0.543	0.519	0.497	0.476	0.456	0.437	0.419	0.402	0.320	0.269	0.223	0.186	0.132
6	0.480	0.456	0.432	0.410	0.390	0.370	0.352	0.335	0.262	0.207	0.165	0.133	0.088
7	0.425	0.400	0.376	0.354	0.333	0.314	0.296	0.279	0.210	0.159	0.122	0.095	0.059
8	0.376	0.351	0.327	0.305	0.285	0.266	0.249	0.233	0.168	0.123	0.091	0.068	0.039
9	0.333	0.308	0.284	0.263	0.243	0.225	0.209	0.194	0.134	0.094	0.067	0.048	0.026
10	0.295	0.270	0.247	0.227	0.208	0.191	0.176	0.162	0.107	0.073	0.050	0.035	0.017
11	0.261	0.237	0.215	0.195	0.178	0.162	0.148	0.135	0.086	0.056	0.037	0.025	0.012
12	0.231	0.208	0.187	0.168	0.152	0.137	0.124	0.112	0.069	0.043	0.027	0.018	0.008
13	0.204	0.182	0.163	0.145	0.130	0.116	0.104	0.093	0.055	0.033	0.020	0.013	0.005
14	0.181	0.160	0.141	0.125	0.111	0.099	0.088	0.078	0.044	0.025	0.015	0.009	0.003
15	0.160	0.140	0.123	0.108	0.095	0.084	0.074	0.065	0.035	0.020	0.011	0.006	0.002
16	0.141	0.123	0.107	0.093	0.081	0.071	0.062	0.054	0.028	0.015	0.008	0.005	0.002
17	0.125	0.108	0.093	0.080	0.069	0.060	0.052	0.045	0.023	0.012	0.006	0.003	0.001
18	0.111	0.095	0.081	0.069	0.059	0.051	0.044	0.038	0.018	0.009	0.005	0.002	0.001
19	0.098	0.083	0.070	0.060	0.051	0.043	0.037	0.031	0.014	0.007	0.003	0.002	0.000
20	0.087	0.073	0.061	0.051	0.043	0.037	0.031	0.026	0.012	0.005	0.002	0.001	0.000
25	0.047	0.038	0.030	0.024	0.020	0.016	0.013	0.010	0.004	0.001	0.001	0.000	0.000
30	0.026	0.020	0.015	0.012	0.009	0.007	0.005	0.004	0.001	0.000	0.000	0.000	0.000
40	0.008	0.005	0.004	0.003	0.002	0.001	0.001	0.001	0.000	0.000	0.000	0.000	0.000
50	0.002	0.001	0.001	0.001	0.000	0.000	0.000	0.000	0.000	0.000	0.000	0.000	0.000

APPENDIX B

Present Value of an Annuity of $1 for *n* Years, Discounted at Rate *k*

Period (*n*)	1%	2%	3%	4%	5%	6%	7%	8%	9%	10%	11%	12%
1	0.990	0.980	0.971	0.962	0.952	0.943	0.935	0.926	0.917	0.909	0.901	0.893
2	1.970	1.942	1.913	1.886	1.859	1.833	1.808	1.783	1.759	1.736	1.713	1.690
3	2.941	2.884	2.829	2.775	2.723	2.673	2.624	2.577	2.531	2.487	2.444	2.402
4	3.902	3.808	3.717	3.630	3.546	3.465	3.387	3.312	3.240	3.170	3.102	3.037
5	4.853	4.710	4.580	4.452	4.329	4.212	4.100	3.993	3.890	3.791	3.696	3.605
6	5.795	5.601	5.417	5.242	5.076	4.917	4.767	4.623	4.486	4.355	4.231	4.111
7	6.728	6.472	6.230	6.002	5.786	5.582	5.389	5.206	5.033	4.868	4.712	4.564
8	7.652	7.325	7.020	6.733	6.463	6.210	5.971	5.747	5.535	5.335	5.146	4.968
9	8.566	8.162	7.786	7.435	7.108	6.802	6.515	6.247	5.995	5.759	5.537	5.328
10	9.471	8.983	8.530	8.111	7.722	7.360	7.024	6.710	6.418	6.145	5.889	5.650
11	10.368	9.787	9.253	8.760	8.306	7.887	7.499	7.139	6.805	6.495	6.207	5.938
12	11.255	10.575	9.954	9.385	8.863	8.384	7.943	7.536	7.161	6.814	6.492	6.194
13	12.134	11.348	10.635	9.986	9.394	8.853	8.358	7.904	7.487	7.103	6.750	6.424
14	13.004	12.106	11.296	10.563	9.899	9.295	8.745	8.244	7.786	7.367	6.982	6.628
15	13.865	12.849	11.939	11.118	10.380	9.712	9.108	8.559	8.061	7.606	7.191	6.811
16	14.718	13.578	12.561	11.652	10.838	10.106	9.447	8.851	8.313	7.824	7.379	6.974
17	15.562	14.292	13.166	12.166	11.274	10.477	9.763	9.122	8.544	8.022	7.549	7.102
18	16.398	14.992	13.754	12.659	11.690	10.828	10.059	9.372	8.756	8.201	7.702	7.250
19	17.226	15.678	14.324	13.134	12.085	11.158	10.336	9.604	8.950	8.365	7.839	7.366
20	18.046	16.351	14.877	13.590	12.462	11.470	10.594	9.818	9.129	8.514	7.963	7.469
25	22.023	19.523	17.413	15.622	14.094	12.783	11.654	10.675	9.823	9.077	8.422	7.843
30	25.808	22.396	19.600	17.292	15.372	13.765	12.409	11.258	10.274	9.427	8.694	8.055
40	32.835	27.355	23.115	19.793	17.159	15.046	13.332	11.925	10.757	9.779	8.951	8.244
50	39.196	31.424	25.730	21.482	18.256	15.762	13.801	12.233	10.962	9.915	9.042	8.304

Discount Rate (k)

APPENDIX B (concluded)

Period (n)	Discount Rate (k)												
	13%	14%	15%	16%	17%	18%	19%	20%	25%	30%	35%	40%	50%
1	0.885	0.877	0.870	0.862	0.855	0.847	0.840	0.833	0.800	0.769	0.741	0.714	0.667
2	1.668	1.647	1.626	1.605	1.585	1.566	1.547	1.528	1.440	1.361	1.289	1.224	1.111
3	2.361	2.322	2.283	2.246	2.210	2.174	2.140	2.106	1.952	1.816	1.696	1.589	1.407
4	2.974	2.914	2.855	2.798	2.743	2.690	2.639	2.589	2.362	2.166	1.997	1.849	1.605
5	3.517	3.433	3.352	3.274	3.199	3.127	3.058	2.991	2.689	2.436	2.220	2.035	1.737
6	3.998	3.889	3.784	3.685	3.589	3.498	3.410	3.326	2.951	2.643	2.385	2.168	1.824
7	4.423	4.288	4.160	4.039	3.922	3.812	3.706	3.605	3.161	2.802	2.508	2.263	1.883
8	4.799	4.639	4.487	4.344	4.207	4.078	3.954	3.837	3.329	2.925	2.598	2.331	1.922
9	5.132	4.946	4.772	4.607	4.451	4.303	4.163	4.031	3.463	3.019	2.665	2.370	1.948
10	5.426	5.216	5.019	4.833	4.659	4.494	4.339	4.192	3.571	3.092	2.715	2.414	1.965
11	5.687	5.453	5.234	5.029	4.836	4.656	4.486	4.327	3.656	3.147	2.752	2.438	1.977
12	5.918	5.660	5.421	5.197	4.988	4.793	4.611	4.439	3.725	3.190	2.779	2.456	1.985
13	6.122	5.842	5.583	5.342	5.118	4.910	4.715	4.533	3.780	3.223	2.799	2.469	1.990
14	6.302	6.002	5.724	5.468	5.229	5.008	4.802	4.611	3.824	3.249	2.814	2.478	1.993
15	6.462	6.142	5.847	5.575	5.324	5.092	4.876	4.675	3.859	3.268	2.825	2.484	1.995
16	6.604	6.265	5.954	5.668	5.405	5.162	4.938	4.730	3.887	3.283	2.834	2.489	1.997
17	6.729	6.373	6.047	5.749	5.475	5.222	4.988	4.775	3.910	3.295	2.840	2.492	1.998
18	6.840	6.467	6.128	5.818	5.534	5.273	5.033	4.812	3.928	3.304	2.844	2.494	1.999
19	6.938	6.550	6.198	5.877	5.584	5.316	5.070	4.843	3.942	3.311	2.848	2.496	1.999
20	7.025	6.623	6.259	5.929	5.628	5.353	5.101	4.870	3.954	3.316	2.850	2.497	1.999
25	7.330	6.873	6.464	6.097	5.766	5.467	5.195	4.948	3.985	3.329	2.856	2.499	2.000
30	7.496	7.003	6.566	6.177	5.829	5.517	5.235	4.979	3.995	3.332	2.857	2.500	2.000
40	7.634	7.105	6.642	6.233	5.871	5.548	5.258	4.997	3.999	3.333	2.857	2.500	2.000
50	7.675	7.133	6.661	6.246	5.880	5.554	5.262	4.999	4.000	3.333	2.857	2.500	2.000

GLOSSARY

accelerated depreciation Any *depreciation*[1] that produces larger deductions for depreciation in the early years of a project's life.

acceptance criterion Any minimum standard of performance in investment analysis (cf. *hurdle rate*).

accounting income An economic agent's *realized income* as shown on financial statements (cf. *economic income*).

accounting rate of return A figure of investment merit, defined as average annual cash inflow divided by total cash outflow (cf. *internal rate of return*).

accounts payable (payables, trade payables) Money owed to suppliers.

accounts receivable (receivables, trade credit) Money owed by customers.

accrual accounting A method of accounting in which *revenue* is recognized when earned and expenses are recognized when incurred without regard to the timing of cash receipts and expenditures (cf. *cash accounting*).

acid test (quick ratio) A measure of *liquidity*, defined as *current assets* less inventories divided by *current liabilities*.

aftertax cash flow Total cash generated by an investment annually, defined as profit after tax plus depreciation or, equivalently, operating income after tax plus the tax rate times depreciation.

allocated costs Costs systematically assigned or distributed among products, departments, or other elements.

annuity A level stream of cash flows for a limited number of years (cf. *perpetuity*).

asset Anything with value in exchange.

asset turnover ratio A broad measure of asset efficiency, defined as net sales divided by total assets.

bankruptcy A legal condition in which an entity receives court protection from its creditors. Bankruptcy can result in *liquidation* or reorganization.

bearer securities Any securities that are not registered on the books of the issuing corporation. Payments are made to whoever presents the appropriate coupon. Bearer securities facilitate tax avoidance.

benefit-cost ratio *Profitability index.*

β-risk (systematic risk, nondiversifiable risk) Risk that cannot be diversified away.

bond Long-term publicly issued debt.

bond rating An appraisal by a recognized financial organization of the soundness of a *bond* as an investment.

book value The value at which an item is reported in financial statements (cf. *market value*).

book value of equity The value of *owners' equity* as shown on the company's balance sheet (cf. *market value of equity*).

break-even analysis Analysis of the level of sales at which a firm or product will just break even.

breakup value The value one could realize by dividing a multibusiness company into a number of separate enterprises and disposing of each individually.

---

1 Words in italics are defined elsewhere in the glossary.

business risk Risk due to uncertainty about investment outlays, operating cash flows, and salvage values without regard to how investments are financed (cf. *financial risk*).

call option Option to buy an asset at a specified exercise price on or before a specified maturity date (cf. *put option*).

call provision Provision describing terms under which a bond issuer may redeem the bond in whole or in part prior to maturity.

capital The amount invested in a venture (cf. *capitalization*).

capital budget List of planned investment projects.

capital consumption adjustment Adjustment to historical-cost depreciation to correct for understatement during inflation.

capitalization The sum of all long-term sources of financing to the firm or, equivalently, total assets less current liabilities.

capital rationing Fixed limit on capital that forces the company to choose among worthwhile projects.

capital structure The composition of the liabilities side of a company's balance sheet. The mix of funding sources a company uses to finance its operations.

cash accounting A method of accounting in which changes in the condition of an organization are recognized only in response to the payment or receipt of cash (cf. *accrual accounting*).

cash budget A plan or projection of cash receipts and disbursements for a given period of time (cf. *cash flow forecast, cash flow statement, pro forma forecast*).

cash cow Company or product that generates more cash than can be productively reinvested.

cash flow The amount of cash generated or consumed by an activity over a certain period of time.

cash flow cycle The periodic transformation of cash through *working capital* and fixed assets back to cash.

cash flow forecast A financial forecast in the form of a *sources and uses statement*.

cash flow from operating activities Cash generated or consumed by the productive activities of a firm over a period of time; defined as profit after tax plus *noncash charges* minus noncash receipts plus or minus changes in *current assets* and *current liabilities*.

cash flow principle Principle of investment evaluation stating that only actual movements of cash are relevant and should be listed on the date they move.

cash flow statement A report of the sources of cash to a business and the uses to which the cash was put over an accounting period

certainty-equivalent A guaranteed amount of money that a decision maker would trade for an uncertain cash flow.

close off the top Financial jargon meaning to foreclose the possibility of additional debt financing.

collection period A ratio measure of control of *accounts receivable*, defined as accounts receivable divided by credit sales per day.

common shares *Common stock*.

common-size financial statements Device used to compare financial statements, frequently of companies of disparate size, whereby all balance sheet entries are divided by total assets and all income statement entries are divided by net sales.

common stock (common shares) Securities representing an ownership interest in a firm.

comparables A method for estimating the *fair market value* of a closely held business by comparing it to one or more comparable, publicly traded firms.

compounding The growth of a sum of money over time through the reinvestment of interest earned to earn more interest (cf. *discounting*).

conglomerate diversification Ownership of operations in a number of functionally unrelated business activities.

constant-dollar accounting System of inflation accounting in which historical-cost items are restated to adjust for changes in the general purchasing power of the currency (cf. *current-dollar accounting*).

constant purchasing power The amount of a currency required over time to purchase a stable basket of physical assets.

consumer price index (CPI) An index measure of the price level equal to the sum of prices of a number of commodities purchased by consumers weighted by the proportion each represents in a typical consumer's budget.

contribution to fixed cost and profits The excess of *revenue* over *variable costs*.

control ratio Ratio indicating management's control of a particular current asset or liability.

conversion ratio Number of shares for which a *convertible security* may be exchanged.

conversion value Market value of shares an investor would own if he or she converted one convertible security.

convertible security Financial security that can be exchanged at the holder's option for another security or asset.

corporate restructuring Any major episodic change in a company's capital or ownership structure.

correlation coefficient Measure of the degree of comovement of two variables.

cost of capital (opportunity cost of capital, hurdle rate, weighted-average cost of capital) Return on new, average-risk investment that a company must expect to maintain share price. A weighted average of the cost to the firm of individual sources of capital.

cost of debt *Yield to maturity* on debt; frequently after tax, in which event it is 1 minus the tax rate times the yield to maturity.

cost of equity Return equity investors expect to earn by holding shares in a company. The expected return forgone by equity investors in the next best equal-risk opportunity.

cost of goods sold (cost of sales) The sum of all costs required to acquire and prepare goods for sale.

coupon rate The interest rate specified on interest coupons attached to bonds. Annual interest received equals coupon rate times the *par value* of the bond.

covenant (protective covenant) Provision in a debt agreement requiring the borrower to do, or not do, something.

coverage ratio Measure of financial leverage relating annual operating income to annual burden of debt (cf. *times-interest-earned ratio, times-burden-covered ratio*).

cumulative preferred stock *Preferred stock* containing the requirement that any unpaid preferred dividends accumulate and be paid in full before common dividends may be distributed.

current asset Any asset that will turn into cash within one year.

current-dollar accounting System of inflation accounting in which historical-cost items are restated to adjust for changes in the price of a specific item (cf. *constant-dollar accounting*).

current liability Any liability that is payable within one year.

current portion of long-term debt That portion of long-term debt that is payable within one year.

current ratio A measure of *liquidity*, defined as current assets divided by current liabilities.

days' sales in cash A measure of management's control of cash balances, defined as cash divided by sales per day.

debt capacity The total amount of debt a company can prudently support given its earnings expectations and equity base.

debt (liability) An obligation to pay cash or other goods or to provide services to another.

debt-to-assets ratio A measure of *financial leverage*, defined as debt divided by total assets (cf. *debt-to-equity ratio*).

debt-to-equity ratio A measure of *financial leverage*, defined as debt divided by shareholders' equity.

default To fail to make a payment when due.

default premium The increased return on a security required to compensate investors for the risk that the company will default on its obligation.

deferred tax liability An estimated amount of future income taxes that may become payable from income already earned but not yet recognized for tax-reporting purposes.

delayed call Provision in a security that gives the issuer the right to call the issue, but only after a period of time has elapsed (cf. *call provision*).

depreciation The reduction in the value of a long-lived asset from use or obsolescence. The decline is recognized in accounting by a periodic allocation of the original cost of the asset to current operations (cf. *accelerated depreciation*).

dilution The reduction in any per share item (such as earnings per share or book value per share) due to an increase in the number of shares outstanding either through new issue or conversion of outstanding securities.

discounted cash flow The method of evaluating long-term projects that explicitly takes into account the time value of money.

discounted cash flow rate of return *Internal rate of return*.

discounting Process of finding the present value of future cash flows (cf. *compounding*).

discount rate Interest rate used to calculate the *present value* of future cash flows.

diversifiable risk That risk that is eliminated when an asset is added to a diversified portfolio (cf. β-*risk*).

diversification The process of investing in a number of different assets.

dividend payout ratio A measure of the level of dividends distributed, defined as dividends divided by earnings.

earnings (income, net income, net profit, profit) The excess of revenues over all related expenses for a given period.

earnings per share (EPS) A measure of each common share's claim on earnings, defined as earnings available for common divided by the number of common shares outstanding.

earnings yield *Earnings per share* divided by stock price.

EBIT Abbreviation for earnings before interest and taxes.

economic income The amount an economic agent could spend during a period of time without affecting his or her wealth (cf. *accounting income*).

economic value added A business's or a business unit's operating income after tax less a charge for the opportunity cost of capital employed.

efficient market A market in which asset prices instantaneously reflect new information.

equity (owners' equity, net worth, shareholders' equity) Ownership interests of common and preferred stockholders in a company. On a balance sheet, equity equals total assets less all liabilities.

equivalence Equality of value of two cash flows occurring at different times if the cash flow occurring sooner can be converted into the later cash flow by investing it at the prevailing interest rate.

Eurodollar Originally a U.S. dollar in Europe, now any currency outside the control of its issuing monetary authority. The Eurodollar market is any market in which transactions in such currencies are executed.

expected return Average of possible returns weighted by their probability.

fair market value (FMV) (intrinsic value) An idealized *market value* defined as the price at which an asset would

trade between two rational individuals, each in command of all of the information necessary to value the asset and neither under any pressure to trade.

figure of merit A number summarizing the investment worth of a project.

Financial Accounting Standards Board (FASB) Official rulemaking body in the accounting profession.

financial asset Legal claim to future cash payments.

financial flexibility The ability to raise sufficient capital to meet company needs under a wide variety of future contingencies.

financial leverage Use of debt to increase the expected return and the risk to equity (cf. *operating leverage*).

first-in, first-out (FIFO) A method of inventory accounting in which the oldest item in inventory is assumed to be sold first (cf. *last-in, first-out*).

Fisher effect Proposition that the nominal rate of interest should approximately equal the real rate of interest plus a premium for expected inflation (cf. *real amount, nominal amount*).

fixed cost Any cost that does not vary over the observation period with changes in volume.

fixed-income security Any security that promises an unvarying payment stream to holders over its life.

forcing conversion Strategy in which a company forces owners of a convertible security to convert by calling the security at a time when its call price is below its conversion value (cf. *call provision, convertible security*).

foreign exchange exposure The risk that an unexpected change in exchange rates will impose a loss of some kind on the exposed party. With **transaction exposure**, the loss is to reported income;

with **accounting exposure**, the loss is to net worth; and with **economic exposure**, the loss is to the market value of the entity.

forward contract A contract in which the price is set today for a trade occurring at a specified future date.

forward market A market in which prices are determined for trade at a specified future date.

free cash flow The *cash flow* available to a company after financing all worthwhile investments; defined as operating income after tax plus depreciation less investment. The presence of large free cash flows is said to be attractive to a corporate raider.

frozen convertible (hung convertible) *Convertible security* that has been outstanding for several years and whose holders cannot be forced to convert because its *conversion value* is below its call price (cf. *forcing conversion*).

funds Any means of payment. Along with cash flow, *funds* is one of the most frequently misused words in finance.

gains to net debtors Increase in debtor's wealth due to a decline in the purchasing power of liabilities.

general creditor Unsecured creditor.

going-concern value The *present value* of a business's expected future *aftertax cash flows*. The going-concern value of *equity* is the present value of cash flows to equity, while the going-concern value of the firm is the present value of cash flows to all providers of capital.

gross margin percentage Revenue minus cost of goods sold divided by revenue.

hedge A strategy to offset investment risk. A perfect hedge is one that eliminates all possibility of gain or loss due to future movements of the hedged variable.

historical-cost depreciation *Depreciation* based on the amount originally paid for the asset.

hurdle rate Minimum acceptable rate of return on an investment (cf. *acceptance criterion, cost of capital*).

income *Earnings*

income statement (profit and loss statement) A report of a company's revenues, associated expenses, and resulting *income* for a period of time.

inflation premium The increased return on a security required to compensate investors for expected inflation.

insolvency The condition of having debts greater than the realizable value of one's assets.

internal rate of return (IRR) *Discount rate* at which project's *net present value* equals zero. Rate at which funds left in a project are *compounding* (cf. *rate of return*).

internal sources Cash available to a company from *cash flow from operations*.

inventory turnover ratio A measure of management's control of its investment in inventory, defined as *cost of goods sold* divided by ending inventory, or something similar.

inventory valuation adjustment Adjustment to historical-cost financial statements to correct for the possible understatement of inventory and *cost of goods sold* during inflation.

investment bank   A financial institution specializing in the original sale and subsequent trading of company securities.

investment value   Value of a *convertible security* based solely on its characteristics as a fixed-income security and ignoring the value of the conversion feature.

junk bond   Any *bond* rated below investment grade.

last-in, first-out (LIFO)   A method of inventory accounting in which the newest item in inventory is assumed to be sold first (cf. *first-in, first-out*).

leveraged buyout (LBO)   Purchase of a company financed in large part by company borrowings.

liability   An obligation to pay an amount or perform a service.

liquid asset   Any asset that can be quickly converted to cash without significant loss of value.

liquidation   The process of closing down a company, selling its assets, paying off its creditors, and distributing any remaining cash to owners.

liquidation value   The cash generated by terminating a business and selling its assets individually. The liquidation value of equity is the proceeds of the asset sale less all company liabilities.

liquidity   The extent to which a company has assets that are readily available to meet obligations (cf. *acid test, current ratio*).

liquidity ratio   Any ratio used to estimate a company's *liquidity* (cf. *acid test, current ratio*).

market for control   The active, competitive trading of controlling interests in corporations, effected by the purchase or sale of sizable blocks of common stock.

market line (securities market line)   Line representing the relationship between *expected return* and β-*risk*.

market value   The price at which an item can be sold (cf. *book value*).

market value of equity   The price per share of a company's *common stock* times the number of shares of common stock outstanding (cf. *book value of equity*).

market value of firm   The market value of *equity* plus the market value of the firm's liabilities.

mark-to-market accounting   The practice of adjusting the carrying value of traded assets and liabilities appearing on a business's balance sheet to their recent market values.

monetary asset   Any asset having a value defined in units of currency. Cash and accounts receivable are monetary assets; inventories and plant and equipment are physical assets.

multiple hurdle rates   Use of different *hurdle rates* for new investments to reflect differing levels of risk.

mutually exclusive alternatives   Two projects that accomplish the same objective so that only one will be undertaken.

net income   *Earnings.*

net monetary creditor   Economic agent having *monetary assets* in excess of *liabilities.*

net monetary debtor   Economic agent having *monetary assets* less than *liabilities.*

net present value (NPV)   *Present value* of cash inflows less present value of cash outflows. The increase in wealth accruing to an investor when he or she undertakes an investment.

net profit   *Earnings.*

net sales   Total sales revenue less certain offsetting items such as returns and allowances and sales discounts.

net worth   *Equity*, shareholders' equity.

nominal amount   Any quantity not adjusted for changes in the purchasing power of the currency due to inflation (cf. *real amount*).

noncash charge   An expense recorded by an accountant that is not matched by a cash outflow during the accounting period.

nondiversifiable risk   β-*risk, systematic risk.*

operating leverage   Fixed operating costs that tend to increase the variation in profits (cf. *financial leverage*).

opportunity cost   Income forgone by an investor when he or she chooses one action over another. Expected income on next best alternative.

opportunity cost of capital   *Cost of capital.*

option   See *call option, put option.*

option premium   The amount paid per unit by an option buyer to the option seller for an option contract.

over-the-counter (OTC) market   Informal market in which securities not listed on organized exchanges trade.

owners' equity   *Equity.*

paid-in capital   That portion of *shareholders' equity* that has been paid in

directly, as opposed to earned profits retained in the business.

par value   An arbitrary value set as the face amount of a security. Bondholders receive par value for their bonds on maturity.

payables period   A measure of a company's use of trade credit financing, defined as accounts payable divided by purchases per day.

payback period   A crude figure of investment merit and a better measure of investment risk, defined as the time an investor must wait to recoup his or her initial investment.

perpetual-growth equation   An equation representing the *present value* of a *perpetuity* growing at the rate of g percent per annum as next year's receipts divided by the difference between the *discount rate* and *g.*

perpetuity   An *annuity* that lasts forever.

plug   Jargon for the unknown quantity in a pro forma forecast.

portfolio   Holdings of a diverse group of assets by an individual or a company.

position diagram   A graph relating the value of an investment position on the vertical axis to the price of an underlying asset on the horizontal axis.

preferred stock   A class of stock, usually fixed-income, that carries some form of preference to income or assets over *common stock* (cf. *cumulative preferred stock*).

premium for control   The premium over and above the existing *market value* of a company's *equity* and acquirer is willing to pay to gain control of the company.

present value   The present worth of a future sum of money.

price-to-earnings ratio (P/E ratio)
Amount investors are willing to pay for
$1 of a firm's current earnings. Price per
share divided by earnings per share over
the most recent 12 months.

principal   The original, or face, amount
of a loan. Interest is earned on the
principal.

private placement   The raising of capital for a business through the sale of
securities to a limited number of well-
informed investors rather than through a
public offering.

profit center   An organizational unit
within a company that produces revenue and for which a profit can be
calculated.

profit margin   The proportion of each
sales dollar that filters down to *income*,
defined as income divided by *net
sales*.

profitability index (benefit-cost ratio)
A figure of investment merit, defined as
the *present value* of cash inflows divided by the present value of cash
outflows.

profits   *Earnings*.

pro forma statement   A financial statement prepared on the basis of some assumed future events.

protective covenant   *Covenant*.

public issue (public offering)   Newly
issued securities sold directly to the public (cf. *private placement*).

purchasing power parity   A theory
stating that foreign exchange rates should
adjust so that in equilibrium, commodities in different countries cost the same
amount when prices are expressed in the
same currency.

put option   Option to sell an asset at a
specified exercise price on or before a
specified maturity date (cf. *call option*).

quick ratio   *Acid test*.

range of earnings chart   Graph relating *earnings per share (EPS)* to earnings
before interest and taxes (EBIT) under alternative financing options.

rate of return   Yield obtainable on an
asset.

ratio analysis   Analysis of financial
statements by means of ratios.

real amount   Any quantity that has
been adjusted for changes in the purchasing power of the currency due to inflation
(cf. *nominal amount*).

realized income   The earning of
income related to a transaction as distinguished from a paper gain.

residual income security   A security
that has last claim on company income.
Usually the beneficiary of company
growth.

residual profits   An alternative to *return on investment* as a measure of *profit
center* performance, defined as *income*
less the annual cost of the capital employed by the profit center.

retained earnings (earned surplus)
The amount of earnings retained and reinvested in a business and not distributed
to stockholders as dividends.

return on assets (ROA)   A measure of
the productivity of assets, defined as
income divided by total assets. A superior but less common definition includes
interest expense and preferred dividends
in the numerator.

return on equity (ROE)   A measure of
the productivity or efficiency with which
shareholders' equity is employed, defined as *income* divided by *equity*.

return on invested capital (ROIC)   A
fundamental measure of the earning
power of a company that is unaffected by

the way the company is financed. It is equal to earnings before interest and tax times 1 minus the tax rate, all divided by *debt* plus *equity*.

return on investment (ROI) The productivity of an investment or a profit center, defined as *income* divided by *book value* of investment or *profit center* (cf. *return on assets*).

revenues *Sales*.

rights of absolute priority Specification in bankruptcy law stating that each class of claimants with a prior claim on assets in liquidation will be paid off in full before any junior claimants receive anything.

risk-adjusted discount rate (cost of capital, hurdle rate) A *discount rate* that includes a premium for risk.

risk aversion An unwillingness to bear risk without compensation of some form.

risk-free interest rate The interest rate prevailing on a default-free bond in the absence of inflation.

risk premium The increased return on a security required to compensate investors for the risk borne.

sales (revenue) The inflow of resources to a business for a period from sale of goods or provision of services (cf. *net sales*).

secured creditor A creditor whose obligation is backed by the pledge of some asset. In liquidation, the secured creditor receives the cash from the sale of the pledged asset to the extent of his or her loan.

Securities and Exchange Commission (SEC) Federal government agency that regulates securities markets.

semistrong-form efficient market A market in which prices instantaneously reflect all publicly available information.

senior creditor Any creditor with a claim on income or assets prior to that of *general creditors*.

sensitivity analysis Analysis of effect on a plan or forecast of a change in one of the input variables.

shareholders' equity *Equity, net worth*.

shelf registration SEC program under which a company can file a general-purpose prospectus describing its possible financing plans for up to two years. This eliminates time lags for new public security issues.

simulation (Monte Carlo simulation) Computer-based extension of *sensitivity analysis* that calculates the probability distribution of a forecast outcome.

sinking fund A fund of cash set aside for the payment of a future obligation. A bond sinking fund is a payment of cash to creditors.

solvency The state of being able to pay debts as they come due.

sources and uses statement A document showing where a company got its cash and where it spent the cash over a specific period of time. It is constructed by segregating all changes in balance sheet accounts into those that provided cash and those that consumed cash.

spontaneous sources of cash Those liabilities, such as accounts payable and accrued wages, that arise automatically, without negotiation, in the course of doing business.

spot market A market in which prices are determined for immediate trade.

spread Investment banker jargon for the difference between the issue price of a new security and the net to the company.

standard deviation of return A measure of variability. The square root of the mean squared deviation from the *expected return.*

statement of changes in financial position A financial statement showing the sources and uses of working capital for the period.

stock *Common stock.*

stock option A contractual privilege sometimes provided to company officers giving the holder the right to purchase a specified number of shares at a specified price within a stated period of time.

striking price (exercise price) The fixed price for which a stock can be purchased in a call contract or sold in a put contract (cf. *call option, put option).*

strong-form efficient market A market in which prices instantaneously reflect all information, public or private.

subordinated creditor A creditor who holds a debenture having a lower chance of payment than other liabilities of the firm.

sunk cost A previous outlay that cannot be changed by any current or future action.

sustainable growth rate The rate of increase in sales a company can attain without changing its profit margin, assets-to-sales ratio, debt-to equity ratio, or dividend payout ratio. The rate of growth a company can finance without excessive borrowing or issuing new stock.

tax shield The reduction in a company's tax bill caused by an increase in a tax-deductible expense, usually deprecia-

tion or interest. The magnitude of the tax shield equals the tax rate times the increase in the expense.

times burden covered A *coverage ratio* measure of *financial leverage,* defined as earnings before interest and taxes divided by interest expense plus principal payments grossed up to their before-tax equivalents.

times interest earned A *coverage ratio* measure of *financial leverage,* defined as earnings before interest and taxes divided by interest expense.

total capital All long-term sources of financing to a business.

trade payables *Accounts payable.*

transfer price An internal price at which units of the same company trade goods or services among themselves.

underwriting syndicate A group of *investment banks* that band together for a brief time to guarantee a specified price to a company for newly issued securities.

unrealized income Earned income for which there is no confirming transaction. A paper gain.

variable cost Any expense that varies with sales over the observation period.

volatility β-*risk.*

warrant A security issued by a company granting the right to purchase shares of another security of the company at a specified price and for a stated time.

weak-form efficient market A market in which prices instantaneously reflect information about past prices.

weighted-average cost of capital *Cost of capital.*

with-without principle Principle defining those cash flows that are relevant to an investment decision. It states that if there are two worlds, one with the investment and one without it, all cash flows that differ in these two worlds are relevant and all cash flows that are the same are irrelevant.

working capital (net working capital) The excess of current assets over current liabilities.

working capital cycle The periodic transformation of cash through current assets and current liabilities and back to cash (cf. *cash flow cycle*).

yield to maturity The *internal rate of return* on a bond when held to maturity.

SUGGESTED ANSWERS TO END-OF-CHAPTER PROBLEMS

Chapter 1

1. Equity = Assets − Liabilities, so a $1 million increase in assets and a $2 million fall in liabilities causes equity to rise $3 million.

2. It means simply that the company's operating activities consumed cash. A combination of three things can cause this: (1) operating losses; (2) increases in working capital, excluding cash, relative to sales; and (3) increases in working capital, excluding cash, in proportion to increase in sales. The first two are potential causes of concern; the last is the natural result of rapid growth and, provided the company can secure the necessary money to offset the negative cash flow from operations, is a positive sign.

3. *a.* The company is better off because it could sell its assets for more; or, should it choose not to sell, the income stream the assets are capable of generating should be higher.

   b. The company is better off because it could retire all its debts at a $10 million lower cost; or, should it choose not to retire its debts, the annual burden of the debt should be lower than that of new debt with the same face value.

   c. I would be indifferent between the two events because the market value of equity rises $10 million in both cases. The only difference is that increased asset value may be due to improved management, whereas falling debt values are usually due to market forces outside the firm. But in terms of the effect on wealth, the two events are identical.

4. Accounting income will be the value of the land sold, less the original purchase price of the parcels sold. So if all parcels are sold, the income is 5 × $1,500,000 + 5 × $600,000 − $10,000,000 = $500,000. Economic income will be the increase in the market value of the land, whether sold or not, over the accounting period. At the end of the first year, this will be $500,000. Answers to each part of this question follow.

Question	Accounting Income	Economic Income
a	$500,000	$500,000
b	0	500,000
c	−2,000,000	500,000
d	2,500,000	500,000

e. Too many companies have tried this. If the market value of a piece of land falls, the owner loses whether or not he sells. The market price of the land fell because people thought the future income stream to the owners was worth less. Continuing to hold the property forces the owner to accept the lower income. Whether or not the loss is recognized might affect accounting earnings, but has nothing to do with reality.

5. a. In 1997 company sales were $78 million, but accounts receivable rose $5 million, indicating that the company received only $73 million in cash. (This ignores possible changes in bad debt reserves.) Letting bop stand for beginning of period and eop for end of period, the equation is

$$\text{Accounts receivable}_{eop} = \text{Accounts receivable}_{bop}$$
$$+ \text{Credit sales} - \text{Collections}$$
$$\text{Collections} = \text{Credit sales} - \text{Change in accounts receivable}$$
$$\$73 \text{ million} = \$78 \text{ million} - \$5 \text{ million}$$

b. During 1997, the company sold $41 million of merchandise at cost, but finished goods inventory fell $1 million, indicating the company produced only $40 million of merchandise. The equation is

$$\text{Inventory}_{eop} = \text{Inventory}_{bop} + \text{Production}$$
$$- \text{Cost of sales}$$
$$\text{Production} = \text{Cost of sales} + \text{Change in inventory}$$
$$\$40 \text{ million} = \$41 \text{ million} - \$1 \text{ million}$$

c. Net fixed assets rose $4 million and depreciation reduced net fixed assets $12 million, so capital expenditures must have been $16 million.

$$\text{Net fixed assets}_{eop} = \text{Net fixed assets}_{bop}$$
$$+ \text{ Capital expenditures } - \text{ Depreciation}$$
$$\text{Capital expenditures} = \text{Change in net fixed assets}$$
$$+ \text{ Depreciation}$$
$$\$16 \text{ million} = \$4 \text{ million} + \$12 \text{ million}$$

6. Because the accountant's primary goal is to measure earnings, not cash generated. She sees earnings as a fundamental indicator of viability, not cash generation. A more balanced perspective is that over the long run, successful companies must be both profitable and solvent; that is, they must have the cash in the bank to pay their bills when due. This means you should pay attention to both earnings and cash flows.

7. *a.* R & E Supplies, Inc. Sources and Uses Statement, 1993–1996 ($000)

Sources of cash:	
Decrease in cash and securities	$ 259
Increase in accounts payable	2,205
Increase in current portion long-term debt	40
Increase in accrued wages	13
Increase in retained earnings	537
Total	$3,054
Uses of cash:	
Increase in accounts receivable	$1,543
Increase in inventories	1,148
Increase in prepaid expenses	4
Increase in net fixed assets	159
Decrease in long-term debt	200
Total	$3,054

b. Insights:

(1) R&E is making extensive use of trade credit to finance a build-up in current assets. The increase in accounts payable equals almost three-fourths of total sources of cash. Increasing accounts receivable and inventories account for almost 90 percent of the uses of cash.

(2) External financing is a use of cash for R&E, meaning it is repaying its loans. A restructuring involving less accounts payable and more bank debt appears appropriate.

8. ZTZ Corporation Cash Flows from Operating Activities, 1997

Net income	$168
Adjustments to reconcile net income to net cash provided by operating activities:	
Depreciation	80
Accrued taxes	40
Changes in current assets and liabilities:	
Accounts receivable	(100)
Inventories	40
Accounts payable	20
Accrued wages	(60)
Net cash flows from operations	$188

9. *a.*

Company	A	B	C
End-of-year cash balance	$50 million	$10 million	$40 million

b. It appears that company C retired more debt than it issued, repurchased more stock than it issued, or some combination of the two.

c. I'd prefer to own company A. A appears to be a growing company as evidenced by the sizable net cash used in financing activities, and its negative net cash flow from operations may well be due to increasing accounts receivable and inventories that naturally accompany sales growth. Company B appears not to be growing, so its negative net cash flows from operations are probably due to losses or to increasing receivables and inventories relative to sales, a trend denoting poor management of current assets.

d. I don't think there is necessarily a cause for concern. It appears company C is a mature, slow-growth company that is returning its unneeded operating cash flows to investors in the form of debt repayment, share repurchase, dividends, or some combination of these. This is a perfectly viable strategy.

10. The general secretary has confused accounting profits with economic profits. Earning $40 million on a $500 million equity investment is a return of only 8 percent. This is too low for the company to continue attracting new equity investment necessary for growth.

Chapter 2

1. *a.* ROE will undoubtedly fall. The numerator of the ratio, net income, will decline because the acquired company is losing money.

b. This is not important to the decision. This is another example of the *timing* problem. If the biotech company has great promise, it may make complete sense to acquire it even though it is currently losing money. The proper way to evaluate the acquisition is to calculate a time-adjusted figure of merit that takes into account the company's future performance. This is the topic of Chapter 9.

2. Your colleague's argument has several holes.

a. He has forgotten the *timing* problem. The investment has consequences over many years, and it is inappropriate to base the decision on only one year's results.

b. Your division's performance system is faulty. Investment return should be judged against a minimum acceptable return, not the division's historical return. An irrational implication of the performance system described is that divisions with very low returns will want to make lots of investments because many will promise returns higher than the division's ROI. Conversely, high-return divisions will find few investments promising returns above division ROI. See Chapter 8 for more on performance appraisal.

    c. As will be discussed beginning in Chapter 7, the appropriate rate of return for evaluating investment opportunities is not the accounting ROI but one that specifically incorporates the time value of money.

3. *a.*

Company	A	B
ROE	21.0%	60.0%
ROA	16.8	12.0
ROIC	18.0	16.8

    b. Company B is much more highly levered than A. A's debt-to-assets ratio is 20 percent, B's is 80 percent. The higher ROE is a natural result of financial leverage.

    c. This is also a result of B's higher leverage. ROA penalizes levered companies by comparing the net income available to equity to the capital provided by owners and creditors.

    d. ROIC abstracts from differences in financing strategy to provide a direct comparison of the earning power of the two companies' assets. On this metric, A is the superior performer. Before drawing any firm conclusions, however, it is important to ask how the business risks the two companies face compare and whether the observed ratios reflect long-run capabilities or transitory events.

4. a. R&E Supplies, Inc., Ratio Analysis

	1993	1994	1995	1996
Profitability ratios:				
Return on equity (%)	30.9	28.6	24.2	16.8
Return on assets (%)	11.3	10.3	7.7	5.0
Return on invested capital (%)	18.7	18.9	17.4	12.9
Profit margin (%)	3.3	2.9	2.4	1.4
Gross margin (%)	16.0	15.0	15.0	14.0
Leverage and liquidity ratios:				
Assets to equity (%)	274.5	276.7	314.4	339.3
Total liabilities to assets (%)	63.6	63.9	68.2	70.5
Total liabilities to equity (%)	174.5	176.7	214.4	239.3
Long-term debt to equity (%)	0.9	0.7	0.6	0.5
Times interest earned (×)	7.7	8.0	7.3	6.9
Times burden covered (×)	3.7	4.3	4.0	2.3
Current ratio (×)	2.8	2.4	1.8	1.7
Acid test (×)	1.8	1.5	1.1	1.0
Turnover control ratios:				
Asset turnover (×)	3.4	3.6	3.2	3.5
Inventory turnover (×)	8.4	8.5	7.1	7.8
Collection period (days)	43.8	47.4	47.5	51.1
Days' sales in cash (days)	21.9	14.6	14.6	7.3
Payables period (days)	39.1	45.0	64.7	66.1
Fixed-asset turnover (×)	87.4	111.0	54.6	71.8

b. Insights:

(1) All of the profitability ratios are down. ROE, while still respectable, has fallen by almost half, and the profit margin is down by more than half. This suggests problems on the income statement.

(2) Leverage is up and liquidity is down. Liabilities now constitute over 70 percent of assets, and the current ratio has fallen almost 40 percent.

(3) Asset turnover has been reasonably steady, although the collection period has risen over 15 percent. The payables period has almost doubled and, at 66 days, appears quite long.

(4) R&E Supplies' rapid growth causes a continuing need for external financing. This need has been exacerbated by falling operating margins. The company appears to have met this need by reducing liquidity (days' sales in cash is down from 21.9 days to 7.3) and increasing trade financing. At the same time, long-term debt to equity is fallen. The company would probably be advised to replace some of its trade financing with a bank loan, part of which is longer term. It also should rethink its pricing-growth strategy. One might argue that R&E has been "buying growth" by underpricing its product.

5. *a.* Collection period = 60.8 days.
   b. Payables period = 36.5 days.
   c. Inventory period = 182.5 days.
   d. (1) Inventory period + Collection period = 243.3 days.
      (2) Payables period = 36.5 days.
      (3) 182.5 + 60.8 − 36.5 = 206.8 days.
   e. Cash cycle = 206.8 days.
   f. A company's cash cycle is the elapsed time between when it pays for merchandise and when it gets paid for the merchandise. During this period, the company must finance the merchandise from a source other than trade credit. Lengthening the cash cycle increases the need for nontrade financing.
   g. The cash cycle is the number of *days* merchandise must be financed. As the *value* of merchandise financed rises, so does the need for nontrade finance.
   h. Reducing the cash cycle to zero might ease financing problems but will likely play havoc with the business. Cutting the collection period, reducing the inventory period, and lengthening the payables period all have important implications for the company's business strategy and customer relations, and should not be done casually.

6. Let L = liabilities, E = equity, and A = assets. By definition, $L = A − E$. If $L/E = 2.00$, $(A − E)/E = 2.00$. So $A/E − 1 = 2.00$, and $A/E = 3.00$.

7. ***a.*** *(1)* Liabilities-to-equity ratio = 50/(80 − 50) = 167%.
   (2) Times interest earned = 10/5 = 2 times.
   (3) Times burden covered = 10/(5 + 2/(1 − 0.40)) = 1.2
   times.
   b. *(1)* % decline in EBIT for times burden covered to fall to
   1.00 = [10 − (5 + 2/(1 − 0.40))]/10 = 16.7%.
   (2) % decline in EBIT before failing to cover common
   dividends:
   1.00 = [10 − (5 + (2 + 0.40 × 5)/(1 − 0.40))]/10 =
   − 16.7%.
   In 1996, the before-tax burden of interest, sinking
   fund, and dividends exceeded EBIT. The company fell
   16.7 percent short of covering these burdens as it was,
   and must have sold assets or raised money from
   external sources to pay its dividend.

8.

	Assets	
Cash		$ 50,000
Accounts receivable		250,000
Inventory		600,000
Total current assets		900,000
Net fixed assets		500,000
Total assets		$1,400,000
	Liabilities and Owners' Equity	
Accounts payable		197,260
Short-term debt		177,740
Total current liabilities		375,000
Long-term debt		325,000
Shareholders' equity		700,000
Total liabilities and equity		$1,400,000

Chapter 3

1. This would tell me I had erred in constructing one or both
   forecasts. Using the same assumptions and avoiding
   accounting and arithmetic errors, estimated external funding
   required should equal estimated cash surplus or deficit for the
   same date.

2. A negative value implies that the company has excess cash above its desired minimum. You can demonstrate this on the balance sheet by setting the external funding requirement to zero and adding the absolute value of the original negative external funding required to cash.

3. New equity equation: = C37 + D28. New net sales equation: = C19 + C19*D4.

4. Pro Forma Forecast for R&E Supplies, 1998

Income Statement

Net sales	$33,496
Cost of goods sold	28,807
Gross profit	4,689
General, selling, and administrative expense	3,685
Interest expense	334
Earnings before tax	671
Tax	302
Earnings after tax	369
Dividends paid	185
Additions to retained earnings	$ 185

Balance Sheet Forecast

Current assets	$ 9,714
Net fixed assets	270
Total assets	$ 9,984
Current liabilities	4,857
Long-term debt	560
Equity	1,990
Total liabilities and shareholders' equity	$ 7,407
External funding required	**$ 2,577**

Projected external funding requirements in 1998 are over $1 million higher than in 1997.

5.

	January	February	March
Cash receipts:			
Sales for cash	$ 80,000	$ 32,000	$ 32,000
Collections from credit sales	640,000	320,000	128,000
Total cash receipts	720,000	352,000	160,000
Cash disbursements:			
Payment for purchases	360,000	800,000	200,000
Wages	120,000	120,000	120,000
Interest payments			60,000
Principal payments			140,000
Dividends			200,000
Tax payments		120,000	
Total cash disbursements	480,000	1,040,000	720,000
Net cash receipts (disbursements)	240,000	(688,000)	(560,000)
Determination of cash needs:			
Beginning cash	200,000	440,000	(248,000)
Net receipts (disbursements)	240,000	(688,000)	(560,000)
Ending cash	440,000	(248,000)	(808,000)
Minimum cash desired	100,000	100,000	100,000
Cash surplus (deficit)	$340,000	($348,000)	($908,000)

Obviously the treasurer had better concern himself with where to borrow money. Michigan Milling will need almost $1 million by the end of March.

6.

Michigan Milling
Income Statement
January 1, 1997–March 31, 1997
($000)

Net sales	$720
Cost of sales at 65%	468
Gross profit	252
Selling and administrative expense	360
Interest	60
Depreciation	20
Net profit before tax	(188)
Tax at 33%	(62)
Net profit after tax	$(126)

**Michigan Milling
Balance Sheet
March 31, 1997
($000)**

Assets

Cash	$ 100
Accounts receivable	128
Inventory	1,092
Total current assets	1,320
Gross fixed assets	600
– Accumulated depreciation	120
Net fixed assets	480
Total assets	$1,800

Liabilities

Bank loan	908
Accounts payable	160
Miscellaneous accruals	40
Current portion long-term debt	100
Taxes payable	18
Total current liabilities	1,226
Long-term debt	560
Shareholders' equity	14
Total liabilities and equity	$1,800

Comments:

(1) Inventory is estimated as follows:

Beginning inventory Jan. 1	$1,200
+ First-quarter purchases	360
– First-quarter cost of goods sold	468
Ending inventory March 30	$1,092

(2) Taxes payable are estimated as follows:

Taxes payable Dec. 31, 1994	$ 200
– Payments	120
+ First-quarter taxes accrued	(62)
Taxes payable March 31	$ 18

(3) Shareholders' equity is estimated as follows

Equity Dec. 31, 1996	$ 340
– Dividends paid	200
+ First-quarter profits	(126)
Equity March 31	$ 14

7.

Michigan Milling
Cash Flow Forecast
First Quarter 1997
($000)

Sources of cash:	
Cash from operations:	
Profit after tax	$ (126)
Depreciation	20
Increase in liabilities or reduction in assets:	
Bank loan	908
Cash	100
Accounts receivable	512
Inventory	108
Total sources	$ 1,522
Uses of cash:	
Dividends	$ 200
Decreases in liabilities or increases in assets:	
Accounts payable	1,000
Current portion long-term debt	40
Taxes payable	182
Long-term debt	100
Total uses	$ 1,522

Chapter 4

1. a. R&E Supplies, Inc., Sustainable Growth Calculations

	1993	1994	1995	1996	1997F
Profit margin (P) (%)	3.3	2.9	2.4	1.4	0.9
Retention ratio (R) (%)	50	50	50	50	50
Asset turnover (A) ($\times$)	3.4	3.6	3.2	3.5	3.3
Financial leverage ($\bar{T}$) ($\times$)	NA	3.2	3.6	3.7	4.5
R&E's sustainable growth rate (g^*) (%)	—	16.7	13.8	9.1	6.7
R&E's Actual growth rate (g) (%)	—	23.0	17.0	28.0	25.0

b. R&E's actual growth rate is well in excess of its sustainable growth rate. Its growth management problems clearly involve finding the money to finance growth.

c. R&E has coped with its growth problems quite poorly.
The profit margin has fallen, contributing to a sizable
reduction in sustainable growth. Dividends continue to
consume half of earnings, and asset turnover has held
constant. The company has essentially financed its rapid
growth by increasing financial leverage, first borrowing
from suppliers, now trying to borrow from the bank. If it
doesn't do something quickly, it will hit its debt capacity
and could find itself in real trouble.

d. There are several possibilities. First, I would work hard to
get the profit margin back up to a reasonable level. This
might involve raising prices. Second, I would prune out
all slow-moving inventory and slow-pay customers. Third,
I would cut or eliminate the dividend. Fourth, I would go
to the bank with a pro forma demonstrating that these
changes will result in reasonable debt ratios and rough
equality between my sustainable and actual growth. If this
failed, I would look for a partner or a buyer.

2. a.

	1991	1992	1993	1994	1995
Sustainable growth rate (%)	36.9	33.5	24.1	10.3	17.3

b. Lindsay's sustainable growth rate in every year has
exceeded its actual growth rate. The company is
generating more cash from operations than it can
productively employ. Its challenge has been what to do
with the excess cash.

c. Lindsay has coped with actual growth below sustainable
levels in two ways. It has allowed its asset turnover to fall
from 1.6 times in 1991 to 1.3 times in 1995, and it has
sharply reduced its debt from 2.5 times in 1991 to 1.3
times in 1995.

d. I would not support the policy. The company has only
modest debt and appears not to be employing its retained
profits productively. It is hard to see how retaining profits
in the business is benefiting owners.

e. Stock repurchase makes sense for Lindsay. It appears to
have little productive use for the money it earns within
the firm, so it should return it to the owners, either as
dividends or in the form of a share repurchase.

3. *a.*

	1991	1992	1993	1994	1995
Sustainable growth rate (%)	2.1	2.2	13.3	20.5	2.2

b. Williams-Sonoma's actual growth in sales is well above its sustainable growth rate; it is growing much too rapidly unless it intends to issue equity in the near future.

c. The company has coped by increasing its financial leverage. The profit margin has been quite low, and after improving for several years, asset turnover fell to a low in 1995.

d. Yes. Williams-Sonoma risks growing broke. One day creditors will refuse to lend more money, and the company could find itself with insufficient cash to pay its bills. The company surely has time to fix the problem, but continually increasing financial leverage is not a long-run option.

Chapter 5

1. *a.* The market value of A's equity is $20 million (4 million shares × $5 per share). The market value of B's is the same (1 million shares × $20 per share).

b. Four hundred A shares are worth $2,000. I would be interested in trading for B shares whenever the value of the B shares exceeded this amount. The offer would have to be for at least 100 B shares ($2,000/$20 per share).

c. Ten percent of A's equity is worth $2 million. One hundred thousand shares of B's stock are also worth $2 million. Therefore, I would want to receive at least 100,000 shares of B stock.

d. The investor should be interested in the percentage of a company's shares owned. This determines the size of her claims on company cash flows and hence the value of her investment. A company's share price is an artifact of the number of shares it has outstanding. It can be arbitrarily changed by splitting the shares. Share price is of interest only to the extent that it helps investors calculate more meaningful dollar or percentage ownership numbers.

2. Earning high returns in an efficient market is like winning at roulette. In any random process, there will be winners and losers. Market efficiency talks about the expected outcome. The presence of investors who earn consistently high returns in the stock market is also not impossible in an efficient market, just as a gambler on a lucky streak is not impossible at the roulette table. The relevant statistical question is whether the length of the streak or the number of repeat winners is inconsistent with blind luck.

3. *a.* The holding period return is 18.1 percent ([$60 +$110]/ $940).

   b. The bond's price might have risen because investor perceptions of its risk declined or because interest rates fell.

4. *a.* The holding period return in yen was 13 percent ([3% × 100,000 + 110,000 − 100,000]/100,000)

   b. You paid $1,000 for the bond (¥100,000/100). At the end of the year, you had interest income and a yen bond worth a total of $1,202.13 (¥113,000/94). Your dollar return was thus 20.2 percent ([$1,202.13 − $1,000]/$1,000).

   c. Your yen return represents 64.4 percent of the dollar return (13%/20.2%). The rest is attributable to changing currency values.

5. *a.*

Stock price	$56.00
− 5% underpricing	2.80
Issue price	$53.20
− 6% spread	3.19
Net to company	$50.01

   Number of shares = $200 million/$50.01 = 399,920 shares.

   b. Investment bankers' revenue = $3.19 × 399,920 = $1,275,745.

   c. Underpricing is not a cash flow. It is, however, an opportunity cost to current owners because it means that more shares must be sold to raise $200 million and each share will represent a smaller ownership interest in the company.

Chapter 6

1. **a.** An increase in the interest rate would lower the debt financing line in the range-of-earnings chart. This would reduce the EPS advantage of debt or increase the disadvantage if EBIT is below the crossover point. It would also increase the crossover EBIT. Both changes would reduce the attractiveness of debt financing.

   b. An increased stock price will reduce the number of shares issued to raise the needed capital, which will increase EPS at all income levels for the equity line. Raising the equity line will improve EPS with equity financing relative to debt and will increase the crossover EBIT. Both changes will make equity more attractive.

   c. The range-of-earnings chart will be unchanged, but increased uncertainty will increase the probability that EBIT will fall below the crossover point. This will make equity more attractive.

   d. Increased common dividends will not affect the range-of-earnings chart. They will reduce the times-common covered ratio and will hence make debt marginally more attractive.

   e. An increase in the amount of debt already outstanding will increase interest expense and lower EPS for all financing options. This will lower both the debt and the equity financing lines in the range-of-earnings chart by the same amount, but will not affect the attractiveness of debt relative to equity, at least as far as the range-of-earnings chart is concerned. Interest coverage obviously falls as existing debt rises, which makes additional debt financing riskier.

2. **a.** EBIT = $40/(1 - .4) + 10 = \$76.7$.
   Interest = $\$10 + .06(\$40) = \$12.4$. Times interest earned = $76.7/12.4 = 6.2$ times.

   b. Burden before tax = $12.4 + (14 + 8)/(1 - .4) = \$49.1$.
   Times burden covered = $66.7/49.1 = 1.4$ times.

   c. EPS = $(66.7 - 12.4)(1 - .4)/16 = \$2.04$.

   d. Times interest earned = $66.7/10 = 6.7$ times. Times burden covered = $66.7/(10 + 14/(1 - .4)) = 2.0$ times. EPS = $(66.7 - 10)(1 - .4)/(16 + 1.6) = \$1.93$.

e. Advice: Interest coverage looks good with debt financing provided Suntone is not in a high-risk business. Burden covered with debt financing might be a bit tight. It depends on whether Suntone has sufficient liquidity to meet a shortfall in EBIT and on how much Suntone will need for new investment. EPS is about 5 percent higher with debt financing, not an especially big income advantage to debt. Adverse signaling effects of issuing new equity should also be considered. I am unwilling to make strong recommendations based on this information.

3. a. Market signaling studies suggest the price of existing shares will fall. One explanation for the decline is that managers know more about their company than outsiders do and that the announcement of an equity sale signals they are worried about the company's prospects.

   b. Expected loss = 30% of issue size = .3($50 million) = $15 million.

   c. 15/50 = 30 percent.

   d. 15/$5 × 100 = 3 percent.

   e. Price per share = 97% of $5.00 = $4.85.

4. a. Each year sources of cash must equal uses of cash. Sources are earnings plus new borrowing. Uses are investments and dividends. So each year an equation of the following form applies: $E + 1.2(E - D) = I + D$, where E is earnings, 1.2 is the debt-to-equity ratio, D is dividends, and I is investment. Solving for D, $D = E - I/2.2$. The following table presents the resulting annual dividend and payout ratio.

   b. Summing dividends and dividing by total earnings, the stable payout ratio is $219/$930 = 24%. Substituting this into our sources and uses equation, $E + 1.2(E - .24E) = I + .24E + CM$, where CM is the change in the marketable securities portfolio. Solving for CM, $CM = 1.67E - I$. The resulting values for CM and the year-end marketable securities portfolio appear in the following table. (Had I carried out the calculations with more accuracy, the ending marketable securities would have equaled the beginning value, $200.)

Year	($ millions)				
	1	2	3	4	5
Dividends ($)	20	−6	34	71	100
Payout ratio (%)	20	−5	20	31	33
Stable payout ratio (%)	24	24	24	24	24
Stable dividend ($)	24	31	41	55	72
Change in marketable securities ($)	−8	−83	−16	43	61
Marketable securities ($)	192	109	93	127	188

    c. The company can do any or some combination of the following: reduce marketable securities, increase leverage, cut dividends, sell new equity.

    d. The options are ranked according to the pecking order as they appear in the answer to question *c*. One might distinguish between using excess borrowing capacity and raising the target debt ratio, with the former ranked above the cut dividends option and the latter below.

    e. The pecking-order theory follows from the desire to avoid negative signaling effects of new equity issues, supplemented by the desire to maintain access to financial markets. If these goals are important to managers, they will naturally follow the pecking order.

Chapter 7

   1. *a.* PV = 100(.564) = $56.40.

     b. PV = 100(.386) = $38.60. Present value is less because the present sum has more time to grow into $100.

     c. PV = 500(.909) + 300(.826) + 1,000(.621) = $1,323.30.

     d. PV = 120(7.606) + 1,000(.239) = $1,151.72.

     e. PV = 8/.10 = $80.00.

     f. FV = 5/.386 = $12.95.

     g. (1/PVF)10 = 20. PVF = .500. Looking in Appendix A at a 10 percent rate, PVF for 7 years = .513 and PVF for 8 years is .467. Interpolating, *n* = 7 years + [(.513 − .500)/(.513 − .467)] × 1% = 7.28 years.

     h. PV = 6.145(5) = 30.725. FV = (1/PVF) × PV = (1/.386) × 30.725 = $79.60.

i. The present value of $100,000 in 15 years is 100,000(.239) = 23,900. The annuity A with this present value is found by solving PVAF $\times A$ = $23,900. Hence, A = $23,900/PVAF = $23,900/7.606 = $3,142.26.

j. NPV = $-$ 342 + 100(PVAF, $r\%$, 6 years) = 0. PVAF, $r\%$, 6 years = 3.42. Looking at Appendix B, PVAF, 19%, 6 years = 3.41, so IRR = almost 19%. Paying less than $342 implies an IRR greater than 19 percent, and vice versa.

k. If the stream lasted forever, PV = 50/.10 = $500. Hence, the stream must be a perpetuity. If the stream lasted only seven years, the salvage value would have to be $500. This is the amount required to be invested at 10 percent to generate $50 per year in perpetuity from year 7 on.

l. NPV = $-$ 100 + 433(PVF, $r\%$, 30 years) = 0. PVF, $r\%$, 30 years = 0.231. Looking at Appendix A for 30 years, the entry for 5% equals 0.231; hence IRR = 5%.

2. *a.* The accounting rate of return = 18/50 = 36%. The payback period = 50/18 = 2.78 years.

b. NPV = $-$ 50 + 18(3.784) = $18,112.

c. BCR = 18(3.784)/50 = 1.36.

d. NPV = 0 = $-$ 50 + 18(PVAF factor, $r\%$, 6 years); (PVAF factor, $r\%$, 6 years) = 2.778. Consulting Appendix B and interpolating, IRR = about 27.8%.

e. The NPV, BCR, and IRR all indicate unambiguously that the investment is worthwhile. The accounting rate of return suggests the same, but is not a reliable indicator of investment value, nor is it comparable to the 15 percent required rate of return on the investment. Because there is no reliable way to transform a 15 percent required rate of return into a maximum acceptable payback period, it is not clear whether a 2.78-year payback period is short enough.

3. Let X equal the end-of-year payment. $10,000 =$X$(3.433); X = $2,912.90. With this annual payment, the NPV on the loan from the bank's perspective is 0, so its IRR is 14 percent.

4. NPV = $-$ 10 + 15.50(PV factor, $r\%$, 9th year) = 0; (PV factor, $r\%$, 9th year) = 0.645. Looking at Appendix A for year 9, PV factor for 5% = 0.645. Therefore, the growth rate is 5 percent.

5. Using the with-without principle, the relevant cash flows are:

Year	0	1	2	3	4	5
Cash flow	–$10	3.1	3.1	3.1	3.1	3.1

The NPV = – 10 + 3.1(3.791) = $1.75 million. Therefore, the campaign is attractive. It avoids a large loss.

6. This is a straightforward replacement problem.

	Old Machine	New Machine
Gross profit	$2,000	$4,000
– Depreciation	1,000	1,500
Profit before tax	1,000	2,500
Tax	450	1,125
Profit after tax	550	1,375
+ Depreciation	1,000	1,500
Aftertax cash flow	$1,550	$2,875

If they keep the old machine, NPV = 1,550(6.144) = $9,523. If they sell the old machine and buy the new one, NPV = −15,000 + 5,000 + 2,875(6.144) = $7,664. Therefore, keep the old machine.

Alternatively, one can look at the difference in the cash flows between the two alternatives. This amounts to analyzing the *incremental* cash flows. Subtracting the old machine cash flows from the new machine cash flows, NPV = – 10,000 + 1,325(PVAF, 10%, 10 years) = – $1,859, indicating that spending an incremental $10,000 to buy the new machine is not attractive. It should not surprise you to learn that this NPV equals the difference in the NPVs of the two options. That is, – $1,849 = $7,664 – $9,523.

The IRR of the incremental cash flow above is 5.5 percent, which, because it is below 10 percent, again indicates the incremental investment is unwarranted.

7. a. Undertake all three investments. The NPV and the IRR indicate that all of the investments are worthwhile.

b. Undertake investment A because it has the highest NPV, and NPV is a direct measure of the increase in wealth from undertaking the investment.

   c. If the capital budget is fixed at $550,000, invest in C and B, and put the remaining $50,000 in A if possible. This is the bundle of investments with the highest *total* NPV. One can select this bundle by ranking investments by their IRRs.

8. The internal rate of return is 13.7 percent. Once again we see the power of compound interest. This is not an especially exciting return inasmuch as it ignores the costs of maintaining, insuring, and protecting a valuable painting and inasmuch as the return on a Van Gogh can be expected to be much higher than the return on a typical fine art investment, even if it is one of his lesser works.

Chapter 8

1. Two arguments are plausible. First, the investment has important "irreducible" benefits that cannot be reflected in the estimated cash flows, such as the investment will increase morale, or the investment will give us an important option to expand in the future. Second, the investment is below the company's average risk; thus, although the return is below the company's cost of capital, the cost of capital is not relevant for the investment. Equivalently, the low risk of the investment places it above the market line. Such investments create value because they promise returns above those available on similar-risk investments.

2. Reducing financial leverage reduces the risks borne by equity investors and hence reduces the cost of equity capital. The company's equity beta will decline as well. Indeed, the falling equity beta causes the cost of equity to fall. Looking at equation 8A–2, the standard deviation of return to equity varies with financial leverage. Figure 6–1 shows the relationship graphically.

3. When the investment lies below the market line, it is possible to make equal-risk investments promising higher expected returns. Conversely, investments above the market line promise expected returns above those available on equal-risk, ready alternatives.

4. *a.* Using the perpetuity equation, IRR = 2/20 = 10%.

   b. $K_W = [(1 - .4)(8\%)(130) + 14\%(100)]/(130 + 100) =$ 8.8%. As long as the market value of debt is given, you might as well use it. As usual, using the book value instead doesn't make much difference. Using the book value, $K_W = 8.9\%$.

   c. IRR exceeds the weighted-average cost of capital and investment is average risk for the company, so it should create value for owners.

5. Divide the cash flows into two periods: a 12-year annuity of $50 and a growing perpetuity beginning in the 12th year. The value of the 12-year annuity is $50(5.660) = $283. The value of the perpetuity at time 12 is $50(1 + .07)/(.14 - .07) = $764.29. Its value at time zero is $764.29(.208) = $158.97. Adding these present values, $283 + $158.97 = $441.97.

6. *a.* NPV = - $100 + $20.7(PVAF, $r\%$, 10 years) = 0. (PVAF, $r\%$, 10 years) = 4.831. Consulting Appendix B for 10 years, $r = 16\%$.

   b. Annual interest and principal payment necessary to amortize an $80 million, 10-year loan at 8 percent is NPV = $80 - $X(6.710) = 0. $X = $11.9 million. So equity cash flows are - $20 million at time zero and $8.8 million per year for 10 years. IRR is NPV = - $20 + $8.8(PVAF, $r\%$, 10 years) = 0. (PVAF, $r\%$, 10 years) = 2.273. From Appendix B, $r = 35\%$.

   c. The IRR from the *entity* perspective is below the weighted-average cost of capital, so the investment is unattractive. The high IRR from the *equity* perspective just reflects the high financial leverage.

7. Here are the first four of 10 years' cash flows. The net present value shown below is the net present value of all 10 years.

	($000 except per-unit figures)				
Year	0	1	2	3	4
Initial cost	– $10,000				
Annual sales (units)		100	100	100	100
Price per unit		$54.00	$58.32	$62.99	$68.02
Variable cost per unit		21.60	23.33	25.19	27.21
Revenue		5,400	5,832	6,299	6,802
Variable cost		2,168	2,333	2,519	2,721
Depreciation		1,000	1,000	1,000	1,000
Income before tax		2,240	2,499	2,779	3,081
Tax		762	850	945	1,048
Income after tax		1,478	1,649	1,834	2,034
+ Depreciation		1,000	1,000	1,000	1,000
ATCF	–$10,000	$2,478	$2,649	$2,834	$3,034
NPV at 18% = $4,894,000					

Here I have discounted the *nominal* cash flows at the nominal discount rate. Alternatively, I could calculate the *real* ATCFs and discount at the *real* discount rate of 10 percent. The NPV is the same either way. It is *incorrect* to calculate the ATCFs ignoring inflation and then discount by the real discount rate because depreciation does not vary with the inflation rate.

8. **a.** ROI before tax = $5/$40 = 12.5%. ROI after tax = $3/$40 = 7.5%.

  b. EVA = $(1 - .4)$5 - .12($40) = - 1.8 million.

  c. The negative EVA suggests the company did not create value for owners last year. Comparing the aftertax ROI to the cost of capital suggests the same thing.

  d. This illustrates a problem with ROI and EVA. They look at performance for one period, while value depends on performance over many future periods. My answer to *c* would certainly change.

Chapter 9

1. Assuming owners want to attain the highest value possible for their business, they will operate it as a going concern if doing so creates the highest value. Conversely, if liquidating

the business generates a higher value, they will liquidate. Hence, the realizable value should always be the higher of the two. If it is not, a raider can profit by gaining control of the business at the lower price (plus a premium) and either selling at the higher price or, if a sale is not possible, operating the business so as to realize the higher value.

2. *a.* Any time one company acquires another, its sales and assets increase. Further, if the acquired company is profitable, earnings will increase as well. This is no surprise.

   b. Value per share before proposal = $100/0.15 = $666.67.

   c. Value per share after proposal = $50/(1 + .15) + ($105/.15)/(1 + .15)^2 = $572.78.

   d. Clearly, owners of Flatbush should oppose the president's plan. It may result in a larger company, but it will destroy shareholder value; that is, stock price will fall under the plan. The problem with the president's plan is that it takes money with an opportunity cost of 15 percent to owners and invests it in a venture yielding only 10 percent ($5 per year added dividend in perpetuity for a $50 investment yields a 10 percent return).

3. Here are my estimates. In coming to these estimates, I judged that Timberland has lower returns on invested capital and equity than three of the four comparable firms and has the highest financial leverage of the group, although none are especially high. On the other hand, Timberland displays the highest five-year growth rate in earnings. The company's rapid earnings growth suggests that its indicator of value for the two income-based ratios should equal or exceed those of the highest comparable companies. A figure about 5 to 10 percent above Wolverine's looks about right. Timberland's low return on invested capital and return-on-equity figures suggest that its indicator of value for the last two, asset-based ratios should be on the low end of the comparable range. Inasmuch as Timberland's asset-based ratios are modestly above those of Wolverine, I have again selected indicators of value somewhat above Wolverine's.

My Estimated Indicator of Value for Timberland

Price/earnings	20.0×
MV firm/EBIT(1 − Tax rate)	18.0×
MV equity/BV equity	2.1×
MV firm/BV firm	1.8×

Implied Value of Timberland Common Stock per Share

Price/earnings	$40.20
MV firm/EBIT(1 − Tax rate)	$50.08
MV equity/BV equity	$35.71
MV firm/BV firm	$44.42

Placing the most weight on the second indicator of value, my best guess is $46.00.

Actual stock price on December 31, 1993 $53.38.

4. *a.*

	($ millions)			
	1999	**2000**	**2001**	**2002**
EBIT(1 − Tax rate)	$ 60	$ 78	$102	$126
+ Depreciation	25	30	50	60
− Capital expenditures	150	90	100	110
− Changes in working capital	20	50	− 10	10
= Free cash flow	− $85	− $32	$ 62	$ 66

b. A negative free cash flow does not necessarily imply that the company is destroying value. It simply means capital expenditures and increases in working capital exceed operating cash flow that year. The capital expenditures will presumably add to EBIT and to free cash flow in following years.

c. FMV = PV{FCF, '99–'02} + PV{Terminal value}. PV{FCF, '99–'02} = − $18.3 million. Terminal value = EBIT(1 − Tax rate)/0.14 = $126/0.14 = $900 million. PV{Terminal value} = $900 million × 0.592 = $532.9 million. Summing, FMV = $514.6 million.

d. FMV of equity = ($514.6 − $300)/50 = $4.29 per share.

e. Terminal value = FCF in 2003/(0.14 − 0.04). FCF in 2003 = $210(1.04)(1 − .4) − 20 − 10 = $101.4. So terminal value = $101.4/.10 = $1,014. Present value of terminal value = $598.2. FMV of company = − $18.3 + $598.2 = $580 million. FMV of equity per share = ($580 − $300)/ 50 = $5.60.

f. Terminal value = Value of equity + Value of interest-bearing liabilities. Value of equity = 8 × Net income in 2002 = 8 × (210 − 0.10 × 200)(1 − .40) = $912 million. Terminal value = $912 million + $200 million = $1,112. Present value of terminal value = $658.4. Therefore, FMV of company on valuation date = − $18.3 + $658.4 = $640.1 million. Value per share = ($640.1 million − $300 million)/50 = $6.80.

INDEX